EXCESSIVE PUNISHMENT

EXCESSIVE PUNISHMENT

HOW THE JUSTICE SYSTEM CREATES MASS INCARCERATION

Edited by Lauren-Brooke Eisen

COLUMBIA UNIVERSITY PRESS NEW YORK

COLUMBIA UNIVERSITY PRESS
Publishers Since 1893
New York Chichester, West Sussex
cup.columbia.edu

Library of Congress Cataloging-in-Publication Data

Names: Eisen, Lauren-Brooke, editor.
Title: Excessive punishment : how the justice system creates mass incarceration / edited by Lauren-Brooke Eisen.
Description: New York : Columbia University Press, [2024] | Includes bibliographical references and index.
Identifiers: LCCN 2023037148 (print) | LCCN 2023037149 (ebook) | ISBN 9780231212168 (hardback) | ISBN 9780231212175 (trade paperback) | ISBN 9780231559249 (ebook)
Subjects: LCSH: Punishment—United States. | Mass incarceration—United States. | Imprisonment—Social aspects—United States. | Criminal justice, Administration of—Social aspects—United States. | Discrimination in criminal justice administration—United States.
Classification: LCC HV9950 .E94 2024 (print) | LCC HV9950 (ebook) | DDC 364.973—dc23/eng/20231122
LC record available at https://lccn.loc.gov/2023037148
LC ebook record available at https://lccn.loc.gov/2023037149

Cover design: Julia Kushnirsky
Cover image: Shutterstock

CONTENTS

PART III. PROSECUTION AND SENTENCING

PART IV. RACISM AND PUNITIVE EXCESS

PART V. UNCOVERING LIFE BEHIND PRISON WALLS

INTRODUCTION

Lauren-Brooke Eisen

AMERICA'S JUSTICE SYSTEM is uniquely punitive.

Although prisons and jails did not always dot the American landscape, today the United States has by far the largest population of incarcerated people in the world. Yet this is a relatively new development. In the country's early days, punishment practices borrowed from England—such as public humiliation, fines, and even corporal punishment—were meted out quickly, with the understanding that people must get back to work. Those who could afford it paid fines as punishment. Colonists with fewer means were often publicly humiliated: thrown in the stockades or whipped in front of crowds.[1] Not until 1829 did the world's first penitentiary, in Philadelphia, open its doors. Inside, those convicted of crimes sat in their cells for almost the entirety of their days, forced to reflect on their sins, read the Bible, and perform solitary labor.[2] As Norval Morris wrote in his 1974 book, *The Future of Imprisonment*, "the prison is an American invention."[3]

It is now nearly two hundred years later, and more than a million Americans today are incarcerated in more than 1,600 prisons.[4] Alongside these prisons are nearly three thousand jails, holding more than half a million other people.[5] Outside these prisons and jails, nearly four million people are out on probation and parole.[6]

This system of punishment is exorbitantly expensive, costing an estimated $182 billion every year.[7]

Public safety is important, and it's critical that we protect victims and support policies that reduce unnecessary incarceration while producing safe and healthy communities. Violence and harm must be addressed. Yet research indicates that reducing crime and promoting more fair and just criminal legal reform policies can—and should—go hand in hand.[8] We need to prioritize reducing crime in ways that are fair, just, practical, and don't contribute to needless incarceration. We can do this by removing guns from our streets, increasing mental health and drug treatment services, investing in afterschool and other youth programs, increasing streetlights, improving health care in our poorest communities, and providing better educational opportunities across the nation.[9]

For those who criticize decarceration because of public safety concerns, let history be your guide. A 2017 study found that nineteen states reduced both imprisonment and crime between the years 2000 and 2015.[10] Similarly, in the decade between 2007 and 2017, thirty-four states reduced both imprisonment and crime rates simultaneously.[11]

The grand irony is that America's experiment with mass incarceration and eternal punishment doesn't produce public safety. Research indicates that 40 percent of those in state and federal prisons don't need to be there for any public safety reason.[12] Further, dozens of research reports indicate that prison is *criminogenic*—mass incarceration actually perpetuates crime.

Why? In prison, people receive few supportive services and become more disconnected from their families, social networks, and jobs. Many prisons don't offer vocational, education, or reentry programs. Many that do have long waiting lists to participate.[13] Incarceration has become about neither rehabilitation nor holding people accountable. Instead, it has become about retribution. Prison is a place of social and physical isolation, of enforced idleness, often without basic necessities, meaningful activities, or adequate medical care.[14] Many jails and prisons have come under investigative scrutiny for routinely violating the constitutional rights of those incarcerated there. At any time, the U.S. Department of Justice is actively conducting investigations or attempting to enforce consent decrees or settlement agreements in dozens of cases regarding constitutional rights violations in prisons, jails, and juvenile detention facilities across the country.[15]

Yet each year, more than six hundred thousand people return home from America's prisons.[16] Many of them are utterly unprepared to rejoin their communities. But even if they are, the effect of criminal convictions has a long tail. What awaits the incarcerated after years in prison? When they attempt to rejoin their family and community, they run up against more than forty thousand rules, laws, and regulations that make it nearly impossible for them to find jobs or housing, or to vote.[17] Millions of low-income people are saddled with fees and fines because of their contact with the justice system. Many are reincarcerated because they cannot pay this debt. In fact, thirty states impose a modern-day poll tax, requiring those with felony convictions to pay all fines and fees related to their convictions before they can vote.[18] Many who return to their communities are already struggling with a host of social problems, with few social services that address them.

How has our nation failed so stunningly to erect guardrails to ward against the justice system's worst harms? How have we failed to rein in its punitive excess?

This book seeks to explore these central questions.

Addressing a vast range of issues—from policing to prosecution, sentencing to incarceration itself—this series of essays highlights how our nation has prioritized punishment as the dominant method of dealing with social harm. These essays illustrate a thread that runs through a maze of local, state, and federal agencies that have all contributed—intentionally or not—to producing this phenomenon. As Jeremy Travis and Bruce Western write in their conclusion to this book, "The long history of punitive excess with its damaging effects on poor people and in Black and Brown communities is itself the product of a grave democracy deficit. The laws that have brought about the era of punitive excess were all passed by our elected representatives." This book's contributors include legal scholars, writers who have experienced incarceration, activists, and those who are currently working to improve the fairness and humaneness of our criminal legal system.

Our country struggles with its deep-rooted impulse to punish people in ways that are far beyond what could be considered proportionate. This includes not just lengthy sentences such as life without parole, but also how we trap individuals in a lifetime of debt with legal financial obligations. This disproportionality is also illustrated in how we create complex posttraumatic stress disorder for the millions who suffer violent and inhumane treatment in prison and jail. We have lost any commitment to proportionality when we erect more and more barriers to reentry, such as restrictions on public housing and job eligibility for those convicted of a felony.

Our nation's justice system fails to live up to the American ideals of equality, fairness, and redemption. These essays ask whether, when, and how we could have made different decisions that would have redirected the evolution of these systems of punishment and social control. Are we finally at a historic moment where we can begin to persuade Americans that our punitive responses to social disorder must change? Or, alternatively, are we always just one uptick in crime away from a return to punitive responses?

While editing these essays, I was reminded of W. H. Auden's poem, "Law Like Love," specifically the fifth stanza:

Others say, Law is our Fate;
Others say, Law is our State;
Others say, others say
Law is no more.
Law has gone away.[19]

Many of the essays in this series provoke the reader to wonder whether in fact law has gone away. Kathy Foer-Morse asks where the justice is in her suffering sexual assault in jail. "How does this embody the rule of law?" she writes. Blake Strode details a married couple who were arrested during a pretextual police stop and spent a month in jail, unable to post bail, never appearing before a judge during that time. Carlton Miller reports on how his brother was convicted of multiple felony crimes by a non-unanimous jury in Louisiana.

Across the pages of this book, the contributors highlight the structural racism that created and sustains America's punitive justice policies. Nkechi Taifa describes how President Nixon's domestic policy advisor John Ehrlichman admitted that the war on drugs was racially motivated. Monica Bell comments on "how punitiveness is the very fabric of how we respond not only to crime, but to Blackness—especially to young Black men." Ted Johnson writes, "In the end, we have a system where justice is delivered unevenly and, at times, arbitrarily. It's as if structural racism compels Lady Justice to lift her blindfold and slant her scales, forcing some of her people at the margins to tumble off the edge beyond her reach."

Another key theme focuses on how those who encounter our nation's law enforcement, criminal courts, jails, and prisons are seen as outsiders or the Other. Rahsaan "New York" Thomas, writing from inside California's San Quentin Prison, notes that correctional officers are "trained not to see us as human; it helps them do their jobs." Christopher Blackwell, writing from a prison in Washington State, describes the dehumanizing experience of having to strip nude in front of a correctional officer, his "naked feet touching the cold, filthy, concrete floor." Peggy McGarry writes, "We seem to be content to waste the lives of those who have broken the law."

Yet if we look deeply enough between the cracks of our nation's broken criminal justice system, we may find seeds of hope starting to sprout. Many places offer promising new approaches for how we treat those who encounter our harsh and unforgiving legal system. Alison Siegler writes about federal legislation that, if passed, could reduce mandatory minimum sentences. David Singleton writes about the work he conducts with Beyond Guilt to creatively work with prosecutors and judges to create pathways of release from prison, where traditional legal avenues offer no hope. Steven Chanenson, Jordan Hyatt, and Synøve Andersen write about their work integrating research and policy to explore whether Scandinavian correctional principles and practices that emphasize human dignity can work effectively in Pennsylvania. Ram Subramanian, writing about humanizing aspects of some northern European prisons currently being piloted in the United States, makes the point that treating people with respect and dignity is essentially free.

Explaining that prisons are uniquely an American creation, Morris also acknowledges that "they are a pervasive American export, like tobacco in their international acceptance, and perhaps also in their adverse consequences."[20] Yet this book explores how countries such as Norway, Germany, and Finland consciously turned away from punitiveness as they built new prisons.

The American system of punishment, however, is different in both structure and design that make wholesale reform challenging. The late professor of law Robert Ferguson wrote in his 2014 book, *Inferno: An Anatomy of American Punishment*, "The instruments of punishment are carefully divided. Legislatures create criminal statutes, police use them to arrest, prosecutors charge, juries decide, judges pronounce sentence, and prison officials carry out the sentence. The approach to punishment is multifaceted in the name of fairness and objectivity, but it serves an exculpatory purpose as well. The separations in the function of punishment mean that no single official ever has to look directly in the abyss. No one punisher need feel the full burden of creating suffering."[21]

These essays bolster Ferguson's assessment of how fragmented America's justice system is. Berkeley professor Malcom Feeley points out that the United States is subdivided into more than three thousand counties.[22] Most of these counties have a jail, usually within the control of an elected sheriff. Law enforcement agencies total more than ten thousand, most funded locally. He writes, "It is as if the separate parts of the machinery of justice were manufactured by one group, assembled by another, and operated by still a third, all working without a common blueprint or meaningful coordination, let alone oversight."[23]

We are left with a dysfunctional maze of agencies that aim for justice, fairness, and due process. But does America's fragmented form of government—reflecting a tradition of localism—make it too difficult to cure the worst excesses of the justice system? How can a nation truly oversee more than 4,400 prisons and jails to ensure that those inside are treated with respect and dignity, and that conditions do not violate the U.S. Constitution? Ferguson points to how, in our current punishment system, no one person in this complex regime feels the full weight of the suffering they create. Yet this also creates a system in which no one person can be held accountable for its failings. It also creates a type of inertia, a momentum that makes reform or—better yet—the coordination of reform difficult within a system that is so fragmented and disconnected.

This book sheds light on where the machinery of justice has stopped working and drives us forward to reimagine America's entire system of punishment.

For decades, a huge swath of policymakers and government officials has weaponized fears about public safety; it is a familiar playbook in the political arena. These essays explore how we, as a nation, can respond to harm or injury without perpetuating such harm ourselves. How do we hold people accountable without passing on the myriad harms we now know are associated with mass incarceration—not only to the individual but also to his or her family and community? What is our ethical obligation to those behind bars?

How we grapple with these questions will determine whether we can carve a path away from punitive excess in our criminal legal system.

NOTES

1. See Marc Mauer, *Race to Incarcerate* (New York: The New Press, 2006), 2.
2. The term *penitentiary* here is used as distinct from *prison* in a general sense to mean an institution ostensibly focused on the rehabilitation of incarcerated people. Eastern State Penitentiary, opened in 1829, used the "Pennsylvania System" of incarceration, which encouraged continuous separate confinement and reflection guided by conversations with wardens and chaplains, as opposed to New York's "Auburn System," in which incarcerated people were required to perform congregate work during the day and be separated in panopticon-style rooms at night, all while maintaining absolute silence. See Harry Barnes, "Historial Origin of the Prison System in America," *Journal of Criminal Law and*

Criminology 12, no. 1 (1921): 35–60, 40–58, https://core.ac.uk/download/pdf/230979849.pdf. However, several punitive prisons predated the 1829 establishment of Eastern State, including Walnut Street, which many consider to have become the first prison in the United States when it was converted from a jail in 1790. See Rex Skidmore, "Penological Pioneering in the Walnut Street Jail, 1789–1799," *Journal of Criminal Law and Criminology* 39, no. 2 (1948): 167–80, https://scholarlycommons.law.northwestern.edu/cgi/viewcontent.cgi?referer=&httpsredir=1&article=3569&context=jclc. Other claimants for the first prison include Newgate in Connecticut, established in 1773. Alexis M. Durham, "Newgate of Connecticut: Origins and Early Days of an Early American Prison," *Justice Quarterly* 6, no. 1 (1989): 89–116.

3. Norval Morris, *The Future of Imprisonment* (Chicago: University of Chicago Press, 1974), 4.
4. Wendy Sawyer and Peter Wagner, *Mass Incarceration: The Whole Pie 2023* (Northampton, MA: Prison Policy Initiative, 2023), https://www.prisonpolicy.org/reports/pie2023.html.
5. Zhen Zeng, "Jail Inmates in 2021—Statistical Tables," NCJ 304888 (Washington, DC: U.S. Department of Justice, Bureau of Justice Statistics, 2022), 1, https://bjs.ojp.gov/sites/g/files/xyckuh236/files/media/document/ji21st.pdf.
6. Wendy Sawyer and Peter Wagner, *Mass Incarceration: The Whole Pie 2023* (Northampton, MA: Prison Policy Initiative, 2023), https://www.prisonpolicy.org/reports/pie2023.html.
7. Prison Policy Initiative, "United States profile," accessed January 26, 2023, https://www.prisonpolicy.org/profiles/US.html.
8. Ames Grawert and Noah Kim, "Myths and Realities: Understanding Recent Trends in Violent Crime" (New York: Brennan Center for Justice, updated May 9, 2023), https://www.brennancenter.org/our-work/research-reports/myths-and-realities-understanding-recent-trends-violent-crime.
9. UChicago UrbanLabs, "Can Street Lighting Reduce Crime?," accessed June 23, 2023, https://urbanlabs.uchicago.edu/projects/crime-lights-study.
10. Don Stemen, *The Prison Paradox: More Incarceration Will Not Make Us Safer* (New York: Vera Institute of Justice, 2017), 4, 12n43, figure 1, https://www.vera.org/downloads/publications/for-the-record-prison-paradox_02.pdf.
11. Cameron Kimble and Ames Grawert, "Between 2007 and 2017, 34 States Reduced Crime and Incarceration in Tandem" (New York: Brennan Center for Justice, August 9, 2019), https://www.brennancenter.org/our-work/analysis-opinion/between-2007-and-2017-34-states-reduced-crime-and-incarceration-tandem.
12. Lauren-Brooke Eisen, James Austin, James Cullen, Jonathan Frank, and Inimai M. Chettiar, *How Many Americans Are Unnecessarily Incarcerated?* (New York: Brennan Center for Justice, 2016), https://www.brennancenter.org

/our-work/research-reports/how-many-americans-are-unnecessarily-incar cerated.

13. See, for example, Ames Grawert and Patricia Richman, *The First Step Act's Prison Reforms* (New York: Brennan Center for Justice, 2022), 6, https://www .brennancenter.org/our-work/research-reports/first-step-acts-prison-reforms.
14. Marta Nelson, Samuel Feineh, and Maris Mapolski, A *New Paradigm for Sentencing in the United States* (New York: Vera Institute of Justice, 2023), 9–10, https://www.vera.org/downloads/publications/Vera-Sentencing-Report -2023.pdf.
15. U.S. Department of Justice, "Special Litigation Section Case Summaries," June 13, 2023, https://www.justice.gov/crt/special-litigation-section-case -summaries/download. See cases listed under "Corrections."
16. Assistant Secretary for Planning and Evaluation, "Incarceration & Reentry," U.S. Department of Health and Human Services, accessed June 23, 2023, https:// aspe.hhs.gov/topics/human-services/incarceration-reentry-0.
17. National Inventory of Collateral Consequences of Conviction, "What Are Collateral Consequences?," accessed June 23, 2023, https://niccc.national reentryresourcecenter.org.
18. An analysis of all fifty states and the District of Columbia's rights restoration schemes reveals thirty jurisdictions in which returning citizens may be required to pay legal financial obligations (LFOs) to regain the right to vote. These schemes fall into two broad categories: those that explicitly require full payment of LFOs as part of the voting rights restoration statutes and those that implicitly require payment of LFOs for voting rights restoration because they condition completion of parole or probation on payment of LFOs. For a definition of LFOs, see Civil Rights Clinic, *Can't Pay, Can't Vote: A National Survey on the Modern Poll Tax* (Washington, DC: Campaign Legal Center, 2019), 20, https://campaignlegal.org/sites/default/files/2019-07/CLC_CPCV_Report _Final_0.pdf.
19. Auden, "Law Like Love," *Another Time*, stanza 5, http://web.mit.edu/cordelia /www/Poems/law_like_love.html.
20. Morris, *The Future of Imprisonment*, 5.
21. Robert A. Ferguson, *Inferno* (Cambridge, MA: Harvard University Press, 2018), 13.
22. Malcolm M. Feeley, "Opening Keynote Address: How To Think About Criminal Court Reform," *Boston University Law Review* 98 (2018): 673–730, 675, https://www.bu.edu/bulawreview/files/2018/06/FEELEY.pdf.
23. Feeley, "Opening Keynote Address."

PART ONE

A HISTORY OF CRIME AND PUNITIVE RESPONSE

1

ADDRESSING VIOLENT CRIME MORE EFFECTIVELY

David Alan Sklansky

IN THE EARLY 2020S, as the United States struggled to address COVID-19, homicides across the country rose sharply and aggravated assaults appeared to increase as well. The numbers were frightening: a nearly 30 percent jump in killings in 2020 and a further increase of roughly 4 percent in 2021.[1] From January 2020 through December 2021, about 44,900 lives were lost to violence in the United States—nearly 11,900 more than would have been killed had homicide rates stayed the same as in 2019.[2]

These numbers paled, of course, beside the 845,000 American deaths from the coronavirus in 2020 and 2021.[3] It's also true that homicide rates across the United States stayed far below their peaks in the early 1980s and early 1990s and about the same as what they were in the early 2000s.[4] Monthly homicide rates also dipped slightly—by about 2 percent—in the first half of 2022.[5] Still, 11,900 killings—let alone 44,900 killings—is a staggering toll. The numbers were even more devastating for Black Americans and Latinos, who are disproportionately the victims of lethal violence in the United States. For Black men under forty-five, homicide is far and away the leading cause of death, accounting for nearly a third of all fatalities; for Latino boys and men age nineteen or younger, it is the second leading cause of death.[6]

The sharp rise in homicides in the early 2020s deserved and received a good deal of attention. Some of the responses, however, doubled down on the kinds of policies that gave us mass incarceration and then helped perpetuate it—in particular, the aggressive use of decades-long, mandatory prison sentences for "violent" crimes.[7] In early 2022, for example, Tennessee adopted a so-called truth-in-sentencing law that eliminated early release for people convicted of a range of violent crimes and narcotics trafficking offenses.[8] There are better ways than this to respond: approaches that have proven effective in reducing extreme violence without driving prison populations even higher.

For the last half century, America's chief strategy for attacking violent crime has been to double down on punishment. More than 40 percent of all people in U.S. jails and prisons are serving time for offenses classified as violent, many of them with mandatory terms prescribed by three-strikes laws adopted in the 1990s.[9] About 36 percent of all California prisoners, for example, were sentenced under the state's three-strikes law.[10]

These laws are part of a web of punitive policies aimed at violent offenders, who also are commonly excluded from diversion programs, problem-solving courts, eligibility for early parole or humanitarian release, opportunities to expunge or seal convictions, and laws allowing re-enfranchisement.[11] In Oklahoma, for instance, defendants charged with violent crimes cannot be diverted to drug courts or mental health courts.[12] If they are convicted of specified violent offenses and sent to prison, they can be paroled only by special order of the governor, and generally will be ineligible to use the state's expungement statute.[13] In 2022, the California legislature passed the nation's broadest records expungement law but excluded violent offenders as well as registered sex offenders from its coverage.[14]

People charged with violent crimes are also often denied procedural protections provided to other defendants. For example, in Nebraska the evidentiary privileges for spouses cannot be invoked by defendants accused of violent offenses.[15] Even before the pandemic, violent crime was something of a third rail for criminal justice reform in the United States, despite the clear, mathematical fact that seriously addressing mass incarceration without radically reducing penalties for violent offenders is impossible.

Three things are wrong with these brute force responses to violent crime. The first is that they impose massive harm for negligible benefit.[16] No evidence indicates that draconian sentences have done much to reduce violence in the United States.[17] They keep offenders locked up long after the individual represents any significant threat, and they don't appreciably increase deterrence, which depends more on the certainty of punishment than on its severity.[18] It's true that crime plummeted in the 1990s, when imprisonment rates were rising, but imprisonment rates also rose during the 1970s and 1980s without any change in crime rates.[19] Further, crime rates during the 1990s—particularly rates of serious violent offenses—dropped just as dramatically in Canada as in the United States, and Canada had no mass incarceration.[20] Decades of research have failed to show any beneficial effect of long U.S. prison sentences on public safety.[21] What is certain is that they destroy lives, tear apart families, hollow out communities, and wreck state budgets.

The second problem, which exacerbates the first, is that violence is a morally freighted term without clear boundaries. Calling a crime violent is a way of placing it beyond the pale, outside the proper sphere of mercy, redemption, or understanding. Legal definitions of *violent crime* are highly arbitrary, reflecting the vagaries of moral condemnation rather than efforts at descriptive accuracy. Burglary is widely classified as violent, for example, even if no one is hurt or even at home when the crime occurs. Arkansas and Rhode Island even treat larceny as a violent offense.[22] Bodily assaults, on the other hand, generally trigger the special penalties for violent crimes only when they are "aggravated" by the infliction of "serious" injury or the involvement of a "deadly" weapon, factors that typically reflect the subjective judgment of police and prosecutors.[23] Whether a crime qualifies as violent can also be heavily influenced by racial bias and other forms of prejudice.

The third and final problem with America's heightened penalties for violent crime is that they treat violence as overwhelmingly a matter of character rather than of circumstances. It takes remarkably few episodes of violence for someone to be labeled a career or habitual offender: three "strikes," or in many places only two. In California, a single previous conviction for a "serious or violent felony" doubles the required prison term for a subsequent offense.[24] In many states, similarly, a single conviction for a violent felony, sometimes only a single arrest, can disqualify a defendant from diversion programs. The assumption underlying modern recidivism enhancements, and the eligibility restrictions on diversion programs, is not that a small subset of murders, rapes, and aggravated assaults are carried out by people who commit violent offenses again and again; it is that anyone who commits two or three violent crimes is likely to be inherently violent.[25] U.S. laws increasingly assume that the roots of violence are in the hearts and minds of offenders, not in the situations in which they find themselves. The powerful social drivers of violence tend to be neglected, from poverty and racism to the wide availability of guns in the United States.

COVID-19 may drive violence as well. It's not clear exactly why homicides spiked in the United States during the pandemic. The same thing didn't happen in the United Kingdom or elsewhere in Europe, and some cities in the United States also bucked the trend. Some of the nationwide increase in killings in 2020 and 2021 may have had to do with the disruption of social services, which were already thinner here than across the Atlantic. Some may have been due to a surge of gun purchases during the pandemic.[26] Some may be traceable to the erosion of trust between the police and public that worsened following the murder of George Floyd in May 2020. Also, significant periods of lock-down and social isolation in 2020 and 2021 exacerbated mental health challenges.

One factor that can be ruled out, though, is the adoption of more lenient criminal justice policies, including the early release of some prisoners, in liberal parts of the country. Killings have risen in all parts of the country, just as much in Republican-led cities as in cities with Democratic mayors, and just as much in counties with and without progressive prosecutors.[27] Ironically, San Francisco—where District Attorney Chesa Boudin was removed from office by a voter recall fueled by concerns about rising crime—saw a much more modest rise in homicides during the pandemic than many other cities.[28]

If COVID-19 in fact increased homicides, simplistic generalizations about "violent crime" in turn worsened the public health emergency. It was clear from early 2020 that overcrowded prisons and jails would help the virus spread rapidly. Government officials across the country, though, Democrats as well as Republicans, have repeatedly balked at releasing violent offenders, even as the death toll from the virus behind bars in the United States surpassed three thousand in November 2022, and even as the definition of violent remains vague and contingent.[29]

Even before the pandemic, far too many people were dying violently in the United States. Fortunately, evidence is growing that gun homicides between non-intimates—the kind of killings that have risen sharply over the past year and a half—can be decreased dramatically by violence reduction programs concentrated on the relatively small number of people, places, and social interactions responsible for most of the street violence in a given city.[30] These programs are not easy to carry out successfully and are even more difficult to sustain over the long term. Pairing focused deterrence with social services and peer-to-peer counseling, they require trust and collaboration between police and community groups, close analysis of local patterns of violence, restraint on the part of police and prosecutors, a strong commitment to helping individuals exit cycles of violence, and an institutional framework that can survive leadership changes, budget crises, and the inevitable calls for tougher approaches when, as in 2020 and 2021, homicide rates begin to climb.

The most famous of these programs, and a model for many of its successors, was Boston's Ceasefire initiative, which dramatically reduced youth homicides by interrupting cycles of retaliatory gang violence.[31] Ceasefire identified a relatively small number of groups responsible for the bulk of youth shootings in Boston and targeted their members with threats of criminal enforcement along with offers of economic support and social services if they refrained from gun violence. The program relied on consultation and coordination between the police department, a range of other municipal agencies and nonprofit groups, and inner-city clergy. A more recent successful version of the Ceasefire approach, in Oakland, California, has focused on adult shooters rather than juveniles (reflecting differences between homicide patterns in Oakland and Boston) and has deemphasized the role of the police while expanding the role of peer-to-peer counseling.[32]

It often takes several tries, stretching over years, before a city finds the right approach, appropriately tailored to local circumstances. Even the most successful programs, though, such as those in Boston and Oakland, are not panaceas: Oakland has seen an increase in gun violence during the pandemic, and firearms arrests among young people in Boston increased significantly in 2022.[33]

Still, we know these programs can work. The one in Boston reduced youth homicides substantially.[34] Those gains began to disappear in the early 2000s when the program was discontinued, then were recovered when the program was restarted. The results in Oakland were similarly impressive: both homicides and nonfatal shootings were cut nearly in half from 2012 to 2018.[35] We also know ways to reduce violent encounters between the police and the public, and ways to curtail prison violence, and ways to help victims of abuse within families and intimate relationships protect themselves from getting killed.[36] The $300 million that the federal government allocated in 2022 for community-based violence intervention programs is a step in the right direction.[37]

None of this is easy, though. Simpler and emotionally cathartic responses, like longer prison sentences for people convicted of violent crimes, have an obvious allure. But we have been down that road before. It leads nowhere good. Violence is a hard problem, and it cannot be ignored or simply wished away. But even the most pressing of crises can be made worse.

NOTES

1. *The Guardian*, "FBI Records Slight Increase in 2021 Homicides—But Data Is Incomplete," October 5, 2022, https://www.theguardian.com/us-news/2022/oct/05/fbi-crime-data-2021-homicides.

2. Federal Bureau of Investigation (FBI), "The Transition to the National Incident-Based Reporting System (NIBRS): A Comparison of 2020 and 2021 NIBRS Estimates," https://www.justfacts.com/document/transition_national_incident-based_reporting_system_2020_2021_nibrs_estimates_fbi_2022.pdf; FBI, "Crime in the United States, 2019: Murder," U.S. Department of Justice, 2020, https://ucr.fbi.gov/crime-in-the-u.s/2019/crime-in-the-u.s.-2019/topic-pages/murder.
3. Farida B. Ahmad, Jodi A. Cisewski, and Robert N. Anderson, "Provisional Mortality Data—United States, 2021," *Morbidity and Mortality Weekly Report* 71, no. 17 (2022), https://www.cdc.gov/mmwr/volumes/71/wr/mm7117e1.htm.
4. Council on Criminal Justice, "Homicide Trends: What You Need to Know," October 5, 2021, https://counciloncj.org/homicide-trends-report.
5. Richard Rosenfeld, Bobby Boxerman, and Ernesto Lopez, "Pandemic, Social Unrest, and Crime in U.S. Cities: Mid-Year 2022 Update" (Washington, DC: Council on Criminal Justice, July 22, 2022), https://counciloncj.org/mid-year-2022-crime-trends.
6. Centers for Disease Control and Prevention (CDC), "Leading Causes of Death—Males—Non-Hispanic black—United States, 2017," November 20, 2019, https://www.cdc.gov/minorityhealth/lcod/men/2017/nonhispanic-black/index.htm; "Leading Causes of Death—Males—Hispanic—United States, 2017," November 20, 2019, https://www.cdc.gov/minorityhealth/lcod/men/2017/hispanic/index.htm.
7. David Alan Sklansky, *A Pattern of Violence* (Cambridge, MA: Harvard University Press, 2021), https://www.hup.harvard.edu/catalog.php?isbn=9780674248908.
8. State of Tennessee, House Bill 2656/Senate Bill 2248, https://www.capitol.tn.gov/Bills/112/Bill/HB2656.pdf; Melissa Brown, "Tennessee General Assembly Passes Controversial 'Truth in Sentencing' legislation," *Nashville Tennessean*, April 21, 2022, https://www.tennessean.com/story/news/politics/2022/04/21/tennessee-general-assembly-passes-controversial-truth-sentencing-legislation/7400115001.
9. Alexi Jones, "Reforms Without Results: Why States Should Stop Excluding Violent Offenses from Criminal Justice Reforms," Press release (Northhampton, MA: Prison Policy Initiative, April 2020), https://www.prisonpolicy.org/reports/violence.html.
10. Mia Bird, Omair Gill, Johanna Lacoe, Molly Pickard, Steven Raphael, and Alissa Skog, *Three Strikes in California* (Berkeley: California Policy Lab, August 2022), 13, https://www.capolicylab.org/wp-content/uploads/2022/08/Three-Strikes-in-California.pdf.
11. Michael O'Hear, "Third-Class Citizenship: The Escalating Legal Consequences of Committing a 'Violent' Crime," *Journal of Criminal Law and Criminology* 109, no. 2 (2019): 165–236, https://scholarlycommons.law.northwestern.edu/cgi/viewcontent.cgi?article=7649&context=jclc.

12. 22 Okla. Stat. § 471.2 (OSCN 2022), Oklahoma Drug Court Act, https://www.oscn.net/applications/oscn/DeliverDocument.asp?CiteID=70501; Oklahoma Department of Mental Health and Substance Abuse Services, "Department of Mental Health and Substance Abuse Services: FY 2012 Budget Request," January 25, 2011, https://oklahoma.gov/content/dam/ok/en/odmhsas/documents/a0002/budgetrequestoutline-1-25-2011-.pdf.
13. 21 Okla. Stat. § 21-13.1 (OSCN 2022); Title 22, § 22-18; Title 57, § 332.16. https://oksenate.gov/sites/default/files/2019-12/os21.pdf.
14. Don Thompson, "California Advances Broadest US Law Sealing Criminal Records," *Seattle Times*, August 18, 2022, https://www.seattletimes.com/nation-world/nation/california-advances-broadest-us-law-sealing-criminal-records/.
15. Neb. Rev. Stat. § 27-505, https://nebraskalegislature.gov/laws/statutes.php?statute=27-505.
16. Mark A. R. Kleiman, *When Brute Force Fails* (Princeton, NJ: Princeton University Press, 2010).
17. Don Stemen, "The Prison Paradox: More Incarceration Will Not Make Us Safer" (New York: Vera Institute of Justice, July 2017), 1–5, https://www.vera.org/downloads/publications/for-the-record-prison-paradox_02.pdf.
18. Daniel S. Nagin, "Deterrence in the Twenty-First Century," *Crime and Justice* 42, no. 1 (2013): 199–263.
19. Franklin E. Zimring, *The Great American Crime Decline* (New York: Oxford University Press, 2006).
20. Zimring, *Great American Crime Decline*, 107–34.
21. Oliver Roeder, Lauren-Brooke Eisen, and Julia Bowling, *What Caused the Crime Decline?* (New York: Brennan Center for Justice, 2019), 7, 21, 25–26, https://www.brennancenter.org/sites/default/files/2019-08/Report_What_Caused_The_Crime_Decline.pdf.
22. O'Hear, "Third-Class Citizenship," 171–76.
23. For more on aggravated assault, see the definition by Cornell University's Legal Information Institute, https://www.law.cornell.edu/wex/aggravated_assault.
24. Bird et al., *Three Strikes in California*, 3.
25. Recidivism sentencing enhancements have been defined as those that "increase criminal sentences for defendants with prior criminal convictions." Sarah French Russell, "Rethinking Recidivist Enhancements: The Role of Prior Drug Convictions in Federal Sentencing," *UC Davis Law Review*, 43, no. 4 (2010): 1135, https://lawreview.law.ucdavis.edu/issues/43/4/articles/43-4_russell.pdf.
26. Matthew Miller, Wilson Zhang, and Deborah Azrael, "Firearm Purchasing During the COVID-19 Pandemic: Results from the 2021 National Firearms Survey," *Annals of Internal Medicine* 175, no. 2 (2022): 219–25, https://www.acpjournals.org/doi/full/10.7326/M21-3423.
27. German Lopez, "2020's Historic Surge in Murders, Explained," *Vox*, March 25, 2021, https://www.vox.com/22344713/murder-violent-crime-spike-surge-2020

-COVID-19-coronavirus; Ames Grawert and Noah Kim, "Myths and Realities"; Todd Fogelson, Ron Levi, Rick Rosenfeld, Heather Schoenfeld, Don Stemen, Jennifer Wood, and Andres Rengifo, *Public Prosecution and Violent Crime: A Review of Data on Homicides and Progressive Prosecution in the United States* (Toronto: Global Justice Lab, 2022), https://munkschool.utoronto.ca/gjl/research/full-report-violent-crime-and-public-prosecution.

28. Jeremy B. White, "San Francisco District Attorney Ousted in Recall Election," *Politico*, June 8, 2022, https://www.politico.com/news/2022/06/08/chesa-boudin-san-francisco-district-attorney-recall-00038002; Susie Neilson, "San Francisco Crime Rates Drastically Shifted in the Pandemic. These Charts Show What's Happening Now," *San Francisco Chronicle*, April 8, 2022, https://www.sfchronicle.com/crime/article/San-Francisco-crime-rate-17065509.php.
29. As of November 28, 2022, the UCLA Law Covid Behind Bars Project reported 3,169 "deaths among incarcerated people," a figure that includes those in jails and prisons as well as immigrants and young people in detention (see https://uclacovidbehindbars.org). Also see Prison Policy Initiative, "The Most Significant Criminal Justice Policy Changes from the COVID-19 Pandemic," accessed November 28, 2022, https://www.prisonpolicy.org/virus/virusresponse.html; Maura Turcotte, Rachel Sherman, Rebecca Griesbach, and Ann Hinga Klein, "The Real Toll from Prison Covid Cases May Be Higher than Reported," *New York Times*, July 7, 2021, https://www.nytimes.com/2021/07/07/us/inmates-incarcerated-covid-deaths.html.
30. Anthony A. Braga, David Weisburd, and Brandon Turchan, "Focused Deterrence Strategies Effects on Crime: A Systematic Review," *Campbell Systematic Reviews* 15 (2019): 1–65, https://onlinelibrary.wiley.com/doi/full/10.1002/cl2.1051.
31. Anthony A. Braga, "Youth Gang Gun Violence in Boston, Massachusetts," in *Problem-Oriented Policing*, ed. Michael S. Scott and Ronald V. Clarke (New York: Routledge, 2020).
32. Samantha Michaels, "Whose Streets?," *Mother Jones*, September/October 2020, https://www.motherjones.com/crime-justice/2020/07/Oakland-ceasefire-shootings-murder-rate-social-services-life-coach-boston-miracle-thomas-abt-david-kennedy-cat-brooks.
33. Susie Neilson, "Gun Violence in Oakland Has Become a 'Pandemic Within the Pandemic.' Here's What's Going On," *San Francisco Chronicle*, December 3, 2021, https://www.sfchronicle.com/crime/article/Gun-violence-in-Oakland-has-become-a-pandemic-16670919.php; Ivy Scott and Travis Andersen, "As Juvenile Gun Arrests Spike in Boston, Wu Launches Youth Safety Task Force," *Boston Globe*, November 27, 2022, https://www.bostonglobe.com/2022/11/27/metro/juvenile-gun-arrests-spike-boston-wu-launches-youth-safety-task-force.
34. Anthony A. Braga, David M. Kennedy, Elin J. Waring, and Anne Morrison Piehl, "Problem-Oriented Policing, Deterrence, and Youth Violence: An

Evaluation of Boston's Operation Ceasefire," *Journal of Research in Crime and Delinquency* 38, no. 3 (2001): 220, https://www.d.umn.edu/~jmaahs/MA%20Theory%20Articles/Braga_problem_oriented%20policing_deterrence.pdf.

35. Mike McLively and Brittany Nieto, *A Case Study in Hope: Lessons from Oakland's Remarkable Reduction in Gun Violence* (San Francisco: Giffords Law Center to Prevent Gun Violence, 2019), 5, https://giffords.org/wp-content/uploads/2019/05/Giffords-Law-Center-A-Case-Study-in-Hope.pdf.
36. Alana Semuels, "How to Fix a Broken Police Department," *The Atlantic*, May 28, 2015, https://www.theatlantic.com/politics/archive/2015/05/Cincinnati-police-reform/393797; Donald Specter, "Making Prisons Safe: Strategies for Reducing Violence," *Washington University Journal of Law & Policy* 22, no. 1 (2006): 125–34, https://journals.library.wustl.edu/lawpolicy/article/id/840; Shon Hopwood, "How Atrocious Prisons Conditions Make Us All Less Safe" (New York: Brennan Center for Justice, August 9, 2021), https://www.brennancenter.org/our-work/analysis-opinion/how-atrocious-prisons-conditions-make-us-all-less-safe; Rachel Louise Snyder, *No Visible Bruises: What We Don't Know About Domestic Violence Can Kill Us* (New York: Bloomsbury Publishing, 2019).
37. Chip Brownlee, "Congress Approved Millions for Gun Violence Prevention. Will It Reach Grassroots Groups?," *The Trace*, August 18, 2022, https://www.thetrace.org/2022/08/biden-gun-violence-grant-application.

2

LOSING OUR PUNITIVE CIVIC RELIGION

Jonathan Simon

LIKE THE MORE THAN ONE MILLION AMERICANS who have died of COVID-19, those subject to the mass suffering and racial disproportionality of our highly punitive legal system—police, prisons, court supervision, immigration detention—bear grave witness to the moral and practical failings of American society and government. Indeed, with the COVID death rate in prisons 20 percent higher than the already high rates for Americans in general, due to overcrowding and health mismanagement, they are in some respects the same problem.[1] American government is simply much better at punishing people than caring for them.

The moral weight of our care deficits and punishment overreach has generated more debate about reforming or even abolishing parts of the criminal legal system than Americans have seen in a generation.[2] But, as the growing backlash to reform talk at the time of this writing in the fall of 2022 highlights, neither reform nor abolition will get very far unless Americans undertake a substantial rethinking of what we want and expect from punishment. The problem is not lack of efforts at reform. Centuries of enthusiastic innovation in punishment, and the police and court systems that go with it, have instead left American culture with too much confidence in punishment. Specifically, this history has embedded into our legal institutions and much else a set of powerful myths about punishment that have in their complementary accumulation turned it into nothing short of an American civic religion—one that offers criminal accountability as a kind of sacrament of legal fidelity and state punishment as a primary source of individual correction and social improvement. It may be more comfortable to celebrate our national fidelity to the rule of law, or even the Constitution, but both repeatedly have been yielded to the imperatives of punishment and racially charged policing.[3]

Some version of these presumptions in favor of punishment can be found throughout the world, products of the imperial spread of European legal system and its punitive criminal law, but in America they have enjoyed an extraordinary degree of popularity from the earliest colonial days to the present. In many societies, crime is either a local concern or a subject for governmental and academic elites, although populism has changed that in many places. But in the United States, not one, but many law and order campaigns since the American Revolution in 1776, and arguably the Salem witchcraft panic in 1692, have helped make crime a primary subject of both popular entertainment and electoral politics and turned criminology into a truly popular science.[4]

To call these cognitive presumptions in favor of punishment myths may seem overly contentious, but their taken-for-granted quality makes them so powerful, leaving many Americans intuitively on the punitive side of every issue from library fines through capital punishment, despite little empirical support that punishing people helps anyone. Repeatedly promoted in courts, legislatures, pulpits, newspapers, and universities, punishment has long been America's preferred response to social crises of all sorts, from wars, to panics over immigration, to natural disasters. It is thus not surprising that despite recent calls for reform many have responded to the social crises of the pandemic by calling for even more police and incarceration.

Perhaps the oldest myth in our punitive civic faith, one with roots in medieval theology, has the high-minded label *accountability*. People who commit crimes must be held accountable; their debt to society must be paid. Left unsaid is why crimes, which generally are complex social events with many causes, should be thought of as creating a debt and punishment as a repayment. The appeal of accountability, of paying a debt to society, is supposed to be reintegration; in reality, it has usually meant the opposite—sanctions into perpetuity.

The reason lies in the history behind this curious exercise in metaphorical or even magical thinking, in fact, a watershed event in the expansion of the state's role in resolving crimes and exacting punishment that left the state as the legal victim of most crimes. Over time, this situation displaced the ability of those harmed by others to seek compensation through the cooperation of families or local secular or clerical authorities (but rarely courts). The state eventually monopolized legal punishment. The most visible product of this legal revolution is the emergence of public control over charging and trying virtually all criminal offenses. Less visible is the shift in the potential scale of punitiveness as harm done by one human being to another to harm done to the sovereign itself. The debt was no longer calculated as an injury to a person but instead as one to the law itself, the damage of which could be considered incalculable. The mediated contest between two relatively equal parties was replaced by a sovereign empowered to control every aspect of the dispute from the extent of the debt created by the crime. This included the ways and means of repayment, such as torture on a scaffold and then, after the eighteenth century, frequently torture in a prison.

The United States is hardly alone in emphasizing the role of punishment as accountability and a way to strengthen law. The same can be found in the penal law of all nations as well as in modern human rights law, which is particularly insistent that crimes against humanity not be forgiven, even as part of reconciliation in conflict-ridden societies.[5] America is unique, though, in the degree of its zeal for exacting full payment. Other countries routinely respond to overcrowding in prisons with pardons and even mass amnesties and use both to make sure that few reach very old age in prison.[6] American states and the federal government routinely allow thousands to die in prison each year of old age, despite compassionate release powers.[7] U.S. courts often pursue even those who avoid incarceration or who eventually win release with demands for financial repayment and ongoing supervision in the community.[8] Alexes Harris and Peggy McGarry's essays in this volume drive home that point (see chapters 27 and 29). In the meantime, talk of using release powers to avoid the excessive prison deaths during COVID-19 was dismissed by governors in blue as well as red states even though the candidates for release, older and sicker prisoners, were deemed a low public safety risk.[9]

The second oldest myth of punishment divides the population into the hardworking and the idle, attributing crime to the latter, and ascribing to punishment the power to discipline the idle and thus reform them. The myth of discipline has ancient roots, but in American culture dates back to the post-revolutionary period; the disruption of war, economic transformation, and increased immigration led to the first of many political turns toward punishment as a way to improve the social order of the new democracy and its concomitant slave society.

The birth of the penitentiary in the Northeast in the early 1800s as a place of forced labor and solitary confinement was perhaps the most famous and influential response.[10] Replacing corporal and capital punishment with confinement in a place of comprehensive control and forced labor, the new prisons sought to reform as well as punish. A less visible form of the merger of forced labor and containment was slavery, especially the carceral form of plantation slavery in the Mississippi Delta during the cotton boom.[11]

Today, the almost religious zeal with which nineteenth-century reformers touted the crime prevention value of forcing the idle to work has slackened somewhat, but in other ways it lingers, especially for the poor. Prisons today are rarely factories, but they still make imprisoned people work at hard and sometimes dangerous jobs without occupational safety rights, collective bargaining rights, or minimum wage compensation.[12] Worse yet, prison work rarely imparts skills translating to employment opportunities on reentry.

This is not a brief against making rehabilitative services available to the people we currently incarcerate or coercively supervise in the community. It is a brief against conflating those services with the primary mandate to punish. As numerous memoirs from and qualitative interviews with Americans incarcerated during the long wave of mass incarceration reflect, many people in prison are coping with multiple obstacles to success in life, including trauma, poor school success, and discrimination often both on the basis of race and criminal legal system status. Tempting as it is to think we can make prisons better by adding rehabilitation, the same accounts from those behind bars show how consistently and totally the imperative of custody and punishment overwhelm the best rehabilitative intentions. Instead, our goal should be to replace punishment with participation in needed services and programs.

Perhaps the most powerful myth about punishment is the belief that our law enforcement institutions—judges, police, prosecutors, prison officials—are experts at identifying a class of truly dangerous repeat criminals whose removal to prison would make society much safer. Beginning in the late nineteenth century, laws began to extend greater power to prosecutors and judges to enhance punishment for those they perceived as dangerous and unamenable to the reformatory power of punishment. These new punitive mechanisms—such as probation, parole, and indeterminate sentencing—gave courts and in some cases prison systems enhanced powers to distinguish between law breakers amenable to reform and those deemed irredeemable and permanently dangerous.

By the 1970s, all these myths were losing their cultural credibility, demonstrated in serious discussions of reducing reliance on imprisonment and reconceiving the concept of public safety.[13] By the end of the decade, however, a new campaign to address social instability through more policing and imprisonment was ascending. A new myth—that cleansing neighborhoods of disorderly people would discourage likely offenders from coming there ("Broken Windows") and reinforce community standards against a tide of violence and poverty—helped justify the largest increase in prisons and policing in America's history.[14] As critics noted early on, both disorder and community standards were racially defined in the United States, and broken windows, whatever its original intentions, soon became a justification for aggressive racial profiling by police.[15] Although this approach is mostly associated with policing and prosecution of low-level crimes that involve disorder or harm to the quality of life in the community, it operates to lock in the other myths about punishment. Reducing aggressive policing and prosecution of low-level crimes is the easiest starting point for progressive prosecutors, around whom so much recent hope for reform has been laid. But as the June 2022 recall of one of the nation's most progressive prosecutors, San Francisco District Attorney Chesa Boudin, indicated, anger about homeless tent encampments and open drug use, which are classic broken windows targets, received the most attention by voters, despite Boudin's favorable record on serious crime.[16]

To take stock, American society is very punitive in part because we have given ourselves many reasons to believe in punishment and to think that it will help make our laws and our society stronger. We believe punishment will repay and restore victims and strengthen the law itself. We believe punishment will reform offenders and remove the dangerous. We believe punishment can make our communities more resilient by reinforcing prosocial norms. If all this punishment leads to a disproportionate impact on minorities, especially Black Americans, too many of us are ready to believe that it is a necessary price to pay for public safety. Punishment, in short, is an entire body of faith, a civic religion, and not, as we sometimes pretend in the academic setting, something that can be tested by experiment. This makes it difficult to shrink the carceral state even in periods, such as now, when many people agree on its flaws.

Our punitive past, however, need not doom us to a punitive future. We are not wrong to care about crime and the harm it does, but as the abolitionist Mariame Kaba puts it, "Our failure to build a culture of care that nurtures human growth and potential, rather than incubating desperation, ensures that more 'criminals' will be created."[17] If we want less crime and more care, we need to invent a new civic faith, one that replaces or reinvents the old myths.

Punishment claimed to repay the debt of crime, reform offenders, deselect the dangerous, and reinforce safe communities, but only through a kind of magical thinking. In fact, real crime victims need real support to heal and commitments from their community to prevent future harm, needs to which our carceral state commits little of its enormous resources. People who harm others need to learn other ways of living but prisons reinforce the harm-doing.[18] Addressing dangerousness and neighborhood safety are problems so soaked with systemic racism in the United States that they cannot be hidden away in a specialized criminal legal system guided by its supposed expertise, but must be politically discussed and collectively addressed.

NOTES

1. USAFacts, "How Many People in Prison Died of Covid-19," September 20, 2022, https://usafacts.org/articles/how-many-people-in-prisons-died-of-covid-19.
2. Marie Gottschalk, *Caught: The Prison State and the Lockdown of American Politics* (Princeton, NJ: Princeton University Press, 2016), 1.
3. On the Supreme Court's approach to policing and the Constituion, see Erwin Chemerinsky, *How the Supreme Court Empowered the Police and Subverted Civil Rights* (New York: Penguin, 2021), xi. One could, however, choose almost any other aspect and find a similar retreat from legality.
4. Jess Blumberg, "A Brief History of the Salem Witch Trials," *Smithsonian Magazine*, October 23, 2007, https://www.smithsonianmag.com/history/a-brief-history-of-the-salem-witch-trials-175162489; Marie Gottschalk, *The Prison and the Gallows: The Politics of Mass Incarceration in America* (Cambridge: Cambridge University Press, 2006), 4.
5. Lisa J. LaPlante, "Outlawing Amnesty: The Return of Criminal Justice in Transitional Justice Schemes," *Virginia Journal of International Law* 49 (2009): 933, https://media.law.wisc.edu/m/zkyjz/lisa_laplante_paper.pdf.
6. Jonathan Simon, "Amnesty Now! Ending Prison Overcrowding Through A Categorical Use of the Pardon Power," *University of Miami Law Review* 70 (2016): 444–88, https://lawreview.law.miami.edu/wp-content/uploads/2016/03/Amnesty-Now-Ending-Prison-Overcrowding-through-a-Categorical-Use-of-the-Pardon-Power.pdf.
7. E. Ann Carson, *Mortality in State and Federal Prisons, 2001–2019—Statistical Tables*, NCJ 300953 (Washington, DC: U.S. Department of Justice, Bureau of Justice Statistics, 2021), 13, https://bjs.ojp.gov/content/pub/pdf/msfp0119st.pdf.

8. Jean Trounstine, "Fighting the Fees that Force Prisoners to Pay for Their Incarceration," *Prison Legal News*, November 6, 2018, https //www.prisonlegalnews .org/news/2018/nov/6/fighting-fees-force-prisoners-pay-their-incarceration.
9. Emily Widra, "State Prisons and Local Jails Appear Indifferent to COVID Outbreaks, Refuse to Depopulate Dangerous Facilities" (Northampton, MA: Prison Policy Initiative, February 10, 2022), https://www.prisonpolicy.org/blog /2022/02/10/february2022_population.
10. Rebecca M. McLennan, *The Crisis of Imprisonment: Protest, Politics, and the Making of the American Penal State, 1776–1941* (Cambridge: Cambridge University Press, 2008), 4.
11. Walter Johnson, *River of Dark Dreams: Slavery and Empire in the Cotton Kingdom* (Cambridge, MA: Harvard University Press, 2013).
12. Jessica Kutz, "The Essential—and Dangerous—Work Prisoners Do," *High Country News*, April 23, 2021, https://www.hcn.org/articles/south-labor-the -essential-and-dangerous-work-prisoners-do.
13. See, for example, President's Commission on Law Enforcement and Administration of Justice, *The Challenge of Crime in a Free Society* (Washington, DC: U.S. Government Printing Office, 1967), https://www.ojp.gov/sites/g/files /xyckuh241/files/archives/ncjrs/42.pdf.
14. Bernard E. Harcourt and Jens Ludwig, "Reefer Madness: Broken Windows Policing and Misdemeanor Marijuana Arrests in New York City, 1989–2000," *Criminology & Public Policy* 6 (2007): 165–82, https://scholarship.law.columbia .edu/cgi/viewcontent.cgi?article=2435&context=faculty_scholarship; George L. Kelling and James Q. Wilson, "Broken Windows," *The Atlantic*, March 1982, https://www.theatlantic.com/magazine/archive/1982/03/broken-windows /304465.
15. Jeffrey Fagan and Garth Davies, "Street Stops and Broken Windows: *Terry*, Race, and Disorder in New York City," *Fordham Law Journal* 28 no. 2 (2000): 457–504.
16. Nicholas Turner and Sam McCann, "Chesa Boudin's Recall Isn't About Crime—It's About Gentrification" (New York: Vera Institute of Justice, July 26, 2022), https://www.vera.org/news/chesa-boudins-recall-isnt-about-crime-its -about-gentrification.
17. Mariame Kaba and Kelly Hayes, "A Jailbreak of the Imagination: Seeing Prisons for What They Are and Demanding Transformation," *Truthout*, May 3, 2018, https://truthout.org/articles/a-jailbreak-of-the-imagination-seeing-prisons -for-what-they-are-and-demanding-transformation.
18. Devah Pager, "The Mark of a Criminal Record," *American Journal of Sociology* 108, no. 5 (2003): 937–75, https://scholar.harvard.edu/files/pager/files/pager _ajs.pdf.

3

MASS INCARCERATION AND VICTIM DISREGARD

Two Sides of the Same Coin

Lenore Anderson

ON JUNE 24, 2017, Chicago resident and nurse Bertha Purnell experienced the unthinkable. Her youngest son, Maurice, who was twenty-eight years old at the time, was killed in front of a barbershop less than a mile from Bertha's home. An acquaintance of her son had pulled out a gun and shot him in the back after a disagreement. Bertha was thrown into a tailspin of paralyzing grief and forced to navigate hardship on top of hardship in the aftermath. Indifferent emergency room staff made her stand outdoors at the hospital as she waited to learn what happened on the night of the tragedy. Unending courtroom appearances included unexplained delays and degrading interactions with lawyers and judges were commonplace. She spent fruitless hours searching for nearby therapeutic help and grappled with additional trauma-induced health challenges that most everyone in her shoes experiences. "I spent most of my days in my car crying," she wrote in 2022. "I walked away from my career as a nurse—I realized I was trying to save lives and I couldn't save my own child."[1]

After five agonizing years, the perpetrator was finally convicted and sentenced to twenty years in prison with 50 percent credits reducing the length to ten years to be served, a sentence considered comparatively short for second-degree murder in today's U.S. criminal court practices. But the well-worn Hollywood tropes of the vengeance-driven victim are quite different from the nuanced and discerning reactions Bertha had after the dreadful process ended. "I have forgiven him. The forgiveness is for me, though. It is not really for him," she reflected. "This is someone who has young children and that really weighed hard on me, even though my son is no longer here. Somehow, I feel like we must break this cycle. I pray that the ten years he has behind bars mean something, that he becomes a better man so he can be a better father for his children."[2]

For Bertha, the most important outcome is not to be found in the toughest punishment possible. It's much deeper than that. "There has to be a purpose for this work," she said. "How do we stop people from thinking the only way to solve problems is to get a gun? We must find answers to stop the bleeding." From her perspective, ending the cycle of violence matters much more. Restorative justice "programming should be mandatory . . . along with reentry, parenting. . . . If he's just left to go back into old ways, it won't help his children."[3]

Although Bertha's wisdom and capacity for empathy are extraordinary, her views about the impact of tough justice on the cycle of trauma are not anomalous. Despite widespread assumptions to the contrary, many victims report sentiments like Bertha's. Most reject mass incarceration policies, preferring instead rehabilitative approaches to safety and justice and an emphasis on providing genuine help, including crisis assistance and healing services, to victims as well as people who've committed harm, to stop recurring trauma.

THE VICTIMS' RIGHTS MOVEMENT CONTRIBUTED TO MASS INCARCERATION

Over the past several decades, as the United States implemented historically unprecedented stringent criminal justice policies, law-and-order politicians constructed a narrative that framed these policies as part of a newfound sensitivity to the plight of crime victims. From the 1970s on, politicians joined with law enforcement associations and a new crop of victims' rights groups to form powerful lobbying coalitions in state capitols across the country, providing grist to the mill for those looking to extend the reach of the carceral system.[4] From the 1980s through the 2010s, thousands of laws, marketed as victims' rights legislation, were enacted around the country.[5] Some of these laws provided victims with new procedural rights in the criminal court process, such as to provide an impact statement, to proceeding notifications, and new opportunities for compensation. However, many others focused more on ratcheting up sentence lengths, expanding arrests, eliminating rehabilitative programs in prison, curtailing opportunities for release, and prohibiting eligibility for many types of jobs and housing to people with records.[6]

These sweeping legislative accomplishments birthed important new programs for victims, such as compensation, relocation, civil legal services, and other types of assistance. But they also fueled dramatic increases in the budgets of justice bureaucracies and the rate of U.S. incarceration. They also set up millions of people with records for a lifetime of poverty and exclusion. As I described in *In Their Names*, the movement for tough justice framed as victims' rights "essentially functioned politically as a steady regimen of steroids for the criminal justice system, resulting in the system's extraordinary growth and power."[7]

Even though many public officials today acknowledge the devastating consequences of the last forty years of extreme incarceration practices, including severe racial disparities, postconviction poverty, and bloated state budgets, too little attention has been paid to the ways in which mass incarceration also hurt victims of crime, the very stakeholders allegedly at the center of concern. Instead, the notion that tough justice serves victims remains a formidable obstacle to criminal justice reform.

Confronting the strained and dysfunctional relationship between the criminal justice system and most victims of crime is long overdue. A close look at the relationship reveals at least two key data points that have the potential to transform American crime policy. First, in line with the views Bertha expressed, extensive research reveals that mass incarceration policies do not align with most victims' preferences. If victims were truly at the center of concern, U.S. justice policies would look very different. Second, most victims never benefited from the enactment of new rights and compensation programs—and that lack of help for victims exacerbates cycles of trauma. Despite rhetoric to the contrary, mass incarceration and chronic victim disregard are two sides of the same coin.

RESEARCH ON VICTIMS' POLICY PREFERENCES REVEALS SUPPORT FOR REHABILITATION

The difference between the cultural myth of a monolithic group of victims demanding revenge and the sophisticated and diverse attitudes and preferences of most people hurt by crime is substantial. Talking about victims is not the same as talking with them. Beginning in 2013 and nearly every year since, my organization, Alliance for Safety and Justice, has been commissioning surveys of thousands of victims around the country—Black and white, rich and poor, young and old, urban and rural, Democrat and Republican—about their experiences with the justice system and their public safety goals.

Three studies have been national in scope and seven state-specific surveys in Arizona, California, Illinois, Michigan, Florida, and Texas have been conducted, totaling roughly ten thousand interviews in ten years.[8]

The results shatter the myth that victims value retribution above all else. To the contrary, surveys have consistently found that victims strongly prefer rehabilitation and options beyond incarceration, such as restorative justice, community service, and treatment, to hold people accountable. They also strongly prefer public investments that build strong communities as the best path to safety, such as violence prevention, mental health services, trauma recovery, job training, and drug addiction treatment, over expanded arrests and incarceration. For example, our September 2022 national study found that, by a nearly two to one margin, victims prefer rehabilitation over punishment; six in ten reported a preference for shorter prison sentences and more spending on prevention over prison sentences that keep people incarcerated for as long as possible; by a two to one margin, victims prefer investing in prevention and crisis assistance over increasing arrests and incarceration; and three in four prefer authorizing credits toward sentence reductions for people who participate in rehabilitation more than requiring completion of full sentences.[9]

These findings hold true across demographic subgroups: majority or plurality support is found among different age, gender, race and ethnicity, and political party affiliation groups. Additionally, majority support for these findings is also found for victims overall as well as for victims of violent crimes, such as victims of rape or murder of a family member.[10] It turns out that victims are far less prone to vengeance-focused grandstanding than most politicians.

For people proximate to repeated patterns of violence, these findings are not surprising. They are sensible. Victims as a demographic group do not have abnormally strong altruistic impulses. Instead, their experiences mean they understand that for others to avoid the harm they endured, stopping preventable cycles is imperative. Simply throwing the book at convicted people is a game of whack-a-mole that, though it might deliver a degree of short-term emotional catharsis for some, many recognize is not effective at making communities safer and stronger in the long term. “Hurt people hurt people,” Bertha summarized. “What good is a justice system that does not help the people they are supposed to help?”[11]

Statistics reveal that most violence happens between people who know each other.[12] That means many victims typically experientially understand much more than most nonvictims about the unresolved troubles many perpetrators exhibit in the lead-up to committing harm—from struggles with addiction to worsening economic desperation to posttraumatic stress disorder (PTSD) or chronic exposure to violence leading to hypervigilance or deteriorating mental stability. For many, it is also plain to see the failings of most criminal justice interventions to bring about needed behavior change. People are arrested one day and released a few months later, only to fall right back into the same patterns. Others are incarcerated for years, only to return unprepared and unable to reintegrate. "People who are reentering in our communities, we need to make sure they have gotten some kind of help," Bertha said. "So when they do come out, they can make a difference—a positive change in their communities."[13]

The policy implications of these insights are urgent. For a decade now, voters have shown impatience with lock-'em-up-and-throw-away-the-key strategies that have cost society a fortune, devastated communities of color in particular, and have scandalously low success rates in making communities durably safer. Despite the recent rise in violence in many American cities (and the resultant increase in tough-on-crime rhetoric), a window in which to develop commonsense reforms that both main political parties could support remains. Key to achieving that is direct and consistent partnership and engagement with survivors—an untapped constituency whose knowledge can break open a deep rethinking of public safety policymaking.

MOST VICTIMS STILL LACK ACCESS TO HELP—AND THE CONSEQUENCES ARE DIRE

Although decades of tough-on-crime legislation missed the mark in aligning with victims' interests, decades of well-intentioned legislation to offer more support to victims have also largely failed to deliver on the promise. Statistics reveal that Bertha's experience of poor treatment by justice system officials and a lack of accessible recovery support are the norm. Despite new rights to compensation and services in the lawbooks, most victims do not get much help. Even though sentences increased, with more people going to prison and spending longer time behind bars, huge numbers of victims have consistently reported feeling entirely ignored by the criminal justice system, their needs for counseling, financial assistance, help relocating to new neighborhoods, and so on far too frequently disregarded. Astoundingly, not even one in ten victims say the justice system was very helpful to them and half reported that their interactions with law enforcement were neither helpful nor reassuring.[14] Worse, nearly 75 percent received no mental health counseling and 87 percent received no financial or economic assistance to help them recover.[15]

The impact of these barriers to help does not fall evenly across the various demographics of victims. Wealthier white victims have far more resources channeled their way than victims of color and low-income victims do.[16] Discriminatory practices mean that victims of color, low-income victims, LGBTQ+ victims, immigrant victims, and victims with criminal records are far less likely to be able to access help.[17] These are also the same demographics of those most likely to be repeatedly hurt by crime. The most harmed are the least helped.

The collateral impacts of this lack of help are widespread. Victims experience mounting debt when they are unable to pay for medical bills or unable to maintain work after an injury. They report developing PTSD, experiencing family and housing instability, and some also fall into depression or struggle with substance use disorder. Disregarding the recovery needs of victims drives many into poverty, chronic illness, addiction, or worse. "As survivors, we are treated horribly at every turn—whether it's how we're treated during the court process or by law enforcement or our lack of access to services in our communities," Bertha explained. "We need access to trauma recovery. We need time to heal. We need law enforcement to provide us information throughout investigations. We need to be treated with respect."[18]

Beyond worsening life outcomes, the long-term consequences on public safety overall that arise from ignoring victims' recovery needs are also significant. Studies estimate that somewhere between 62 and 87 percent of the men entering U.S. jails and prisons daily have histories of unaddressed trauma.[19] It is not uncommon for those who commit crimes to have been victims long before, often never getting help to recover or ever getting access to safety in the aftermath. When we don't help people being hurt, we are setting them up for long-term difficulties and, for some, that includes resorting to violence or crime themselves. The standard punishments issued at conviction, all too often, add trauma to trauma. Most U.S. jails and prisons were designed to cut people off from humanity: concrete cells, isolation, sensory deprivation, rampant violence, daily hostility. In the name of victims, the U.S. approach to public safety developed into a justice system that simultaneously discriminates against most victims and sends perpetrators to incarceration facilities better designed for retriggering trauma than turning lives around.

KEY TO A NEW APPROACH: SURVIVOR LEADERSHIP

As heart-wrenching as these lessons are, they also hold the key to a new approach to safety and justice, one focused on stopping the cycle of trauma. As Bertha described, "If we get these services, we reduce the cycle of violence, because people who have been affected by trauma often end up being touched in the criminal justice system. Healing healthy would stop that."[20] Abandoning "tough justice" and instead channeling public dollars into a range of effective programs that have been demonstrated to heal trauma can help more victims recover, improve public safety, and reduce incarceration at the same time. Examples of these programs are popping up all over the country—often led by survivors who, after experiencing disregard, turned their own healing into action and built solutions for others.

After searching for community-accessible help and coming up empty handed, Bertha Purnell decided to create her own program. "It's time for people to stop sitting in rooms telling us what we need without asking us what we need," she said.[21] In 2018, she founded Mothers OnA Mission 28—a reference to her son Maurice's age when he was murdered. The grassroots organization supports survivors with a range of services: a bimonthly healing group, one-to-one services, compensation application information, and help arranging funerals, along with additional referrals and body-based healing practices like yoga and meditation.[22] Mothers OnA Mission 28 helps dozens of people every year, survivors experiencing trauma similar to what Bertha experienced herself years before.

Mothers OnA Mission 28 is one of hundreds of survivor-led and community-based victims services programs transforming lives in neighborhoods across the country. Despite little government backing and limited resources or official recognition, these programs offer a lifeline to thousands of people in the darkest moments of their lives. They model what it looks like to prioritize dignity and healing, to give people the kind of support and connection that everyone needs to recover from traumatic harm.

Day by day, leaders like Bertha are building a new victims' rights movement. "It is very important to me that survivors be at the center of policymaking, because there are policies being made surrounding what we need—and if you don't hear our voices as to what we need, how are those policies going to be effective?"[23] This new movement is different. It's not about political slogans or expanding justice bureaucracies. This time, it's about equipping communities with capacity to build the solutions needed to stop the cycle of trauma. And that begins with listening first and then following survivors' lead.

NOTES

1. Alliance for Safety and Justice, *Crime Survivors Speak 2022: National Survey of Victims Views on Safety and Justice*, 2022, 38, https://allianceforsafetyandjustice.org/wp-content/uploads/2022/09/Alliance-for-Safety-and-Justice-Crime-Survivors-Speak-September-2022.pdf.
2. Bertha Purnell, interview by the author, June 1, 2023.
3. Purnell, interview, 2023.
4. For a brief overview of this movement, see Marlene Young and John Stein, *The History of the Crime Victims' Movement in the United States* (Washington, DC: National Organization for Victim Assistance, 2004), https://www.ncjrs.gov/ovc_archives/ncvrw/2005/pg4c.html. Also see Jill Lepore, *New Yorker*, "The Rise of the Victims'-Rights Movement," May 21, 2018, https://www.newyorker.com/magazine/2018/05/21/the-rise-of-the-victims-rights-movement.
5. Sarah Brown Hammond, "Enforcing and Evaluating Victims' Rights Laws," *LegisBrief* 13, no. 13 (March 2005): 1, http://janmcquaid.com/WVU-NCSL-05LBMar-enforce-VictimsRights.pdf.
6. Jill Lepore, "The Rise of the Victims'-Rights Movement," *New Yorker*, May 21, 2018, https://www.newyorker.com/magazine/2018/05/21/the-rise-of-the-victims-rights-movement; Bill Ainsworth, "A Marriage of Convenience," *Sacramento Bee*, December 11, 1994, https://sacbee.newspapers.com/newspage/626713526; Candace McCoy, *Politics and Plea Bargaining* (Philadelphia: University of Pennsylvania Press, 1993), 28–30, https://www.pennpress.org/9780812214338/politics-and-plea-bargaining; Markus Dirk Dubber, *Victims in the War on Crime* (New York: New York University Press, 2002), 3, https://nyupress.org/9780814719299/victims-in-the-war-on-crime.
7. Lenore Anderson, *In Their Names* (New York: The New Press, 2022). 7.
8. Alliance for Safety and Justice (ASJ), *Crime Survivors Speak 2022*; *Crime Survivors Speak: The First-Ever National Survey of Victims' Views on Safety and Justice*, 2017, https://allianceforsafetyandjustice.org/crimesurvivorsspeak; *Crime Survivors Speak: Arizona Victims' Views on Safety and Justice*, 2022, https://allianceforsafetyandjustice.org/wp-content/uploads/2022/05/CSSJ_SSAZ CRIMESURVERY_V4-INT.pdf; *Crime Survivors Speak: Florida Victims' Views*

on Safety and Justice, 2018, https://allianceforsafetyandjustice.org/wp-content/uploads/2018/02/ASJ_FloridaCrimeSurvivorBrief-online.pdf; Californians for Safety and Justice, *California Crime Victims' Voices*, 2017, https://safeandjust.org/wp-content/uploads/CA-Crime-Victims-Report-8_24_17.pdf; *California Crime Survivors Speak: A Statewide Survey of California Victims' Views on Safety and Justice*, 2018, https://allianceforsafetyandjustice.org/wp-content/uploads/2019/04/201904-CALIFORNIA-REPORT-FINAL-FINAL.pdf; *Toward Shared Safety: The First-Ever National Survey of America's Safety Gap*, 2020, https://weshare-safety.us/wp-content/themes/shared-safety/assets/downloads/NatlSafetyGaps-09142020.pdf; *Crime Survivors Speak: Texas Victims' Experiences with Recovery and Views on Criminal Justice*, 2019, https://allianceforsafetyandjustice.org/wp-content/uploads/2019/04/201904-ASJ-Texas-Report-Full-FINAL.pdf; *Illinois Crime Victims' Voices: The First-Ever Survey of Illinois Victims' Views on Safety and Justice*, 2017, https://allianceforsafetyandjustice.org/wp-content/uploads/2016/12/ASJ-Illinois-Crime_survivors-FINAL-online.pdf; *Crime Survivors Speak: Michigan Victims' Views on Safety and Justice*, 2018, https://allianceforsafetyandjustice.org/wp-content/uploads/2018/07/ASJ_MichiganCrimeSurvivorBrief-F2-ONLINE.pdf.

9. ASJ, *Crime Survivors Speak 2022*, 6.
10. ASJ, *Crime Survivors Speak 2022*, 6.
11. Bertha Purnell, unpublished video from an event in Chicago, January 2023.
12. Katie Smith, "'Random' Crime Makes Headlines, but How Common Is It Really?," *News Nation*, August 31, 2022, https://www.newsnationnow.com/us-news/midwest/crime-involving-strangers.
13. Bertha Purnell, unpublished video, 2023.
14. ASJ, *Crime Survivors Speak 2022*, 18, 16.
15. ASJ, *Crime Survivors Speak 2022*, 20.
16. Heather Warnken, "A Vision for Equity in Victim Services: What Do the Data Tell Us About the Work Ahead?," video presentation, U.S. Department of Justice, Office for Victims of Crime, June 8, 2021, https://ovc.ojp.gov/media/video/12971#transcript%E2%80%940; Heather Warnken and Janet L. Lauritsen, *Who Experiences Violent Victimization and Who Accesses Services? Findings from the National Crime Victimization Survey for Expanding Our Reach*, U.S. Department of Justice, Office of Justice Programs, https://www.ojp.gov/ncjrs/virtual-library/abstracts/who-experiences-violent-victimization-and-who-accesses-services.
17. Anderson, *In Their Names*, 91–99; see also Claudia Lauer and Mike Catalini, "Every State Offers Victim Compensation. For the Longs and Other Black Families It Often Isn't Fair," Associated Press, May 17, 2023, https://apnews.com/article/crime-victims-compensation-racial-bias-58908169e0ee05d4389c57f975eae49b.
18. ASJ, *Crime Survivors Speak 2022*, 38.

19. See Rafael A. Javier, Elizabeth Owen, and Jemour A. Maddux, *Assessing Trauma in Forensic Contexts* (Cham: Springer, 2020). Nancy Wolff and Jing Shi, "Childhood and Adult Trauma Experiences of Incarcerated Persons and Their Relationship to Adult Behavioral Health Problems and Treatment," *International Journal of Environmental Research and Public Health* 9, no. 5 (May 2012): 1908–26, https://www.ncbi.nlm.nih.gov/pmc/articles/PMC3386595; Nancy Wolff, Jessica Huening, Jing Shi, and B. Christopher Frueh, "Trauma Exposure and Posttraumatic Stress Disorder Among Incarcerated Men," *Journal of Urban Health* 91, no. 4 (August 2014), 715–16, https://pubmed.ncbi.nlm.nih.gov/24865800; Bonnie L. Green, Jeanne Miranda, Anahita Daroowalla, and Juned Siddique, "Trauma Exposure, Mental Health Functioning, and Program Needs of Women in Jail," *Crime and Delinquency* 51, no. 1 (2005): 133–51.
20. Bertha Purnell, "Crime Survivors for Safety and Justice," YouTube, 2023, https://www.youtube.com/watch?v=-MmSZ4h-r2w.
21. Purnell, unpublished video, 2023.
22. Mothers OnA Mission28, https://www.mothersonamission28.org.
23. Purnell, "Crime Survivors."

4

CRIME, THE IDEA

Emile DeWeaver

CRIME IS NOT REAL. This assertion flies in the face of common sense and consensus. *Of course crime is real*, one would be justified in thinking—we see "crime" every day on the news. Charles Manson was, in fact, responsible for nine murders.[1] Dylann Roof did, in fact, enter the Emanuel African Methodist Episcopal Church and kill nine people.[2] Crime rates are, in fact, either up or down or stable on a given day in every city in the United States.

So how could crime be a fiction? You the reader and I likely agree that people hurt others and transgress moral boundaries. We may also agree that communities have the job of figuring out how to prevent and remedy such transgressions because a basic precondition for happiness is safety. If, however, we are actually to create a society that is safe for everyone, we'll profit from challenging our belief in the "reality" of crime.

Begin this challenge by considering race. For hundreds of years, race's realness was a "fact," but today scientists understand that race is not real.[3] What *real* means is well described by journalist Jenée Desmond-Harris.[4] "By 'real,' I mean based on facts that people can even begin to agree on. Permanent. Scientific. Objective. Logical. Consistent. Able to stand up to scrutiny." *Racism* is real, as real as Dylan Roof. *Race*, however, is a fiction, and the creation of this fiction was a political project aimed at a political end.

It is in this sense that crime is also fiction, and I offer one more example before I come to my point. Consider the difference between a person and a person's mythology—specifically, consider King Arthur of medieval England. Historians debate whether Arthur was a historical person whose accomplishments have been wildly exaggerated (his legend features sorcerers, an unbreakable sword that cuts through anything, and a lady who lives beneath a lake) or pure fiction.[5]

As a thought experiment, let's say he was a historical figure around which a fictional legend arose. You would be justified in saying that King Arthur is real; his mythology is not. What if, however, this distinction isn't available to you? Would it make sense to say King Arthur is real if we make no distinction between his historical person and a king who killed giants and dragons with a magic sword?

The national conversation about crime engages a similar mythology: prevailing narratives routinely deny us the ability to make the distinction between myth and reality. These narratives are, like racial narratives, political projects aimed at political ends. Given the conflation of myth and reality, it makes as much sense to call crime real as it does to call the legend of King Arthur real. If we want to call crime real, we have to locate the truth of what it is and what it isn't. We have to dispel the mythologies of crime.

One myth is that we punish people for committing crimes. The truth is, we punish people less because of what they do and more because of who they are. If I kill a stranger on the street for disobeying my orders, I'm a murderer. Law enforcement officers routinely kill unarmed people for, according to police claims, resisting arrest—arrests, as in the case of George Floyd, where no meaningful crime has been committed—but we don't treat police forces like criminal institutions.

If I steal toilet paper from a convenience store, I'm a thief who deserves incarceration, but when Donald Trump and his "university" steal $25 million from students, he's merely someone who has to return a good portion of the money he stole.[6] On January 6, 2021, Trump incited an insurgency in the nation's capital that resulted in multiple deaths.[7] If Patrisse Cullors, a cofounder of Black Lives Matter, incited an insurgency at the Capitol, she'd likely be shot to death on the street without a trial.

In these comparisons, there's no moral difference that justifies criminalizing me or Cullors but not police officers or Trump. Yet popular narratives in the United States have manufactured a moral difference. Such fabricated differences often rest on narratives about how the actions of a so-called criminal harm people or society. But when we compare the scale of harm done to society by Trump or Officer Derek Chauvin to the harm done by, say, a sixteen-year-old drug dealer, crime (or the absence of it) is no longer a function of the harm a person causes—it's a function of privilege, which necessarily implicates the perpetuation of white supremacy. In other words, the truth beneath the mythology of crime is that many Americans feel justified in punishing people not because of what the people have done but because of their social position relative to the white power structure.

Then the second myth, that crime is an act committed by an individual. Calling an act a crime is instead a choice we make as a society about how we respond to harms committed in our community. I recently experienced how this myth operates while standing in line at a local Walgreens.

I was about to check out at the cash register when I looked up from my phone and noticed a security guard becoming excited, even agitated. He alternated between whispering to a store clerk and positioning himself to track someone in the surveillance mirrors on the store's ceiling.

The scene awakened trauma in my body. I remembered all the times I'd been caught shoplifting as a child, how quickly and easily our criminal legal system could destroy a young life, family, and community in the name of justice. I began to scan the security mirrors too, thinking *please don't let this be some kid.* The security guard ducked into an aisle. I tracked him in the mirrors to determine his target. The person stealing wasn't a kid.

I sighed with only slight relief because the person's age was of little consolation. From the state of his hoodie, it seemed likely that he was a homeless person. We're in the middle of a pandemic, I thought, and he's struggling to survive. The security guard intercepted him. By then, more and more people—both staff and customers—had realized what was happening. The store grew tense, fearful.

I watched the guard escort the man along the back of the store. When I was eighteen, I was a security guard; I knew that the next step for the guard was to call the police. I was about to pay for the coffee I had bought, so I asked the clerk to ring up the sale and told her I'd be right back. The security guard moved toward the store exit with his charge. I stopped them and addressed the homeless man.

"Hey, man," I tried to sound as casually authoritative as I could. "Go back, get whatever you want, and I'll pay for it."

Something quite phenomenal happened.

The store's tense, fearful atmosphere evaporated. A look of deep relief washed over the security guard, and he stepped back without protest. The people standing in line relaxed. A woman working in the photo department left her post to open a third checkout stand specifically to get this homeless man checked out. She smiled and treated him like a human being. It's true that I had to buy this treatment for him ($30 for toilet paper, food, and a razor), but that did not make the decisions everyone made in that store any less real or less important. All it would have taken is for one person to insist on police involvement, and that homeless man would have been arrested. It took the entire community waiting in that store to save this man.

The homeless man had in one second gone from a criminal whom people feared and even reviled to a member of a community who needed support. Not only did this community—the people in the store—choose to support him, they seemed hungry to do it. They'd just needed to be shown a path and given the opportunity to be the community that the man deserved. The difference between crime and not-crime wasn't the homeless man's actions or his intent. It was his community's response.

NOTES

1. Steve Rubenstein, "Charles Manson, 'Helter Skelter' Mass Murderer, Dies at 83," *SFGATE*, November 19, 2017, https://www.sfgate.com/crime/article/Charles-Manson-Helter-Skelter-mass-12370465.php.
2. Rebecca Hersher, "Jury Finds Dylann Roof Guilty in S.C. Church Shooting," NPR, *The Two-Way*, December 15, 2016, https://www.npr.org/sections/thetwo-way/2016/12/15/505723552/jury-finds-dylann-roof-guilty-in-s-c-church-shooting.
3. Audrey Smedley and Brian D. Smedley, "Race as Biology Is Fiction, Racism as a Social Problem Is Real: Anthropological and Historical Perspectives on the Social Construction of Race," *American Psychologist* 60, no. 1 (2005): 16–26, https://doi.org/10.1037/0003-066X.60.1.16.
4. Jenée Desmond-Harris, "11 Ways Race Isn't Real," *Vox*, October 10, 2014, https://www.vox.com/2014/10/10/6943461/race-social-construct-origins-census.
5. N. J. Higham, *King Arthur: Myth-Making and History* (New York: Routledge, 2002).
6. Tom Winter and Dartunorro Clark, "Federal Court Approves $25 Million Trump University Settlement," NBC News, February 6, 2018, https://www.nbcnews.com/politics/white-house/federal-court-approves-25-million-trump-university-settlement-n845181.
7. Nicole Gaouette, "Terrifying Scope of Capitol Attack Becoming Clearer as Washington Locks Down for Biden's Inauguration," CNN, January 16, 2021, https://www.cnn.com/2021/01/16/politics/insurrection-investigation-washington-lockdown/index.html.

PART TWO

FEDERAL FUNDING DRIVES PUNITIVE JUSTICE

5

THE FEDERAL FUNDING THAT FUELS MASS INCARCERATION

Lauren-Brooke Eisen

MANY OF THE ESSAYS in this volume highlight how sentencing laws and other criminal legal policies created a system of mass incarceration resulting in today's nearly 1.2 million people confined to federal and state prisons, and approximately seven hundred thousand more locked up in local jails.[1] Discussed far less frequently is how federal funding for law enforcement and prison construction played a key role in creating America's vast carceral landscape. For more than half a century, federal dollars have incentivized and rewarded disproportionately punitive responses to crime.

Since the late 1960s, federal funding has fueled local criminal justice policy in ways that have resulted in more arrests, more incarceration or probation, harsher sentencing laws, and more contacts with the criminal justice legal apparatus. These federal dollars incentivized and rewarded criminal justice agencies and actors to punish beyond what could be considered proportionate and combat crime in increasingly more militaristic ways, funding this excess punitiveness that pervades our criminal legal system. As Yale University associate professor of history and professor of African American studies Elizabeth Hinton has pointed out, federal grants were often tied to arrests, which encouraged more apprehensions in low-income, often urban neighborhoods that were earmarked for "special law-enforcement programs."[2]

Today, Washington spends billions of dollars each year subsidizing state and local criminal justice agencies. The Department of Justice (DOJ) by itself distributes more than $5 billion in federal grants to state and local governments annually, not including the funding that law enforcement agencies across the nation get from the Department of Homeland Security.[3] Hundreds of millions more come through the Department of Defense, which facilitates the transfer of military-grade weapons and armored vehicles to police departments—for instance, a $705,000 armored mine-resistant vehicle for Bridgeport, Connecticut.[4] Even the Department of Agriculture has gotten involved, providing $360 million to build jails in rural communities since 1996.[5]

The history of such punitive funding stretches back to President Lyndon Johnson's signing of the Omnibus Crime Control and Safe Streets Act of 1968, which earmarked $400 million for law enforcement purposes.[6] Four years later, President Richard Nixon, who had ascended to the presidency after running a campaign focused on law and order, announced that since 1969, his administration had doled out $1.5 billion in state and local law enforcement grants, relative to just $22 million during the final three years of the Johnson administration.[7]

From 1960 to 1980, violent crime across the nation soared 270 percent.[8] In New York City alone, 141 murders were recorded in 1967, yet 390 were by 1972. By 1980, the city that never sleeps reported 1,814.[9]

In the ensuing years, as crime increased—particularly crime related to the spread of crack cocaine—so did the flow of federal dollars. The Anti-Drug Abuse Act of 1986, signed by President Ronald Reagan, increased funding for law enforcement and mandated harsher penalties in federal drug cases, including life imprisonment.[10] The legislation not only dedicated more than $1 billion to state and federal law enforcement agencies, including an authorization of $96.5 million for new federal prisons, but also expanded the use of no-knock warrants, such as the one Louisville police used in 2020 when they killed Breonna Taylor as she slept in her home.[11]

Then came the legislation that showed how policy had been fully separated from reality. Crime in the United States peaked in 1991, but even as it declined Washington's appetite for crueler penalties and overreaching enforcement increased.[12] The watershed moment was the enactment of the Violent Crime Control and Law Enforcement Act, often referred to as the 1994 Crime Bill, signed into law by President Bill Clinton, rows of uniformed law enforcement officers standing behind him.[13]

By the time the bill was enacted, the violent crime rate had already fallen by 6 percent.[14] By the time it took effect the following year, the rate was down by 10 percent.[15] Yet over the next decade, despite what would become the most dramatic drop in crime in the nation's history, politicians chose not to lead the nation in urgently necessary conversations about the proper role of enforcement and punishment, but to instead feed the punitive machine they had built.

The 1994 Crime Bill banned nineteen types of semiautomatic firearms (defined as assault weapons) as well as restricted the characteristics of firearms that could be sold legally. It also implemented the Violence Against Women Act, intended to protect victims of domestic violence.[16] However, the legislation also mandated harsher penalties for people caught in the criminal legal system. It authorized the death penalty for dozens of existing and newly defined federal crimes, and required life imprisonment for any conviction for a third violent felony, the infamous "three strikes and you're out" policy. It also established a funding mechanism that incentivized and rewarded states for sending people to prison for very long periods.

The 1994 Crime Bill also offered federal grants to states to expand their prison capacity, and made the grants contingent on states' increasing the length of incarceration of those convicted of violent crimes. Through the bill's Violent Offender Incarceration and Truth-in-Sentencing (TIS) Incentive Grants Program, the legislation authorized $12.5 billion in grants to fund incarceration, nearly 50 percent of which was earmarked for states that adopted tough TIS laws that scaled back parole. Specifically, states were rewarded for having or enacting laws requiring those convicted of violent crimes to serve at least 85 percent of the sentence imposed, making it difficult for those convicted of violent crimes to earn early release based on rehabilitative principles. Eleven states adopted TIS laws in 1995, one year after the bill was signed.[17] By 1998, incentive grants had been awarded to twenty-seven states and the District of Columbia.[18]

In addition to the financial incentives, states found significant symbolic value in the program's messaging. In 1999, the authors of an Urban Institute study on the legislation's impact interviewed a staff member of Connecticut's Office of Policy and Management. They wrote, "When asked about Connecticut's motivation in moving to an 85 percent truth in sentencing law, [the staff member] responded that Connecticut liked to be 'ahead of the curve' on national reforms, and she implied that the state government might be viewed negatively if it did not seek federal funds to help with its perceived crime problem."[19]

Another creation of the 1994 Crime Bill was the Community Oriented Policing Services Program, a division of the Justice Department that has provided billions of dollars to police departments to hire new officers.[20] Between 1995 and 1999, the annual appropriation for the program averaged nearly $1.4

billion.[21] At the same time—as journalist Radley Balko demonstrated in his 2013 book, *Rise of the Warrior Cop: The Militarization of America's Police Forces*—the federal government ceded some control over the use of this money, resulting in many law enforcement agencies spending funds not on community policing, but on the militarization of their forces.

And so it continued. Even as the frequency of crime declined, the federal response was more spending on more enforcement and more punishment. In 2005, when reauthorizing the Violence Against Women Act, Congress expanded previous laws providing funding for local police to create the Justice Assistance Grant (JAG) program.[22] All fifty states plus Washington, DC, six U.S. territories, and more than a thousand local governments now use JAG funds, which amount to $300 to $500 million yearly and support almost any criminal justice activity covered by the federal statute.

For many years, civil rights groups criticized the program for funding drug task forces that were often unnecessary for the protection of public safety. These task forces provide avenues for agencies across governments to share personnel, equipment, intelligence, and other resources. Critics, including the Brennan Center, pointed out that federal officials asked JAG recipients to report the number of arrests made, but not their crime rates. The DOJ also measured the amount of cocaine seized, but not whether those arrested were screened for drug addiction. The department's own metrics sent a signal to states and local governments that JAG funding was implicitly conditioned on more arrests, more cocaine busts, and more prosecutions—inevitably at the expense of crime prevention activities or programs that could divert people from the criminal legal system.[23]

Today, recognition is emerging that federal dollars have helped deepen today's devastating fissures between police and the communities they purport to serve, perpetuating trauma and harm through mass incarceration and criminal legal system overreach. Under the Barack Obama administration, the Justice Department revised JAG performance measures to better steer recipients toward the development of programs that would reduce crime and incarceration rather than increase enforcement and arrest activity.[24] For example, the DOJ stopped asking how many people were arrested and how many drugs were seized, and instead started asking about the number of citations issued in lieu of arrest, and whether prosecutors routinely recommend alternatives to prison.

The ripple effects from mass incarceration are causing generations of damage. So many children—nearly 5.3 million under age eighteen, which according to a recent estimate is nearly one in ten—have experienced parental incarceration that in 2013 *Sesame Street* felt it necessary to add a Muppet named Alex, whose father is incarcerated, to reach out to children grappling with how to grow up with a parent behind bars.[25]

It is important to acknowledge the difficulty of criticizing decades of funding decisions, some that were made during times of increased crime rates and some that may have had the best of intentions. Yet as the federal government thinks through how best to use its unique power of the purse to support and create safe and thriving communities across the nation, it is critical to understand the consequences of past funding decisions that tore apart neighborhoods and destroyed families. It is also necessary to include people who have been most harmed by mass incarceration in these funding decisions.

Attempting to spur Congress to reverse course on the last half century of funding the nation's addiction to overincarceration, the Brennan Center for Justice recently proposed a new, federal funding program, called the Public Safety and Prison Reduction Act, which would incentivize states to focus on reducing unnecessary incarceration while promoting humane and fair criminal-justice policies that preserve public safety.[26] Senator Cory Booker (D-NJ) and Representative Tony Cárdenas (D-CA) introduced a bill modeled on the Brennan Center's proposal called the Smart Sentencing Adjustments Act, which rewards states that use these grant dollars to shrink their prison populations by 20 percent over three years by providing an extra three years of funding.[27] If the twenty-five states with the largest prison populations used these grant dollars to reduce imprisonment by 20 percent, 180,000 fewer people in the United States would be imprisoned—in context, about twenty thousand more than the entire federal prison system incarcerates.[28] The bill would establish subgrants for organizations that are led by formerly incarcerated individuals or that serve high numbers of people who have been arrested or convicted.

In a 2015 speech before the NAACP, Bill Clinton publicly apologized for the harm the 1994 Crime Bill caused.[29] "I signed a bill that made the problem worse, and I want to admit it," he said. "In that bill there were longer sentences, and most of these people were in prison under state law, but the federal law set a trend. And that was overdone. We were wrong about that."

This remarkable and rare acknowledgment of how far afield policymakers and governments strayed by overfunding the growth of the U.S. police and carceral state offers a glimpse of the regret of a nation.

NOTES

1. Jacob Kang-Brown, Chase Montagnet, and Jasmine Heiss, "People in Jail and Prison in Spring 2021" (New York: Vera Institute of Justice, 2021), 1, https://www.vera.org/publications/people-in-jail-and-prison-in-spring-2021.
2. Elizabeth Hinton, "Why We Should Reconsider the War on Crime," *Time*, March 20, 2015, https://time.com/3746059/war-on-crime-history.
3. Mike Crowley and Betsy Pearl, "Reimagining Federal Grants for Public Safety and Criminal Justice Reform" (Washington, DC: Center for American Progress, 2020), 2, https://www.americanprogress.org/article/reimagining-federal-grants-public-safety-criminal-justice-reform; Spencer Ackerman, "US Police Given Billions from Homeland Security for 'Tactical' Equipment," *The Guardian*, August 20, 2014, https://www.theguardian.com/world/2014/aug/20/police-billions-homeland-security-military-equipment.
4. Brian Barrett, "The Pentagon's Hand-Me-Downs Helped Militarize Police. Here's How," *Wired*, June 2, 2020, https://www.wired.com/story/pentagon-hand-me-downs-militarize-police-1033-program; Ana Radelat and Gregory B. Hladky, "Connecticut Police Receive Millions of Dollars in Military Equipment from Program That's Under Fire," *CT Mirror*, June 12, 2020, https://ctmirror.org/2020/06/12/connecticut-police-receive-millions-of-dollars-in-military-equipment-from-program-thats-under-fire.
5. Jack Norton and Jacob Kang-Brown, "Federal Farm Aid for the Big House" (New York: Vera Institute of Justice, October 22, 2018), https://www.vera.org/in-our-backyards-stories/federal-farm-aid-for-the-big-house.
6. Omnibus Crime Control and Safe Streets Act of 1968, Pub. L. No. 90-351, 82 Stat. 197 (1968), codified at 34 U.S.C. § 10101, et seq.
7. Richard Nixon, "Radio Address on Crime and Drug Abuse" (nationwide radio broadcast, Camp David, MD, October 15, 1972), https://www.presidency.ucsb.edu/documents/radio-address-crime-and-drug-abuse.
8. James Austin and Lauren-Brooke Eisen with James Cullen, and Jonathan Frank, *How Many Americans Are Unnecessarily Incarcerated?* (New York: Brennan Center for Justice, 2016), 3, https://www.brennancenter.org/sites/default/files/publications/Unnecessarily_Incarcerated_0.pdf.
9. Leonard Buder, "1980 Called Worst Year of Crime in City History," *New York Times*, February 24, 1981, https://www.nytimes.com/1981/02/25/nyregion/1980-called-worst-year-of-crime-in-city-history.html.
10. Anti-Drug Abuse Act of 1986, Pub. L. No. 99-570, 100 Stat. 3207 (1986), codified at 21 U.S.C. § 801, et seq.
11. Matthew Brown and Tessa Duvall, "Fact Check: Louisville Police Had a 'No-Knock' Warrant for Breonna Taylor's Apartment," *USA Today*, June 30, 2020, https://www.usatoday.com/story/news/factcheck/2020/06/30/fact-check-police-had-no-knock-warrant-breonna-taylor-apartment/3235029001.

12. Ames Grawert, Matthew Friedman, and James Cullen, *Crime Trends: 1990–2016* (New York: Brennan Center for Justice, 2017), 1, https://www.brennancenter.org/our-work/research-reports/crime-trends-1990-2016.
13. Violent Crime Control and Law Enforcement Act of 1994, Pub. L. No. 103-322, 108 Stat. 1796 (1994). For signing, see Signing the Violent Crime Control and Law Enforcement Act of 1994 on the South Lawn, September 13, 1994 Public Papers Book II Folio D (September 13, 1994), https://www.govinfo.gov/app/details/PPP-PHOTOS-1994-book2/PPP-PHOTOS-1994-book2-folio-D.
14. Statista, "Reported Violent Crime Rate in the United States from 1990 to 2021," accessed December 14, 2022, https://www.statista.com/statistics/191219/reported-violent-crime-rate-in-the-usa-since-1990.
15. Statista, "Reported Violent Crime Rate."
16. National Network to End Domestic Violence, "Violence Against Women Act," accessed December 14, 2022, https://nnedv.org/content/violence-against-women-act.
17. Paula M. Ditton and Doris James Wilson, *Truth in Sentencing in State Prisons*, NCJ 170032 (Washington, DC: Bureau of Justice Statistics, 1999), 1, https://bjs.ojp.gov/content/pub/pdf/tssp.pdf.
18. Ditton and Wilson, *Truth in Sentencing*, 1.
19. William J. Sabol, Katherine Rosich, Kamala Mallik Kane, David P. Kirk, and Glenn Dubin, *The Influences of Truth-in-Sentencing Reforms on Changes in States' Sentencing Practices and Prison Populations* (Washington, DC: Urban Institute, 2002), 27, https://webarchive.urban.org/UploadedPDF/410470_FINALTISrpt.pdf.
20. Community Oriented Policing Services, "About the COPS Office," U.S. Department of Justice, accessed December 14, 2022, https://cops.usdoj.gov/aboutcops.
21. Nathan James, "Community Oriented Policing Services (COPS) Program," *In Focus* 10922 (Washington, DC: Congressional Research Service, 2022), 1, https://sgp.fas.org/crs/misc/IF10922.pdf.
22. Inimai Chettiar, Lauren-Brooke Eisen, and Nicole Fortier with Timothy Ross, *Reforming Funding to Reduce Mass Incarceration* (New York: Brennan Center for Justice, 2019), 18, https://www.brennancenter.org/sites/default/files/2019-08/Report_Reforming-Funding-Reducee-Mass-Incarceration.pdf.
23. Chettiar et al., *Reforming Funding*, 4.
24. Jonathan Frank, "Justice Department Issues Changes to Largest Criminal Justice Grant" (New York: Brennan Center for Justice, January 8, 2016), https://www.brennancenter.org/our-work/analysis-opinion/justice-department-issues-changes-largest-criminal-justice-grant.
25. Data Resource Center for Child & Adolescent Health, "2018–2019 National Survey of Children's Health, Question: Parent or Guardian Served Time in Jail," accessed December 14, 2022, https://www.childhealthdata.org/browse/survey

/results?q=7919&r=1; Sesame Workshop, "Incarceration," accessed December 14, 2022, https://sesamestreetincommunities.org/topics/incarceration.

26. Hernandez Stroud, Lauren-Brooke Eisen, and Ram Subramanian, "A Proposal to Reduce Unnecessary Incarceration" (New York: Brennan Center for Justice, 2023), https://www.brennancenter.org/our-work/policy-solutions/proposal-reduce-unnecessary-incarceration.
27. Smart Sentencing Adjustments Act, S.1342, 118th Congress (2023), https://www.congress.gov/bill/118th-congress/senate-bill/1342/text?s=1&r=2.
28. Federal Bureau of Prisons, "Statistics," accessed December 20, 2022, https://www.bop.gov/about/statistics/population_statistics.jsp.
29. Peter Baker, "Bill Clinton Concedes His Crime Law Jailed Too Many for Too Long," *New York Times*, July 15, 2015, https://www.nytimes.com/2015/07/16/us/politics/bill-clinton-concedes-his-crime-law-jailed-too-many-for-too-long.html.

6

THE ROLE OF FEDERAL FUNDING IN IMPROVING AMERICAN JUSTICE

Ed Chung

A DEBATE THAT HAS CONSISTENTLY EMERGED when studying the rise of mass incarceration in the United States centers on the role of the federal government in this phenomenon. Lauren-Brooke Eisen's essay in this book (see chapter 5) summarizes the background, tracing federal policy decisions that have contributed to mass incarceration since the early 1970s. Some view federal actions as less consequential given the dispersed nature of U.S. criminal justice systems.[1] Others, however, argue that policies such as the war on drugs and the imposition of federal mandatory minimum sentences were catalysts for states to create and impose similar state criminal laws and enforcement schemes. At the very least, these and other federal policies like the Violent Crime Control and Law Enforcement Act of 1994 served as cheerleaders of a movement that was well under way—a motivating effect, providing significant resources to states to further tough-on-crime policies while creating a prison expansion boom for decades.[2]

Over the last several years, the country has witnessed some retrenchment of these policies. States have enacted reforms such as rolling back mandatory minimum sentences.[3] Efforts to clear and expunge criminal records and provide those leaving prison access to jobs are steadily increasing.[4] Innovations in public health approaches to preventing violence have taken root.[5] These are steps in the right direction, but they barely scratch the surface on the work that needs to happen to dramatically reduce mass incarceration.

But now that the push to reverse the harms of mass incarceration is increasingly part of the national public consciousness, what if anything can the federal government do to support it? Can federal policies be a galvanizing force for transformation—or at least something more than a cheerleader?

THE LEVERS OF THE FEDERAL GOVERNMENT

These questions have been on my mind for the past decade plus. I have had the honor of serving in the federal government and helping shape national policies related to public safety and criminal justice—in the Justice Department, the U.S. Senate, and the White House. Since leaving federal government at the end of 2016, I have been pushing for change "on the outside" by working with researchers to develop evidence, advocates to press for change, and practitioners to implement effective policies. Through all of these interactions and experiences, I have seen the justice reform field and the public at large continue to hold out hope that the federal government can play an instrumental role in moving the country's criminal justice policies in the opposite direction from an enforcement-centric approach.

There are some real hurdles to overcome to make this a reality, starting with the will and commitment by our political leaders to prioritize this issue. Ending mass incarceration—or supporting the more accepted notion of criminal justice reform—is growing both in awareness and importance to lawmakers in DC, but most still hew to a traditional view of public safety and criminal justice.[6] That they do was demonstrated by the two-year roller-coaster ride following the 2020 murder of George Floyd by Minneapolis Police Department officers. As protests and uprisings quickly emerged across the country, a growing chorus of politicians echoed the demonstrators' call to "defund the police," but among many Democrats this push shifted a mere two years later to a "fund the police" mantra leading up to the midterm elections.[7] Lawmakers may be open to changing the system to be more effective and just, but they also express weariness and reluctance to institute transformative changes.

Even if the president and Congress favored wholesale changes to the criminal justice system, they do not have a magic wand to wave. No one does. In the United States, the federal government's levers to affect local and state criminal justice systems are powerful because of their potential to influence systems across the country but limited because they do not have direct authority or control over counties and states. Congress, for example, has the power to pass statutes that are enforced and implemented by federal authorities and processed through federal courts. The overwhelming majority of criminal laws, however, are enacted and enforced through state criminal justice systems, which are governed by local and state officials.

The federal lever most akin to a magic wand is the president's constitutionally authorized clemency power, which President Obama wielded in an unprecedented way. During the last three years of his administration, Obama commuted the sentences of more than 1,700 people, significantly reducing the federal prison population in a short period.[8] The process by which clemency applications were considered came under scrutiny, but the effect of the initiative was tangible: Obama commuted more sentences than the thirteen presidents who preceded him combined.[9] This was the first time in American history that the president used this power in such a broad manner with the specific intent to reform the federal criminal justice system.[10] Yet, even in this example, the clemency power is limited to those who have been convicted of a federal offense; it does not touch convictions under state law.

Moreover, our federal legislative system also makes passing as well as repealing laws an arduous path, regardless of whether the national political climate resembles modern times or something less polarized. This is the primary reason the laws from the war on drugs era of the 1980s and 1990s endure. In only a few instances over the past twenty years have significant federal laws pushed a criminal justice reform agenda. In 2007, Congress passed the Second Chance Act to provide funding and grants for substance use treatment, mentoring, and transitional services for people leaving prison.[11] President Obama signed the Fair Sentencing Act in 2010, which reduced "the disparity in the amounts of powder cocaine and crack cocaine required for the imposition of mandatory minimum sentences."[12] In 2018, President Donald Trump signed the First Step Act, a law that included improvements to the federal Bureau of Prisons and sentencing reforms such as retroactively applying the Fair Sentencing Act.[13]

Another federal government tool is a president's use of existing executive branch powers. The president and the cabinet have megaphones to reach community and government partners, and the message from the bully pulpit can be augmented through executive actions carried out by federal agencies. After Michael Brown was killed in 2014 by police officers in Ferguson, Missouri, the Obama administration was spurred to action by mass uprising and protests across the country.[14] The Justice Department increased investigations into local law enforcement practices that resulted in systemic misconduct.[15] The president convened the Task Force on 21st Century Policing, which provided recommendations on how to transform law enforcement agencies by, for example, changing policies to limit the use of force, holding officers accountable when they violate policies and the law, and improving training to ensure that best practices are implemented.[16] I was personally invested in these policy changes, having led the federal government's effort to create policies to curtail the transfer of military equipment to local police departments and build programs to enhance trust between law enforcement and communities.[17]

Executive actions can be drafted and signed quickly—many of these policy pushes were put in motion within a matter of weeks—but the downside is how easy it is for subsequent administrations to undo or discontinue them. For example, very few of the post-Ferguson policy pushes were embedded in a permanent structure, and the incoming Trump administration discarded many of them in its first year through orders and memorandums—literal strokes of the pen.[18] This dealt a significant setback to widespread adoption of reforms that needed time to take hold and a consistent push from the president to shore up local leaders committed to change. Witnessing the hard work that my colleagues and I put in over three years seemingly vanish overnight was a real wake-up call.

THE PROMISE OF FEDERAL FUNDING

Of the remaining levers, perhaps federal funding to support local and state efforts provides the most promise. One of the most rewarding experiences of my career was working as a senior advisor in the Office of Justice Programs (OJP), a little-known agency with the U.S. Department of Justice that is responsible for managing north of $5 billion of federal grants related to public safety and criminal justice.[19] Before working there, I had little appreciation for the power and influence that federal funding can have on what takes place locally. Funding has been a key driver of the reform movement over the past fifteen years by supporting the testing and piloting of interventions that could replace harmful practices, evaluating them for long-term effectiveness, putting coalitions together to coordinate messages and disseminate information, and shaping public opinion to show policymakers the need to change course. Federal funding levers can combine the relative speed and flexibility of executive actions with a sense of permanence that comes from legislative action to press for transformative change. This authority, though, needs to be wielded with intent and careful deliberation of several important considerations.

One key factor that plays a tremendous role in determining how transformative the change can be is the dollar amount set for reform efforts. The investment must be significant. The Brennan Center, for example, proposed legislation that would devote $1 billion over ten years to fund grants that reverse the harmful effects of mass incarceration.[20] Even though a bill modeled on that legislation was introduced in Congress, the federal government has yet to move forward on that or other proposals that would devote a substantial amount of funding specifically for reform efforts. Thus far, the most robust dedicated funding to transform the criminal justice system is the Second Chance Act, which has appropriated around $1 billion in grants to support reentry efforts since it was enacted more than fifteen years ago.[21] Today, reentry is one of the most popular, bipartisan, and effective areas of justice reform and championed by a variety of social sectors such as educational institutions, community groups, the business community, sports, and entertainment.

Another essential element to ensuring the effectiveness of federal funding is to clearly articulate the purpose of the grant and specify the activities for which the grantee can use the funds. Changing the status quo requires an intentional, directive approach. Unfortunately, most of the large funding streams currently provide a great deal of deference to localities and states on how to allocate federal public safety and criminal justice dollars. Without specific direction, the default posture of lawmakers—as well as the public at large—toward safety and the criminal justice system will continue to reflect a traditional approach that overemphasizes arrests and incarceration.

A prime example of this is illustrated in how states use federal funding received through the Byrne Justice Assistance Grants (JAG).[22] This funding stream provides every state and several localities a large block of flexible money determined by a formula to use for public safety and criminal justice purposes. Local policymakers have significant leeway on how they will spend these funds (such as for salaries or equipment) if the purpose of those expenditures fall within one of nine broad program areas that have been developed over time.[23] Although some of the purpose areas such as prevention and reentry are more aligned with reforming the criminal justice system, a 2019 analysis by the Center for American Progress showed that states chose to use more than half of all Byrne JAG funding for law enforcement.[24] Additionally, states used a significant portion of the remaining dollars for other traditional carceral and enforcement purposes like corrections and court processes.

The lack of specificity and guardrails has repercussions. This was clear when the federal government made $350 billion available to localities through the 2021 American Rescue Plan Act, which supported local government agencies to improve their economic recovery at the height of the COVID-19 pandemic. The Treasury Department provided guidance to local and state governments on how they could allocate those resources. The guidance, though, did not include specific definitions or restrictions on what the money could be used to accomplish.[25] According to an analysis by the Marshall Project in 2022, nearly half of the total amount allocated to cities and counties—at that point to replace tax revenues—went to projects that mentioned police, law enforcement, courts, jail, or prison.[26]

Finally, the federal government should make every effort to intentionally incorporate ideas and information from a wide array of experts in the field to shape federal funding priorities and avoid making funding decisions in a bubble. This can certainly be done through traditional methods such as task forces and advisory committees, but even those fall prey to relying on the same external voices. An overlooked mechanism to diversify who has input in determining how public safety and justice reform grants are awarded is the peer review process.[27] In general, applications for grants offered by the Department of Justice and the Office of Justice Programs are reviewed both by government staff as well experts from the field. The peer reviewers score each application according to the grant criteria, and their combined assessment influences the final decisions that OJP makes.

However, the type of expertise that OJP seeks in its peer reviewers is both vague and unclear. The publicly available information, for example, describes the topic areas in which potential reviewers should have experience and expertise in an academic way (such as crime control and prevention). This could dissuade people who have different experiences—such as those in service delivery or with conviction histories—from considering the opportunity. OJP has not made a significant public push to call attention to this important role or recruit experts from more diverse backgrounds. Without expanding the pool of peer reviewers, the grant application process becomes stagnant, the same type of reviewer prioritizing the same type of applicant. In other words, the federal government could inadvertently be closing the door on entire classes of promising grantees with the potential to transform communities simply because it has not changed who has input into the process.

CONCLUSION

Federal funding has the potential to spur the transformation of the country's criminal justice systems, but it is not an easy road. Policymakers must make a sustained commitment to reversing mass incarceration. The investment cannot be small. A substantial amount of resources is required, along with an intentional approach to use the power of federal funding for change rather than to maintain the status quo.

NOTES

1. German Lopez, "Why You Can't Blame Mass Incarceration on the War on Drugs," Vox, May 30, 2017, https://www.vox.com/policy-and-politics/2017/5/30/15591700/mass-incarceration-john-pfaff-locked-in.
2. Rashawn Ray and William A. Galston, "Did the 1994 Crime Bill Cause Mass Incarceration?" (Washington, DC: Brookings Institution, August 28, 2020), https://www.brookings.edu/articles/did-the-1994-crime-bill-cause-mass-incarceration; Glenn Kessler, "Joe Biden's Defense of the 1994 Crime Bill's Role in Mass Incarcerations," *Washington Post*, May 16, 2019, https://www.washingtonpost.com/politics/2019/05/16/joe-bidens-defense-crime-bills-role-incarceration-trend.
3. FAMM, "State Reforms to Mandatory Minimum Sentencing Laws," updated October 30, 2020, https://famm.org/wp-content/uploads/Chart-STATE-REFORMS-TO-MANDATORY-MINIMUM-SENTENCING-LAWS-2018.pdf.
4. Clean Slate Initiative, "Clean Slate in the States," accessed January 2, 2023, https://www.cleanslateinitiative.org/states#states.
5. Nazish Dholakia and Daniela Gilbert, "Community Violence Intervention Programs Explained" (New York: Vera Institute of Justice, September 1, 2021), https://www.vera.org/community-violence-intervention-programs-explained.
6. David A. Graham, "How Criminal-Justice Reform Fell Apart," *The Atlantic*, May 26, 2022, https://www.theatlantic.com/ideas/archive/2022/05/george-floyd-anniversary-police-reform-violent-crime/630174.
7. Alex Seitz-Wald, "How Democrats Went from Defund to Refund the Police," NBC News, February 6, 2022, https://www.nbcnews.com/politics/politics-news/democrats-went-defund-refund-police-rcna14796.
8. Neil Eggleston, "A Nation of Second Chances: President Obama's Record on Clemency," The White House, January 19, 2017, https://obamawhitehouse.archives.gov/issues/clemency; U.S. Department of Justice, "Obama Administration Clemency Initiative," updated January 12, 2021, https://www.justice.gov/archives/pardon/obama-administration-clemency-initiative.
9. Office of the Inspector General, "Review of the Department's Clemency Initiative," U.S. Department of Justice, August 2018, https://oig.justice.gov/reports/2018/e1804.pdf; Eggleston, "A Nation of Second Chances."

10. Barack Obama, "The President's Role in Advancing Criminal Justice Reform," *Harvard Law Review* 130, no. 811 (January 5, 2017): 811–66, https://harvardlawreview.org/2017/01/the-presidents-role-in-advancing-criminal-justice-reform.
11. The White House, "Fact Sheet: President Bush Signs Second Chance Act of 2007," Press release, April 9, 2008, https://georgewbush-whitehouse.archives.gov/news/releases/2008/04/20080409-15.html.
12. Jesse Lee, "President Obama Signs the Fair Sentencing Act," *The White House* (blog), August 3, 2010, https://obamawhitehouse.archives.gov/blog/2010/08/03/president-obama-signs-fair-sentencing-act.
13. The White House, "President Donald J. Trump Is Committed to Building on the Successes of the First Step Act," Briefing statement, April 1, 2019, https://trumpwhitehouse.archives.gov/briefings-statements/president-donald-j-trump-committed-building-successes-first-step-act.
14. AP News, "Timeline of Events in Shooting of Michael Brown in Ferguson," August 8, 2019, https://apnews.com/article/shootings-police-us-news-st-louis-michael-brown-9aa32033692547699a3b61da8fd1fc62.
15. Civil Rights Division, *The Civil Rights Division's Pattern and Practice Police Reform Work: 1994–Present* (Washington, DC: U.S. Department of Justice, January 2017), https://www.justice.gov/crt/file/922421/download.
16. President's Task Force on 21st Century Policing, *Final Report of the President's Task Force on 21st Century Policing.* (Washington, DC: Office of Community Oriented Policing Services, 2015), https://cops.usdoj.gov/pdf/taskforce/taskforce_finalreport.pdf.
17. Christi Parsons, "Obama Bars Some Military Equipment from Going to Local Police," *Los Angeles Times*, May 18, 2015, https://www.latimes.com/nation/la-na-obama-military-equipment-police-20150518-story.html; National Initiative for Building Trust and Justice, accessed January 2, 2023, https://trustandjustice.org.
18. Justin George, "Trump Has Already Demolished Obama's Criminal-Justice Legacy," Vice Media Group, January 22, 2018, https://www.vice.com/en/article/mbpnkb/trump-has-already-demolished-obamas-criminal-justice-legacy.
19. U.S. Department of Justice, "Office of Justice Programs," accessed January 2, 2023, https://www.ojp.gov; Office of Justice Programs, "FY 2021 Budget Request at a Glance," accessed January 2, 2023, https://www.justice.gov/doj/page/file/1246791/download.
20. Hernandez Stroud, Lauren-Brooke Eisen, and Ram Subramanian, "A Proposal to Reduce Unnecessary Incarceration" (New York: Brennan Center for Justice, 2023), https://www.brennancenter.org/our-work/policy-solutions/proposal-reduce-unnecessary-incarceration.
21. Author's analysis based on the following sources: U.S. Department of Justice, "FY 2019 Performance Budget: Office of Justice Programs," February 2018,

https://www.justice.gov/jmd/page/file/1034426/download; "FY 2021 Performance Budget: Office of Justice Programs," February 2020, https://www.justice.gov/doj/page/file/1246736/download; "FY 2022 Performance Budget: Office of Justice Programs," May 2021, https://www.justice.gov/jmd/page/file/1399261/download; Council of State Governments Justice Center, Bureau of Justice Assistance, and the National Reentry Resource Center, "The Second Chance Act," April 2018, https://csgjusticecenter.org/wp-content/uploads/2020/02/July-2018_SCA_factsheet.pdf.

22. Bureau of Justice Assistance, "Edward Byrne Memorial Justice Assistance Grant (JAG) Program," U.S. Department of Justice, accessed January 2, 2023, https://bja.ojp.gov/program/jag/overview.
23. The current program areas are (1) law enforcement; (2) prosecution and court; (3) prevention and education; (4) corrections and community corrections, including reentry; (5) drug treatment and enforcement; (6) planning, evaluation, and technology improvement; (7) crime victim and witness initiatives; (8) mental health programs and related law enforcement and corrections programs, including behavioral programs and crisis intervention teams; and (9) implementation of state crisis intervention court proceedings. Bureau of Justice Assistance, "Fact Sheet: Edward Byrne Memorial Justice Assistance Grant Program," U.S. Department of Justice, accessed January 2, 2023, https://bja.ojp.gov/doc/jag-program-fact-sheet.pdf.
24. Ed Chung, Betsy Pearl, and Lea Hunter, "The 1994 Crime Bill Continues to Undercut Justice Reform—Here's How to Stop It" (Washington, DC: Center for American Progress, March 26, 2019), https://www.americanprogress.org/article/1994-crime-bill-continues-undercut-justice-reform-heres-stop.
25. U.S. Department of the Treasury, *Coronavirus State & Local Fiscal Recovery Funds: Overview of the Final Rule,* January 2022, https://home.treasury.gov/system/files/136/SLFRF-Final-Rule-Overview.pdf.
26. Anastasia Valeeva, Weihua Li, and Susie Cagle, "Rifles, Tasers and Jails: How Cities and States Spent Billions of COVID-19 Relief" (Washington, DC: The Marshall Project, September 7, 2022), https://www.themarshallproject.org/2022/09/07/how-federal-covid-relief-flows-to-the-criminal-justice-system.
27. Office of Justice Programs, "Peer Reviewers," U.S. Department of Justice, May 4, 2021, https://www.ojp.gov/funding/peer-reviewers#resources.

PART THREE

PROSECUTION AND SENTENCING

7

THE PROSECUTOR PROBLEM

Paul Butler

I BECAME A PROSECUTOR because I don't like bullies. I stopped being a prosecutor because I don't like bullies.

I grew up on the south side of Chicago in an all-Black neighborhood. My family had direct experience with crime—our house was broken into and my mother was held up at gunpoint. As a young Black man, I also had some bad experiences with police officers, such as getting stopped for no reason and being the object of suspicion every time I rode my bike into a white neighborhood.

So I went into the prosecutor's office in the District of Columbia as an undercover brother, hoping I could create change from within. I wanted to help keep people safe from criminals, and I wanted to help keep Black people as safe as possible in a racist criminal justice system.

What I instead found was that rather than my changing the system, the system was changing me. Like many lawyers, I was competitive and ambitious, and the way for a young lawyer to move up in the prosecutor's office was to lock up as many people as possible for as long as possible. It turned out I was good at it. I started to think of that work as the best way to serve my community.

At some point, though, I began to see things differently. Virtually all the defendants were Black or Latino. In Washington, as in many American cities, if you visit criminal court, you would think that white people don't commit crime. I came to realize that I did not go to law school to put Black people in prison, especially for the drug crimes that I was prosecuting—crimes that white folks were also committing but didn't get arrested for. I also didn't feel that my work sending so many people to prison—especially Black men—was making communities any safer. On the contrary, I learned that too many prosecutors use their power in a way that has contributed to the radical increase in incarceration.

As the most powerful actors in the criminal legal system, local and federal prosecutors have a huge amount of discretion and are subject to little judicial oversight—oversight that might moderate their misuse of prosecutorial power. For example, they decide not only whether to charge someone with a crime, but if so, what crime. Even if a judge does not agree with the prosecutor's decision to charge someone with a particular crime, the judge is powerless to undo the prosecutor's action. Because punishment for a crime is largely determined by the sentence that lawmakers have established in the criminal code, the prosecutor often has more power over how much punishment someone convicted of a crime receives than the judge who does the actual sentencing.[1]

Let's say that a person has been arrested for possessing five pounds of weed (in a jurisdiction where marijuana possession and selling is criminalized). The prosecutor can choose not to charge that person (no sentence, obviously), charge them with simple possession (usually a sentence of limited duration or severity), or charge them with possession with intent to distribute, which can require—by statute—several years in prison. Most prosecutor offices are not transparent about what factors would lead them to which charging decision—and that's assuming that the office even has uniform standards. Many offices don't, and decide these issues on an ad hoc basis, which risks allowing inappropriate considerations like race to influence who gets charged.

Plea bargaining exacerbates the problem. This is because prosecutors typically offer an accused person a deal to avoid going to trial. Some 95 percent of criminal cases are resolved this way. If the defendant agrees to confess their guilt, the prosecutor recommends a sentence to the judge that is less punitive than what the prosecutor would recommend if the defendant goes to trial, and loses. This threat by prosecutors—to throw the book at defendants who are found guilty—radically dilutes the defendant's constitutional right to a trial.

Unfortunately, the Supreme Court authorized this practice in a 1978 case, *Bordenkircher v. Hayes*.[2] Lewis Hayes had been charged with forgery and faced a two- to ten-year prison sentence. Prosecutors offered to pursue a five-year sentence if Hayes pleaded guilty and saved them from "the inconvenience and necessity of a trial."[3] If he refused to plead guilty, prosecutors said they would seek an indictment under the Kentucky Habitual Crime Act. Because Hayes had previously been convicted of two felonies, a conviction would mandate a sentence of life imprisonment. Hayes exercised his constitutional right to a trial, prosecutors charged him under the Habitual Crime Act, and he was found guilty and sentenced to a life term.

Hayes challenged his conviction on the grounds that his Fourteenth Amendment due process rights were violated when prosecutors threatened to reindict him on more serious charges if he did not plead guilty to the original, less serious forgery offense. In its 5–4 decision, the Supreme Court rejected the challenge. According to the Court, the plea bargain system is an "important component of this country's criminal justice system," and no constitutional violation occurs as long as pleas are made "knowingly and voluntarily."[4] The Court did recognize that punishing a person because he "has done what the law plainly allows him to do" is "a due process violation of the most basic sort."[5] But it rejected the idea that Hayes was being punished, claiming instead that he was just being presented with "difficult choices."[6]

Since *Bordenkircher*, plea bargaining has become so institutionalized that Justice Anthony Kennedy noted, in a case decided in 2012, that plea bargaining "is not some adjunct to the criminal justice system; it *is* the criminal justice system."[7] Despite this standard, a growing number of prosecutors have pledged not to punish individuals for exercising their right to a fair and speedy trial.[8] Other prosecutors have opted to charge individuals with restraint. For example, Dan Satterberg, a prosecutor from Seattle, began using charging standards that protected against disproportionate sentences and discouraged filing a case in every instance where one could be filed.[9]

Prosecutors have also contributed to the racial disparities that are an endemic feature of the U.S. criminal legal system. In 2014, the Vera Institute of Justice published research that examined racial disparities at play in the Manhattan District Attorney's office and concluded that "race remained a statistically significant independent factor" at most discretionary points in the legal process.[10] In Vera's report, based on the analysis of more than two hundred thousand cases, researchers found that Black and Latino people charged with drug offenses were more likely to receive more punitive plea offers than white defendants, particularly offers that included incarceration. Black and Latino defendants were also more likely than similarly situated whites and Asian Americans to be detained before trial. The study did find that prosecutors treated Black and Latino defendants more favorably in at least one respect: they were more likely than whites to have cases dismissed before they went to trial—probably, the report argued, because "police were more likely to bring them in on bogus or unsubstantiated charges" in the first place.

Many of these policies and practices are being reexamined in jurisdictions across the country, in part thanks to reformers who have won district attorney elections. The "progressive prosecutor" movement owes its start to Angela Davis's 2009 book, *Arbitrary Justice: The Power of the American Prosecutor,* which argued that prosecutors should use their discretion to reduce mass incarceration and racial disparities.

Reform-minded prosecutors have different approaches, but they all reject incarceration as a knee-jerk response to social ills. In Chicago, Cook County State's Attorney Kim Foxx declined to prosecute low-level offenses such as small-scale retail theft as felonies. In New York, Manhattan District Attorney Alvin Bragg instructed his office to seek incarceration only for the most serious offenses, such as murder and sexual assault, and to refrain from requesting sentences longer than twenty years, unless "exceptional circumstances" are a consideration.[11] Philadelphia District Attorney Larry Krasner requires prosecutors in his office to state on the record the costs and benefits of any prison sentences they recommend to judges.[12] In San Francisco, District Attorney Chesa Boudin ended the use of three-strikes laws prior to being recalled in June 2022.[13]

Despite the ongoing efforts by progressive prosecutors across the country, their discretion and policies are under attack by politicians and other skeptical parties in their communities. Boudin, for example, was recalled after instituting progressive policies in his office. Before taking office as head prosecutor in San Francisco in 2020, Boudin served as a public defender, but his connection to the criminal legal system began much earlier. When he was an infant, his mother, Kathy Boudin, was sentenced to twenty years to life after acting as the unarmed getaway driver in a robbery north of New York City that left three people dead.[14] His father was incarcerated for his involvement in the same robbery.[15]

Boudin, motivated by his experiences, went to law school and then took a job as a public defender in San Francisco. After years of serving as a public defender, he decided to run for San Francisco district attorney—the same office that Vice President Kamala Harris formerly held.[16] His platform included promises to limit the use of incarceration, increase police accountability, and address systemic racial inequalities in San Francisco's criminal legal system. Days after his historic win, those in opposition to his policies and positions launched a recall effort. Leaders of this effort were members of Boudin's party. Mary Jung, the former chair of the Democratic Party in San Francisco, led the campaign to recall him. In response to the campaign's success, Jung stated that "San Francisco needed a change and this is just really a validation of what a lot of us were feeling."[17] Those feelings included frustration over street conditions, such as drug sales, homeless encampments, and untreated mental illness.

Despite Boudin pointing out on multiple occasions that he was not responsible for many of those street conditions, the recall prevailed, which may have also been motivated by the rise in crime rates in San Francisco. When Boudin first took office, he eliminated cash bail and announced that gang affiliation would no longer be used in sentencing or in prosecuting cases where officers stopped a car as pretext for a drug search. Spurred by deteriorating conditions in jails and prisons during the COVID-19 pandemic, Boudin began to push for decarceration, reducing San Francisco's jail population from a daily average of 1,200 to seven hundred people by May 2020. Although crime overall had dropped by 30 percent between March 2020 and December 2020, burglaries rose by 40 percent and car thefts rose by more than 20 percent between January 2020 and July 2020.[18] Despite the Democratic County Central Committee in California voting 20–2 to oppose Boudin's recall (the two nays being former opponents in the district attorney race), the recall movement prevailed. More than 60 percent of voters approved the recall.[19]

Other progressive prosecutors faced similar fates, such as Aramis Ayala and Andrew Warren in Florida. Ayala, the first Black person elected head prosecutor in Florida, served from 2017 to 2021 as the state attorney for the Ninth Judicial Circuit.[20] In 2017, she announced that her office would not seek the death penalty in any case during her tenure.[21] This announcement came during a press conference regarding the prosecution of a man accused of killing his pregnant ex-girlfriend and a police officer. Believing that pursuing the death penalty was not in the best interests of justice or her community, Ayala stated that her office would not pursue one should a guilty verdict be issued.

This prompted then Florida Governor Rick Scott to remove Ayala from the case. In her place, Scott appointed Brad King, a white male prosecutor from another district.[22] Ayala continued to face resistance from the governor during her term as she prosecuted cases without seeking the death penalty. Scott removed Ayala from at least twenty-six other murder cases, replacing her with King each time. Ayala challenged the governor's actions in court, but the Florida Supreme Court ultimately upheld Scott's removal of Ayala in a 5–2 vote.[23]

More recently, Andrew Warren was removed from office as head prosecutor by current Florida Governor Ron DeSantis.[24] In 2019, Warren, then state attorney for Hillsborough County in Florida, signed a letter from the progressive organization Fair and Just Prosecution denouncing Florida laws that punished doctors for providing gender-affirming care to transgender individuals. After the Supreme Court struck down the constitutional right to an abortion in June 2022, Warren signed another letter by Fair and Just Prosecution in which he pledged to refrain from using his prosecutorial discretion and the resources of the criminal legal system to prosecute individuals who seek, provide, or otherwise support abortions.[25]

Warren's signature on both petitions prompted DeSantis to remove Warren from office via executive order.[26] Governors under Florida law are empowered to remove "any county officer" for "malfeasance, misfeasance, neglect of duty, drunkenness, incompetence, permanent inability to perform official duties, or commission of a felony."[27] DeSantis asserted that Warren's pledge not to prosecute individuals involved in gender-affirming care and abortions was a "neglect of duty" showing "incompetence" that is "beyond just exercising discretion."[28]

However, despite signing both letters, Warren had taken no action in his office to carry out the pledges made in the letters. Warren believes that "the governor's order is just based on pure conjecture and lies about what he thinks I'm going to do with cases that haven't even come before me yet."[29] Ultimately, the Florida Senate has the final say on the matter.

The progressive prosecutor movement is new but promising. Despite the obstacles that progressive prosecutors face, their work is still necessary. Because prosecutors are one of the primary sources of the problem of mass incarceration and excessive punishment, they must also be part of the solution.

NOTES

1. Jamila Hodge and Kelsey Reid, "Unlocking the Black Box of Prosecution" (New York: Vera Institute of Justice, 2019), https://www.vera.org/unlocking-the-black-box-of-prosecution.

2. Bordenkircher v. Hayes, 434 U.S. 357 (1978).
3. *Bordenkircher*, 434 U.S. at 358.
4. *Bordenkircher*, 434 U.S. at 361–62.
5. *Bordenkircher*, 434 U.S. at 363.
6. *Bordenkircher*, 434 U.S. at 364.
7. Missouri v. Frye, 566 U.S. 134 (2012) at 7, citing Robert Scott and William Stuntz, "Plea Bargaining as a Social Contract," *Yale Law Journal* 101, no. 8 (1992): 1912, https://scholarship.law.columbia.edu/faculty_scholarship/317.
8. See generally Jamie Fellner, *An Offer You Can't Refuse: How U.S. Federal Prosecutors Force Drug Defendants to Plead Guilty* (New York: Human Rights Watch, December 5, 2013), https://www.hrw.org/report/2013/12/05/offer-you-cant-refuse/how-us-federal-prosecutors-force-drug-defendants-plead.
9. Fair and Just Prosecution, *21 Principles for the 21st Century Prosecutor* (New York: Brennan Center for Justice and The Justice Collaborative, 2018), https://fairandjustprosecution.org/wp-content/uploads/2018/12/FJP_21Principles_Interactive-w-destinations.pdf.
10. Besiki Kutateladze, Whitney Tymas, and Mary Crowley, "Race and Prosecution in Manhattan" (New York: Vera Institute of Justice, 2014), https://www.vera.org/downloads/publications/race-and-prosecution-manhattan-summary.pdf.
11. Jonah E. Bromwich, "Manhattan D.A. Acts on Vow to Seek Incarceration Only for Worst Crimes," *New York Times*, January 6, 2022, https://www.nytimes.com/2022/01/06/nyregion/alvin-bragg-manhattan-da.html.
12. Bobby Allyn, "Philly DA Wants Prison Costs Included as Judge Calculates Offender's Debt to Society," WHYY/PBS, March 28, 2018, https://whyy.org/segments/philly-da-wants-prison-costs-included-as-judge-calculates-offenders-debt-to-society.
13. Thomas Fuller, "Voters in San Francisco Topple the City's Progressive District Attorney, Chesa Boudin," *New York Times*, June 8, 2022, https://www.nytimes.com/2022/06/07/us/politics/chesa-boudin-recall-san-francisco.html.
14. Miriam Pawel, "How Chesa Boudin's Life Made Him a Lightning Rod for the Progressive Prosecutor Movement," *Los Angeles Times*, March 30, 2022, https://www.latimes.com/politics/story/2022-03-30/chesa-boudin-san-francisco-recall-profile.
15. Pawel, "Chesa Boudin's Life," 2022.
16. Benjamin Wallace-Wells, "The Trial of Chesa Boudin," *The New Yorker*, July 29, 2021, https://www.newyorker.com/news/annals-of-inquiry/the-trial-of-chesa-boudin.
17. Fuller, "Voters Topple Chesa Boudin," 2022.
18. Wallace-Wells, "Trial of Chesa Boudin."
19. Fuller, "Voters Topple Chesa Boudin."

20. Paul Butler, "Progressive Prosecutors Are Not Trying to Dismantle the Master's House, and the Master Wouldn't Let Them Anyway," *Fordham Law Review* 90, no. 5 (2022): 1995, https://ir.lawnet.fordham.edu/cgi/viewcontent.cgi?article=5923&context=flr.
21. Jordan Smith, "The Power to Kill," *The Intercept*, December 3, 2019, https://theintercept.com/2019/12/03/death-penalty-reform-prosecutors.
22. Bernie Woodall, "Florida Prosecutor Sues Governor to Remain on Murder Cases," Reuters, April 11, 2017, https://www.reuters.com/article/florida-prosecutor/florida-prosecutor-sues-governor-to-remain-on-murder-cases-idUSL1N1HJ1O8.
23. Ayala v. Scott, No. SC17-653 (Fla. 2017), https://caselaw.findlaw.com/fl-supreme-court/1872696.html.
24. Patricia Mazzei, "DeSantis Suspends Tampa Prosecutor Who Vowed Not to Criminalize Abortion," *New York Times*, August 4, 2022, https://www.nytimes.com/2022/08/04/us/desantis-tampa-prosecutor-abortion.html.
25. Steve Contorno, "DeSantis Suspends Tampa Prosecutor Who Took Stance Against Criminalizing Abortion Providers," CNN, August 4, 2022, https://www.cnn.com/2022/08/04/politics/desantis-suspends-prosecutor/index.html.
26. Fla. Exec. Order 22-176 (August 4, 2022), https://www.flgov.com/wp-content/uploads/2022/08/Executive-Order-22-176.pdf.
27. Contorno, "DeSantis Suspends Tampa Prosecutor."
28. Contorno, "DeSantis Suspends Tampa Prosecutor."
29. Kathryn Varn, "Ousted Florida Prosecutor Andrew Warren's 'Woke' Politics Helped Crack Decades-Old Murder Cases," *Tallahassee Democrat*, August 11, 2022, https://www.tallahassee.com/story/news/2022/08/11/andrew-warrens-former-florida-prosecutor-woke-politics-helped-solve-two-florida-cold-cases/10225763002.

8

THE TRIAL PENALTY

Coercive Plea Bargaining

Martin Sabelli

EVERY CULTURE CELEBRATES ITS IDENTITY in the form of an origin myth—the story that relates the creation of the social order that governs that society. In America, we tell ourselves that our ancestors came to this land to escape the monarchical tyranny of their homelands and, to ensure the success of their mission, pioneered a republican form of government characterized by institutions designed to protect individual freedoms and liberties. Perhaps the most celebrated of these institutions is the jury trial, which places our peers between the juggernaut of the state and the freedom and liberty of the individual.

In fact, as shocking as this may be to the modern American mindset, our forebears considered the right to trial by jury to be as fundamental to freedom and liberty as the right to vote.[1] The Framers of the Constitution imagined a legal system characterized by trials under the watchful gaze of both jurors drawn from the community and judges charged with ensuring equilibrium between the power of the state and the individual accused.

In America today, we have abandoned the system of public jury trials envisioned by the Framers, and embedded in the Bill of Rights, in favor of a shadow system of guilty pleas driven by the logic of prosecutorial power—power rooted most significantly in mandatory sentencing laws.[2] The silver screen celebrates an idealized world of trials. The modern criminal legal system operates as an assembly line of guilty pleas following a weakened, unrecognizable parody of an adversarial process. We maintain the form of the adversarial process envisioned by the Framers but nurture profound asymmetries of power between prosecutors and the accused that allow the state to effectively coerce pleas from the innocent and guilty alike by threatening exponentially higher posttrial sentences. Turn down five years' probation and serve five years in prison after trial. Two years now or twenty after trial. These threats fill the corridors of our courthouses marking the drumbeat of guilty plea after guilty plea because we have shifted power in court from citizen jurors and professional judges to prosecutors. To be painfully clear, this power imbalance not only causes many to accept brutal sentences despite having a legal defense but also incentivizes innocent people to plead guilty.[3]

How does this happen from day to day in virtually every criminal court throughout the nation? The process is simple: the prosecutor conveys a settlement offer to the defense attorney, threatening a posttrial sentence much greater than the pretrial offer.[4] This discrepancy—the substantial and coercive difference between an offer and a sentence—is often referred to as the trial penalty or trial tax. The defense attorney—very often before having had an opportunity to review the evidence, investigate the case, or establish a relationship with the client—conveys the offer to the client. The client must then choose between challenging the sufficiency and legality of the prosecution's evidence, on the one hand, and, on the other, the unavoidable risk of losing at trial and—thanks to mandatory minimum sentences—suffering a draconian posttrial sentence often dictated by the prosecutor.

In this brave new world, nothing is sacred. The trial penalty has also eliminated true bargaining, especially for the most vulnerable, including people of color and the poor who lack the resources to resist prosecutorial power. You cannot bargain if your opponent has, legally, placed a gun to your head in the form of a twenty-year mandatory minimum sentence—used more often against people of color—in a context of systemic racism and implicit bias.[5] A process is not truly adversarial and bargaining is not bargaining, given the profound asymmetry of power.

Going to trial, of course, triggers the most extreme forms of the trial penalty. Take, for example, the case of Rogel Aguilera-Mederos—a twenty-six-year-old truck driver with no criminal record—who received a 110-year sentence for accidentally killing four people because his brakes failed as he approached stalled traffic on a Colorado highway. Aguilera-Mederos received this severe term, the equivalent of a life sentence, not because he had acted with malice—he did not—but because he rejected a plea offer and exercised his right to trial.[6] Because he elected to exercise this constitutional right, prosecutors invoked Colorado's mandatory sentencing laws, which required the 110-year term and effectively stripped the sentencing judge of any discretion to fashion a just sentence.[7]

Fortunately for Aguilera-Mederos, fellow truck drivers immediately rallied to his side, initiating a boycott of Colorado and a petition to reduce his sentence signed by almost five million people. Then, with the national spotlight focused on the case, the district attorney retracted her support for the brutal sentence her office had requested and, ten days after the sentencing, Colorado Governor Jared Polis commuted the sentence to ten years.[8] Likewise, Kevin O'Brien Allen, a Black man, was charged in Louisiana for selling $20 worth of marijuana. Prosecutors offered him five years, but Mr. Allen opted to go to trial, lost, and is now serving life without parole.[9] Both men suffered for exercising their right to trial illustrating why the vast majority of accused simply take the deal whether they have a defense or not.

The unchecked power of prosecutors has resulted in the disappearance of trials, as the National Association of Criminal Defense Lawyers found. Approximately 95 percent of felony charges result in plea deals—in federal court, less than 2 percent.[10] Why? Because those who elect to go to trial suffer, across the board, penalties three times higher than those who plead and, in some types of cases, eight times higher, the rational response, given the uncertainty of trial, is therefore often to surrender a valid defense and plead guilty.[11] Essentially, the trial penalty has virtually eliminated trials by breaking the will of one accused individual after another.[12]

Second, we can thank the trial penalty for aggravating mass incarceration because individuals facing the trial penalty routinely agree to severe sentences to avoid even more severe sentences. Empirically, the increased reliance on plea bargaining coincides with the explosion of our prison population at both the state and federal levels.[13] Many of my clients of color agree to extreme sentences to avoid even more extreme sentences that would effectively end their lives in prison. Across the system, with more and more people pleading to longer sentences, we fill our prisons at a rate much higher than other democracies.[14]

Third, although the trial penalty affects all accused people, it punishes the vulnerable most harshly, especially racial and ethnic minorities and the poor, thanks to the effects of systemic racism and other bargaining inequalities. I have sat across the table from indigent clients, many clients of color, who "choose" to plead guilty in this context of legalized coercion. Although some may have the economic resources to minimize the most abusive aspects of the trial penalty—including the overuse of pretrial detention—people of color and the poor are easy pickings in our prosecutor-driven justice system.

Fourth, we can thank the trial penalty for a greater degree and frequency of police and prosecutor misconduct. On a systemic level, fewer trials translate to less citizen oversight of the police and prosecutorial functions. By allowing jury trials to fade away, we have effectively stripped juries of the authority to curb government power and judges of the power to mete out individualized justice case by case.

To explore the relationship between the disappearance of trials and police misconduct, imagine a police officer choosing to pepper spray a nine-year-old girl as she sat in handcuffs in a patrol car crying for her father.[15] What could have been in the mind of this officer when he acted with violence toward a child? I cannot fathom what this officer was thinking, but he likely did not consider, even for a millisecond, the potential that his conduct would be subject to public scrutiny in a court of law. I am certain that this officer was not troubled, let alone even deterred, by the thought that anyone would cross-examine him about his use of force during a suppression hearing or criminal trial. Our assembly line system of guilty pleas—uninterrupted by the suppression hearings and trials framed in the Fourth, Fifth, and Sixth Amendments—often insulates police from accountability for their day-to-day, street-level decisions.

Fifth, plea agreements routinely require waivers of other rights that the Bill of Rights guarantees, including the right to bail, the right to know the evidence against you, and the right to appeal. Request bail? No deal. Request discovery? No deal. Demand Brady material? No deal. More and more frequently, individuals plead guilty without exercising the rights that the Framers ensconced in the Bill of Rights simply because prosecutors demand waivers of these rights as a condition for not being punished to the full extent permitted under severe mandatory sentencing laws.

The Framers who designed our criminal legal system would not recognize today's justice system. They envisioned a system of trials designed to protect the accused, protect rights for all, and to shine light into every stage of the process. Having surrendered this vision of justice, we have failed to protect ourselves, our families, and our communities from police misconduct, mass incarceration, and wrongful convictions. To restore the balance, we must revoke mandatory minimum sentencing, elect prosecutors who will choose to use their power constitutionally rather than coercively, and empower judges to impose rational sentences as the Constitution requires. These policies will better provide the foundation for the democratic, just, and humane criminal legal system the Framers envisioned.

NOTES

1. In the words of John Adams, "representative government and trial by jury are the heart and lungs of liberty. Without them we have no other fortification against being ridden like horses, fleeced like sheep, worked like cattle, and fed and clothed like swine and hounds." *The Revolutionary Writings of John Adams*, ed. C. Bradley Thompson (Indianapolis, IN: Liberty Fund, 2000), 55.
2. See, for example, Vera Institute of Justice, "Unlocking the Black Box of Prosecution" (New York: Vera Institute of Justice, 2018), https://www.vera.org/unlocking-the-black-box-of-prosecution.
3. National Registry of Exonerations, "Innocents Who Plead Guilty," November 24, 2015, https://www.law.umich.edu/special/exoneration/Documents/NRE.Guilty.Plea.Article1.pdf.
4. Norman L. Reimer and Martín A. Sabelli, "The Tyranny of the Trial Penalty: The Consensus That Coercive Plea Practices Must End," *Federal Sentencing Reporter* 31, nos. 4/5 (2019): 215–221, https://online.ucpress.edu/fsr/article/31/4-5/215/109287/The-Tyranny-of-the-Trial-Penalty-The-Consensus.
5. M. Marit Rehavi and Sonja B. Starr, "Racial Disparity in Federal Criminal Sentences," *Journal of Political Economy* 122, no. 6 (2014): 1320–54, https://repository.law.umich.edu/articles/1414.
6. Prosecutors acknowledged that the accident did not involve malice. See Billy Binion, "Rogel Aguilera-Mederos Rejected a Plea Deal. So He Got 110 Years in Prison," *Reason*, December 22, 2021, https://reason.com/2021/12/22/rogel-aguilera-mederos-rejected-a-plea-deal-so-he-got-110-years-in-prison. The parties have not released the terms of the pretrial offer.
7. Judge A. Bruce Jones stated that "if I had the discretion, it would not be my sentence," noting that Colorado's mandatory sentencing laws gave him no choice. See Billy Binion, "He Was Sentenced to 110 Years in Prison for Causing a Fatal Traffic Accident. The Judge Isn't Happy About It," *Reason*, December 15, 2021, https://reason.com/2021/12/15/he-was-sentenced-to-110-years-in-prison-for-causing-fatal-traffic-accident-colorado-judge-mandatory-sentencing.
8. Marisa Sarnoff, "'You Will Serve Your Just Sentence': Colorado Governor Cuts Prison Time for Truck Driver Sentenced to 110 Years for Fatal 2019 Crash," *Law & Crime*, December 31, 2021, https://lawandcrime.com/high-profile/you-will-serve-your-just-sentence-colorado-governor-cuts-prison-time-for-truck-driver-sentenced-to-110-years-for-fatal-2019-crash.
9. Last Prisoner Project, "Kevin's Story," accessed February 14, 2023, https://www.lastprisonerproject.org/freekevinallen.
10. The United States Sentencing Commission reports that in 2021, 98.3 percent of cases were resolved through guilty pleas consistent with the pattern over the past twenty years. See "Fiscal Year 2021 Overview of Federal Criminal

Cases," April 2022, 8, https://www.ussc.gov/sites/default/files/pdf/research-and-publications/research-publications/2022/FY21_Overview_Federal_Criminal_Cases.pdf.

Even the Supreme Court has admitted that our criminal legal system has become "a system of pleas, not a system of trials." See Lafler v. Cooper, 566 U.S. 156 (2012); see also Benjamin Weiser, "Trial by Jury, a Hallowed American Right, Is Vanishing," *New York Times*, August 7, 2016, https://www.nytimes.com/2016/08/08/nyregion/jury-trials-vanish-and-justice-is-served-behind-closed-doors.html; John Gramlich, "Only 2% of federal criminal defendants go to trial, and most who do are found guilty," Pew Research Center, June 11, 2019, https://www.pewresearch.org/short-reads/2019/06/11/only-2-of-federal-criminal-defendants-go-to-trial-and-most-who-do-are-found-guilty.

11. Rick Jones, Gerald B. Lefcourt, Barry J. Pollack, Norman L. Reimer, and Kyle O'Dowd, *The Trial Penalty: The Sixth Amendment Right to Trial on the Verge of Extinction and How to Save It* (Washington, DC: National Association of Criminal Defense Lawyers, 2018), 20–21, https://www.nacdl.org/trialpenaltyreport.
12. "[Plea bargaining] presents grave risks of prosecutorial overcharging that effectively compels an innocent defendant to avoid massive risk by pleading guilty to a lesser offense." Lafler v. Cooper, 566 U.S. 156, 185 (2012) (Scalia, J. dissenting). See Lucian E. Dervan and Vanessa A. Edkins, "The Innocent Defendant's Dilemma: An Innovative Empirical Study of Plea Bargaining's Innocence Problem," *Journal of Criminal Law & Criminology* 103 (2013): 1–48, https://papers.ssrn.com/sol3/papers.cfm?abstract_id=2071397.
13. Albert W. Alschuler, "Plea Bargaining and Mass Incarceration," *New York University Annual Survey of American Law* 76, no. 1 (2021): 205–34, https://annualsurveyofamericanlaw.org/wp-content/uploads/2022/01/76.2-Alschuler.pdf.
14. The United States imprisons approximately 650 people for every hundred thousand, a much higher rate than Western democracies and higher than authoritarian regimes, including Russia and China. See Emily Widra and Tiana Herring, "States of Incarceration: The Global Context 2021" (Northampton, MA: Prison Policy Initiative, September 2021), https://www.prisonpolicy.org/global/2021.html.
15. NBC News, "9-Year-Old Girl Pepper-Sprayed: New Video Shows Police Interactions Before and After," February 12, 2021, https://www.nbcnews.com/video/bodycam-footage-shows-9-year-old-rochester-girl-being-pepper-sprayed-100937797791.

9

END MANDATORY MINIMUMS

Alison Siegler

TO DISMANTLE America's dehumanizing and racially skewed "human caging" system, we need to eliminate mandatory minimum sentences.[1] Forget swinging the pendulum from tough-on-crime to leniency; it always swings back. Instead, we need a paradigm shift. A paradigm shift occurs in three phases: it starts with a dominant paradigm, moves through a crisis phase, and ends with "a revolutionary change in world-view" that constitutes a new dominant paradigm.[2]

Currently, the dominant paradigm in the criminal legal system is the myth that locking people of color in cages to serve harsh mandatory minimum sentences is necessary to keep white people safe. At the federal level alone, mandatory minimum penalties are the cornerstone of the human caging system. Prosecutors' choice to pursue mandatory minimums in more than half of all federal cases disproportionately affects poor people of color and has driven the exponential growth in the federal prison population in recent decades.[3] All fifty states and the District of Columbia also have mandatory minimum sentencing laws.[4]

The principle that underlies mandatory minimums is dehumanization. As Isabel Wilkerson writes, our country's racial "caste system relies on dehumanization to lock the marginalized outside the norms of humanity so that any action against them is seen as reasonable."[5] So many of the horrors Wilkerson catalogs in the "program of purposeful dehumanization" instituted by the Nazis and by the United States during chattel slavery have analogs in today's carceral state: anonymous uniforms replacing clothing, inmate numbers supplanting names, the shaving of heads, the roll calls.[6]

Racial disparities in the application of mandatory minimums are a particularly stark illustration of Wilkerson's thesis. Mandatory minimums dehumanize people by—in the words of Judge Stephanos Bibas—acting as "sledgehammers rather than scalpels," falling with equal force on people whose circumstances are dramatically different from one another and preventing judges from calibrating punishment to suit the person or the crime.[7] One commentator has described how mandatory minimums "were developed to be weapons focused on Black communities, and they have caused their intended damage."[8] Mandatory minimums, especially for drug offenses, may also deviate from constitutional principles by sacrificing a person's liberty without advancing any clear public interest.[9]

Over the past century, the mandatory minimums paradigm has moved into the second phase of a paradigm shift—the crisis phase—becoming the subject of dispute and controversy. Congress first enacted mandatory minimums for drug offenses in the early twentieth century.[10] Reformers pushed back, however, and by the middle of the century a rehabilitative sentencing model began to replace the punitive model. In 1970, Congress repealed most drug-related mandatory minimums, taking more of a "public health approach" to drug policy.[11]

However, in keeping with the chaos that arises from a paradigm shift, by the mid-1970s, anti-imprisonment and antidiscrimination reformers on the left began railing against the rehabilitative model because it gave judges too much discretion, precipitating disparities.[12] Paradoxically, by criticizing so-called arbitrary sentencing practices, these reformers (chief among them, Senator Edward Kennedy of Massachusetts) ultimately helped usher in the current tough-on-crime era. In the mid-1980s, mandatory minimums reentered the federal system with a vengeance as a pillar of President Reagan's war on drugs.[13] In one of the most powerful illustrations of America's failure to rein in our punitive excess, by the end of the 1980s, all fifty states had enacted mandatory minimums.[14]

Since then, the mandatory minimums paradigm has come under fire for three primary reasons: the reallocation of power from judges to prosecutors, the extension of racism and classism, and the failure to advance community safety.

CONSTRAINING JUDGES, EMPOWERING PROSECUTOR ABUSE

Mandatory minimums shackle judges. Although sentencing is supposed to be carried out by a neutral judge, mandatory minimums upend this system by positioning one adversary—the prosecutor—as the ultimate decision-maker, barring the judge from considering a person's history, culpability, or family responsibilities. If a prosecutor charges someone with an offense carrying a twenty-year mandatory minimum at the outset of a case and that person is found guilty, the judge is legally bound to sentence that person to prison for at least twenty years regardless of whether they were a leader or a lackey. Mandatory minimums prohibit the judge from considering that person's individual circumstances and tie their hands when it comes to showing mercy.

Judges routinely condemn mandatory minimums for preventing them from meting out individualized justice and for transferring sentencing authority to prosecutors. One former federal judge, for example, elaborated: "I was often prohibited from assessing a defendant's history, personal characteristics or role in the offense. In sentencing, where judgment should matter most, I could not exercise my judgment."[15] Another recalled, "The most unjust sentence I ever imposed was [a] twenty-five-year mandatory minimum sentence I had to give . . . because the Government deliberately structured its sting operation to make that mandatory minimum applicable."[16] Research into judicial attitudes about mandatory minimums confirms that "the majority of judges feel stifled by mandatory minimum sentencing statutes and perceive that these statutes sometimes prevent them from properly carrying out their sentencing role by reducing the discretion they have to do their jobs effectively."[17]

Other problems flow from this perversion of the power balance. For most people charged with an offense carrying a mandatory minimum, the only hope for avoiding a high mandatory sentence is to cooperate with the prosecution against others. Mandatory minimums thus "provide prosecutors with weapons to bludgeon defendants into effectively coerced plea bargains."[18] This produces the cooperation paradox: big fish who are more culpable and have information about other criminal activity can avoid mandatory minimum sentences by collaborating in the prosecution of others.[19] Meanwhile, the less culpable little fish are yoked with high mandatory minimum sentences.[20] They become casualties of a process that sets aside proportionality and mercy in favor of increasing the number of convictions. Consequently, the least culpable players incur severe punishments, and the most culpable leverage their knowledge into lenient plea deals.

Prosecutors' control over mandatory minimums creates a host of perverse incentives that fuel systemic injustice. When someone's only hope of seeing their children grow up is to cooperate with the government, they may well say whatever the prosecutor wants to hear. In fact, "lying cooperators account for an astounding fifteen to forty-five percent of wrongful convictions."[21] Prosecutors also leverage their power over mandatory minimums to strong-arm people into abdicating their right to seek pretrial freedom. One federal judge described the injustice wrought when prosecutors punish people who win pretrial release by refusing to let them cooperate: "From time to time, an AUSA would brazenly say something like, 'we have no interest in cooperation [with the arrestee] if you release them [pending trial].'"[22]

CREATING RACIAL AND ECONOMIC DISPARITIES

Prosecutors' power over mandatory minimums creates racial disparities, obliterating any pretense of an unbiased system. A 2014 study found that prosecutors' discretionary use of charges carrying mandatory minimum sentences resulted in Black individuals spending more time in prison than white people for the exact same crimes.[23] Concerningly, prosecutors bring charges carrying mandatory minimums "*65 percent more often* against [B]lack defendants," all else equal.[24] Evidence also shows that, when prosecuting drug crimes, some federal prosecutors charge Black and Latino individuals more often than white individuals with a quantity of drugs just sufficient to trigger a mandatory minimum; the disparity is highest "in states with higher levels of racial animus."[25]

Additionally, mandatory minimums produce disparities linked with poverty.[26] In particular, "Congress chose to establish mandatory minimums for crimes 'that most affect people in poverty,' and prosecutors disproportionately charge minimums for such crimes."[27]

DIMINISHING COMMUNITY SAFETY, HARMING INDIVIDUALS

Although mandatory minimums purportedly protect the public, research proves that they are antithetical to community safety. For example, lengthy prison sentences increase the risk of future crime because "incarceration is inherently criminogenic."[28] Mandatory minimums only exacerbate this problem. Florida experienced a 50 percent spike in crime after enacting mandatory minimums.[29] Our overreliance on prisons also makes us less safe by diverting resources from other critical public safety and community needs.[30]

In contrast, studies show that shorter sentences in drug cases neither diminish public safety nor increase drug abuse.[31]

Mandatory minimums exact a high social cost. While in jail pending trial and later in prison, incarcerated individuals are at greater risk of violence and disease; many are unable to obtain adequate health care.[32] During the pretrial phase, individuals in custody often lack access to doctors and are unable to obtain essential prescription medication.[33] Incarcerated individuals also face high levels of sexual victimization.[34] In the federal system, these dangers are exacerbated by severe overcrowding of jails and prisons.[35]

Long sentences also make it more difficult for people to reintegrate into society. Even after release from prison, people face protracted unemployment and other collateral consequences.[36] "Children of incarcerated parents have been found to exhibit more negative behavioral, academic, and emotional outcomes, and are more likely than their peers to end up in prison."[37] This creates a pernicious cycle: "The longer a parent is incarcerated, the risk of that punishment being visited upon their children increases exponentially."[38] Having a parent incarcerated for a significant period also imparts on children "greater risks of health and psychological problems, and lower economic well-being and educational attainment."[39] As one federal judge concluded, "the long-term price of mass incarceration is too high to pay, not just in economic terms, but also in terms of shared social values."[40]

EXECUTIVE BRANCH NEEDS TO CURB ITS USE OF MANDATORY MINIMUMS

The dominant paradigm of mandatory minimums is vulnerable, and instituting a new paradigm is both possible and crucial. President Biden and his attorney general have denounced mandatory minimums, as did former Attorney General Eric Holder in 2013.[41] President Biden's 2022 Safer America Plan, which offers funding to states for law enforcement, requires jurisdictions to "repeal mandatory minimums for non-violent crimes and change other laws that contribute to increased incarceration rates."[42] Even though federal prosecutors—all of whom are subject to supervision by the Department of Justice (DOJ)—have long been the primary proponents of mandatory minimums, Attorney General Merrick Garland disavowed mandatory minimums during his confirmation hearings: "We should . . . as President Biden has suggested, seek the elimination of mandatory minimum[s]."[43]

Yet, during the first two years of Garland's term, Biden's DOJ gave no sign that it would stop pursuing mandatory minimums. In fact, in 2021, Garland reinstated a harsh policy from the Obama era that incorporated a long-standing directive requiring federal prosecutors to levy charges carrying mandatory minimum sentences in every case where they might conceivably apply.[44]

Finally, in December 2022, Garland issued two policy directives that discourage prosecutors from charging offenses carrying mandatory minimums. One memo reverses the described directive, replacing it with one that directs prosecutors to charge offenses linked to mandatory minimums only where "the remaining charges . . . would not sufficiently reflect the seriousness" of the offense.[45] The other memo revivifies and improves on a 2013 Eric Holder policy that directed prosecutors to decline to seek mandatory minimums for low-level, nonviolent drug offenses.[46] This second directive explicitly acknowledges that mandatory minimum sentences in drug cases have "resulted in disproportionately severe sentences for certain defendants and perceived and actual racial disparities in the criminal justice system."[47]

Although the new directives are encouraging, they are long delayed, coming after two years in which people continued to be charged according to the old mandatory minimum policies. The decision to reinstate the 2013 policy is significant, given that research suggests that "federal prosecutors were responsive to *internal* DOJ policies like the Holder 2013 memo that encourage less aggressive use of these punitive 'legal hammers.'"[48] In fact, the 2013 memo "was associated with a 32 percent decrease in the odds of receiving a binding minimum relative to the pre-Holder 2010 period."[49] However, empirical evidence nevertheless suggests that such changes in prosecutors' mandatory minimums policies only marginally mitigate the problem, underscoring the need for broader reform. Although prosecutors charged fewer mandatory minimums for eligible individuals in the wake of the 2013 memo, the end result was only a mild decrease in sentence length for most people.[50] Empirical evidence also suggests that Holder's 2013 memo failed to mitigate racial disparities in sentencing, even though mandatory minimums are one critical cause of such inequalities.[51]

Moreover, the Biden administration undermined its commitment to ending the use of mandatory minimums by extending "overly punitive mandatory minimum sentencing laws [for] the broad class of fentanyl-related compounds."[52] This policy disproportionately harms Black people and is "a haunting echo of the crack/cocaine disparity," with "fentanyl analogues . . . punished more harshly than fentanyl itself, without the science to back it."[53]

The House passed the HALT Fentanyl Act in 2023 with the Biden administration's endorsement, a big step toward making this punitive and retrograde mandatory minimums policy permanent.[54]

In sum, this administration's progressive mandatory minimums policies are undermined by its approach to fentanyl analogs. Also, DOJ policy directives are inherently transitory. Garland's reform efforts can easily be rolled back by future administrations.

CONGRESS NEEDS TO ABOLISH MANDATORY MINIMUMS

Given that reform efforts by DOJ would provide, at best, a temporary fix, congressional action is needed to shift the paradigm and mitigate racial inequity. Congress needs to repeal federal mandatory minimums, make the change retroactive for those already serving mandatory minimum sentences, and incentivize states to follow suit.[55]

The most comprehensive solution introduced in recent years was the Mandatory Minimum Reform Act of 2017 and 2020, which would have repealed all mandatory minimums for federal drug crimes.[56] The bipartisan Smarter Sentencing Act of 2023 would enact a narrower reform, reducing mandatory minimums for certain nonviolent drug offenses and making other reforms retroactive.[57] In 2021, the House passed Senator Cory Booker's EQUAL Act by a bipartisan vote—more than half of the bill's twenty-one cosponsors were Republicans—with the Biden administration's endorsement.[58] That legislation was reintroduced in 2023 but would not end mandatory minimums.[59]

Even if Congress fails to pass meaningful legislation abolishing or limiting mandatory minimums, second look and second chance legislation could provide a safety valve for some serving mandatory minimums.[60] Such legislation "would allow courts to reevaluate a person's sentence after a significant period of time served in prison and determine if that sentence is still necessary."[61] In 2020, for example, the District of Columbia enacted second look legislation that allows people convicted under the age of twenty-five to petition for resentencing after serving fifteen years of a sentence.[62] In the federal system, the Second Look Act of 2019 and 2022 would have allowed prisoners to petition a federal court for a sentence reduction if they had been sentenced to more than ten years and had served at least ten years in custody.[63] Similarly, the Model Penal Code was updated in 2019 to include a second look provision that would authorize a "judicial decisionmaker to hear and rule upon applications for modification of sentence from prisoners who have served 15 years of any sentence."[64] The National Association of Criminal Defense Lawyers lauded both the Second Look Act of 2019 and the Model Penal Code revision as "a critical backstop that enhances other efforts to turn around mass incarceration."[65]

Finally, Senator Durbin's Smarter Pretrial Detention for Drug Charges Act of 2023 would eliminate a pretrial jailing provision that bolsters lengthy postconviction incarceration, including mandatory minimums.[66] Currently, every person facing a federal drug charge carrying a mandatory minimum penalty is also saddled with a harsh "presumption of detention" at the outset of the case that makes it very difficult to secure pretrial release at the outset of the case.[67] That presumption falls heavily on people of color and results in the unnecessary pretrial jailing of people who pose little risk to society.[68] Senator Durbin's bill would eliminate the presumption of detention in all drug cases, making it easier for those facing federal mandatory minimum drug charges to secure pretrial release.[69] This, in turn, would enable more people to avoid the application of harsh mandatory penalties at sentencing.[70]

Any of the preceding legislative reforms would be a step toward establishing a new paradigm that abjures mandatory minimums and respects human dignity.[71] Abolishing mandatory minimums altogether, though, is the best way to return sentencing power to judges, mitigate racism, and advance community safety. Attempts to stitch up the tattered old paradigm are futile and will not eradicate the spreading stain of racial inequity. We should instead heed Justice Sonia Sotomayor's message that, until we value the lives, rights, and liberties of those on the receiving end of the system, "our justice system will continue to be anything but."[72]

NOTES

1. Alec Karakatsanis, "Policing, Mass Imprisonment, and the Failure of American Lawyers," *Harvard Law Review Forum* 128 (2015): 255, 262, https://harvardlawreview.org/wp-content/uploads/2015/04/vol128-Karakatsanis.pdf.
2. John Naughton, "Thomas Kuhn: The Man Who Changed the Way the World Looked at Science," *The Guardian*, August 28, 2012, https://www.theguardian.com/science/2012/aug/19/thomas-kuhn-structure-scientific-revolutions.
3. Rachel E. Barkow, "Categorical Mistakes: The Flawed Framework of the Armed Career Criminal Act and Mandatory Minimum Sentencing," *Harvard Law Review* 133 (2019): 214n123; Charles Colson Task Force on Federal Corrections, *Transforming Prisons, Restoring Lives* (Washington, DC: Urban

Institute, 2016), 9, 23, https://www.urban.org/sites/default/files/publication/77101/2000589-Transforming-Prisons-Restoring-Lives.pdf.

4. Claire Kebodeaux, "Rape Sentencing: We're All Mad About Brock Turner, But Now What?," *Kansas Journal of Law and Public Policy* 27 (2017): 36, https://lawjournal.ku.edu/wp-content/uploads/2020/08/Kebodeaux-V27I1.pdf .
5. Isabel Wilkerson, *Caste: The Origins of Our Discontents* (New York: Random House, 2020), 142.
6. Wilkerson, *Caste.*
7. Stephanos Bibas, "Plea Bargaining Outside the Shadow of Trial," *Harvard Law Review* 117 no. 8 (2004): 2487, https://scholarship.law.upenn.edu/cgi/viewcontent.cgi?article=1923&context=faculty_scholarship.
8. Jelani Jefferson Exum, "Addressing Racial Inequities in the Criminal Justice System Through a Reconstruction Sentencing Approach," *Ohio Northern University Law Review* 47 no. 3 (2021): 583, https://digitalcommons.onu.edu/cgi/viewcontent.cgi?article=1304&context=onu_law_review.
9. See Alec Karakatsanis, *Usual Cruelty: The Complicity of Lawyers in the Criminal Injustice System* (New York: The New Press, 2019), 31–32:

   > [A]n entire strand of constitutional law—due process jurisprudence requiring the government to demonstrate a good reason to deprive a person of her bodily liberty—is ignored to enforce drug laws. . . . [T]he principle of the 'rule of law' cannot be applied at the same time to the law requiring a mandatory ten-year prison sentence for a crack cocaine offense and to the law that the government must prove that depriving a person of a fundamental liberty interest such as physical freedom is necessary to serve an identifiable public good.

10. Mona Lynch, *Hard Bargains: The Coercive Power of Drug Laws in Federal Court* (New York: Russell Sage Foundation, 2016), 15, cited in Erica Zunkel and Alison Siegler, "The Federal Judiciary's Role in Drug Law Reform in an Era of Congressional Dysfunction," *Ohio State Journal of Criminal Law* 18 (2020): 295, https://chicagounbound.uchicago.edu/cgi/viewcontent.cgi?article=13989&context=journal_articles. The first mandatory minimum, passed in 1914, concerned opium manufacture and was influenced by anti-Chinese prejudices.
11. However, even the law which repealed these minimums, the Comprehensive Drug Abuse Prevention and Control Act of 1970, contained additional mandatory minimum penalties for some drug offenses. Stephanie Holmes Didwania, "Mandatory Minimum Entrenchment and the Controlled Substances Act," *Ohio State Journal of Criminal Law* 18, no. 1 (2020): 28–29, https://kb.osu.edu/handle/1811/92262; Michael Tonry, "Mandatory Penalties," *Crime & Justice* 16 (1992): 251.
12. Zunkel and Siegler, "Federal Judiciary's Role," 297.

13. Danielle Snyder, "One Size Does Not Fit All: A Look at the Disproportionate Effects of Federal Mandatory Minimum Drug Sentences on Racial Minorities and How They Have Contributed to the Degradation of the Underprivileged African-American Family," *Hamline Journal of Public Law & Policy* 36, no. 1 (2017): 89–95, https://digitalcommons.hamline.edu/cgi/viewcontent.cgi?article=1012&context=jplp.
14. Tonry, "Mandatory Penalties," 244.
15. Shira A. Scheindlin, "I Sentenced Criminals to Hundreds More Years Than I Wanted to. I Had No Choice," *Washington Post*, February 17, 2017, https://www.washingtonpost.com/posteverything/wp/2017/02/17/i-sentenced-criminals-to-hundreds-more-years-than-i-wanted-to-i-had-no-choice; see also Alison Siegler, "Shift the Paradigm on Mandatory Minimums," American Bar Association, October 18, 2021, https://www.americanbar.org/groups/criminal_justice/publications/criminal-justice-magazine/2022/winter/shift-paradigm-mandatory-minimums.
16. Chief Judge Colleen McMahon, "(Re)views from the Bench: A Judicial Perspective on Second-Look Sentencing in the Federal System," *American Criminal Law Review* 58, no. 4 (2021): 1617, 1622, https://www.law.georgetown.edu/american-criminal-law-review/wp-content/uploads/sites/15/2021/07/58-4_McMahon-ReViews-from-the-Bench.pdf.
17. The sample included forty-one state judges. Esther Nir & Siyu Liu, "The Challenge of Imposing Just Sentences Under Mandatory Minimum Statutes: A Qualitative Study of Judicial Perceptions," *Criminal Justice Policy Review* 33 (2022): 197, https://scholarsphere.psu.edu/resources/b54d8ba6-d618-4a6f-82a9-7a89f732076c.
18. Jed. S. Rakoff, "Mass Incarceration: The Silence of the Judges," *New York Review*, May 21, 2015, https://www.nybooks.com/articles/2015/05/21/mass-incarceration-silence-judges.
19. *Hearing Before the U.S. Sentencing Commission* (May 27, 2010) (statement of Stephen J. Schulhofer, Robert B. McKay, professor at the New York University School of Law), https://www.ussc.gov/sites/default/files/pdf/amendment-process/public-hearings-and-meetings/20100527/Testimony_Schulhofer.pdf.
20. *Hearing* (Schulhofter statement), 14–15.
21. "Who wouldn't tell the prosecutors whatever they want to hear if it means getting back to your family before you die?" Alison Siegler, Judith P. Miller, and Erica K. Zunkel, "Reforming the Federal Criminal System: Lessons from Litigation," *Journal of Gender, Race & Justice* 25 (2022): 123–24 and n.112.
22. Alison Siegler, *Freedom Denied: How the Culture of Detention Created a Federal Jailing Crisis* (Chicago: University of Chicago, 2022), 67 (quoting federal magistrate judge), https://freedomdenied.law.uchicago.edu/report. Such

coercion can have devastating consequences. Studies show that pretrial detention, independent of other factors, can itself increase the likelihood of a higher sentence and decrease the likelihood of avoiding the application of a mandatory minimum. Stephanie Holmes Didwania, "The Immediate Consequences of Federal Pretrial Detention," *American Law and Economics Review* 22, no. 1 (2020): 24–74, 26.

23. See M. Marit Rehavi and Sonja B. Starr, "Racial Disparity in Federal Criminal Sentences," *Journal of Political Economy* 122 (2014): 1324, 1349, 1350, https://repository.law.umich.edu/cgi/viewcontent.cgi?article=2413&context=articles.
24. Rehavi and Start, "Racial Disparity," 1350 (emphasis added).
25. Cody Tuttle, "Racial Disparities in Federal Sentencing: Evidence from Drug Mandatory Minimums" (job market paper, University of Maryland, October 19, 2019), 5, https://economics.yale.edu/sites/default/files/tuttle_mandatory_minimums.pdf.
26. "Mandatory minimums also have a disparate impact on indigent individuals." Siegler, "Shift the Paradigm."
27. Michael Stamm, "Between a Rock and Discriminatory Place: How Sentencing Guidelines and Mandatory Minimums Should Be Employed to Reduce Poverty Discrimination in the Criminal Justice System," *Georgetown Journal on Poverty Law & Policy* 24, no. 3 (2017): 399, 410, 400. Cited in Siegler, "Shift the Paradigm."
28. Shon Hopwood, "Improving Federal Sentencing," *UMKC Law Review* 87, no. 1 (2018): 80, 91 ("When a defendant spends long sentences in deplorable and oppressive prison conditions away from their community, with few meaningful opportunities for rehabilitation, and surrounded by others who have committed crimes, it increases the chance the defendant will engage in future crimes"). See also Office of the President of the United States, *Economic Perspectives on Incarceration and the Criminal Justice System* (2016), 39 ("a growing body of work has found that incarceration increases recidivism"), https://obamawhitehouse.archives.gov/sites/default/files/page/files/20160423_cea_incarceration_criminal_justice.pdf. Evidence also demonstrates that prison sentences do not reduce recidivism. See, for example, Francis T. Cullen et al., "Prisons Do Not Reduce Recidivism: The High Cost of Ignoring Science," *Prison Journal* 91, no. 3 (2011): 48S, 50S, https://doi.org/10.1177/0032885511415224. See also Damon M. Petrich, Travis C. Pratt, Cheryl Lero Jonson, and Frances T. Cullen, "Custodial Sanctions and Reoffending: A Meta-Analytic Review," *Crime and Justice* 50 (2021): 353, 401 ("Consensus that custodial sanctions, overall, do not reduce reoffending is universal").
29. See Mirko Bagaric, Gabrielle Wolf, and Daniel McCord, "Nothing Seemingly Works in Sentencing: Not Mandatory Penalties; Not Discretionary

Penalties—But Science Has the Answer," *Indiana Law Review* 53, no. 3 (2020): 499–544, 513, https://mckinneylaw.iu.edu/ilr/pdf/vol53p499.pdf.

30. See Lauren Jones, Sandra van den Heuvel, and Amanda Lawson, *The Cost of Incarceration in New York State: How Counties Outside New York City Can Reduce Jail Spending and Invest in Communities* (New York: Vera Institute of Justice, 2021), 1–3, https://www.vera.org/publications/the-cost-of-incarceration-in-new-york-state.
31. Nancy Gertner and Chiraag Bains, "Mandatory Minimum Sentences Are Cruel and Ineffective. Sessions Wants Them Back," *Washington Post*, May 15, 2017, https://www.washingtonpost.com/posteverything/wp/2017/05/15/mandatory-minimum-sentences-are-cruel-and-ineffective-sessions-wants-them-back; Greg Newburn and Sal Nuzzo, "Mandatory Minimums, Crime, and Drug Abuse; Lessons Learned, Paths Ahead" (James Madison Institute, 2019), 9, https://jamesmadison.org/wp-content/uploads/2019/02/PolicyBrief_MandatoryMinimums_Feb2019_v04.pdf.
32. See Siegler, *Freedom Denied*, 63–66; Charles Colson Task Force, *Transforming Prisons, Restoring Lives*, 17, 31 (finding that BOP facility understaffing and overcrowding has led to increased violence); David Reutter, "BOP Settles Medical Negligence Claim for $600,000," *Prison Legal News*, June 3, 2015, https://www.prisonlegalnews.org/news/2015/jun/3/bop-settles-medical-negligence-claim-600000 (describing a "lawsuit alleging officials at USP Coleman Low caused a prisoner to suffer permanent injuries due to their negligent provision of medical care"); C. J. Ciaramella, "Judge Holds Federal Bureau of Prisons in Contempt for Allowing Man to Waste Away from Untreated Cancer," *Reason*, October 10, 2022, https://reason.com/2022/10/10/judge-holds-federal-bureau-of-prisons-in-contempt-for-allowing-man-to-waste-away-from-untreated-cancer ("Medical neglect in U.S. prisons and jails is an ongoing constitutional disaster.").
33. Siegler, *Freedom Denied*, 63–64; see also Laura M. Maruschak, Marcus Berzofsky, and Jennifer Unangst, *Medical Problems of State and Federal Prisoners and Jail Inmates, 2011–12* (Washington, DC: Bureau of Justice Statistics, 2016), 11 https://bjs.ojp.gov/content/pub/pdf/mpsfpji1112.pdf.
34. Siegler, *Freedom Denied*, 64–65 ("For every 1,000 individuals held in jails and prisons, nearly 13 alleged an act of sexual victimization. The actual number of assaults is likely much higher, as *staff* members perpetrated 56% of these reported assaults"). See also Emily Buehler, *Sexual Victimization Reported by Adult Correctional Authorities, 2016–2018* (Washington, DC: Bureau of Justice Statistics, 2021), 1, https://bjs.ojp.gov/content/pub/pdf/svraca1618.pdf. The most recent year for which such statistics are available is 2018.
35. Siegler, *Freedom Denied*, 63 ("Rampant overcrowding in federal jails exacerbates medical neglect while introducing incarcerated people to a litany of other risks"), 66 (describing how understaffing during the pandemic led to medical

neglect for detainees in the Miami Federal Detention Center with detainees who were "diabetics, hypertensives, [and suffered from] cardiomyopathy and HIV . . . not being provided their medication. It was reported that over 750 prescriptions [went] unfilled"). Joshua Ceballos and Alex Deluca, "Employees at Understaffed Miami Prison Say Inmates, Guards, and Public Are at Risk," *Miami New Times*, May 24, 2022, https://www.miaminewtimes.com/news/fdc-miami-staffing-shortage-spurs-complaints-from-inmates-and-prison-guards-14521728. See also Michael Balsamo and Michael R. Sisak, "The Jail Where Jeffrey Epstein Killed Himself Is Crumbling," AP News, September 23, 2021 (documenting how the crumbling prison infrastructure created health and safety risks for incarcerated individuals), https://apnews.com/article/health-prisons-new-york-manhattan-coronavirus-pandemic-5113a1e33a0c3967787e04c0523e406b.

36. See Jamiles Lartey, "How Criminal Records Hold Back Millions of People" (Washington, DC: The Marshall Project, April 1, 2023), https://www.themarshallproject.org/2023/04/01/criminal-record-job-housing-barriers-discrimination; Margaret Colgate Love, *The Many Roads from Reentry to Reintegration: A National Survey of laws Restoring Rights and Opportunities after Arrest or Conviction* (Washington, DC: Collateral Consequences Resources Center, 2022), 96, https://ccresourcecenter.org/wp-content/uploads/2022/08/MRFRTR_8.24.22.pdf.
37. Charles Colson Task Force, *Transforming Prisons, Restoring Lives*, 15.
38. Shon Hopwood, "Second Looks and Second Chances," *Cardozo Law Review* 41 no. 1 (2019): 101, 111, https://cardozolawreview.com/second-looks-second-chances.
39. Hopwood, "Second Looks."
40. Rakoff, "Mass Incarceration," 2015.
41. "The Biden Plan for Strengthening America's Commitment to Justice," Biden-Harris 2020 campaign website (archived November 15, 2021), https://perma.cc/9QDU-MMA7; U.S. Department of Justice (DOJ), "Attorney General Eric Holder Delivers Remarks at the Annual Meeting of the American Bar Association's House of Delegates," Press release, August 12, 2013, https://www.justice.gov/opa/speech/attorney-general-eric-holder-delivers-remarks-annual-meeting-american-bar-associations.
42. The White House, "Fact Sheet: President Biden's Safer America Plan," Press release, August 1, 2022, https://www.whitehouse.gov/briefing-room/statements-releases/2022/08/01/fact-sheet-president-bidens-safer-america-plan-2.
43. U.S. Senate Judiciary Committee, "The Nomination of the Honorable Merrick Brian Garland to be Attorney General of the United States: Day 1," February 22, 2021, https://www.judiciary.senate.gov/committee-activity/hearings/the-nomination-of-the-honorable-merrick-brian-garland-to-be-attorney-general-of-the-united-states-day-1.

44. For Garland's directive, see Office of the Attorney General, "Interim Guidance on Prosecutorial Discretion, Charging, and Sentencing," DOJ, January 29, 2021, https://www.justice.gov/ag/page/file/1362411/download. For the previous guidance, see "Department Policy on Charging and Sentencing," May 19, 2010, https://www.justice.gov/sites/default/files/oip/legacy/2014/07/23/holder-memo-charging-sentencing.pdf; *Justice Manual* § 9-27.300: Selecting Charges—Charging the Most Serious Offenses, https://www.justice.gov/jm/jm-9-27000-principles-federal-prosecution#9-27.300.
45. Office of the Attorney General, "General Department Policies Regarding Charging, Pleas, and Sentencing," U.S. Department of Justice, December 16, 2022, 3, https://www.justice.gov/media/1265326/dl?inline.
46. Office of the Attorney General, "Additional Department Policies Regarding Charging, Pleas, and Sentencing in Drug Cases" (Garland memorandum revivifying 2013 Holder memorandum), DOJ, December 16, 2022, 1, https://www.justice.gov/media/1265321/dl?inline; see also Office of the Attorney General, "Department Policy on Charging Mandatory Minimum Sentences and Recidivist Enhancements in Certain Drug Cases" (2013 Holder memorandum), DOJ, August 12, 2013, https://www.justice.gov/sites/default/files/oip/legacy/2014/07/23/ag-memo-department-policypon-charging-mandatory-minimum-sentences-recidivist-enhancements-in-certain-drugcases.pdf.
47. Office of the Attorney General, "Additional Department Policies," 1.
48. Mona Lynch, Matt Barno, and Marisa Omori, "Prosecutors, Court Communities, and Policy Change: The Impact of Internal DOJ Reforms on Federal Prosecutorial Practices," *Criminology* 59, no. 3 (2021): 480–519, 514 (emphasis in original), https://escholarship.org/uc/item/63s7374d.
49. Lynch, Barno, and Omori, "Prosecutors, Court Communities," 498.
50. Stephanie Holmes Didwania, "Charging Leniency and Federal Sentences," *Univ. of Wisconsin Legal Studies Research* no. 1746 (2020), 43, https://papers.ssrn.com/sol3/papers.cfm?abstract_id=3556138; see also Lynch, Barno, and Omori, "Prosecutors, Court Communities," 506 ("The results . . . after controlling for changes in caseload characteristics demonstrate that the Holder 2013 memo was associated with a slight decrease in final sentence lengths"); Karakatsanis, *Usual Cruelty*, 2019, 76 (noting that Holder "[fought] against retroactive application of [the Fair Sentencing Act] . . . that would reduce the disparity between the punishment of crack and powder cocaine. And he quietly intervened to prevent the release of tens of thousands of black federal prisoners detained illegally for drug offenses").
51. Didwania, "Charging Leniency," 43. But see Lynch, Barno, and Omor, "Prosecutors, Court Communities," 513 (finding that the Sessions memo that rescinded Holder's 2013 memo appears to have caused "more aggressive use of

federal drug prosecutions in places where non-Whites are especially likely to be prosecuted for drug crimes" with prosecutors targeting "less serious defendants in these jurisdictions").

52. Leadership Conference on Civil and Human Rights, letter to Attorney General Merrick Garland, December 14, 2021, 7, http://civilrightsdocs.info/pdf/policy/letters/2021/12132021_Leadership_Conference_Letter_to_DOJ_Regarding_Criminal_Legal_Reform_and_Racial_Equity.pdf; see also White House, "Biden-Harris Administration Provides Recommendations to Congress on Reducing Illicit Fentanyl-Related Substances," press release, September 2, 2021, https://www.whitehouse.gov/ondcp/briefing-room/2021/09/02/biden-harris-administration-provides-recommendations-to-congress-on-reducing-illicit-fentanyl-related-substances.
53. Beth Schwartzapfel, "Biden Could Have Taken the War on Drugs Down a Notch. He Didn't" (Washington, DC: The Marshall Project, June 16, 2021), https://www.themarshallproject.org/2021/06/16/biden-could-have-taken-the-war-on-drugs-down-a-notch-he-didn-t.
54. The Biden administration is facing pushback for backing the Halt All Lethal Trafficking of (HALT) Fentanyl Act (H.R. 467) and failing to condemn that bill's expansion of mandatory minimums. See Jacob Sullum, "Panicked by Fentanyl Analogs, Biden Embraces the Mandatory Minimums He Claims to Oppose," *Reason*, May 25, 2023, https://reason.com/2023/05/25/panicked-by-fentanyl-analogs-biden-embraces-the-mandatory-minimums-he-claims-to-oppose; see also Criminal Justice Organizations, letter to President Joe Biden, May 23, 2023, https://drugpolicy.org/sites/default/files/cj_letter_re_sap_on_halt_act_5.23.23_0.pdf.
55. See, for example, *Controlled Substances: Federal Policies and Enforcement: Hearing Before the H. Subcomm. on Crime, Terrorism, and Homeland Security* (Statement of Alison Siegler, Erica Zunkel, and Judith P. Miller), 116th Cong., 1st sess. (March 11, 2021), https://www.govinfo.gov/content/pkg/CHRG-116hhrg44670/pdf/CHRG-116hhrg44670.pdf.
56. Mandatory Minimum Reform Act of 2017, H.R. 3800, 115th Cong. (2017); Mandatory Minimum Reform Act of 2020, H.R. 7194, 116th Cong. (2020).
57. Smarter Sentencing Act, S. 1152, 118th Cong. (2023).
58. EQUAL Act, S. 79, 117th Cong. (2021); Sean Sullivan and Seung Min Kim, "Biden Administration Endorses Bill to End Disparity in Drug Sentencing Between Crack and Powder Cocaine," *Washington Post*, June 22, 2021, https://www.washingtonpost.com/politics/biden-drugs-sentencing-cocaine/2021/06/21/cd0c5e26-d2dc-11eb-ae54-515e2f63d37d_story.html.
59. EQUAL Act, S. 524.
60. See generally Hopwood, "Second Looks and Second Chances."

61. FAMM "Second Look Sentencing," accessed September 7, 2022, https://famm.org/secondlook.
62. Omnibus Public Safety and Justice Amendment Act of 2020, D.C. Law 23-274, 68 DCR 1034 (2020).
63. Second Look Act, S. 2146, 116th Cong. (2019); Second Look Act, S. 5193, 117th Cong. (2022), https://www.congress.gov/bill/116th-congress/senate-bill/2146/text?r=6&s=1.
64. Model Penal Code § 305.6 (2019).
65. JaneAnne Murray, Sean Hecker, Michael Skocpol, and Marissa Elkins, "Second Look = Second Chance: Turning the Tide Through NACDL's Model Second Look Legislation," *Federal Sentencing Reporter* 33 (2021): 342, https://scholarship.law.umn.edu/cgi/viewcontent.cgi?article=1751&context=faculty_articles.
66. See Smarter Pretrial Detention for Drug Charges Act, S. 1056, 118th Cong. (2023).
67. 18 U.S.C. § 3142(e)(2)–(3). Release or detention of a defendant pending trial.
68. Siegler, *Freedom Denied*, 152, 165–66; Amaryllis Austin, "The Presumption for Detention Statute's Relationship to Release Rates," *Federal Probation* 81 (2017): 52–63, 55, https://www.uscourts.gov/sites/default/files/81_2_7_0.pdf.
69. See Smarter Pretrial Detention for Drug Charges Act, S. 1056, 118th Cong. (2023); see also Siegler, *Freedom Denied*, 158 ("Our courtwatching data show that arrestees were detained at much higher rates in presumption-of-detention cases than non-presumption cases").
70. See Didwania, "Immediate Consequences," 26.
71. Ram Subramanian, "How Some European Prisons Are Based on Dignity Instead of Dehumanization" (New York: Brennan Center for Justice, November 29, 2021), https://www.brennancenter.org/our-work/analysis-opinion/how-some-european-prisons-are-based-dignity-instead-dehumanization ("Putting the brakes on American punitive excess can and should be accomplished by centering human dignity as a foundational, organizing principle of the nation's corrections system").
72. Utah v. Strieff, 136 S. Ct. 2056, 2071 (2016) (Sotomayor, J., dissenting).

10

THE AMERICAN "PUNISHER'S BRAIN"

Andrew Cohen

AMERICA'S PENCHANT FOR PUNITIVE SENTENCING goes back beyond the Constitution or the Pilgrims or even British common law, further than the Magna Carta or the Code of Hammurabi or the Talmud, back to the dawn of human history, when small groups of people adopted concepts of culpability and punishment as a matter of basic survival.[1] Our ancient ancestors shamed and weeded out the rule-breakers among them, sometimes with leniency, usually in harsh ways, to protect the integrity and the unity of their tribe.[2]

All humans may be hardwired to be cruel in a fashion. But as Robert Ferguson argued in his 2014 masterwork, *Inferno*, the United States has allowed these instincts to dominate criminal justice policy. "Prisoners in this country have been put away, silenced, beaten, sadistically tormented, and most of all forgotten—frequently enough for their entire lives," Ferguson wrote. "They have been relegated to conditions and circumstances and physical degradation that shame us as well as them and that no one wants to recognize even though the failure in recognition defines a part of us. No human being deserves that much punishment."[3]

As Asia Johnson (chapter 13), Shon Hopwood (chapter 16), and Michele Deitch (chapter 22) point out in their essays, this is the current state of affairs in most jails and prisons in the United States.

As other essays in this book detail, over the past half century we have experienced an unprecedented era of mass incarceration. On any given day, almost two million people are locked up in the nation's five thousand or so prisons and jails, many serving sentences grossly disproportionate to the nature of their crimes.[4] That doesn't include another thirty thousand or so effectively imprisoned in federal immigration detention centers.[5]

A 2016 report by the Brennan Center for Justice concluded that nearly 40 percent of the prison population at the time—nearly six hundred thousand people, more than the entire population of Atlanta or Albuquerque—were imprisoned without any legitimate public safety justification.[6] Advocates have recommended significant changes to sentencing laws that would ensure "default sentences that are proportional to the specific crime committed and in line with social science research."[7] Meaningful sentencing reform also would include alternatives to incarceration for low-level crimes and shorter sentences for crimes warranting incarceration. Some of these policy initiatives have found legislative and judicial support. Others have not.

Moreover, as The Sentencing Project recently revealed, more people are serving life sentences today across the nation—some 206,000 people in federal and state prisons—than there were people in prison altogether in the United States in 1970.[8] Since 1984, the number of people serving such sentences, at great taxpayer cost, has more than quadrupled, a rate of growth even more explosive than the overall rise in incarceration rates during that time.[9] In fact, 83 percent of the world's population of life-without-parole prisoners are living behind American bars and nearly one-third of them are over the age of fifty-five.[10]

But if retributive justice is in our DNA, if punishment comes down to us from prehistory, why is American justice so much harsher than it is in other Western democracies? The Netherlands, for example, imprisons its citizens at a per capita rate that is one-tenth the U.S. per capita rate for all sorts of criminal offenses.[11]

One obvious root of this exceptionalism is America's endless struggle over racial justice. We endured punitive sentencing in the racist Black Codes that sprung up in southern states after the Civil War to incarcerate or force newly freed slaves into a form of indentured servitude.[12] We saw it in convict leasing.[13] We saw the same in the formation of Jim Crow laws sanctioned by the Supreme Court and in the discriminatory housing and employment practices and policies the law allowed.

Modern punitive sentencing schemes began to take root half a century ago, when the Nixon administration began its so-called war on drugs, a futile battle the nation is still waging.[14] These punitive efforts metastasized in the late 1980s and early 1990s, when a nationwide crime wave generated a fierce, punitive corrections-based response that led to the creation and enforcement of three-strikes laws, expanded the scope of mandatory minimum sentences, and fueled truth-in-sentencing measures. All of these, together, vastly expanded the number of people sent to federal and state prisons.

The prevailing narrative at the time was tough on crime, Nkechi Taifa writes in her essay (see chapter 15). "It was a narrative that caused then-candidate Bill Clinton to leave his presidential campaign trail to oversee the execution of a mentally challenged man in Arkansas. It was the same narrative that brought about the crack–powder cocaine disparity, supported the transfer of youth to adult courts, and popularized the myth of the Black child as 'super predator.'" No surprise, really, given that at least one former Nixon official conceded decades ago that the administration created the war on drugs as a political ploy to criminalize Black society and its progressive defenders.[15]

Those policies are largely still with us, three decades later, despite recent reforms and a decades-long decline in violent crime.[16] So, in some jurisdictions, is capital punishment. At the same time, excessively punitive sex offender laws have exploded, requiring registration on lists, imposing residency restrictions, and even imprisoning people for "treatment" long after their prison terms have been completed.[17]

Roughly twenty such "civil commitment programs" are now in place in various states, and many of the people in them may be indefinitely detained.[18] We also see the American "punisher's brain," as Colorado Judge Morris Hoffman has put it, in the often inhumane ways in which the condemned are forced to serve out these sentences in dangerous, dirty prisons bereft of adequate health care.[19] We see it all even though compelling evidence justifying excessively punitive sentences seems scant.[20] In fact, a growing body of evidence has undermined long-perceived links between public safety and the length of prison sentences.[21]

The rise of habitual offender three-strikes laws is a good example of the excessively punitive dynamic in sentencing. These laws, a by-product of the 1990s' law and order push, generally require judges to mete out life-without-parole sentences to defendants who commit at least three offenses if the most recent of them is considered a serious felony. Judges and legislators in some states have used particularly broad definitions of these triggering offenses. In Washington, for example—the first state to enact a three-strikes law—second-degree robbery was for decades a three-strike-triggering offense even though it was statutorily defined as a crime without a weapon and without significant injury to the victim.[22] The state legislature revised the related sentencing law in 2021.[23]

These three-strikes laws, though still popular among those who believe that longer sentences deter crime, have resulted in absurd results in some cases. Let's talk just about food, for instance. A Navy veteran suffering from substance addiction was given a life sentence for robbing a Subway store of $107 and a $5 gift card.[24] A Texas resident served a life sentence for stealing a tuna-on-sourdough sandwich from a Whole Foods.[25] As Matt Taibbi wrote about California's three-strikes regime:

> Have you heard the one about the guy who got life for stealing a slice of pizza? Or the guy who went away forever for lifting a pair of baby shoes? Or the one who got 50 to life for helping himself to five children's videotapes from Kmart? How about the guy who got life for possessing 0.14 grams of meth? That last offender was a criminal mastermind by Three Strikes standards, as many others have been sentenced to life for holding even smaller amounts of drugs, including one poor sap who got the max for 0.09 grams of black-tar heroin.[26]

Truth-in-sentencing state laws, also spawned during the 1980s and early 1990s, are another good example of the ways in which American policymakers have imposed particularly harsh sentencing regimes. These laws were enacted to require prisoners to serve a higher proportion of their sentences than had been the practice, with much less time off for good behavior and much less deference given to the judgments of local parole boards. Once again, Washington was the first state to enact such a measure, in 1984, and, within two decades, forty-two states and the District of Columbia had some form of these laws on their books.[27]

Mandatory minimum sentences are similarly widespread. The last seventy-five years or so have seen the tide of federal mandatory minimums ebb and flow. From the 1950s to 1970s, it swelled. Then it receded. The Comprehensive Drug Abuse Prevention and Control Act of 1970, a progressive law from the Nixon era, abolished mandatory minimum sentences for almost all drug offenses.[28] Then the politics of crime and justice turned again toward harsher punishment, and more incarceration. From the mid-1980s until just a few years ago, Congress churned out one new mandatory minimum sentencing scheme after another, even after doubts were raised about their effectiveness.[29]

The harshness of these sentencing regimes is magnified when they are compared with those in other countries. For example, American laws have long granted trial judges the freedom to impose consecutive sentences on separate charges related to the same crime—in many instances effectively lengthening a defendant's sentence to life without parole, but without saying so. Some U.S. prisoners are sitting in their cells with two-hundred-year sentences. By contrast, only since 2011 have Canadian trial judges even been allowed to issue consecutive sentences, and only in murder cases, specifically to ensure longer sentences before parole eligibility.[30] In May 2022, the Canadian Supreme Court ruled that sentences of life without parole are unconstitutional.[31]

Disparities in sentencing are especially stark relative to practices in such European countries as Germany and the Netherlands. The laws and criminal justice policies of these nations don't just differ from their American counterparts in the details—they differ in philosophy. The U.S. punisher's brain is absent from European justice models, which emphasize rehabilitation and resocialization. Germany's Prison Act, for example, specifically states that the very purpose of incarceration is to help prisoners lead lives of "social responsibility free of crime upon release."[32]

Most defendants convicted of crimes in Germany and the Netherlands—even what we would consider crimes of violence in the United States—never spend any measurable time in prison. Most are diverted into other programs, or forced to pay fines, or given suspended sentences. As noted in Ram Subramanian's essay (see chapter 23), these practices, and the emphasis on rehabilitation for those prisoners who are kept behind bars, go hand in hand with low crime and recidivism rates in those countries.[33]

When it comes to punitive sentencing regimes, Canada sits somewhere in between the U.S. and European models. Only twenty-nine crimes in Canada's criminal code carry a mandatory minimum sentence, most having to do with firearm-related offenses in a nation that has no equivalent of a Second Amendment.[34] Canada did enact its own truth-in-sentencing law in 2009—federal legislators wanted to be more punitive—but five years later a unanimous Supreme Court held that people "can receive extra credit for time spent in custody before they are sentenced."[35]

American sentencing laws are still harsher than those of counterparts in many other democracies, and the United States is still by far the world's incarceration leader. Yet recent bipartisan justice reforms on both a federal and state level have begun to change the American punishment narrative. Citing evidence-based practices and relying on statistics undermining long-held justifications for many punitive sanctions, justice reformers across the country have convinced some policymakers that the costs of excessive sentences don't just fall on the incarcerated or their families but rather on everyone.

NOTES

1. Morris B. Hoffman, *The Punisher's Brain: The Evolution of Judge and Jury* (New York: Cambridge University Press, 2014).
2. Andrew Cohen, "How Evolution Explains the Conflicted Death-Penalty Debate," *The Atlantic*, May 6, 2014, https://www.theatlantic.com/politics/archive/2014/05/the-evolution-of-punishment-explains-our-dance-with-the-death-penalty/361674.
3. Robert A. Ferguson, *Inferno* (Cambridge, MA: Harvard University Press, 2018), 238.
4. Christopher Ingraham, "The U.S. Has More Jails Than Colleges. Here's a Map of Where Those Prisoners Live," *Washington Post*, January 6, 2015, https://www.washingtonpost.com/news/wonk/wp/2015/01/06/the-u-s-has-more-jails-than-colleges-heres-a-map-of-where-those-prisoners-live.
5. Immigration Detention Quick Facts, Transactional Records Access Clearinghouse, updated October 31, 2022, https://trac.syr.edu/immigration/quickfacts/detention.html.
6. James Austin and Lauren-Brooke Eisen with James Cullen and Jonathan Frank, *How Many Americans Are Unnecessarily Incarcerated?* (New York: Brennan Center for Justice, 2016), 7, https://www.brennancenter.org/our-work/research-reports/how-many-americans-are-unnecessarily-incarcerated; U.S. Census Bureau, "City and Town Population Totals, 2020–2021," https://www.census.gov/data/tables/time-series/demo/popest/2020s-total-cities-and-towns.html.
7. Austin and Eisen, *How Many Americans*, 6–7.
8. The Sentencing Project, *People Serving Life Exceeds Entire Prison Population of 1970* (Washington, DC: Campaign to End Life Imprisonment, February 2020), 1, https://www.sentencingproject.org/app/uploads/2022/08/People-Serving-Life-Exceeds-Entire-Prison-Population-of-1970.pdf.
9. Ashley Nellis, *Still Life: America's Increasing Use of Life and Long-Term Sentences* (Washington, DC: The Sentencing Project, 2017), 5, https://www.sentencingproject.org/app/uploads/2022/10/Still-Life.pdf.
10. Sentencing Project, *People Serving Life*; Ashley Nellis, *No End in Sight: America's Enduring Reliance on Life Imprisonment* (Washington, DC: The Sentencing Project, 2021), 4, https://www.sentencingproject.org/app/uploads/2022/08/No-End-in-Sight-Americas-Enduring-Reliance-on-Life-Imprisonment.pdf.

11. Danielle Batist, "How the Dutch Are Closing Their Prisons," *U.S. News & World Report*, May 13, 2019, https://www.usnews.com/news/best-countries/articles/2019-05-13/the-netherlands-is-closing-its-prisons.
12. Equal Justice Initiative, "Convict Leasing," November 1, 2013, https://eji.org/news/history-racial-injustice-convict-leasing.
13. Equal Justice Initiative, "Convict Leasing."
14. Dan Baum, "Legalize It All: How to Win the War on Drugs," *Harper's Magazine*, April 2016, https://harpers.org/archive/2016/04/legalize-it-all.
15. Baum, "Legalize It All."
16. Alexandra Thompson and Susannah N. Tapp, *Criminal Victimization, 2021*, NCJ 305101 (Washington, DC: U.S. Department of Justice, Bureau of Justice Statistics, 2022), 1, https://bjs.ojp.gov/content/pub/pdf/cv21.pdf.
17. Paul M. Renfro, "Sex Offender Registries Are Fueling Mass Incarceration—And They Aren't Helping Survivors," *Jacobin*, June 22, 2020, https://jacobin.com/2020/06/sex-offender-registries-mass-incarceration; Maurice Chammah, "What to Do with Violent Sex Offenders" (Washington, DC: The Marshall Project, September 24, 2017), https://www.themarshallproject.org/2017/09/24/what-to-do-with-violent-sex-offenders.
18. Chammah, "What to Do."
19. Morris B. Hoffman, "Op-Ed: Why the Rule of Law Requires the Bite of Punishment," *Los Angeles Times*, September 24, 2017, https://www.latimes.com/opinion/op-ed/la-oe-hoffman-sentencing-deterrence-20141002-story.html.
20. Marc Mauer, *Long-Term Sentences: Time to Reconsider the Scale of Punishment* (Washington, DC: The Sentencing Project, 2018), https://www.sentencingproject.org/reports/long-term-sentences-time-to-reconsider-the-scale-of-punishment.
21. David J. Harding, "Do Prisons Make Us Safer?," *Scientific American*, June 21, 2019, https://www.scientificamerican.com/article/do-prisons-make-us-safer.
22. For historical context, see Tom James, "Lifer Inmates Excluded from Washington '3 Strikes' Change," Associated Press/*Seattle Times*, updated May 22, 2019, https://www.seattletimes.com/seattle-news/its-just-wrong-3-strikes-sentencing-reform-leaves-out-62-washington-state-inmates.
23. Nina Shapiro, "Legislature Moves to Resentence up to 114 People Serving Life without Parole under Washington's Three-Strikes Law," *Seattle Times*, April 8, 2021, https://www.seattletimes.com/seattle-news/politics/up-to-114-people-serving-life-without-parole-to-get-resentenced-as-washington-legislature-eases-three-strikes-law; Washington State Legislature, "SB 5164-2021-22," https://app.leg.wa.gov/billsummary?BillNumber=5164&Initiative=false&Year=2021.
24. Nina Shapiro and Manuel Villa, "New Laws Lead Some Washington Prosecutors to Rethink Three-Strike Life Sentences," *Seattle Times*, January 3, 2021,

https://www.seattletimes.com/seattle-news/new-laws-lead-some-washington-prosecutors-to-rethink-three-strike-life-sentences.

25. Alex Hannaford, "No Exit," *Texas Observer*, October 3, 2016, https://www.texasobserver.org/three-strikes-law-no-exit.
26. Matt Taibbi, "Cruel and Unusual Punishment: The Shame of Three Strikes Laws," *Rolling Stone*, March 27, 2013, https://www.rollingstone.com/politics/politics-news/cruel-and-unusual-punishment-the-shame-of-three-strikes-laws-92042.
27. Joe Watson, "Harsh Sentencing Laws in Washington State to Blame for Growing Lifer Population, Says University Study," *Prison Legal News*, December 28, 2016, https://www.prisonlegalnews.org/news/2016/dec/28/harsh-sentencing-laws-washington-state-blame-growing-lifer-population-says-university-study; William J. Sabol, Katherine Rosich, Kamala Mallik Kane, David P. Kirk, and Glenn Dubin, *The Influences of Truth-in-Sentencing Reforms on Changes in States' Sentencing Practices and Prison Populations* (Washington, DC: Urban Institute, 2002), 7, https://www.urban.org/sites/default/files/publication/60401/410470-The-Influences-of-Truth-in-Sentencing-Reforms-on-Changes-in-States-Sentencing-Practices-and-Prison-Populations.PDF.
28. Comprehensive Drug Abuse Prevention and Control Act of 1970, Pub. L. 91-513, 84 Stat. 1236, https://www.govinfo.gov/content/pkg/STATUTE-84/pdf/STATUTE-84-Pg1236.pdf; *CQ Almanac*, "Comprehensive Drug Control Bill Cleared by Congress," 1970, https://library.cqpress.com/cqalmanac/document.php?id=cqal70-1293935.
29. Pew Charitable Trusts, "Federal Drug Sentencing Laws Bring High Cost, Low Return," 2015, 1–2, https://www.pewtrusts.org/-/media/assets/2015/08/federal_drug_sentencing_laws_bring_high_cost_low_return.pdf.
30. Protecting Canadians by Ending Sentence Discounts for Multiple Murders Act, S.C. 2011, c. 5, https://www.canlii.org/en/ca/laws/astat/sc-2011-c-5/latest/sc-2011-c-5.html.
31. Amanda Coletta, "Canadian Supreme Court Rules All Killers Must Have Chance at Parole," *Washington Post*, May 27, 2022, https://www.washingtonpost.com/world/2022/05/27/canada-supreme-court-life-without-parole-bissonnette.
32. Ram Subramanian and Alison Shames, *Sentencing and Prison Practices in Germany and the Netherlands: Implications for the United States* (New York: Vera Institute for Justice, 2013), 7, https://www.prisonstudies.org/sites/default/files/resources/downloads/european-american-prison-report.pdf.
33. Maurice Chammah, "Prison Without Punishment" (Washington, DC: The Marshall Project, September 25, 2015), https://www.themarshallproject.org/2015/09/25/prison-without-punishment; Subramanian and Shames, *Sentencing and Prison Practices*, 7.

34. Government of Canada, *Mandatory Sentences of Imprisonment in Common Law Jurisdictions: Some Representative Models*, updated August 17, 2022, https://www.justice.gc.ca/eng/rp-pr/csj-sjc/ccs-ajc/rr05_10/p2.html.
35. The Canadian Press, "Supreme Court Softens Tories' Tough-on-Crime Sentencing Law," CBC, April 11, 2014, https://www.cbc.ca/news/politics/supreme-court-softens-tories-tough-on-crime-sentencing-law-1.2606789.

11

PUNISHMENT OVER PREVENTION

U.S. Drug Policy

Morgan Godvin

THE UNITED STATES holds some dubious titles. It is both the world's leader in incarceration and the world's leader in fatal drug overdoses. As the specter of fentanyl looms over the land, people are clamoring for the government to do something. Despite fault lines in the drug war and a softening of the rhetoric toward a public health approach, that something is rarely the thing needed to reduce harm.

The war on drugs is increasingly recognized as a policy failure, as Nkechi Taifa writes in her essay (see chapter 15). If incarceration were the cure for substance use, the country would be in good shape. Instead, it has an overdose rate twenty times the global average.[1] Many of its policies are mocked internationally; the irony that the self-appointed international defender of human rights abroad flagrantly violates human rights at home is lost on no one but Americans.

American drug policy has touched every facet of my life. I've survived half a dozen overdoses, lost my mother and four friends to accidental overdoses, and lost years of my life to incarceration. Nowhere is the harm more visible than in my friendship with Justin Delong.

"What does heroin smell like?" Justin asked me wryly from the passenger seat of my car, teeing up a joke.

"I don't know, what?" Whatever it was, it wafted from the spoon jammed in the gap below my car stereo and filled the car with its pungent odor as Justin applied the lighter's flame.

"Vinegar and broken dreams!" He descended into a deep belly laugh. He'd been released from prison just a few months before, and here we were again, like so many years that came before, doing heroin in my car.

The joke was gallows humor—our dreams laid in tattered shreds behind us, never to be thought of again. Black tar heroin has a distinctive vinegar smell, and after five years of use, one that was emotionally correlated to despair and brokenness. Both of us resigned ourselves to lives and deaths in heroin addiction; fleeting moments of resolve would bring us into recovery only for the siren song to topple us again.

We'd met around the time we should have been graduating high school if we hadn't dropped out. We both boarded the OxyContin-to-Heroin express train in 2008 during Oxy's heyday; about twelve thousand people died from opioid overdoses that year.[2] The U.S. government forced a major reduction in Oxy supply by slashing prescriptions, but demand stayed flat. In the vacuum that followed, heroin stepped in. Never again could we know the precise milligram dosage of the drug we were using, nor that it wasn't cut with poison or infected with toxic bacteria.

Where graduation photos should be were only mug shots. From his eighteenth birthday until his death, he was persecuted and prosecuted for his addiction. There's the booking photo from when he "resisted arrest," battered and blue. The officers tightened his handcuffs so tightly they dug into his flesh. He contracted MRSA in an overcrowded holding cell, where he was left for days without medical care.[3] The state treated him as a criminal for his drug use, full stop.

I was able to evade arrest for a longer time than Justin could, being white, female, employed, and culturally middle class in underpoliced neighborhoods. Eventually, I was also arrested for felony drug possession.

Drug court was billed as a kinder, gentler alternative to incarceration. I complied with all of their requirements except the one to stop using heroin. In practice, it was simply a rhetorical rebranding of punishment.[4] Naively, my first time in jail I voluntarily requested it. I was hoping to get restabilized on my buprenorphine after a setback. Regrettably, I showed up to my drug court check-in with my medication, a letter from my doctor, and the prescription and asked to be taken into custody.[5] The nurse at the jail scoffed at the request to provide my prescribed medication. I was forced to kick my addiction cold turkey in a jail dormitory under fluorescent lights that never turned off, puking in a trash can in front of seventy-seven strangers. Seven days later, I was released back into the same situation; the only thing that changed was my bitterness.

Buprenorphine and methadone slash overdose mortality. They are the gold standard treatments for opioid use disorder. The primary government response to opioid use disorder, however, remains incarceration. Most jails refuse to provide these medications, even today.[6] In April 2022, under Attorney General Merrick Garland, the Department of Justice finally released a clarifying opinion, stating that it is a violation of the Americans with Disabilities Act to do to others what was done to me.[7] Although access is improving—mostly due to successful litigation—it remains woefully inadequate.[8]

At the time of my arrest, I was in college for my paramedic's license and working as a pizza delivery driver. The felony triggered a financial aid revocation and a mandatory license suspension. The Anti-Drug Abuse Act of 1988 facilitated the denial of various federal benefits for any drug offense, from public housing to the Pell Grant.[9] As of 2016, mandatory license suspensions affected more than 191,000 people per year.[10] For me, it meant unemployment for the first time in my addiction. Homelessness soon followed. Nevertheless, at each check-in with my probation officer, I was required to pay a supervision fee of $60 for the privilege of not being sent back to jail. Fines and fees have expanded in tandem with the drug war, disproportionately affecting the poorest and least able to pay.[11]

The first drug delivery resulting in death law, also known as *drug-induced homicide*, was passed in 1986. Basketball legend Len Bias died of a cocaine overdose in June that year, shocking the U.S. public. Partly in reaction to his high-profile death, the 1986 Anti-Drug Abuse Act sailed through Congress with bipartisan support, calling for life imprisonment for anyone selling drugs resulting in an overdose death.[12]

Twenty-seven years later, I was charged with the very law that President Ronald Reagan had signed. The mandatory minimum sentence for the crime I was charged with was twenty years. The maximum was life without parole.

A few months after that night in the car when we laughed over the smell of vinegar and broken dreams, Justin texted me looking for a gram of heroin. I wasn't a dealer by any means, but my mom's recent passing had left me with what felt like a fortune; it would be gone by the next month. In the meantime, I could buy more than a single day's worth of heroin at a time.

Justin's dealer had car trouble on the way to deliver him his gram. I learned that through the discovery while sitting in jail. I was little more than a backup, a middleman. Except that day, I had a gram to spare.

"Can you help me out? I need a G," read his text to me.

"Ya," was my curt response. I texted him my address—you don't think to cover your tracks when you don't see yourself as a dealer or criminal—and he showed up at my front door.

He'd once risked arrest to save my life after finding me crumpled on the bathroom floor, not breathing and blue. In the days before the Good

Samaritan laws protected us from arrest for calling 911 during an overdose, it was risky to seek help. He dragged my limp body out of the bathroom, gave rescue breaths, called 911, and slipped out the back door and into the night as the police arrived.

I would have done anything to save my Justin. I tried to cajole him into staying and hanging out, but his ride was waiting, he told me. "Let me grab your wallet at least"—he'd left it the last time we'd hung out.

"Next time," he said, and gave me one of his famous bear hugs good-bye.

The next night, Justin texted me again. He asked for two grams and a delivery, which I refused. He knew that I did not deliver and that I was too depressed to leave my house under any circumstance. It should have been a red flag. Justin was already dead and the police were pretending to be him from his phone. This is how they secured a warrant, I presume.

That night, I was sitting on my couch watching television when my front door was breached by SWAT. Black-clad soldiers pointed M4 rifles at me and screamed, "We have a warrant!" It was an infamous no-knock raid, of the type that would kill Breonna Taylor and countless others.

When the police searched my bedroom, they found Justin's wallet that he'd left behind. The only thing it contained was his Clackamas County Jail identification card, reality as metaphor, life as art.

"You are under arrest for the overdose death of Justin Delong," said the detective as he tightened handcuffs around my wrists, one of which was swollen from an abscess. "Drug delivery resulting in death is a federal crime with a twenty-year mandatory minimum sentence." I tried to process both pieces of information simultaneously: my best friend was dead, and I was being held liable as if I'd murdered him.

While he lived, the government treated Justin as a criminal. He had been arrested a dozen times, spent countless months in jail, and he had done one prison stint. He was still on postprison supervision the night he died. Had he been pulled over on the way home from my apartment, he would have received a felony drug possession charge and held fully liable to the maximum extent of the law. Instead, he arrived home safely and died alone in his bedroom with a needle still sticking out of his elbow.

My paperwork read "Morgan Godvin v. The United States Government," so absurd I had to laugh at it. I had been found in possession of seven-tenths of a gram of heroin and $90. The full weight of the federal government had been unleashed on me all the same. I was a criminal history category three for two prior possession of heroin felonies and for being on felony probation (for these prior felonies); my prospective prison term was increased 25 percent because I had a history of addiction.

My codefendants and I were sentenced to a total of sixty years in prison for Justin's death. My roommate, his dealer, and two men above him were all ensnared in the investigation, the latter of whom remain in prison after being subjected to a trial tax and sentenced to twenty years.[13] For my mere five-year sentence, I consider myself lucky.

Justin's family opposed the prosecution entirely, having watched us struggle with addiction together for years. Victims' voices are lauded when they align with the punitive interests of the prosecution and are utterly disregarded otherwise. His mother was subjected to court testimony of her son's autopsy results and traumatized anew, in the name of justice.

While he lived, the government was content to punish Justin for his drug use. Only on his death did he become a victim, and only insofar as his death could be used to incarcerate other human beings. The federal government spent nearly two million dollars on my and my codefendant's incarceration alone, not counting investigation and prosecution fees.[14] Where were those resources while Justin lived? What if Justin had been offered medications for opioid use disorder in jail or prison? What if I had?

Despite vague assertions that laws on drug delivery resulting in death are used for kingpins, data from the Action Lab at Northeastern University proves otherwise.[15] In more than half of all convictions, the victim and the defendant were friends, partners, or siblings.[16] Take the case of Aaron Wodzinski.[17] He entered treatment after the overdose death of a friend and was arrested, with a newborn baby at home, more than one year into successful recovery. He was sentenced to twenty years in prison. Justin Morgan is accused of providing $29 worth of fentanyl to his friend with whom he relapsed during quarantine early in the COVID-19 pandemic.[18] He is facing life in prison in Pennsylvania. In all of our cases, the same government that appears to lack resources to provide drug treatment, or medications for opioid use disorder in jail, or naloxone, has seemingly unlimited resources to prosecute and incarcerate people for overdose deaths.

What other wealthy democracies spend on people's welfare, the United States spends on punishment. In a policy approach seemingly designed to wait for harm to occur and then punish for it, its drug policy is no different. Harm reduction has been bolstered by decades of robust academic research. Decriminalization, medications for opioid use disorder, syringe exchange, and safe consumption all reduce mortality and morbidity.[19] Yet these interventions face opposition in the United States. Syringe exchanges have proven themselves universally effective since the 1980s; West Virginia, which boasts the highest overdose rate in the country, recently eliminated theirs.[20] Governor Gavin Newsom of California used his veto powers to overturn a bill passed by the legislature to permit that state's first safe-consumption site.[21] In contrast with Canada, Australia, and the United Kingdom, the United States has a much more punitive and less efficient system of methadone delivery.[22]

Justin and I had engaged in literally hundreds of drug transactions among ourselves. He had never overdosed, and law enforcement had never become involved in our private, consensual transactions. Despite the United States' abhorrent overdose rate, it remains true that most opioid use does not result in overdose. One study showed that even among opioid overdoses almost 94 percent of people survive if they receive naloxone.[23] There is no statistical way that anyone engaging in drug sales knows with any certainty that they will be caught for any crime, much less for the improbable occurrence of overdose and the even more improbable prosecution of drug-induced homicide.

Drug-induced homicide prosecutions do little more than exacerbate grief, funnel money into punishment over prevention, and make drug users more afraid to call 911 during a medical emergency; no Good Samaritan law protects against charges of drug delivery resulting in death. A rhetorical shift reframing the overdose crisis as a poisoning crisis is bolstering the expansion of drug-induced homicide laws, led by upper-middle-class white parents adept at taking advantage of the political winds.[24] Meanwhile, the parents of Black and Brown children will continue to see them carried out in handcuffs.

The specter of fentanyl looms large in the land. Despite being a medication used in hospitals across the country thousands of times per day, fentanyl is imbued with magical properties and framed as a bogeyman. Illicitly manufactured fentanyl differs from pharmaceutical fentanyl chiefly by the fact that its dosage is unknown, not because it is a fundamentally different substance. It does not require a fundamentally different response than other opioids. Calls have been made to execute fentanyl dealers or lock them up for life.[25] In pushback against the limited progress toward reform that has been achieved, Colorado recently voted to refelonize fentanyl possession.[26] With deaths reaching tragic heights, the nation has never had more of an impetus to adopt evidence-based interventions. Instead, it reaches for its old familiar friend, punishment.

Punitiveness is so baked into the American psyche that we reach for it reflexively. But punitiveness and prevention are mutually exclusive. If one prefers to punish, one must wait for the harm to occur. If one prefers to prevent, one prevents not only harm but also the need to punish for it.

My life bears the scars of our American drug policy. Every one of my friends who overdosed on heroin was incarcerated repeatedly, none so often as Justin. I implore the government to prevent further harm before it occurs instead of waiting for someone to punish. I cannot bear to bury any more friends.

NOTES

1. Regan Morris, "Fentanyl Overdose: US Teens Fastest Growing Group to Die," BBC News, October 16, 2022, https://www.bbc.com/news/world-us-canada-63206753.
2. National Institute on Drug Abuse, "Overdose Death Rates," figure 4, January 20, 2022, https://nida.nih.gov/research-topics/trends-statistics/overdose-death-rates.
3. The Centers for Disease Control and Prevention (CDC) defines MRSA, methicillin-resistant *Staphylococcus aureus*, as "a type of bacteria that is resistant to several antibiotics" and causes health problems, some severe, in health-care settings and beyond. "Methicillin-Resistant Staphylococcus Aureus (MRSA): General Information," June 26, 2019, https://www.cdc.gov/mrsa/community/index.html; Andrew Cohen, "Criminal Justice Reform Must Include Better Medical Treatment in Prisons and Jails" (New York: Brennan Center for Justice, May 24, 2015), https://www.brennancenter.org/our-work/analysis-opinion/criminal-justice-reform-must-include-better-medical-treatment-prisons-and.
4. United Nations Human Rights Special Procedures, "Drug Courts Pose Dangers of Punitive Approaches Encroaching on Medical and Health Care Matters, UN Experts Say," March 20, 2019, https://www.unodc.org/documents/commissions/CND/2019/Contributions/UN_Entities/InfoNote20March2019.pdf.
5. Morgan Godvin, "I Thought Jail Would Help Me Get Clean. I Was Dead Wrong" (Washington, DC: The Marshall Project, September 3, 2020), https://www.themarshallproject.org/2020/09/03/i-thought-jail-would-help-me-get-clean-i-was-dead-wrong.
6. Ashish P. Thakrar, G. Caleb Alexander, and Brendan Saloner, "Trends in Buprenorphine Use in US Jails and Prisons from 2016 to 2021," *JAMA Network,*

December 14, 2021, https://jamanetwork.com/journals/jamanetworkopen/fullarticle/2787100.

7. U.S. Department of Justice, Office of Public Affairs, "Justice Department Issues Guidance on Protections for People with Opioid Use Disorder Under the Americans with Disabilities Act," News release no. 22-328, April 5, 2022, https://www.justice.gov/opa/pr/justice-department-issues-guidance-protections-people-opioid-use-disorder-under-americans.
8. Pew Charitable Trusts, "Opioid Use Disorder Treatment in Jails and Prisons," April 2020, 2, https://www.pewtrusts.org/en/research-and-analysis/issue-briefs/2020/04/opioid-use-disorder-treatment-in-jails-and-prisons.
9. Bradley D. Custer, "Federal Financial Aid for College Students With Criminal Convictions" (Washington, DC: Center for American Progress, December 17, 2020), https://www.americanprogress.org/article/federal-financial-aid-college-students-criminal-convictions.
10. Joshua Aiken, *Reinstating Common Sense: How Driver's License Suspensions for Drug Offenses Unrelated to Driving Are Falling out of Favor* (Northampton, MA: Prison Policy Initiative, 2016), https://www.prisonpolicy.org/driving/national.html.
11. Fines & Fees Justice Center and Reform Alliance, "National Examination of Probation & Parole Fees Finds Widespread Imposition in Nearly All 50 States," Press release, May 10, 2022, https://finesandfeesjusticecenter.org/2022/05/10/press-release-national-examination-of-probation-parole-fees-finds-widespread-imposition-in-nearly-all-50-states.
12. Jonathan Gabler, "How Len Bias's Death Helped Launch the US's Unjust War on Drugs," *The Guardian*, June 29, 2021, https://www.theguardian.com/sport/2021/jun/29/len-bias-death-basketball-war-on-drugs.
13. Brian D. Johnson, "Trials and Tribulations: The Trial Tax and the Process of Punishment," *Crime and Justice* 48 (2019): 313–63, https://www.journals.uchicago.edu/doi/10.1086/701713.
14. "Annual Determination of Average Cost of Incarceration Fee (COIF)," *Federal Register* 86, no. 167 (September 1, 2021): 49060, https://www.federalregister.gov/documents/2021/09/01/2021-18800/annual-determination-of-average-cost-of-incarceration-fee-coif.
15. Health in Justice Action Lab, "Drug-Induced Homicide," Northeastern University, accessed December 5, 2022, https://www.healthinjustice.org/drug-induced-homicide.
16. Health in Justice Action Lab, "Drug-Induced Homicide."
17. Morgan Godvin, "When Accidental Overdose Is Treated as Murder" (Boston, MA: Health in Justice Action Lab, Northeastern University, 2019), 8, https://www.healthinjustice.org/_files/ugd/3bbb1a_9a50168a658e4ab29461d2d887e707d0.pdf.

18. Hanna O'Reilly, "Scranton Man Charged for Victim's Overdose Death," FOX56, May 14, 2020, https://fox56.com/news/local/scranton-man-charged-for-mans-overdose-death.
19. Lauren Vogel, "Decriminalize Drugs and Use Public Health," *Canadian Medical Association Journal* 186, no. 10 (2014): E356, https://www.ncbi.nlm.nih.gov/pmc/articles/PMC4081223; Marc R. Larochelle, Dana Bernson, Thomas Land, Thomas J. Stopka, Na Wang, Ziming Xuan, Sarah M. Bagley, Jane M. Liebschutz, and Alexander Y. Walley, "Medication for Opioid Use Disorder After Nonfatal Opioid Overdose and Association with Mortality: A Cohort Study," *Annals of Internal Medicine* 169, no. 3 (2018): 137–45, https://pubmed.ncbi.nlm.nih.gov/29913516; CDC, "Summary of Information on the Safety and Effectiveness of Syringe Services Programs (SSPs)," May 23, 2019, https://www.cdc.gov/ssp/syringe-services-programs-summary.html; Jennifer Ng, Christy Sutherland, and Michael R. Kolber, "Does Evidence Support Supervised Injection Sites?," *Canadian Family Physician* 63, no. 11 (2017): 866, https://www.ncbi.nlm.nih.gov/pmc/articles/PMC5685449.
20. CDC, "Drug Overdose Mortality Rate," March 1, 2022, https://www.cdc.gov/nchs/pressroom/sosmap/drug_poisoning_mortality/drug_poisoning.htm; Lauren Peace, "Judge Rules Law Restricting West Virginia Needle Exchange Programs Can Stand," West Virginia Public Broadcasting, July 15, 2021, https://www.wvpublic.org/health-science/2021-07-15/judge-rules-law-restricting-west-virginia-needle-exchange-programs-can-stand.
21. Brian Mann, "California Gov. Newsom Vetoes Public Safe Drug-Use Clinics as Overdoses Surge," NPR, August 23, 2022, https://www.npr.org/2022/08/23/1119036357/california-gov-newsom-vetoes-public-safe-drug-use-clinics-as-overdoses-surge.
22. Zoe Adams, Noa Krawczyk, Rachel Simon, Kimberly Sue, Leslie Suen, and Paul Joudrey, "To Save Lives from Opioid Overdose Deaths, Bring Methadone into Mainstream Medicine," *Health Affairs*, May 27, 2022, https://www.healthaffairs.org/do/10.1377/forefront.20220524.911965.
23. Nadia Kounang, "Naloxone Reverses 93% of Overdoses, But Many Recipients Don't Survive a Year," CNN, October 30, 2017, https://www.cnn.com/2017/10/30/health/naloxone-reversal-success-study/index.html.
24. Morgan Godvin, "Language Matters: Is This a Drug Overdose or Drug Poisoning Crisis?," TalkingDrugs, June 9, 2022, https://www.talkingdrugs.org/is-this-a-drug-overdose-or-drug-poisoning-crisis.
25. Brett Samuels, "Trump in DC Speech Calls for Death Penalty for Convicted Drug Dealers," *The Hill*, July 26, 2022, https://thehill.com/homenews/campaign/3575157-trump-in-dc-speech-calls-for-death-penalty-for-convicted-drug-dealers; Erin Davis, "Drafted Legislation Creates Mandatory Minimum Sentences for Fentanyl," WSFA 12 News, September 14, 2022, https://www.wsfa.com

/2022/09/14/drafted-legislation-creates-mandatory-minimum-sentences-fentanyl.

26. Mike Littwin, "Opinion: We're Moving Backwards on Fentanyl Crisis," *Colorado Springs Indy*, April 20, 2022, https://www.csindy.com/opinion/columnists/fairandunbalanced/opinion-we-re-moving-backwards-on-fentanyl-crisis/article_8c2ccd98-c014-11ec-aa0f-47ce2c895ec7.html.

12

IMPROVING SENTENCING POLICIES TO IMPROVE TRUST AND LEGITIMACY

Adam Gelb

IN 2001, Governor Roy Barnes of Georgia established a state sentencing commission and appointed me as executive director. I was eager for him to select members and proceed apace but was lucky he didn't.

The delay in seating the commission gave me a chance to jump in my car and drive to courthouses around the state, from the massive concrete complexes in metro Atlanta to majestic neoclassical gems at the center of town squares in places like Metter and Valdosta. I spent hundreds of hours chatting with judges, prosecutors, defenders, corrections and parole officials, and others in what turned out to be an invaluable crash course in courtroom dynamics and idiosyncrasies involving how decision-makers apply the law.

Through this fascinating set of conversations—and many more over the years since—three things became clear. First, sentences handed down in court reflect a wide range of factors that are completely divorced from a pure sense of how someone should be held accountable for their actions. Second, in a highly indeterminate sentencing system such as Georgia's, the real power of sentencing isn't in the courtroom at all but instead at the back end of the system, in the hands of the parole board. Third, the widespread use of the term *early release* is inaccurate, distorts sentencing decisions, and significantly undermines faith in the criminal justice system.

These three observations may feel pedestrian, especially for experienced denizens of America's halls of justice. In my experience, however, they're rarely explicitly discussed and even more seldom considered in policy decisions. If they were, my guess is that we would see individual sentencing decisions and overall punishment policies and sentencing structures that are more fair and more effective, less expensive, and more deserving of public trust.

THE ROLE OF POLICY AND THE REALITY OF THE COURTROOM

Policy discussions about sentencing typically make a big mistake: they assume that sentencing decisions in individual cases have something to do with policy. They should, of course. Do we want to reserve our prisons for people who've committed serious violent crimes? Should we expand drug treatment courts and other community-based sentencing alternatives? Those kinds of questions are decided on a broad basis by legislatures that determine budgets, define elements of crimes, and set the ranges of possible penalties. Sentencing courts must then follow the parameters of the statutes and should be sensitive to the most current information about what works to reduce reoffending or restore victims and survivors.

The stuff of policy debates, though, is typically far removed from the everyday exigencies of the courtroom. Plea negotiations, where some 95 percent of sentencing decisions are made, have nothing whatsoever to do with the size or composition of the prison population. Instead, they turn on the facts and circumstances of the instant case itself: the defendant's role in the crime, the severity of the harm caused, the strength of physical evidence, the credibility of witnesses, and so on. Critically, a plea deal might reflect even less about the elements of the case than about the relative negotiating skills of the prosecutor and defense counsel, not to mention how much pressure they're under to simply resolve the matter, move on to the next case, and keep the court calendar from grinding to a halt.

In the policy realm, these real-world factors magically vanish once the sentence is pronounced. One perception is that the sentence is a policy judgment that expresses the court's highly considered assessment about what is the most appropriate consequence for the crime. If a sentence is deemed too severe or lenient, the interpretation is that the court was simply more severe or lenient than it should have been given the damage the offense caused the community. What it really represents is just the best deal that the parties could strike.

None of this is to suggest that policy has no role. I've spent nearly my entire professional career trying to infuse policy analysis and research more deeply into sentencing practices, educating governors, legislators, judges, prosecutors, and others about what works to reduce recidivism and to increase proportionality and parsimony. Policy conversations should be more cognizant of the practicalities of the courtroom and plea-bargaining process. When they do, their observations and critiques will resonate more—both with courtroom actors and policymakers.

THE ROLE OF PAROLE AND ANTICIPATORY SENTENCING

The most striking discovery I made in my travels around Georgia was how judges and prosecutors thought about their jobs in relation to parole. Georgia had (and continues to have) one of the most indeterminate sentencing structures in the nation. The statutory penalties for many crimes, including high volume offenses such as burglary, range from probation to twenty years in prison. After sentencing, the parole board has nearly complete discretion to release someone virtually immediately or to require them to serve every last day of the court-ordered term behind bars. In sentencing nerd parlance, the front door and the back door in Georgia are wide open.

It turned out that courts held polar opposite views of whether they should take this parole discretion into account in their sentencing decisions and plea negotiations. Half of the judges and prosecutors I spoke with said it was improper, even unethical, to consider when the defendant would likely be released on parole. After accounting for all the case processing considerations discussed, these court actors believed if you wanted someone to serve ten years, you should sentence (or plead) them to ten years. If the parole board let them out after seven, or five, or three years, that was their business.

The other half of my rolling focus group thought this approach was absurd. "How could you possibly ignore the reality of parole release?" they asked. "If you want someone to serve ten years in prison and you expect they will serve about 50 percent of the maximum term, you need to inflate the sentence to twenty years. That's the only way to achieve the just outcome you desire." I came to call this practice *anticipatory sentencing*.

Further complicating the situation was a thick computer printout showing the average percentage of sentence served for every criminal offense in the Georgia code. The state Corrections Department had distributed these stacks—picture that old continuous printer paper with green and white rows and holes on both sides—something like a decade earlier, but anticipatory sentencers treated them like the gospel or at least the best information that they could use to guide their decisions. Maybe by now the average burglar was serving about 25 percent or 70 percent of their court-ordered sentences, but the book says 40 percent so if I want four years behind the walls, I've got to sentence to ten.

Interestingly, views on anticipatory sentencing seemed to have little alignment with sentencing philosophies or political affiliations. That is, some of the judges and prosecutors who had reputations as severe sentencers did not engage in speculation about parole release, and some known as more lenient routinely consulted the old release data and said they inflated sentence lengths accordingly. I never was able to discern another pattern or explanation for the variance. When I asked why some felt one way or the other, the answer was always, "Well, that's just the way I feel about it."

Rationality, consistency, and predictability are hallmarks of a system that is perceived as just. Yet these anticipatory dynamics introduce a troubling element of randomness. That randomness grows when the release window expands, such as when time-to-serve requirements are relaxed or good and earned time credits are increased. More determinate sentencing schemes have plenty of their own challenges, but the greater discretion there is at the back end of the system, the more sentences at the front end become a guessing game based on individual court actors' perceptions of their proper roles in the system.

EARLY RELEASE AND THE ROLE OF LANGUAGE

As an erstwhile drummer, I was drawn to the movie *Whiplash*, in which an abusive music instructor played by J. K. Simmons pushes his promising drum student nearly over the brink in his pursuit of perfection. At one point, Simmons tells him, "There are no two words in the English language more harmful than 'good job.' "

You may take issue with that harsh theory of behavior motivation, but when it comes to criminal justice, it's hard to argue that the two most dangerous words aren't "early release." The fear that someone who has been released "early" from prison will commit a serious crime is probably the single biggest driver of longer prison sentences and more restrictive parole policies—and, in turn, the historic rise in American imprisonment. Legislators, judges, prosecutors, parole board members, probation and parole officers—anyone who makes decisions about who goes to prison and how long they serve—still lives to a certain extent in the shadow of Willie Horton.[1]

Yet the early release terminology we use is fundamentally inaccurate and misleading. It is used casually and nearly universally—by journalists and by reform advocates and opponents alike—to describe anyone who is released at anything shy of 100 percent of the maximum possible sentence. Recent examples include "Minnesota Pardon Board agenda won't include early release for ex-cop Kimberly Potter" (Axios Twin Cities) and "Woman granted early release from time served in prison overdose death" (CBS affiliate in Youngstown, Ohio).[2] Google "early release" and click the News tab to see just how common this is.

The phrase strongly implies that the system has failed to deliver what it promised. It said it was going to do one thing but turned around and did another. It cheated. The term breeds mistrust and cynicism. It does immense damage to the credibility of the justice system and to government in general.

But as discussed, everyone involved in the criminal justice process—victims and survivors included—knows that laws and policies not only permit but also encourage people to gain release before the expiration of their sentence. A recent report for the Council on Criminal Justice Task Force on Long Sentences by the Robina Institute of Criminal Law and Criminal Justice does a thorough job of explaining the legal "release window"—the interaction between parole discretion and various statutory sentence credits for good behavior and program participation that determine the minimum and maximum boundaries of a prison term.[3] Arkansas, for example, has a large release window: people may serve as little as 17 percent of the possible maximum sentence before release. Windows are smaller in states that adopted truth-in-sentencing policies, such as Arizona, where 85 percent of the maximum must be served before release.

Whether the release window is large or small, the lawyers—and reporters—understand the combination of release mechanisms means defendants are highly unlikely to serve every last day of their maximum sentence behind bars. As such, there's nothing early whatsoever about the release of someone who has completed certain programs or convinced a paroling authority that he or she is ready to return home. Nor is there anything untoward and deceptive about it. It's the law, and everyone knows it.

People have tried to come up with various substitutes for the term *early release* to get around the problem. *Accelerated* and *expedited* are among them. So far, nothing has really stuck. Finding something that does isn't a matter of political messaging or spin. It's acknowledging that when someone goes home before they max out their prison sentence, the system isn't pulling one over on the public. It's functioning exactly as designed.

It's tempting to assemble these observations into an argument for a particular type of sentencing system. If I were starting with a blank sheet of paper, I'd keep the front door and the back door fairly tight, similar to what they do in North Carolina, Minnesota, or Kansas. Such systems have myriad advantages. At the individual level, for crime victims and survivors, greater certainty about when assailants will be released may bring more peace of mind. Defendants and incarcerated people may be more likely to believe that their sentences and release dates are based on fair, objective, and consistent criteria rather than arbitrary discretion, and they may feel more confident about planning for the future. Corrections systems are better able to schedule and prioritize in-prison and postprison programming and plans, including housing and employment.

Although those objectives are critical, even more is at stake. Striking the right balance of power between the courts and parole offers greater assurances of equity and fairness, the degree to which similarly situated people convicted of similar offenses both receive and serve similar sentences. At a time when many Americans question the legitimacy of every element of the justice system, enhancing public confidence is perhaps the most important goal of all.

NOTES

1. In prison in Massachusetts on a life sentence for murder, Horton was released on a weekend furlough in the mid-1980s and committed a rape. His case was used against the Massachusetts governor, Michael Dukakis, in the 1988 presidential election and has become an enduring metaphor for policies characterized as soft on crime.
2. Torey Van Oot, "Minnesota Pardon Board Agenda Won't Include Early Release for Ex-Cop Convicted in Fatal Shooting," Axios, December 19, 2022, https://www.axios.com/local/twin-cities/2022/12/19/kim-potter-sentence-commutation-request-daunte-wright; Jennifer Rodriguez, "Woman Granted Early Release from Time Served in Prison Overdose Death," WKBN, December 22, 2022, https://www.wkbn.com/news/local-news/woman-granted-early-release-from-time-served-in-prison-overdose-death.
3. Julia Laskorunsky, Gerald G. Gaes, and Kevin Reitz, *Factors Affecting Time Served in Prison: The Overlooked Role of Back-End Discretion* (Washington, DC: Council on Criminal Justice, 2022), 1–23, https://counciloncj.org/wp-content/uploads/2022/11/Factors-Affecting-Time-Served.pdf.

PART FOUR

RACISM AND PUNITIVE EXCESS

13

HOW PUNITIVE EXCESS IS A MANIFESTATION OF RACISM IN AMERICA

Theodore R. Johnson

A WIDELY ACCEPTED NARRATIVE about incarceration in the United States goes something like this:

> At the dawn of the Reagan era in a nation of 229 million Americans, the incarcerated population was about 567,000, with 8 percent behind bars for drug offenses as of 1982.[1] The war on drugs that raged throughout the 1980s and into the next decade—bringing with it statutory reforms that relied heavily on increased policing, incarceration, and mandatory sentencing—meant the imprisonment rate for drug offenses was more than twelve times greater in 2018 than it had been in 1973.[2] At the end of 2019, 14 percent of people in prisons nationwide were serving time for drug offenses.[3] Nearly two million people are locked up in the United States.[4] And the march toward this mass incarceration occurred with Black Americans squarely underfoot, trampling their communities and imprinting racial disparity onto the nation's criminal justice system.[5]

That story isn't wrong, but it is incomplete. In this all-too-common telling, punitive excess, mass incarceration, and racial disparity are commingled—a grim tale of three tragic characters arising together from the carceral policies of the last four decades. It would follow, then, that to address one of them would be to make inroads against them all. This logic, though, is much too thin, mostly serving to make a long story short.

The more accurate account of imprisonment in the United States reveals that punitive excess, mass incarceration, and racial disparity are distinct phenomena. If the incarcerated population were cut by 75 percent overnight, the nation would wake the following morning to a disproportionate number of imprisoned people of color and inhumane abuses continuing in jails and prisons. Should punitive excess vanish in the blink of an eye, an exceedingly large number of people would still confined in correctional facilities and people of color would still be overrepresented. One need only catalog the experiences of racial and ethnic minorities to discern that if both mass incarceration and punitive excess were abolished, racial disparities in imprisonment rates would still exist. Moreover, given how race factors into the range of socioeconomic factors that influence a person's life chances, people of color would remain unduly exposed to whatever punishment and social penalties were to take the place of confinement.

Although racial disparity in the nation's prisons and jails is neither the root cause of injustice nor the primary deficiency in U.S. legal institutions, it is an especially valuable heuristic for identifying the critical flaws and shortcomings in the criminal justice system. That is, efforts to address racial disparities are likely to have outsize impacts on reducing the incidence of punitive excesses as well as the overall number of incarcerated people.

This likelihood spotlights an ugly truth within the nation's structures and policies, one that the criminal justice system crystallizes with astonishing clarity: the unwillingness to confront a history of racial oppression and the continued devaluation of people of color make full equality and justice in America unattainable. To establish a fair and unbiased justice system loosened from punitive excess and mass incarceration, we need to reckon with the central role race plays in systemic outcomes.

The entrenchment of racial hierarchy in the United States began before the nation came to be and has long endured. The nation's founding era featured forced displacements, chattel slavery, indentured servitude, outright denials of citizenship, and dehumanization of Native Americans, Black people, and immigrants of different races and ethnicities arriving in the New World. Less than two years after the Constitution was ratified, Congress passed the Naturalization Act of 1790 that limited eligibility for citizenship to "free white person[s] . . . of good moral character."[6] In the infamous *Dred Scott v. Sandford* opinion of 1857, the Supreme Court declared the United States was grounded in a culture that considered Black people to be "beings of an inferior order" and possessing "no rights which the white man was bound to respect."[7]

Even a civil war could not straighten out the racial oppression that the nation had wrought. After hundreds of thousands of casualties, the assassination of Abraham Lincoln once he had declared his intention to enfranchise

Black men, and the ratification of three constitutional amendments abolishing slavery and granting citizenship to freedmen and many immigrants as well as prohibiting racial discrimination when citizens exercised voting rights, people of color were systemically targeted with violence and legislation to force them to the bottom of the racial caste.

Although the civil rights movement a century later helped the nation painstakingly move toward becoming a more inclusive democracy, race remained a primary social determinant of the measure of justice and citizenship one could access. Racial hierarchy and inequality coursed in the nation's bloodstream, infecting every aspect of U.S. society and pooling in the criminal justice system.

Its fingerprints are everywhere. White segregationists' sanctioned vigilantism and terrorism during the Jim Crow era focused on Black people. The federal government forcibly corralled more than 120,000 Japanese Americans in internment camps during World War II while sparing nearly all Americans of German and Italian descent.[8] Today, Latino immigrants and undocumented denizens are caged in detention facilities and separated from their families, and Black Americans are incarcerated at alarmingly high rates, overrepresented in punitive excesses such as solitary confinement and the death penalty. For example, one study found that the risk of solitary confinement for Black men is more than eight times that for white men—and that Latino men were 2.5 times likelier than white men to be held in such extreme isolation.[9] Further, although Black Americans make up less than 14 percent of the U.S. population, they account for 42 percent of those on death row.[10]

This history and the policies it birthed resulted in a conflated ontology of race, social threats, and crime. That is, sociologists and political scientists have found that, in a society with a built-in racial hierarchy, the visual markers of race and ethnicity create boundaries of trust and empathy, leading to civic and social distance among citizens.[11] When certain communities of color are treated like a scourge and caricatured as incompatible with American values, their very presence can create a heightened sense of insecurity in the broader society. The criminal justice system has been fashioned to manage these societal anxieties by exerting control over the population deemed a danger to the American way of life.

The Black American experience at the turn of the twentieth century is an example of this sociology in motion. In the early decades of the Great Migration, when millions of Black Americans left the brutality and economic insecurity of the South to seek opportunities in northern and midwestern states, they encountered communities of white European immigrants who were themselves often discriminated against and treated as second-class citizens. The ensuing competition for employment and housing—as well as a desire for social advancement—caused many white citizens to set aside nativist resentments toward white European immigrants and unite in opposition to the Black arrivals.

These immigrants were able to secure patronage jobs, particularly in law enforcement, as a buffer between Black Americans and white political and economic elites. Research reveals that the rate of arrest and incarceration of Black Americans in Great Migration destination cities increased as the proportion of white immigrants on local police forces increased.[12] Charges for petty offenses against Black people skyrocketed, turning accusations of crimes such as suspicious behavior, disorderly conduct, and public drunkenness into instruments for social control.

As Martin Luther King Jr. said in remembrance of the work of renowned sociologist and historian W. E. B. Du Bois, so long as the devaluation of Black people persisted, "the brutality and criminality of conduct toward the Negro was easy for the conscience to bear. The twisted logic ran—If the black man was inferior, he was not oppressed."[13]

In the end, the United States has a system in which justice is delivered unevenly and at times arbitrarily. It's as if structural racism compels Lady Justice to lift her blindfold and slant her scales, forcing some of her people at the margins to tumble off the edge beyond her reach. Nkechi Taifa's essay (see chapter 15) demonstrates how such racism operates by detailing the crack-to-powder cocaine sentencing disparity. Discussing federal drug laws, she notes that people convicted of distributing 5 grams of crack cocaine (about what two pennies weigh) received a mandatory prison term of five years, whereas it took 500 grams of powder cocaine (more than the weight of a soccer ball) for one to receive the same five-year sentence. This reality should be of little surprise considering that crack cocaine is stereotyped as Black and low-class and that powder cocaine is often associated with posh white users.

Any serious attempts at reform and making our justice system truly just will require a direct confrontation with what African American studies scholar Eddie Glaude Jr. calls the value gap.[14] This is the idea that the true plague in American society is that people of color, particularly Black people in a nation where chattel slavery featured so prominently, are simply valued less. Thus, no matter what law or policy is implemented with racial justice and equality as its goal, if the value gap is left unaddressed, Glaude argues, "our systems will always produce the same results: racial inequality."[15] We do not need to look far to find evidence of this assertion. When states and localities enacted "ban the box" laws, which prohibit employers from asking about criminal history on job applications, researchers found that companies began using an applicant's race as a proxy for criminal history, effectively increasing racial discrimination in the hiring process.[16] As decriminalization and legalization of marijuana becomes more commonplace, possession of which led to the disproportionate arrests and incarceration of Black and Hispanic Americans, upward of 80 percent of business owners in the booming cannabis industry are white and just 10 percent are Black or Hispanic.

There is no way around this quandary. It is a product of U.S. history that people of color remain overly exposed to the darkest corners and worst impulses of the U.S. criminal justice system, its institutions and practices, and its actors. Reimagining justice in America requires a color-conscious approach to policy, employing measures and taking actions that account for people's disparate paths and experiences. Perhaps this is why in her initial conception, Lady Justice wore no blindfold—when a system is truly just, it doesn't need to be blind to be impartial or equitable.[17]

At the same time, policy reforms to end mass incarceration and cease excessive punishment are critical. Treating the threat of incarceration as a last resort rather than a first response to any social problem is an unassailable good for any fair and just society. Respecting the humanity and dignity of all people by refusing to subject them to cruel and unusual punishments not only helps us live up to our constitutional principles, but also ushers the United States one step closer to being the more perfect union outlined in its national canon.

That goal, however, remains a distant one—no other people imprison each other more than Americans. Louisiana embodies this peculiarity in superlative fashion. It has the highest incarceration rate in the country, and Fair Bryant knows this better than anyone. Bryant, a Black man who served time in the state's infamous prison known as Angola, was sentenced to life after being convicted of attempting to steal hedge clippers in 1997.[18] His fate was the product of punitive excess hallmarks—habitual offender laws, harsh mandatory sentencing, and forced field labor in an institution that owns the horrific distinction of holding two men in solitary confinement for nearly four decades, the longest period in American history.

For Bryant, like too many others, the criminal justice system has been anything but fair. Bryant's life is a stark reminder that ending mass incarceration and eradicating punitive excess should neither shake us from being clear-eyed about the outsize role race plays in America nor stuff these policy reforms into racial justice frames for political expediency's sake. We must tell the complete story of incarceration in the United States, complete with its ugly bits and filled with all its details, complexities, and nuances. Only then will we be able to bring our system to justice.

NOTES

1. Bureau of Justice Statistics (BJS), "Key Statistics: Total Correctional Population," accessed December 19, 2022, https://bjs.ojp.gov/data/key-statistics; The Sentencing Project, "Fact Sheet: Trends in U.S. Corrections," 2022, 2–3, https://www.sentencingproject.org/app/uploads/2022/08/Trends-in-US-Corrections.pdf; Steven R. Schlesinger, Benjamin H. Renshaw III, and Joseph M. Bessette, "Crime and Justice Facts, 1985" (Washington, DC: U.S. Department of Justice, Bureau of Justice Statistics, 1986), 26, https://bjs.ojp.gov/content/pub/pdf/cjf85.pdf.
2. BJS, "Key Statistics"; David Stockman, "How to Drain the Swamp: End the Failed War on Drugs, Part 1" (Fairfax, VA: Future of Freedom Foundation, June 1, 2018), https://www.fff.org/explore-freedom/article/how-to-drain-the-swamp-end-the-failed-war-on-drugs-part-1.
3. E. Ann Carson, *Prisoners in 2020—Statistical Tables*, NCJ 302776 (Washington, DC: Bureau of Justice Statistics, 2021), table 14, 28, https://bjs.ojp.gov/content/pub/pdf/p20st.pdf.
4. Jacob Kang-Brown, Chase Montagnet, and Jasmine Heiss, *People in Jail and Prison in Spring 2021* (New York: Vera Institute of Justice, 2021), 1, https://www.vera.org/publications/people-in-jail-and-prison-in-spring-2021; Wendy Sawyer and Peter Wagner, "Mass Incarceration: The Whole Pie 2022," Press release, March 14 (Northampton, MA: Prison Policy Initiative, 2022), https://www.prisonpolicy.org/reports/pie2022.html.
5. Wendy Sawyer, "Visualizing the Racial Disparities in Mass Incarceration," *Prison Policy Initiative* (blog), July 27, 2020, https://www.prisonpolicy.org/blog/2020/07/27/disparities.
6. "H.R. 40, Naturalization Bill, March 4, 1790," accessed December 19, 2022, https://www.visitthecapitol.gov/artifact/h-r-40-naturalization-bill-march-4-1790.
7. Scott v. Sandford, 60 U.S. 19 (1856), https://www.archives.gov/milestone-documents/dred-scott-v-sandford.
8. Molly Enking, "The First-Ever List of Japanese Americans Forced into Incarceration Camps Is 1,000 Pages Long," *Smithsonian Magazine*, November 18, 2022, https://www.smithsonianmag.com/smart-news/list-japanese-americans-internment-camps-ireicho-180981133.

9. Hannah Pullen-Blasnik, Jessica T. Simes, and Bruce Western, "The Population Prevalence of Solitary Confinement," *Science Advances* 7, no. 48 (2021): 5, https://doi.org/10.1126/sciadv.abj1928.
10. Ranya Shannon, "3 Ways the 1994 Crime Bill Continues to Hurt Communities of Color" (Washington, DC: Center for American Progress, May 10, 2019), https://www.americanprogress.org/article/3-ways-1994-crime-bill-continues-hurt-communities-color.
11. Juliet Hooker, *Race and the Politics of Solidarity* (Oxford: Oxford University Press, 2009).
12. Christopher Muller, "Northward Migration and the Rise of Racial Disparity in American Incarceration, 1880–1950," *American Journal of Sociology* 118, no. 2 (2012): 281–326, http://users.soc.umn.edu/~uggen/Muller_AJS_12.pdf.
13. Martin Luther King Jr., "Honoring Dr. Du Bois" (speech, Carnegie Hall, New York, February 23, 1968), *Freedomways* No. 2, https://www.crmvet.org/info/68mlkweb.htm.
14. Eddie S. Glaude Jr., "We Need to Begin Again," *The Atlantic*, July 18, 2020, excerpted from Glaude's *Begin Again: James Baldwin's America and Its Urgent Lessons for Our Own* (New York: Penguin Random House, 2020), https://www.theatlantic.com/ideas/archive/2020/07/why-we-need-begin-again/614326.
15. Eddie S. Glaude Jr., *Democracy in Black: How Race Still Enslaves the American Soul* (New York: Crown, 2016), 34.
16. Amanda Agan and Sonja Starr, "Ban the Box, Criminal Records, and Racial Discrimination: A Field Experiment," *Quarterly Journal of Economics* 133, no. 1 (2018): 1, 24–25, https://law.yale.edu/sites/default/files/area/workshop/leo/leo16_starr.pdf.
17. Valérie Hayaert, "The Paradoxes of Lady Justice's Blindfold," in *The Art of Law*, ed. Stefan Huygebaert, Georges Martyn, Vanessa Paumen, Eric Bousmar, and Xavier Rousseau (Cham: Springer, 2018), 201.
18. Nick Chrastil, "Fair Wayne Bryant, Man Given Life Sentence for Stealing Hedge Clippers, Granted Parole," *The Lens*, October 15, 2020, https://thelensnola.org/2020/10/15/fair-wayne-bryant-man-given-life-sentence-for-stealing-hedge-clippers-granted-parole.

14

WE MUST END THE CARCERALITY IN OUR OWN HEARTS

Monica Bell

ON AUGUST 24, 2019, Elijah McClain stopped by a gas station in his hometown of Aurora, Colorado, to buy iced tea for himself and his cousin. As he waited in line holding the cans of tea, he adjusted his face-covering runner's mask and, as he left the store, he gave his customary "gratitude bow" to the cashier before leaving.[1]

Shortly after he left the 7–11 and began walking home, listening to music with his earbuds, a caller named Juan reported Elijah to 911:

> He's walking south on Billings Street; he has a mask on. . . . when I passed by him, he put his hands up. He does all these kinds of. . . . I don't know. He looks sketchy. He might be a good person or a bad person. He has a full-on mask on.[2]

Although nothing about this call suggested that anything approximating crime, violence, or danger was occurring, the 911 operator told the caller she would "put a call in so officers can go see what's going on."[3] Officers came to the scene and stopped Elijah a block from home.

> "Stop. Stop. I have a right to stop you 'cause you're being suspicious!"[4]

Aurora police officer Nathan Woodyard rushed toward twenty-three-year-old Elijah, one hand balled into a fist with index finger and thumb extended, pointing at Elijah as if to mimic a gun.[5]

Elijah—"Eli," to some—was confused. He stopped the music he was listening to and began pulling his headphones out of his ears to better hear and understand what was happening. But before he could process the interruption to his evening walk from the gas station, two other officers, Jason Rosenblatt and Randy Roedema, had joined the scene. The first officer began to grip and stroke Elijah's torso, back, and waist.[6]

Early in the encounter, Elijah entreated officers to stop touching him so forcefully. He told them that as an "introvert" he was uncomfortable with all of this unexpected touching and pleaded with officers to "please respect the boundaries that I am speaking." Yet, the swarm persisted. One officer commanded Elijah to "stop tensing up" and "relax." Of course, demanding that a person stop being tense and stressed is not an effective way of discouraging those feelings. When Elijah insisted that he was merely "going home" to a place that was one block away, Woodyard responded in a threatening tone: "Relax—or I am going to have to *change* this situation."[7] The three officers pushed Elijah onto the ground and began applying "control techniques" including a now-banned hold in which officers deliberately apply pressure to the carotid artery to cut off blood flow to the brain and induce unconsciousness.[8]

After a struggle, throughout which Elijah was vomiting into his mask, struggling to breathe, and apologizing for upsetting the officers, the officers called in paramedics to subdue this 140-pound anemic man. The officers called Elijah's strength "superhuman."[9] Paramedics arrived, hastily diagnosing an inconsistently conscious Elijah with "excited delirium"—a condition that many experts do not consider a legitimate medical diagnosis but rather one developed solely to justify the use of chemical restraints during police stops.[10] The so-called rescuers injected Elijah with an overdose of a sedative, ketamine.

Less than ten minutes later, Elijah's heart stopped. After several days in a coma, his brain and breath stopped too. With hopes of his recovery snuffed out, his family removed his swollen and bruised body from life support.[11]

Since Elijah died in August 2019, much change has occurred in Aurora. Despite the protestations of the Aurora Police Association—which initially insisted that "there is no evidence that APD officers caused [Elijah McClain's] death" and criticized "the hysterical overreaction to this case"—none of the officers involved are still paid employees of the department.[12] An independent investigative report commissioned by the city determined that the officers behaved illegally and in violation of Aurora Police Department policy, but also found that Aurora's policies were insufficient to prevent future incidents.[13]

In November 2021, the City of Aurora entered a state consent decree with the Colorado attorney general that requires oversight of the Aurora Police Department, Aurora Fire Rescue, and Aurora Civil Service Commission as they improve their training and policies on addressing racial bias in policing, use of force, documentation of stops, use of sedatives as restraint, recruitment, hiring, promotion, accountability, transparency, and dispute resolution.[14] Although criminal proceedings against three police officers and two paramedics are ongoing, the city settled with Elijah's family for $15 million. Elijah's mother, Sheneen McClain, morosely called the settlement "blood money."[15]

Since Elijah's death, many have rightly focused outrage and activism against the officers and paramedics who killed him. His death underscores the interlocking problems of police authoritarianism, violence, and state failure to execute its duty of care for Black life.

Yet few have asked why the police and paramedics were interacting with Elijah at all. Why did the 911 dispatcher so quickly send police to stop Elijah when the caller did not report any dangerous behavior? Why call 911 in the first place? Although these moments of discretion seem more difficult to regulate than police and paramedic discretion may be, in them lies a key—but often ignored—set of components of "police reform."

Implicit in the caller's decision to call 911, and the 911 dispatcher's choice to send officers merely "to see what was going on" were two assumptions. First was that unusual behavior on its own, regardless of whether it seems remotely connected to dangerousness, warrants response and investigation from armed agents of the state. Second was that, if in doubt about the dangerousness of a situation, a person should err on the side of bringing police in rather than leaving them out. To make lasting change in our responses to crime and violence, these assumptions must fall. In this essay, I focus primarily on the actions of the caller to explore and critique both premises.

"I'M JUST DIFFERENT, THAT'S ALL": THE "SKETCHINESS" OF ELIJAH MCCLAIN

By many accounts, including his own, Elijah was an unusual person. One of his former coworkers at Massage Envy, the spa where he was employed, described him as a "one-of-a-kind eccentric" who "naturally marched to his own drum."[16] Another coworker called him an "an earthly angel" who was "inspired by everything."[17] One of his long-term massage clients took note of his "child-like spirit," appreciating that he "lived in his own little world. He was never into, like, fitting in. He just was who he was."[18] As he pleaded with officers as they choked him, "I'm just different, that's all." The police and paramedics killed Elijah and they are responsible for doing so. Yet the chain of events that led to his death started simply because Juan—the person who called 911—thought Elijah was strange.

Juan could not understand why Elijah was wearing a runner's mask or why he waved his arms, and he thought this confusion was a sufficient reason to call the authorities. When officers on the scene sought more details, Juan reiterated that he did not see any signs of dangerousness or criminality.[19] According to Officer Alicia Ward, Juan "didn't feel threatened or anything" and "just thought it was weird." Sergeant Dale Leonard, also on the scene, realized the caller hadn't claimed to observe any criminal behavior, though he surmised that Elijah's behavior must mean "he's on something, obviously."[20] A 2021 independent investigator's report on the matter, ordered by the Aurora City Council, determined that these officers did not meet the constitutional standard to justify their decision to stop, search, and detain Elijah: they did not have "reasonable suspicion" that he was part of any criminal activity.[21]

"Sketchiness" and "suspiciousness" are curious characterizations, seeming to arise from a correlated set of unspoken circumstances. Although the caller made much of Elijah's runner's mask, wearing a runner's mask on its own cannot be considered "suspicious"—certainly not given that Elijah was a long-distance runner, and these masks protect runners' faces from wind and cold weather. Elijah was not running at the time, but we hardly classify people as suspicious simply because they wear the incorrect attire for an occasion. In addition to the fact that Elijah was often cold, some of Elijah's friends think he liked wearing the mask to cope with his sometimes crippling social anxiety.[22]

Juan said Elijah put his hands up as he passed, which the 911 dispatcher described to officers as "waving his arms."[23] But of course, handwaving is not an obvious prelude to criminal behavior either. There is some irony that the very position officers often demand from citizens they search, especially Black men—to raise their hands, to "assume the position"—was held out as a reason for suspicion.[24] Elijah's friends surmised that the handwaving and gesticulation was probably his dancing.[25] Of course, Elijah might have been viewed as "sketchy" for other unspoken reasons—his race, his neighborhood, his gender, all the reasons that are rarely acknowledged explicitly these days, but that have long fed into Americans' ideas about crime and danger.[26]

BLACK NONCONFORMITY AND AMERICAN VALUES

Although demands for conformity in the United States are certainly intense, in some settings we view nonconformity as a characteristic worthy of protection or even celebration. For example, journalist Olga Khazan wrote an entire book glorifying human eccentricity, *Weird: The Power of Being an Outsider in an Insider World*.[27] In *Weird*, Khazan argues that being unusual, not seeming to fit in with the mainstream, confers advantages in creativity and resilience.

Beyond such psychological considerations, U.S. constitutional principles—such as privacy and free expression—underscore the purported value of nonconformity at a collective level. In recent years, the appreciation of unusual perspectives and unusual behavior has been invoked not only to protect historically excluded viewpoints but as a key element of "anti–cancel culture" rhetoric. When more than 150 prominent scholars and writers signed a controversial letter, published in *Harper's Magazine* in 2020, they emphasized how much they "need a culture that leaves us room for experimentation, risk taking, and even mistakes."[28] More recently, the Massachusetts Institute for Technology issued a new proposed statement in support of free expression, touting its "tradition of celebrating provocative thinking, controversial views, and nonconformity" and proclaiming that such expression "is essential to the search for truth and justice."[29]

Obviously, the particular forms of nonconformity that these elite speakers are defending are not of the same type as Elijah's quirky clothing choices and dancing in the street. One might argue that unusual expression directly intended to communicate an idea is more democratically or educationally salient than the type of self-expression Elijah exhibited that August night.

However, it is hard to shake the sense that had Elijah been a professor who lost his job for his unusual or even abhorrent views, rather than a massage therapist who lost his freedom and ultimately his life for unusual but noncriminal behavior, outrage at the state discipline against him would have been far greater in the first place. As much as America embraces free expression and nonconformity in principle, it has rejected those values as applied to Black men, among whom the slightest deviation from norms can provoke fear, policing, and punishment.[30] Although Elijah's masking and dancing were not a purposeful communication of ideas, they were in themselves repudiations of the narrow range of presentations Black men are allowed, part of a larger way of being that bucked expectations of Black masculinity and stoicism. As one Black male commentator recently explained, "sensitive Black boys are not a rare breed—they exist in droves—but the world does its best to beat it out of them."[31]

SEEING NOTHING AND SAYING TOO MUCH: THE PROBLEM OF PRIVATE CARCERALITY

Even those who are horrified by the police and paramedic killing of Elijah might be slower to criticize the 911 caller for reporting unusual behavior. Juan was not sure what was occurring and made a choice to err in favor of calling in police, hoping that even if he had summoned authorities when there was no danger, they would look for themselves and behave responsibly. Remember, even in the initial call, Juan was openly ambivalent about whether any danger was present. "He might be a good person or a bad person," he told the dispatcher.[32] There is a world in which individuals would be able to report unusual activity to the police and trust them to be able to discern true risks. We live, however, in another one, especially when it comes to race and class-polarized communities.

One reason for discomfort with criticizing the caller is that, especially in the two decades since 9/11, America has embraced mutual surveillance. As the slogan goes, "If you see something, say something." A 2016 *Washington Post* op-ed called the catchphrase "the unofficial slogan of post-9/11 America."[33] A New York advertising executive developed the phrase on September 12, 2001, and eventually it became a campaign of the U.S. Department of Homeland Security. As the *Washington Post* author mused, "The expression makes us vigilant, but it also makes us paranoid."[34] Good citizenship now requires watching other people closely to take note of "something" and report it to authorities. This mentality originated with concerns over international terrorism but is now so culturally embedded that it has knock-on effects for domestic policing as well.[35] Within this "if you see something, say something" framework, it seems callous and bizarre to chastise the 911 caller. Yet the forms of "something" that warrant a report are rarely well defined.[36] Thus 911 calls become a pathway along which the mundane activities of Black people are evidence of suspiciousness.

One change necessary for shrinking the role of policing in harm to Black people is complicating "if you see something, say something" culture. This culture encourages people to call authorities but exercises little discernment about whether public safety is truly at risk. Thus it misidentifies paranoid surveillance as good citizenship.

However, 911 calls are only one example of the ways that private suspicion, based on shallow notions of normalcy, has been weaponized for punishment. Long-standing programs such as Neighborhood Watch and newer social media-driven approaches such as NextDoor are among the various techniques private individuals use in attempting to build safety in their communities. These tools present unaccounted-for risks to anyone who seems unusual or out of place.[37] Indeed, aware of this risk, NextDoor now provides information about antiracism on its website, and it warns new members that one of four primary rules is not to engage in "racism, hateful language, or discrimination of any kind."[38] Yet, even as it offers resources on dynamics like implicit bias and racial privilege, it does not—perhaps cannot—directly confront prevalent private bias. The rise of private policing, too, presents a challenge for those who aim to change policing, whether from a reform-focused or abolitionist perspective.[39]

In this book's conclusion, Bruce Western and Jeremy Travis note that "punishment not only describes what criminal justice institutions do, but also signifies a relationship between the state and its citizens." Yet punishment also describes a bundle of private relationships, those between human beings like Elijah and others like Juan. This is only one essay in a volume of thirty-eight that heartbreakingly illustrate that and how punitiveness is the very fabric of how we respond not only to crime, but also to Blackness—especially to young Black men like Elijah, trying to live free in a world that refuses to allow it. When members of the public see every deviation from the norm as a threat and policing as the only reasonable response to threat, policing flourishes even outside the direct confines of the state. Transforming policing and ending mass incarceration requires structural and policy change. It also demands that we eradicate the carcerality in our hearts.

NOTES

1. Grant Stringer, "Unlikely Suspect: Those Who Knew Elijah Balk at Aurora Police Account of His Death," *Sentinel Colorado*, October 27, 2019, https://sentinelcolorado.com/news/metro/unlikely-suspect-those-who-knew-elijah-balk-at-aurora-police-account-of-his-death.
2. Aurora Police, "911 Dispatch Call Regarding Elijah McClain," YouTube, November 22, 2019, Video, 4:09, https://www.youtube.com/watch?v=pdD3mvNP2QQ.
3. Aurora Police, "911 Dispatch Call," 2:02.
4. Allison Sherry, "In Colorado, Aurora City Leaders Look at Next Steps in Elijah McClain Case," NPR, February 23, 2021, https://www.npr.org/2021/02/23/970672241/in-colorado-aurora-city-leaders-look-at-next-steps-in-elijah-mcclain-case.
5. Aurora Police, "Body Worn Camera Regarding the In-Custody Death of Elijah McClain," YouTube, November 22, 2019, Video, 3:08:30, 9:31–9:33, https://www.youtube.com/watch?v=q5NcyePEOJ8.
6. Jonathan Smith, Melissa Costello, and Roberto Villaseñor, *Investigation Report and Recommendations Pursuant to a City Council Resolution Approved July 20, 2020* (City of Aurora, Colorado, February 22, 2021), 3, https://cdn5-hosted.civiclive.com/UserFiles/Servers/Server_1881137/File/News%20Items/Investigation%20Report%20and%20Recommendations%20(FINAL).pdf.
7. Aurora Police, "Body Worn Camera," 34:27–34:39.
8. Aaron Keller, "Elijah McClain's Death: Our First Look at Police Officers and Paramedics After Grand Jury Indictment," Law & Crime, September 2, 2021, https://lawandcrime.com/high-profile/elijah-mcclains-death-our-first-look-at-police-officers-and-paramedics-after-grand-jury-indictment.
9. Allison Sherry, "Elijah McClain's Autopsy Report Changed to Death by Ketamine," Colorado Public Radio, September 23, 2022, https://www.cpr.org/2022/09/23/elijah-mcclain-death-by-ketamine-autopsy-report-changed.
10. Sherry, "Elijah McClain's Autopsy Report"; American Medical Association, "New AMA Policy Opposes 'Excited Delirium' Diagnosis," June 14, 2021, https://www.ama-assn.org/press-center/press-releases/new-ama-policy-opposes-excited-delirium-diagnosis.
11. Elise Schmelzer, "Aurora Man to Be Taken Off Life Support After Confrontation with Police Left Him Brain Dead," *Denver Post*, August 30, 2019, https://www.denverpost.com/2019/08/30/elijah-mcclain-aurora-police-death.
12. Kyla Guilfoil, "Judge Finds Sufficient Evidence to Continue Elijah Mcclain Case," ABC News, July 19, 2022, https://abcnews.go.com/US/judge-finds-sufficient-evidence-continue-elijah-mcclain-case/story?id=87065423. One officer involved was among four fired for making fun of Elijah's death; other involved officers were suspended without pay pending the resolution of the

criminal cases against them, which are still outstanding at the time of writing. See, for example, Lucy Tompkins, "Here's What You Need to Know About Elijah McClain's Death," *New York Times*, January 18, 2022, https://www.nytimes.com/article/who-was-elijah-mcclain.html.

13. Smith, Costello, and Villaseñor, *Investigation Report*, 73, 146.
14. Colorado ex rel. Weiser v. City of Aurora, Joint Motion to Enter Judgment of Stipulated Consent Decree and Judgment Under C.R.S. Section 24-31-113, (D. Colo., November 22, 2021), https://cdn5-hosted.civiclive.com/UserFiles/Servers/Server_1881137/File/Residents/Public%20Safety/Consent%20Decree%20-%20Fully%20Negotiated%20Final%20Form%20of%20Agreement.pdf. In April 2022, the Aurora police chief who had shepherded much of these efforts at change was fired, which some have speculated was because of her connection to the local Black community and commitment to reforms, though there may have been other issues. Virginia Langmaid, "Police Chief Who Took over Colorado Department During Fallout over Elijah McClain's Death Is Fired," CNN, April 7, 2022, https://www.cnn.com/2022/04/07/us/aurora-colorado-police-chief-fired.
15. Sophie Kasakove, "Family of Elijah McClain to Receive $15 Million in Settlement," *New York Times*, November 20, 2021, https://www.nytimes.com/2021/11/20/us/elijah-mcclain-settlement.html; Allison Sherry, "Case Against Aurora Police and Paramedics in Elijah McClain's Death Delayed Again," Colorado Public Radio, November 4, 2022, https://www.cpr.org/2022/11/04/elijah-mcclain-case-delayed-again.
16. Miranda Bryant, "'He Was Inspired by Everything:' Friends and Family Pay Tribute to Elijah McClain," *The Guardian*, June 30, 2020, https://www.theguardian.com/us-news/2020/jun/30/elijah-mcclain-aurora-colorado-tributes-police-killing.
17. Bryant, "He Was Inspired."
18. Stringer, "Unlikely Suspect."
19. Aurora Police, "911 Dispatch Call," 2:27, 3:23.
20. Smith, Costello, and Villaseñor, *Investigation Report*, 23–24.
21. Smith, Costello, and Villaseñor, *Investigation Report*, 2–4.
22. Stringer, "Unlikely Suspect." For a broader discussion of how criminal law treats mere nonnormative behavior as criminal, see Jamelia N. Morgan, "Rethinking Disorderly Conduct," *California Law Review* 109, no. 5 (2021): 1637–702, https://californialawreview.org/print/rethinking-disorderly-conduct.
23. Aurora Police, "911 Dispatch Call," 1:49; Smith, Costello, and Villaseñor, *Investigation Report*, 75.
24. See Nikki Jones, *The Chosen Ones: Black Men and the Politics of Redemption* (Berkeley: University of California Press, 2018), 110.
25. Stringer, "Unlikely Suspect."

26. Khalil Gibran Muhammad, *The Condemnation of Blackness: Race, Crime, and the Making of Modern Urban America* (Cambridge, MA: Harvard University Press, 2010).
27. Olga Khazan, *Weird: The Power of Being an Outsider in an Insider World* (New York: Hachette, 2020).
28. *Harper's Magazine*, "A Letter on Justice and Open Debate," July 7, 2020, https://harpers.org/a-letter-on-justice-and-open-debate.
29. Ad Hoc Working Group on Free Expression, "MIT Statement on Freedom of Expression and Academic Freedom," Massachusetts Institute of Technology, September 1, 2022, https://facultygovernance.mit.edu/sites/default/files/reports/2022-09_Proposed_MIT_Statement_on_Freedom_of_Expression_and_Academic_Freedom.pdf.
30. See, for example, Maria R. Lowe, Angela Stroud, and Alice Nguyen, "Who Looks Suspicious? Racialized Surveillance in a Predominantly White Neighborhood," *Social Currents* 4, no. 1 (2017): 34–50; see also Turea Michelle Hutson, Elizabeth McGhee Hassrick, Sherira Fernandes, et al., "'I'm Just Different—That's All—I'm So Sorry . . .': Black Men, ASD and the Urgent Need for DisCrit Theory in Police Encounters," *Policing: An International Journal* 45, no. 3 (2022): 524–37.
31. Stephen A. Crockett Jr., "Elijah McClain Was a Sensitive Black Man and That Still Didn't Save His Life," *Huffpost*, September 30, 2022, https://www.huffpost.com/entry/elijah-mcclain-sensitive-black-man_n_6335e077e4b04cf8f360dc1a.
32. Aurora Police, "911 Dispatch Call," 1:48.
33. Hanson O'Haver, "How 'If You See Something, Say Something' Became our National Motto," *Washington Post*, September 23, 2016, https://www.washingtonpost.com/posteverything/wp/2016/09/23/how-if-you-see-something-say-something-became-our-national-motto.
34. O'Haver, "If You See Something."
35. See Amna A. Akbar, "National Security's Broken Windows," *UCLA Law Review* 62 (2015): 834–907, https://www.uclalawreview.org/wp-content/uploads/2019/09/Akbar-final-article-5.29.15.pdf.
36. DHS specifies what might constitute "something" worth reporting in the context of a terrorism threat, and explicitly notes that appearance should be excluded. U.S. Department of Homeland Security, "Recognize Suspicious Activity," accessed November 5, 2022, https://www.dhs.gov/see-something-say-something/recognize-the-signs.
37. See, for example, Rahim Kurwa, "Building the Digitally Gated Community: The Case of Nextdoor," *Surveillance & Society* 17, no. 1/2 (2019): 111–117, https://ojs.library.queensu.ca/index.php/surveillance-and-society/article/view/12927/8483.

38. NextDoor, "Policies to prevent racism & discrimination," accessed December 10, 2022, https://help.nextdoor.com/s/article/Do-nct-discriminate?language=en_US.
39. Indeed, some libertarian commentators drew on the occasion of calls to defund the police to argue for police privatization as a related alternative. See, for example, John Osterhoudt, "Don't 'Abolish the Police.' Privatize Them," *Reason*, July 21, 2020, https://reason.com/video/2020/07/21/dont-abolish-the-police-privatize-them.

15

RACE, MASS INCARCERATION, AND THE DISASTROUS WAR ON DRUGS

Nkechi Taifa

THE WAR ON DRUGS was a racially motivated crusade to criminalize Blacks and the antiwar Left, Nixon's domestic policy advisor John Ehrlichman revealed in a 1994 interview.

Although not surprised to read his confession, I must admit I was infuriated at his decades-later candor, in the midst of a mass incarceration of more than two million people, disproportionately Black, unmatched worldwide.[1]

"We knew we couldn't make it illegal to be either against the war or black, but by getting the public to associate the hippies with marijuana and blacks with heroin, and then criminalizing both heavily, we could disrupt those communities. We could arrest their leaders, raid their homes, break up their meetings, and vilify them night after night on the evening news. Did we know we were lying about the drugs? Of course we did."[2]

Before the war on drugs, overt racist lynching and explicitly blatant discrimination—as opposed to today's mass incarceration—were in vogue for Black people. Why focus on incarcerating people or due process of law, when a fully functioning extrajudicial system was in place? With the advent of the racially targeted drug war against Black people, however, mass incarceration became the punishment of choice.

Mass incarceration was the gradual progeny of a number of congressional bills, also touched on in Lauren-Brooke Eisen's essay on decades of punitive federal funding strategies (see chapter 5), most notably, the 1984 Comprehensive Crime Control and Safe Streets Act, which eliminated parole in the federal system, eventually resulting in an upsurge of geriatric prisoners; the 1986 Anti-Drug Abuse Act, which established mandatory minimum sentencing schemes, including the infamous hundred-to-one quantity ratio between crack and powder cocaine; and the 1988 Anti-Drug Abuse Act, which added overly broad interpretations of conspiracy to the mix.[3] These laws authorizing harsh penalties for drug-related crimes were responsible for flooding the federal system with people convicted of low-level and nonviolent drug offenses.

I have a long view of the criminal punishment system, having been in the trenches for more than forty years. During the early 1990s while policy counsel for a civil liberties organization, I walked the halls of Congress lobbying against the various omnibus crime bills that culminated in the granddaddy of them all—the now infamous Crime Bill of 1994, the Violent Crime Control and Safe Streets Act.[4] This bill featured the largest expansion of the federal death penalty in modern times; the gutting of habeas corpus; the evisceration of the exclusionary rule; the trying of thirteen-year-olds as adults for certain crimes; prohibiting Pell educational grants for prisoners; the implementation of the federal three strikes law; the refusal to equalize the crack/powder disparity; a hundred thousand new cops on the streets and the explosion in racial profiling that followed; and monetary incentives to states to enact truth-in-sentencing laws that spurred an astronomical rise in prison construction across the country, lengthening the amount of time served by an ever-growing national prison population, and solidifying a mentality of meanness.[5]

The prevailing narrative at the time—tough on crime—caused then candidate Bill Clinton to leave his presidential campaign trail to oversee the execution of a mentally challenged man in Arkansas.[6] It was the same narrative that brought about the crack/powder cocaine sentencing disparity. The narrative that supported the transfer of youth to adult courts and popularized the myth of the Black child as superpredator.

During the height of the war on drugs with the proliferation of mandatory minimum sentences, unnecessarily lengthy prison terms were robotically meted out with seemingly callous abandon. Shockingly severe punishments over the past forty years of ten, twenty, thirty years, and life imprisonment for drug offenses hardly raised an eyebrow.[7] Traumatizing sentences that snatched parents from children and loved ones and furthered the destabilization of families and communities were commonplace. Such punishments should offend our society's standard of decency. Why haven't they?

A Supreme Court case decided in 1991 ruled that mandatory life imprisonment for a first time drug offense was not cruel and unusual punishment.[8] I was flabbergasted; the rationale sounded so ludicrous. The Court held that although the punishment was cruel, it was not unusual. The twisted logic reminded me of another Supreme Court case decided a few years earlier, in 1987.[9] There, the Court allowed the execution of a man, despite overwhelming evidence of racial bias, because of fear that the floodgates would be opened to racial challenges in other parts of criminal sentencing as well. So, lengthy sentences are cruel, but they are usual. Systemic racism exists, but it is the norm.

The United States has the world's highest rate of incarceration rate, with almost two million people behind bars.[10] A primary driver of this shameful and destructive statistic is the disproportionate representation and unequal treatment Blacks face at each stage of the criminal punishment continuum—from racially discriminatory profiling and wealth-based bail discrimination to nondiverse juries and harshly severe sentencing laws. In many instances, laws today are facially neutral and do not intentionally discriminate. However, disparate treatment is often ingrained within the structural fabric of social institutions, allowing discrimination without the need of an overt act by a specific person. Today's racism, in many cases, is subtle and structurally embedded in many police departments, prosecutors' offices, and courtrooms. It is found in laws that look fair but nevertheless have a racially discriminatory impact.

An egregious example is the way the drug war has accelerated since the late 1980s. The combination of federal law enforcement, prosecutorial practices, and legislation resulted in Black people's being disproportionately arrested, convicted, and imprisoned using the gross disparity in penalty between crack and powder cocaine. People convicted of distributing five grams of crack cocaine, less than the equivalent of two packets of sugar, received a mandatory prison term of five years, but it took 500 grams of powder cocaine for the same sentence.[11] Although the U.S. Department of Health and Human Services' National Survey on Drug Use and Health has revealed larger numbers of documented white crack cocaine users, the overwhelming number of people sentenced came from Black communities and were disproportionately affected by the facially neutral, yet unreasonably harsh, crack penalties.[12]

The system of mass incarceration fueled by the war on drugs decimates not only individuals, families, and communities, but generations of Black people as well. It does not matter whether the subject is police brutality, unjust sentencing, or white supremacist terrorism, a double standard of justice appears enshrined within the fabric of America.

For the system to be just, the public must be confident that at every stage of the process—from the initial investigation of crimes by police to the prosecution or punishment of that crime—that people in like circumstances are treated the same. Today, however, as yesterday, the criminal legal system strays far from that ideal, causing African Americans to often question, is it justice or "just-us"?

This doubt was prevalent over two decades ago when 10 to 15 percent of the Black people of the little Texas town of Tulia in 1999 were arrested; most were convicted and imprisoned on drug trafficking charges.[13] Despite trials and pleas marred by serious due process violations, the convictions were based on the sole, uncorroborated testimony of a white narcotics officer with a racist background whose modus operandi was to record purported drug buys on his arms and legs.[14] The undercover officer was characterized by a judge as "the most devious, non-responsive law enforcement witness this court has witnessed in 25 years on the bench," resulting in the Tulia defendants' pardons in 2003. The shamed former deputy was part of a federally funded narcotics task force under which law enforcement officers and at least one prosecutor combined their efforts to fight the war on drugs.[15] Such drug task forces have been found to be a national disgrace, rife with scandal, corruption, perverse incentives, and racial disparities, with scant federal oversight. Indeed, the role that the federal government has played in financially incentivizing the astronomical rise of mass incarceration must be illuminated and rectified.[16]

For a while, it appeared as though the tough-on-crime chorus was fading away and a new narrative developing on the horizon. This manifested with the 2008 signing of the Second Chance Act.[17] The Fair Sentencing Act of 2010 also became law, reducing the disparity between crack and powder cocaine.[18] It was exhilarating to experience these winds of change. Indeed, the narrative on criminal justice appeared to be shifting and justice system change seemed not the lightning rod it was decades ago.

I smiled when the 2012 Supreme Court *Miller v. Alabama* ruling came out, because it held that mandatory life without parole sentences for children violated the Eighth Amendment's prohibition against cruel and unusual punishment.[19]

I was delighted when former Attorney General Holder announced his Smart on Crime policies, which focused federal prosecutions on large-scale drug traffickers rather than bit players.[20] I applauded President Obama's executive clemency initiative to provide relief for many serving inordinately lengthy mandatory minimum sentences.[21] I celebrated the Sentencing Reform and Corrections Act, a carefully negotiated bipartisan bill passed out of the Senate Judiciary Committee in 2015, despite its failure to become law, and I am glad that some of its provisions were incorporated as part of the 2018 First Step Act.[22] All these reforms would have been unthinkable when I first embarked on criminal legal system reform.

TOUGH-ON-CRIME REFORM BACKLASH

The budding new narrative fell quiet as violent crime sharply rose over the last several years, many law enforcement officials and policymakers arguing that criminal justice reform is to blame. The best available research, however, dictates otherwise. The Brennan Center's analysis, "Myths and Realities: Understanding Recent Trends in Violent Crime," illuminates this mistaken narrative about public safety, pointing out that violent crime has indeed risen since 2020, but in ways that defy politicized attempts to blame "blue" jurisdictions and reform policies.[23] The report documents other popular but mistaken narratives about public safety and explains why they are flawed. For example, although rising crime in New York has been attributed to bail reform, what we know thus far suggests that bail reform did not drive the increases in crime.[24] Even so, criminal justice reforms and reformers alike have faced extensive criticism.

Perhaps most notably, the recall of District Attorney Chesa Boudin in San Francisco was painted as a case of voters rejecting progressive prosecutors and criminal justice reform.[25] These claims go too far; others have argued instead that his recall speaks more to the "unique political structure" of San Francisco.[26] In addition, recent efforts to recall Los Angeles's district attorney, also a "progressive prosecutor," have failed, and in Tennessee and Vermont, reformist district attorneys continue to win elections.[27] Louisiana has weakened some of its previous (and altogether insufficient) decarceration efforts in response to recent crime spikes.[28] Additionally, New York's partial rollback of its bail reform laws demonstrates that legislators, even in blue states, are reacting to public fears that reform contributes to violent crime.[29]

Despite considerable backlash, some progressive legislation continues to advance, proof of the need and space for meaningful work to be done. For example, despite the 2010 reduction in penalty between crack and powder cocaine, the disparity was never abated. In 2021, the EQUAL Act, which would finally rectify the situation, passed the House of Representatives with an overwhelming majority of 361 to 66.[30] Despite receiving the endorsement of the Department of Justice and widespread bipartisan support from lawmakers and law enforcement, the act died in the Senate after a last-ditch effort to include it in a year-end omnibus bill.[31] It has since been reintroduced.[32]

Other innovative ideas have also begun to gain traction. In 2019, Senator Cory Booker and Representative Karen Bass (mayor of Los Angeles since December 2022) introduced the Second Look Act, a bill that would allow a defendant who has served at least ten years to petition a federal court for a sentence reduction provided they are not a danger to society, are ready for reentry, and the interests of justice warrant such reduction.[33] Although the bill did not advance, the District of Columbia has passed and expanded second look legislation, and other states are exploring the idea as well.[34]

Of course, major challenges also remain on the horizon. In 2018, the Trump administration issued an emergency order designating fentanyl analogs as Schedule I controlled substances, more broadly allowing prosecutors to charge people with federal drug crimes. Though this scheduling order is temporary, it has been extended multiple times.[35] This continues a pattern of enforcement-first responses to drug-related public health crises and exacerbates disparities in the criminal justice system; indeed, federal prosecutions involving fentanyl analogs have skyrocketed since fiscal year 2016.[36]

The First Step Act changed thousands of lives—roughly 4,200 people as of August 2022 benefited from a sentence reduction pursuant to the provision making the 2010 Fair Sentencing Act retroactive, and according to the Bureau of Prisons, the Act has led to grants of compassionate release in more than 4,500 other cases.[37]

Although we should have learned from the unintentional consequences resulting from failed attempts to ameliorate the crack epidemic of the 1980s, the Food and Drug Administration's proposed ban on menthol cigarettes also has the potential to harm the very communities it seeks to help. Advocates fear a ban on flavored cigarettes will encourage increased policing of Black people, given that a large majority of Black smokers prefer menthol cigarettes.[38] Thus, in addition to the harm policymakers feel they will be solving from banning flavored tobacco, these same communities could now be at increased risk from overzealous law enforcement practices.[39] Moreover, another consequence of such prohibition will likely be the growth of underground markets. At a time when the war on marijuana is winding down with the growing legalization of cannabis, the sentiment should not be to replace it with a war on tobacco—in essence, the criminalization of smoking. Although tobacco smoking has fueled a massive public health epidemic for decades, some people will always smoke tobacco, just as some people will always abuse or be addicted to drugs, alcohol, caffeine, or sugar. A public health approach relying on harm reduction is a more sensible path to addressing addiction than demanding and assuming that everyone will just say no.

We need to avoid the repetition of policies that may have been well intentioned, yet instead resulted in overcriminalization and racism. We have been down that slippery slope in the past, with disastrous consequences.

Black communities have experienced nearly four decades of misguided, knee-jerk policy decisions mandated as part of the flawed war on drugs. However, for a just and equitable society to survive and thrive, the racist policies and severe sentences the war on drugs has wrought need to end. We need to guard against new manifestations of injustice as progressive bills are introduced and passed. Indeed, this is not the time to be content with piecemeal reform and baby-step progress. This is the time for courageous bold change. Whether one's primary entry point to criminal legal system reform is stringent sentencing, overfederalization, racial discrimination, cost savings, or redemption, we should not be satisfied with the numbing norm, but instead work toward institutionalizing our shared demand of a standard of decency that values transformative change.

NOTES

1. Dan Baum, "Legalize It All: How to Win the War on Drugs," *Harper's Magazine*, April 2016, https://harpers.org/archive/2016/04/legalize-it-all.
2. Tom LoBianco, "Report: Aide Says Nixon's War on Drugs Targeted Blacks, Hippies," CNN, March 23, 2016, https://www.cnn.com/2016/03/23/politics/john-ehrlichman-richard-nixon-drug-war-blacks-hippie/index.html.
3. Comprehensive Crime Control Act of 1984, Pub. L. No. 98-473, 98 Stat. 1976 (1984), https://www.congress.gov/bill/98th-congress/senate-bill/1762; Anti-Drug Abuse Act of 1986, Pub. L. No. 99-570, 98 Stat. 3207 (1986), https://www.congress.gov/bill/99th-congress/house-bill/5484; Deborah J. Vagins and Jesselyn McCurdy, "Cracks in the System: Twenty Years of the Unjust Federal Crack Cocaine Law" (New York: American Civil Liberties Union, 2006), i, https://www.aclu.org/other/cracks-system-20-years-unjust-federal-crack-cocaine-law; Anti-Drug Abuse Act of 1988, Pub. L. No. 100-690, 102 Stat. 4181 (1988), https://www.congress.gov/bill/100th-congress/house-bill/5210.

4. Violent Crime Control and Law Enforcement Act of 1994, Pub. L. No. 103-322, 108 Stat. 1796 (1994), https://www.congress.gov/bill/103rd-congress/house-bill/3355/text.
5. Cornell Law School's Legal Information Institute (LII) describes habeas corpus as "Latin for 'that you have the body.' In the US system, federal courts can use the writ of habeas corpus to determine if a state's detention of a prisoner is valid." See https://www.law.cornell.edu/wex/habeas_corpus. According to LII, the exclusionary rule "prevents the government from using most evidence gathered in violation of the United States Constitution" (see https://www.law.cornell.edu/wex/exclusionary_rule).
6. Perry Bacon Jr., "In a First, Democrats' Platform to Call for Death Penalty Abolition," NBC News, July 10, 2016, https://www.nbcnews.com/meet-the-press/first-democrats-platform-call-death-penalty-abolition-n605946.
7. Jennifer Turner, *A Living Death: Life Without Parole for Nonviolent Offenses* (New York: American Civil Liberties Union, 2013), https://www.aclu.org/report/living-death-life-without-parole-nonviolent-offenses.
8. Harmelin v. Michigan, 501 U.S. 957 (1991).
9. McCleskey v. Kemp, 481 U.S. 279 (1987).
10. Wendy Sawyer and Peter Wagner, *Mass Incarceration: The Whole Pie 2022* (Northampton, MA: Prison Policy Initiative, 2022), https://www.prisonpolicy.org/reports/pie2022.html.
11. Vagins and McCurdy, *Cracks in the System*, i.
12. Vagins and McCurdy, *Cracks in the System*, i.
13. American Civil Liberties Union, "Racist Arrests in Tulia, Texas," June 30, 2003, https://www.aclu.org/other/racist-arrests-tulia-texas.
14. Dan Canon, "This Cop Framed One out of Every Ten Black People in a Texas Town," *Medium*, October 22, 2021, https://medium.com/i-taught-the-law/this-cop-framed-one-out-of-every-ten-black-people-in-a-texas-town-760f1e3d3b6f.
15. Adam Liptak, "$5 Million Settlement Ends Case of Tainted Texas Sting," *New York Times*, March 11, 2004, https://www.nytimes.com/2004/03/11/us/5-million-settlement-ends-case-of-tainted-texas-sting.html.
16. Brennan Center for Justice, "Changing Incentives," accessed November 18, 2022, https://www.brennancenter.org/issues/end-mass-incarceration/changing-incentives.
17. The White House, "Fact Sheet: President Bush Signs Second Chance Act of 2007," April 9, 2008, https://georgewbush-whitehouse.archives.gov/news/releases/2008/04/20080409-15.html.
18. Fair Sentencing Act of 2010, Pub. L. No. 111-220, 124 Stat. 2372 (2010), https://www.congress.gov/111/plaws/publ220/PLAW-111publ220.pdf.

19. Equal Justice Initiative, "U.S. Supreme Court Bans Mandatory Life-Without-Parole Sentences for Children Convicted of Homicide," June 25, 2012, https://eji.org/news/supreme-court-bans-mandatory-life-without-parole-sentences-for-children-miller-v-alabama.
20. U.S. Department of Justice, "The Attorney General's Smart on Crime Initiative," updated March 9, 2017, https://www.justice.gov/archives/ag/attorney-generals-smart-crime-initiative.
21. U.S. Department of Justice, "Obama Administration Clemency Initiative," updated January 12, 2021, https://www.justice.gov/archives/pardon/obama-administration-clemency-initiative.
22. First Step Act of 2018, Pub. L. 115-391, 132 Stat. 5194 (2018), https://www.congress.gov/115/plaws/publ391/PLAW-115publ391.pdf.
23. Ames Grawert and Noah Kim, "Myths and Realities: Understanding Recent Trends in Violent Crime" (New York: Brennan Center for Justice, July 12, 2022), https://www.brennancenter.org/our-work/research-reports/myths-and-realities-understanding-recent-trends-violent-crime.
24. Ames Grawert and Noah Kim, "The Facts on Bail Reform and Crime Rates in New York State" (New York: Brennan Center for Justice, March 22, 2022), https://www.brennancenter.org/our-work/research-reports/facts-bail-reform-and-crime-rates-new-york-state.
25. Ross Barkan, "The Backlash Has Begun," *New York Magazine*, June 8, 2022, https://nymag.com/intelligencer/2022/06/chesa-boudin-recall-is-the-beginning-of-a-backlash.html.
26. Joshua Davis, "Why San Francisco's District Attorney Recall Vote Isn't What It Seems," *Washington Post*, June 6, 2022, https://www.washingtonpost.com/opinions/2022/06/06/chesa-boudin-san-francisco-recall.
27. Sam Levin, "Bid to Recall Los Angeles District Attorney Fails, a Win for Criminal Justice Reform," *The Guardian*, August 15, 2022, https://www.theguardian.com/us-news/2022/aug/15/los-angeles-district-attorney-george-gascon-recall; Adrienne Johnson Martin, Brittany Brown and Jacob Steimer, "Steve Mulroy Blows Out Weirich; Tarik Sugarmon Wins as Well," MLK50, August 5, 2022, https://mlk50.com/2022/08/05/steve-mulroy-blows-out-weirich-tarik-sugarmon-wins-as-well; Colin Flanders, "Chittenden State's Attorney Sarah George Fends Off Primary Challenge," *Seven Days*, September 6, 2022, https://www.sevendaysvt.com/vermont/chittenden-states-attorney-sarah-george-fends-off-primary-challenge/Content?oid=36202720.
28. Mark Ballard, "Amid Crime Spike, Are Louisiana Criminal Justice Bills 'Rollbacks' or 'Needed Tweaks?,'" *The Advocate*, June 14, 2022, https://www.theadvocate.com/baton_rouge/news/politics/legislature/article_32809c38-ec2a-11ec-973b-2ff96ef173f4.html.

29. Joseph Spector and Anna Gronewold, "New York Democrats Pare Back Nation-Leading Bail Reform Amid Crime Wave," *Politico*, April 11, 2022, https://www.politico.com/news/2022/04/11/new-york-democrats-pare-back-nation-leading-bail-reform-amid-crime-spikes-and-election-fights-00024361.
30. Sarah N. Lynch, "U.S. House Passes Bill to End Disparities in Crack Cocaine Sentences," Reuters, September 28, 2021, https://www reuters.com/world/us/us-house-passes-bill-end-disparities-crack-cocaine-sentences-2021-09-28.
31. Lynch, "U.S. House Passes Bill"; Justice Action Network, "Senate Failure to Include EQUAL Act in Omnibus Bill Will Have Tragic Consequences," December 20, 2022, https://www.justiceactionnetwork.org/news/newsnbspsenate-failure-to-include-equal-act-in-omnibus-bill-will-have-tragic-consequencesnbspnbsp.
32. EQUAL Act, S. 524, 118th Cong. (2023), https://www.congress.gov/bill/118th-congress/senate-bill/524.
33. Cory Booker, "Booker, Bass to Introduce Groundbreaking Bill to Give 'Second Look' to Those Behind Bars," U.S. Senator Cory Booker, July 15, 2019, https://www.booker.senate.gov/news/press/booker-bass-to-introduce-groundbreaking-bill-to-give-and-ldquosecond-look-and-rdquo-to-those-behind-bars.
34. FAMM Foundation, "Second Look Sentencing Explained," accessed August 10, 2023, https://famm.org/secondlook.
35. Renuka Rayasam, "'This Is Crack 2.0,'" *Politico*, March 13, 2022, https://www.politico.com/news/magazine/2022/03/13/fentanyl-analogues-drug-war-00016805.
36. Human Rights Watch, "Groups Urge US to End Emergency Scheduling of Fentanyl-Related Substances," April 8, 2021, https://www.hrw.org/news/2021/04/08/groups-urge-us-end-emergency-scheduling-fentanyl-related-substances; Kristin M. Tennyson, Charles S. Ray, and Kevin T. Maass, *Fentanyl and Fentanyl Analogues: Federal Trends and Trafficking Patterns* (Washington, DC: U.S. Sentencing Commission, 2021), 2, https://www.ussc.gov/sites/default/files/pdf/research-and-publications/research-publications/2021/20210125_Fentanyl-Report.pdf.
37. U.S. Sentencing Commission, "First Step Act of 2018 Resentencing Provisions Retroactivity Data Report," August 2022, table 1, https://www.ussc.gov/sites/default/files/pdf/research-and-publications/retroactivity-analyses/first-step-act/20220818-First-Step-Act-Retro.pdf; Federal Bureau of Prisons, "First Step Act," accessed June 1, 2023, https://www.bop.gov/inmates/fsa.
38. U.S. Food & Drug Administration, "FDA Proposes Rules Prohibiting Menthol Cigarettes and Flavored Cigars to Prevent Youth Initiation, Significantly Reduce Tobacco-Related Disease and Death," Press release, March 19, 2015, https://www.fda.gov/news-events/press-announcements/fda-proposes-rules

-prohibiting-menthol-cigarettes-and-flavored-cigars-prevent-youth-initiation; Jacob Sullum, "The FDA's Menthol Cigarette Ban Is a 'Racial Justice' Issue, but Not in the Way Its Supporters Mean," *Reason*, April 28, 2022, https://reason.com/2022/04/28/the-fdas-menthol-cigarette-ban-is-a-racial-justice-issue-but-not-in-the-way-its-supporters-mean; Christopher Rhodes, "Ben Crump Warns of Racial Bias in Proposed Menthol Cigarette Ban," *Blavity*, April 25, 2022, https://blavity.com/ben-crump-warns-of-racial-bias-in-proposed-menthol-cigarette-ban; Cristine D. Delnevo, Ollie Ganz, and Renee D. Goodwin, "Banning Menthol Cigarettes: A Social Justice Issue Long Overdue," *Nicotine & Tobacco Research* 22, no. 10 (2020): 1673–75, https://www.ncbi.nlm.nih.gov/pmc/articles/PMC7542641.

39. Ayanna Alexander, "Black Cops Fear Menthol Ban Will Bring Heavy Police Crackdown," *Bloomberg Law*, April 30, 2021, https://news.bloomberglaw.com/social-justice/black-cops-fear-menthol-ban-will-bring-heavy-police-crackdown.

PART FIVE

UNCOVERING LIFE BEHIND PRISON WALLS

16

HOW ATROCIOUS PRISON CONDITIONS MAKE US ALL LESS SAFE

Shon Hopwood

IMAGINE ONE OF THOSE DYSTOPIAN MOVIES in which some character inhabits a world marked by dehumanization and a continual state of fear, neglect, and physical violence—*The Hunger Games*, for instance, or *Mad Max: Fury Road*. Now imagine that the people living in those worlds return to ours to become your neighbors. After such brutal traumatization, is it any wonder that they might struggle to obtain stable housing or employment, manage mental illness, deal with conflict, or become a better spouse or parent?

This is no fantasy world. American prisons cage millions of human beings in conditions similar to those movies. Of the more than 1.2 million people incarcerated in American prisons, more than 95 percent will be released back into the community at some point.[1] Given those numbers, we should ensure that those in our prisons come home better off, not worse—for their sake, but for society's as well.

Yet U.S. prisons fail miserably at preparing people for a law-abiding and successful life after release. A long-term study of recidivism rates of people released from state prisons from 2005 to 2014 found that 68 percent were arrested within three years of their release and 83 percent within nine years.[2] Evidence confirms the great irony of the American criminal justice system: long periods of incarceration do not appear to have any effect on whether someone is rearrested, but do make people less employable after their release, increasing the likelihood that they will have to resort to criminalized behaviors for survival.[3] The data tell us that people are spending more time in prisons and the longest prison terms just keep getting longer, and thus the U.S. system of mass incarceration all but ensures high rates of recidivism.[4]

It is not difficult to understand why U.S. prisons largely fail at preparing people to return to society successfully. American prisons are dangerous.

Most are understaffed and overpopulated. Today, a major problem is a critical staffing shortage. To recruit new corrections staff, numerous states are not only raising salaries but also reducing the minimum age to apply for these roles to eighteen and offering one-time hiring bonuses.[5] Because of inadequate supervision, people in our prisons are exposed to incredible amounts of violence, including sexual violence. In 2019, the Civil Rights Division of the U.S. Department of Justice concluded that Alabama's prison system failed to protect prisoners from astounding levels of homicide and rape.[6] A single week in 2017 tallied four stabbings (one of which was fatal), three sexual assaults, several beatings, and one person's bed set on fire as he slept.[7] In 2022, the Civil Rights Division found that conditions at the Mississippi State Penitentiary—the state's oldest prison, known as Parchman—violate the Eighth and Fourteenth Amendments to the U.S. Constitution.[8] The investigation revealed that "violence against incarcerated persons runs rampant" at the facility and found that a stabbing occurred at a time when one correctional officer was assigned to watch 180 incarcerated people.[9] Three hours later, an incarcerated person at the prison was able to alert that correctional officer, but the stabbing victim (who was incarcerated and stabbed by another incarcerated person) was already dead. These are just two of thousands of examples of inhumane conditions in American prisons that violate the U.S. Constitution.

Prisons are so violent that they meaningfully affect the rehabilitation efforts for those inside them. The fear of violence is ever present in these gladiator-style prisons, where people have no protection from it. Incarcerated people who frequently witness violence and feel helpless to protect against it can experience posttraumatic stress symptoms—such as anxiety, depression, paranoia, and difficulty with emotional regulation—that last years after their release from custody.[10] Because escalating conflict is the norm for those serving time (often provoking violence as a self-defense mechanism), when they face conflict after being released, they are ill equipped to handle it in a productive way. If the number of people affected by prison violence were small, this situation would still be unjust and inhumane. But when more than 113 million adults in the United States have had a close family member in jail or prison, the social costs can be cataclysmic.[11]

Part of the reason U.S. prisons are so violent is the idleness that occurs in them. As prison systems expanded over the last four decades, many states rejected the role of rehabilitation and reduced the number of available rehabilitation and educational programs.[12] Florida, the nation's third largest prison system, has virtually no education programs for prisoners, even though research shows that those programs reduce violence in prison and the recidivism rate for those released from prison.[13] In Montana, the largest prison in the state reported a 2022 waiting list of seven hundred incarcerated people for a substance use disorder program that could only handle one hundred participants a year.[14] In the federal Bureau of Prisons, the waiting list for the agency's literacy program includes sixteen thousand people.[15]

It is not just the violence that is harmful. How American prisons are designed negatively affects the ability of people to be self-reliant after their release. Prisons create social isolation by taking people from their communities and placing them behind razor wire, in locked cages. Through strict authoritarianism, rules, and control, prisons lessen personal autonomy and increase institutional dependence. This ensures that people learn to rely on the free room and board and daily structure only a prison can offer, rendering them less able to cope with economic and social demands on release unless they have transitional support.[16]

The location of prisons also causes harm. Many prisons are located far away from cities and hundreds of miles from prisoners' families.[17] Consequently, family relationships deteriorate, affecting both prisoners and their loved ones.[18] Approximately 2.7 million children in America have a parent who is currently in prison or jail; more than five million have had a parent in prison or jail at some point in their lives.[19] In fact, the United States has the second highest rate of incarcerating women across the globe; only Thailand has a higher rate.[20] On Mother's Day, more than 150,000 imprisoned mothers can typically spend the day apart from their children.[21] Because children with an incarcerated parent run greater risks of health and psychological problems, lower economic well-being, and decreased educational attainment, the aggravating effect of imprisonment far from family is obvious.[22]

The ill-considered location of prisons also increases the likelihood of inadequate attention paid to people with serious mental issues, who are widely present in U.S. prisons. In fact, 37 percent of those incarcerated report a history of mental illness, a rate twice that among the overall adult population.[23] Prisons in remote and rural areas fail to hire and retain mental health professionals, and, given the lack of such resources, misdiagnosis of serious mental health issues is more likely.[24] Further, as Homer Venters writes in his essay in this book (see chapter 21), a "lack of oversight and interest among our national and state health bodies has reinforced the horrible reality that harming health is part of the punishment of incarceration." Not only is the treatment of such prisoners inadequate, but false negative determinations can also make it more difficult for them to receive disability benefits or treatment once released.

Prisons tend to rinse away the parts that make us human. They continue to use solitary confinement as a mechanism for dealing with idleness and misconduct, despite studies showing that it creates or exacerbates mental illness.[25] U.S. prisons also foster an environment that values dehumanization and cruelty. At the federal prison in which I served for more than a decade, I watched correctional officers handcuff and then kick a friend of mine who had a softball-sized hernia protruding from his stomach. Because he was asking for medical attention, they treated him like a dog. There was little empathy in that place. And for more than ten years of my life, when those in authority addressed me, it was with the label *inmate*. The message every day, both explicitly and implicitly, was that I was unworthy of respect and dignity. Such an environment leads people to have a diminished sense of self-worth and personal value, affecting a person's ability to empathize with others.[26] The ability to empathize is a vital step toward rehabilitation, and when prisons fail to rehabilitate, public safety ultimately suffers.

In sum, if you were to design a system to perpetuate intergenerational cycles of violence and imprisonment in communities already overburdened by criminal justice involvement, then the American prison system is what you would create. It routinely and persistently fails to produce the fair and just outcomes that will make us all safer.

What can be done? One of the reasons U.S. prison systems are so immune to change is because the worst of prison abuses occur behind closed doors, away from public view.[27] As Michele Deitch's essay in this series details (see chapter 22), few prison systems have the independent oversight and transparency needed to ensure that they implement the best policies or comply with constitutional protections such as the Eighth Amendment prohibition on cruel and unusual punishment.[28]

There is no reason why U.S. prisons should not be modeled on the principle of human dignity, which respects the worth of every human being.[29] If you translated that into policy, it would mean that people in prison would both be protected from physical, sexual, and emotional abuse and be provided with adequate mental health and medical treatment. It would mean that prison systems would foster interpersonal relationships by placing people in facilities close to their loved ones and allowing ample in-person, phone, and video visitation. It would mean providing training on how to become better citizens, spouses, and parents. It would mean offering educational and vocational programs designed to provide job skills for reentry, and behavioral programs designed to create empathy and autonomy, thereby preparing former prisoners to lead law-abiding and successful lives.

NOTES

1. Jacob Kang-Brown, Chase Montagnet, and Jasmine Heiss, "People in Jail and Prison in Spring 2021" (New York: Vera Institute of Justice, 2021), 1, https://www.vera.org/downloads/publications/people-in-jail-and-prison-in-spring-2021.pdf; Nathan James, *Offender Reentry: Correctional Statistics, Reintegration into the Community, and Recidivism*, CRS report no. RL34287 (Washington, DC: Congressional Research Service, 2015), 1, https://sgp.fas.org/crs/misc/RL34287.pdf.
2. Mariel Alper, Matthew R. Durose, and Joshua Markman, *2018 Update on Prisoner Recidivism: A 9-Year Follow-up Period (2005–2014)*, NCJ 250975 (Washington, DC: Bureau of Justice Statistics, 2018), 1, https://bjs.ojp.gov/content/pub/pdf/18upr9yfup0514.pdf.
3. Michael Mueller-Smith, "The Criminal and Labor Market Impacts of Incarceration" (working paper, University of Michigan, August 18, 2015), https://sites.lsa.umich.edu/mgms/wp-content/uploads/sites/283/2015/09/incar.pdf. For the relation between incarceration and recidivism, see Pew Charitable Trusts, "Prison Time Served and Recidivism," October 8, 2013, https://www.pewtrusts.org/en/research-and-analysis/fact-sheets/2013/10/08/prison-time-served-and-recidivism; Elizabeth Berger and Kent S. Scheidegger, "Sentence Length and Recidivism: A Review of the Research" (working paper, Criminal Justice Legal Foundation, May 2021), https://www.cjlf.org/publications/papers/SentenceRecidivism.pdf.
4. Urban Institute, "Trends: The Hidden Story of Rising Time Served," 2017, accessed December 9, 2022, https://apps.urban.org/features/long-prison-terms/trends.html.
5. David Montgomery, "Prison Staff Shortages Take Toll on Guards, Incarcerated People," *Stateline* (Pew Charitable Trusts blog), September 26, 2022, https://www.pewtrusts.org/en/research-and-analysis/blogs/stateline/2022/09/26/prison-staff-shortages-take-toll-on-guards-incarcerated-people.
6. Civil Rights Division, *Investigation of Alabama's State Prisons for Men* (Washington, U.S. Department of Justice, 2019), 1, https://www.splcenter.org/sites/default/files/documents/doj_investigation_of_alabama_state_prisons_for_men.pdf.

7. Katie Benner and Shaila Dewan, "Alabama's Gruesome Prisons: Report Finds Rape and Murder at All Hours," *New York Times*, April 3, 2019, https://www.nytimes.com/2019/04/03/us/alabama-prisons-doj-investigation.html.
8. U.S. Department of Justice, Office of Public Affairs, "Justice Department Finds Conditions at Mississippi State Penitentiary Violate the Constitution," Press release, April 20, 2022, https://www.justice.gov/opa/pr/justice-department-finds-conditions-mississippi-state-penitentiary-violate-constitution.
9. Civil Rights Division, *Investigation of the Mississippi State Penitentiary (Parchman)*, Press release (Washington: U.S. Department of Justice, 2022), 7–8, https://www.justice.gov/opa/press-release/file/1495796/download.
10. Meghan A. Novisky and Robert L. Peralta, "Gladiator School: Returning Citizens' Experiences with Secondary Violence Exposure in Prison," *Victims & Offenders* 15, no. 5 (2020): 594–618, https://www.researchgate.net/publication/339118610_Gladiator_School_Returning_Citizens'_Experiences_with_Secondary_Violence_Exposure_in_Prison.
11. Brian Elderbroom, Laura Bennett, Shanna Gong, Felicity Rose, and Zoë Towns, *Every Second: The Impact of the Incarceration Crisis on America's Families*, (Washington, DC: FWD.us, 2018), 13, https://everysecond.fwd.us/downloads/everysecond.fwd.us.pdf.
12. Julilly Kohler-Hausmann, *Getting Tough: Welfare and Imprisonment in 1970s America* (Princeton, NJ: Princeton University Press, 2017), 19–23. Also see Arit John, "A Timeline of the Rise and Fall of 'Tough on Crime' Drug Sentencing," *The Atlantic*, April 22, 2014, https://www.theatlantic.com/politics/archive/2014/04/a-timeline-of-the-rise-and-fall-of-tough-on-crime-drug-sentencing/360983.
13. Ryan McKinnon and Josh Salman, "Wasted Minds," *USA Today*, July 10, 2019, https://stories.usatodaynetwork.com/wastedminds; Amanda Pompoco, John Wooldredge, Melissa Lugo, Carrie Sullivan, and Edward J. Latessa, "Reducing Inmate Misconduct and Prison Returns with Facility Education Programs," *Criminology & Public Policy* 16, no. 2 (2017): 515–47, https://doi.org/10.1111/1745-9133.12290; Emily Mooney and Shon Hopwood, "Reinstate Pell Grants for Prisoners," *National Review*, June 10, 2019, https://www.nationalreview.com/2019/06/reinstate-pell-grants-prisoners-step-right-direction.
14. Seaborn Larson, "700 Inmates on Waiting List for Treatment at State Prison," *Independent Record*, January 18, 2022, https://helenair.com/news/state-and-regional/govt-and-politics/700-inmates-on-waiting-list-for-treatment-at-state-prison/article_f2680272-eb18-57e1-a42c-dff7985dac0c.html.
15. Federal Prison System, *FY 2019 Performance Budget Congressional Submission: Salaries and Expenses* (Washington, DC: U.S. Department of Justice, updated 2022), 27, https://www.justice.gov/jmd/page/file/1034421/download.

16. Pamela Valera, Laura Brotzman, Woodrow Wilson, and Andrea Reid, "'It's Hard to Reenter When You've Been Locked Out': Keys to Offender Reintegration," *Journal of Offender Rehabilitation* 56, no. 6 (2017): 412–31, https://doi.org/10.1080/10509674.2017.1339159.
17. Beatrix Lockwood and Nicole Lewis, "The Long Journey to Visit a Family Member in Prison" (Washington, DC: The Marshall Project, December 18, 2019), https://www.themarshallproject.org/2019/12/18/the-long-journey-to-visit-a-family-member-in-prison.
18. Meghan Mitchell, Kallee McCullough, Di Jia, and Xa Zhang, "The Effect of Prison Visitation on Reentry Success: A Meta-Analysis," *Journal of Criminal Justice* 47 (2016): 74–83, https://doi.org/10.1016/j.crimjus.2016.07.006.
19. Lindsey Cramer, Margaret Goff, Bryce Peterson, and Heather Sandstrom, *Parent-Child Visiting Practices in Prisons and Jails* (Washington, DC: Urban Institute, 2017), 1, https://www.urban.org/sites/default/files/publication/89601/parent-child_visiting_practices_in_prisons_and_jails_0.pdf.
20. Susan Hatters Friedman, Aimee Kaempf, and Sarah Kauffman, "The Realities of Pregnancy and Mothering While Incarcerated," *Journal of the American Academy of Psychiatry and the Law* 48, no. 3 (2020): 1, https://jaapl.org/content/jaapl/early/2020/05/13/JAAPL.003924-20.full.pdf.
21. Wendy Sawyer and Wanda Bertram, "Prisons and Jails Will Separate Millions of Mothers from Their Children in 2022" (Northhampton, MA: Prison Policy Initiative, May 4, 2022), https://www.prisonpolicy.org/blog/2022/05/04/mothers_day/.
22. Eric Martin, "Hidden Consequences: The Impact of Incarceration on Dependent Children," *NCJ Journal* 278 (March 2017), 3, https://nij.ojp.gov/topics/articles/hidden-consequences-impact-incarceration-dependent-children.
23. National Alliance on Mental Illness, "Mental Health Treatment While Incarcerated," accessed December 9, 2022, https://www.nami.org/Advocacy/Policy-Priorities/Improving-Health/Mental-Health-Treatment-While-Incarcerated.
24. Christie Thompson and Taylor Elizabeth Eldridge, "Treatment Denied: The Mental Health Crisis in Federal Prisons" (Washington, DC: The Marshall Project, November 21, 2018), https://www.themarshallproject.org/2018/11/21/treatment-denied-the-mental-health-crisis-in-federal-prisons.
25. Peter Scharff Smith, "The Effects of Solitary Confinement on Prison Inmates: A Brief History and Review of the Literature," *Crime and Justice* 34, no. 1 (2006): 441–528,
26. Craig Haney, "The Psychological Impact of Incarceration: Implications for Post-Prison Adjustment" (paper presented at From Prison to Home, conference of the U.S. Department of Health and Human Services, January 30–31, 2002), 10, https://aspe.hhs.gov/sites/default/files/migrated_legacy_files//42351/Haney.pdf.

27. Michele Deitch, "Independent Oversight Is Essential for a Safe and Healthy Prison System" (New York: Brennan Center for Justice, November 3, 2021), https://www.brennancenter.org/our-work/analysis-opinion/independent-oversight-essential-safe-and-healthy-prison-system.
28. Kevin Ring, "Congress should support independent oversight of federal prisons," *The Hill*, September 14, 2020, https://thehill.com/opinion/criminal-justice/515854-congress-should-support-independent-oversight-of-federal-prisons; Families for Justice Reform, "The Need For Independent Oversight of Prisons" (Washington, DC: FAMM, 2020), 1–2, https://famm.org/wp-content/uploads/FAMM-Prison-Oversight-Principles.pdf; Farmer v. Brennan, 511 U.S. 825 (1994).
29. Cinnamon Janzer, "North Dakota Reforms its Prisons, Norwegian Style," *U.S. News & World Report*, February 22, 2019, https://www.usnews.com/news/best-states/articles/2019-02-22/inspired-by-norways-approach-north-dakota-reforms-its-prisons; Ram Subramanian, "How Some European Prisons Are Based on Dignity Instead of Dehumanization" (New York: Brennan Center for Justice, November 29, 2021), https://www.brennancenter.org/our-work/analysis-opinion/how-some-european-prisons-are-based-dignity-instead-dehumanization.

17

WHAT DID YOU CALL ME?

Rahsaan "New York" Thomas

IT ALL STARTS WITH A LABEL. Nazi Germany, Rwanda, and American slavery all hold that in common. In each case, targeted groups were assigned names that had the psychological effect of dehumanizing. Once you're not seen as a human, you don't see yourself as human—and inhuman treatment begins that could cause your end.

Mass incarceration started with labels too. The n-word accompanied the Black Code laws that returned freed slaves to plantations to work the fields, unpaid (under convict leasing schemes) for minor, often made-up offenses such as vagrancy or not signing a labor contract with a white plantation owner.[1] Under President Richard Nixon, when it had become politically inconvenient to call Black people the n-word, they called us *criminals* and proceeded to build prisons focused on punishment rather than rehabilitation to discipline behavior born of oppression and intergenerational trauma rather than offering reparations or healing. The tag *superpredators* launched the locking up of kids, sentencing teenagers to multiple life terms, then housing them in adult institutions. One label ran alongside all the others and helped balloon the prison population in the United States to more than 2.3 million. That term is *inmate.*

Webster's defines *inmate* as "a person confined with others in a prison or mental institution." But calling a person an inmate doesn't describe where you are, it says *who* you are. It identifies you as your incarceration, as an outcast. You are "Other," as Peggy McGarry notes in her essay (see chapter 29).

Not all labels are harmful, of course. Calling someone a student or a mother brings up positive images and reactions. Not so the word *inmate.*

With more than twenty years in prison and counting, I hear correctional officers use the word constantly with an inflection in their voice that sounds like they're talking about someone less than human. I remember a correctional officer giving a new officer a tour of the media center at San Quentin. "This is where the inmates record the *Ear Hustle* podcast," he said, meaning to express pride in what we did—but because of his use of the word *inmate*, what I heard in my mind was "This is where the monkeys we trained record *Ear Hustle*."

Correction officers are trained not to see us as human; it helps them do their jobs. They are trained to be able to pepper spray or even shoot us without warning if it appears necessary. It helps them maintain that "professional" distance by seeing us as different from them, less than them, as *inmates*.

I think society must see people in jails and prisons as less than human as well. Even some social justice advocates and news reporters use the word *inmate* without regard for the damage it causes. I've seen incarcerated people internalize that word, lose touch with their personhood, and do nothing with their prison time but mop floors.

If you think that word is harmless, close your eyes and tell me what image comes to mind when you hear the word *inmate*.

Language is obviously important. Why do newspapers and even the California prison system respect the pronouns and language of the LGBTQ community? Why did news reporters stop calling undocumented immigrants *illegals*?

As Emile DeWeaver pointed out in his article "Moving the Needle on Black Liberation,"[2] mass incarceration harms more Black people than police shootings. In 2017,[3] the police killed 223 Black people but nearly three-quarters of a million were imprisoned.[4] People fight for their lives "Monday through Friday . . . in the courtroom around the country," raps Plies in his hit "100 Years." Yet as I watch my fifteen-inch flat screen TV from the top bunk of a six by nine cell, I don't see armies of protesters marching against the much larger problem of mass incarceration.

I believe we allowed mass incarceration to happen right in front of our faces because we lost sight of the fact that prisons contain people. We lost sight of the inhumanity of putting a sixteen-year-old in an adult maximum-security prison or sentencing a burglar to sixty-six years to life. We didn't care about *inmates* because we forgot they're human beings.

Calling someone housed in a correction facility *a person in prison* or an *incarcerated person* is very different from calling him or her an *inmate*. If we use *person* as the noun and *incarcerated* as the adjective, we keep their humanity front and center.

We are people despite our mistakes. I've been in hundreds of prison self-help group sessions and heard the backstories of hundreds of men incarcerated for violent crimes. They all eventually took accountability for the harm they caused. Remorse drives many of them to help stop cycles of further violence. From hearing their backstories and studying behavioral science, I see their humanity and that they often committed crimes for really human reasons. When we call any of them *inmate*, we disconnect from the person, and we don't take accountability for our role in failing them before they made the decision that failed us.

Consider my own circumstances. Growing up, I was a nerd who attended Catholic schools from first grade through eleventh. I played video games on a Commodore 64 computer, rode a skateboard, collected Marvel comic books, watched *Star Trek*, and played Dungeons & Dragons just like the guys in *The Big Bang Theory* and *Stranger Things*.

However, I grew up in New York City's murder capital—Brownsville, Brooklyn. Being an awkward extra-light-skinned kid was hell. I faced bullying daily. When bullied, when robbed, when beat up, I had three choices: endure physical harm, call the cops and face ridicule from the police and ostracism from my peers, or fight back. I chose to become pugnacious toward the oppression. Although I have always hated violence, I hated feeling helpless and being bullied even more. So I fought my neighbor—for acceptance, for respect, and to be left alone.

Things accelerated when I was seventeen. A sixteen-year-old with a gun tried to rob me and my little brother. I refused to give up my gold ring; I ran; my little brother was shot. After that day I started carrying a gun and using it when faced with similar circumstances. Fast-forward to age twenty-nine, when two armed men were robbing my friend right before my eyes. I opened fire, killing one and wounding the other.

Today I realize that my real enemies weren't my neighbors or the police. The real enemies were post–Jim Crow segregation accomplished through redlining, employment discrimination, policing policies rooted in maintaining white supremacy, gun show loopholes, addressing criminal behavior and addiction through violence, the lack of emotional intelligence education in the school-to-prison pipeline, felony disenfranchisement, and untreated trauma.

My growth took place in prison. However, it wasn't by design. I started my time in a maximum-security facility wanting help, but all they had was Narcotics Anonymous, Jesus, Buddha, and Mohammed. It took thirteen years for me to reach San Quentin and get real help, real opportunities, and only by God's grace did I make it here.

I owe San Quentin for being a unique correctional facility that offers rare opportunities. In my nine years here, I've accomplished so much, including graduating from college, becoming a Pulitzer Prize finalist with the *Ear Hustle* podcast team, effectively counseling kids through the SQUIRES program, creating the Empowerment Avenue program (which supports incarcerated artists and writers), completing ten self-help groups, directing a film called *Friendly Signs* and submitting it to film festivals, and so much more. Had I thought of myself only as someone in a correctional facility, I would not have so many accomplishments in conjunction with community members that transcend the prison walls.

Seeing myself as part of society rather than part of a prison has garnered community support that governors are recognizing.

On January 13, 2022, California governor Gavin Newsom commuted my fifty-five-to-life sentence and sent me before a parole board.[5] On August 21, 2022, the Board of Parole Hearings found me suitable for release—to walk out of the long-dark tunnel of incarceration into the light of freedom in February 2023.

New York Governor Kathy Hochul sees the importance of language. In August of 2022, she signed into law a bill that replaces the word *inmate* with *incarcerated person* when referring to people serving prison time.[6]

Still some people call me an *inmate*. Good thing I know I'm not, or I would have wasted these last twenty-two years just mopping floors and getting face tattoos.

NOTES

1. V. Camille Westmont, "Dark Heritage in the New South: Remembering Convict Leasing in Southern Middle Tennessee Through Community Archaeology," *International Journal of Historical Archaeology* 26, no. 1 (2022): 1–21, https://www.ncbi.nlm.nih.gov/pmc/articles/PMC7884100.
2. Emile DeWeaver, "Moving the Needle on Black Liberation," *Truthout*, July 9, 2017, https://truthout.org/articles/moving-the-needle-on-black-liberation.
3. NAACP, "Criminal Justice Fact Sheet," accessed November 1, 2022, https://naacp.org/resources/criminal-justice-fact-sheet.
4. According to the U.S. Department of Justice, 475,900 Black people were in state and federal prisons at the end of 2017 and 250,100 were in jails nationwide as of

midyear 2017. See Jennifer Bronson and E. Ann Carson, *Prisoners in 2017*, NCJ 252156 (Washington, DC: Bureau of Justice Statistics, 2019), 17, table 8, https://bjs.ojp.gov/content/pub/pdf/p17.pdf; Zhen Zeng, *Jail Inmates in 2017*, NCJ 251774 (Washington, DC: Bureau of Justice Statistics, 2019), 5, table 3, https://bjs.ojp.gov/content/pub/pdf/ji17.pdf.

5. Hayley Smith, "Newsom Grants Clemency to San Quentin Inmate, Podcast Host Rahsaan Thomas," *Los Angeles Times*, January 14, 2022, https://www.latimes.com/california/story/2022-01-14/newsom-grants-clemency-to-san-quentin-inmate-and-podcast-host.
6. Governor Kathy Hochul, "Governor Hochul Signs Legislative Package to Promote Greater Fairness and Restore Dignity for Justice-Involved Individuals," New York State, August 8, 2022, https://www.governor.ny.gov/news/governor-hochul-signs-legislative-package-promote-greater-fairness-and-restore-dignity-justice.

18

THE INHUMANITY OF SOLITARY CONFINEMENT

Christopher Blackwell

"LET'S GO, YOU KNOW THE DRILL," the impatient guard yells at me. Fighting the urge to scream "FUCK OFF!" at him at the top of my lungs through the thick door, I obey the demeaning command. I honestly have no choice. Fighting the situation would only make it worse. There is nothing more inhumane than having to strip down in front of another human, especially when they are demanding that you do so in an aggressive tone. No matter how many years I've been in prison or how many times I've been forced to participate in this barbaric practice, which is far more times than I can count, it never gets easier.

I strip all the way down until I have nothing on at all. My naked feet touch the cold, filthy, concrete floor. I can feel the dirt, grime, and who knows what else on the soles of my feet. I'm sure the floor hasn't been cleaned in weeks, and I cringe at the thought. I feel powerless, weak, and angry. I know I had no choice but to follow the correctional officer's directive, but I hate myself for doing it.

Once I'm fully nude, the guard's invasive eyes look me up and down. It takes everything I have to hold my head up high, but I do. In this moment, I must retain something—my dignity, or humanity, at least what's left of it.

One of the guards starts barking commands; stripping down is only the initial part of the degrading process. "Run your hands through your hair. Shake it out." He moves his head back and forth intensively looking through my hair as if a weapon will fall from hiding behind a lock of hair at any moment. "Bend your ears back, let me see behind, open your mouth. Run your fingers through your gum lines. Now lift your arms. Now your nuts. Turn around and bend over. Spread 'em and cough. Okay, let me see the bottoms of your feet. Get dressed." It's clear he's done this far too many times.

Through the slot, the guard throws an oversized orange jump suit and a roll of ratty looking pink under clothes—stained and worn—on the floor of the cell. I'm finally allowed to cover my naked body. I get dressed as quickly as I can, trying not to let the guard strip me of my dignity as he did my clothes, but that might be impossible.

This is just one of the countless dehumanizing ways prisoners are abused in solitary confinement across the United States. Prisoners are forced to live and participate in unnatural ways to survive the horrific experience; an experience that should have no place within our society.

An estimated forty-one thousand to forty-eight thousand people are in solitary confinement in American prisons.[1] Recent data indicates that more than six thousand prisoners have spent at least one year in solitary confinement and more than 1,400 have been isolated for longer than six years.[2]

I was twelve the first time I was sent to solitary confinement. It was then that I felt the experience of the brutal place we called the hole. We called it that because that's exactly where it felt like you were—a dark, deep hole, with nothing but your own mind to pull you through.

My destructive behavior in society caused me to continue going into and out of juvenile detention centers, and later adult prisons. Because of this, I came to know solitary confinement quite well. I was incredibly prideful, full of toxic masculinity, and felt like I always had something to prove. Now, at forty-one years old and still living with the trauma of what I have experienced in solitary, it's hard for me to be around people, exist comfortably in social situations, or be in crowded areas at all. I feel compelled to share some of the irreparable damage caused by a practice still in place today, a practice countless scientific studies have warned will cause lifelong consequences to those forced to endure its harsh conditions. For example, research has proven the mental and physical health effects that result from subjecting people to solitary confinement—including increased paranoia, hallucinations, posttraumatic stress disorder, increased risks of depression, anxiety, and suicide.[3] Yet, as a society, we sit by and continue to allow the use of this torturous practice as it is weaponized against millions of men, women, and children who are currently locked away within the carceral system.

Solitary confinement works to desensitize by dehumanizing those forced to endure its abuse. The effects often remain throughout individuals' lives, denying its victims the chance for a healthy reintegration into their communities.

When I have been placed in solitary confinement, I have only been allowed to leave the cell in restraints (handcuffed and shackled), often with a dog leash clipped to my shackles. That's how I was escorted by two corrections officers to showers and recreation yards. I was frequently strip searched before a shower or during recreational time, a practice even some U.S. courts have called humiliating.

While in solitary, I was fed all meals through a slot on the metal door—like an animal caged in a zoo. My meals were often small and served cold to lukewarm at best. Mail from my loved ones was thrown on the ground and kicked under the door, as if it were a discarded piece of trash in the way of a guard's path. If an envelope was too thick—containing precious photos of loved ones—it would be severely damaged in the process. When I protested, I was met with a dismissing comment and left screaming and banging on the door in anger as the officer casually walked away.

I have been forced to endure the yelling and banging of other prisoners who have mental health issues—individuals that become exceedingly worse with long periods of isolation. The yelling and banging often went on for hours or days at a time.

I've been placed in a *strip cell* (when one is deemed a behavioral issue or has expressed thoughts of suicide, all items—including most clothing and toilet paper—are taken).[4] I was left alone in a cell with nothing but my cold body and the pale concrete around me.

I've been placed in cells where the heat is extremely hot or the cold is extremely cold, forcing me into a constant state of being uncomfortable with my mind off balance, focused only on survival.

The negative impacts of solitary confinement are so dramatic that the United Nations refers to prolonged isolation as torture in its Standard Minimum Rules for the Treatment of Prisoners (known as the Nelson Mandela Rules).[5] In fact, the Nelson Mandela Rules state that prolonged solitary confinement is defined as "a time period in excess of 15 consecutive days."

Approximately 95 percent of prisoners are released back into the community, it's inevitable society will feel the effects of these damaged humans.[6]

During my time in solitary, I became lost in my head reliving childhood abuse I suffered at the hands of my biological father.

I lived with the fear of possibly going insane, like the many who surrounded me, those who were flooding their cells with toilet water, banging for hours on their steel doors, talking to themselves (yelling and having arguments with themselves), causing self-harm, and even playing with bodily fluids.

While in solitary, I knew my emotions could drag me to a place from which they would never recover. When I looked for logic in an illogical situation and wished I would be treated like a human in an inhumane place, I was let down time and again. Those of us who have spent time in solitary confinement respond to this by turning off our emotions and pursuit of logic while in the hole. It takes time to return to our feeling once we're out of the hole. Sometimes people don't recover.

A prisoner can descend into a mental abyss—a fog-like state—in which alertness, attention, and concentration can all become impaired.

Furthermore, the effects reach far beyond those forced to endure the conditions of solitary confinement firsthand, often damaging prisoners' support networks.[7] Families and friends of those who have suffered in solitary must confront how desensitized their loved ones have become while they struggle to support their emotional breakdowns. They have to live with a feeling of powerless when unable to help their loved ones, let alone communicate with them. When in solitary, calls to our family and friends outside prison are not set on a regular schedule. I've had to call my wife in the middle of her workday. She was a teacher and couldn't take my call if she was in class. Worse, in some cases, those in solitary are stripped of phone privileges entirely, making it impossible to communicate with loved ones at all.

It's impossible to express all the damage caused to the victims of solitary confinement. Even though those who are locked away in solitary confinement represent only 6 to 8 percent of America's prison population, they remain about 50 percent of those who die by suicide.[8] The pressure of being locked in isolation twenty-three hours a day, sometimes more, can take every ounce of one's mental, emotional, and physical will to survive and maintain their sanity. Even short periods spent in solitary can cause permanent effects to those forced to experience its torturous grasp. Just ask the prison administrators who've tried to spend mere hours in there. For example, former director of the Colorado Department of Corrections, Rick Raemisch, who eventually ended long-term solitary confinement in Colorado in agreement with the Nelson Mandela Rules, spent twenty hours in solitary confinement in 2014. Writing about his experience for the *New York Times*, Raemisch noted, "If I was troubled by the experience after such a relatively short time, then I had to say, 'Enough.'"[9]

We need to put a stop to this abuse. Inflicting these harms on prisoners is wrong and morally unsound. That solitary confinement has existed this long is a travesty. We know it's wrong, we know it causes severe damage to human beings, yet we still allow the practice to continue. We must stop this monstrous practice of harming humans and begin to heal those who have been forced to endure its abuse. Continuing this shameful practice isn't an attack only on those forced to experience it, but on our communities as well.

Having served more than forty years in solitary confinement, Albert Woodfox, rest his soul, a former member of the Black Panther Party and one of the wrongfully convicted Angola 3, said it best: "There is a part of me . . . that is gone, that has been taken—my soul. I had to sacrifice that part in order to survive."[10] No one should be forced to make such a sacrifice, especially in a world as advanced as ours. We have the studies, and we know the harm that is being caused. No longer can we look away and act like what's happening is beneficial to anyone involved.

NOTES

1. See Correctional Leaders Association and the Arthur Liman Center for Public Interest at Yale Law School (CLA and Liman Center), *Time-in-Cell: A 2021 Snapshot of Restrictive Housing Based on a Nationwide Survey of U.S. Prison Systems* (New Haven, CT: Yale Law School, 2022), xi, 61, https://law.yale.edu/sites/default/files/area/center/liman/document/time_in_cell_2021.pdf.
2. These numbers reflect self-reported data from thirty-four state prison systems and the federal Bureau of Prisons as of July 2021. CLA and Liman Center, *Time-in-Cell*, viii.
3. See Jeffrey L. Metzner and Jamie Fellner, "Solitary Confinement and Mental Illness in U.S. Prisons: A Challenge for Medical Ethics," *Journal of the American Academy of Psychiatry and the Law* 38 (2010): 104–105, http://jaapl.org/content/jaapl/38/1/104.full.pdf; Lauren Brinkley-Rubinstein, Josie Sivaraman, David L. Rosen, David H. Cloud, Gary Junker, Scott Proescholdbell, Meghan E. Shanahan, and Shabbar I. Ranapurwala, "Association of Restrictive Housing During Incarceration with Mortality after Release," *JAMA Network Open* 10 (2019), https://jamanetwork.com/journals/jamanetworkopen/fullarticle/2752350; Stuart Grassian, "Psychiatric Effects of Solitary Confinement," *Washington University Journal of Law & Policy* 22 (2006): 328, 332, 335, 349, https://openscholarship.wustl.edu/cgi/viewcontent.cgi?article=1362&context=law_journal_law_policy.
4. Sal Rodriguez, "Utah Supermax Prisoners Report Being 'Treated Like an Animal,'" Solitary Watch, February 15, 2013, https://solitarywatch.org/2013/02/15/utah-supermax-prisoners-report-being-treated-like-an-animal.
5. United Nations, *Nelson Mandela Rules*, A/RES/70/175, Rule 43.1(a) and (b) (2015), https://documents-dds-ny.un.org/doc/UNDOC/GEN/N15/443/41/PDF/N1544341.pdf.

6. Nathan James, *Offender Reentry: Correctional Statistics, Reintegration into the Community, and Recidivism*, CRS report no. RL34287 (Washington, DC: Congressional Research Service, 2015), 1, https://sgp.fas.org/crs/misc/RL34287.pdf.
7. Annalena Wolcke, "The Collateral Consequences of Solitary Confinement" (Washington, DC: Solitary Watch, 2022), https://solitarywatch.org/wp-content/uploads/2022/09/SW-Fact-Sheet-2-Collateral-Consequences-v220909.pdf.
8. Tiana Herring, "The Research Is Clear: Solitary Confinement Causes Long-Lasting Harm" (Northampton, MA: Prison Policy Initiative, December 8, 2020), https://www.prisonpolicy.org/blog/2020/12/08/solitary_symposium; Terry A. Kupers, "What to Do with the Survivors? Coping with the Long-Term Effects of Isolated Confinement," *Criminal Justice and Behavior* 35 (2008): 1009, http://www.nrcat.org/storage/documents/usp_kupers_what_do_with_survivors.pdf.
9. Rick Raemisch, "Why We Ended Long-Term Solitary Confinement in Colorado," *New York Times*, October 12, 2017, https://www.nytimes.com/2017/10/12/opinion/solitary-confinement-colorado-prison.html.
10. International Coalition to Free the Angola 3, "The Angola 3 Case: What You Need to Know," accessed November 28, 2022, https://angola3.org/the-case; Albert Woodfox, *Solitary: Unbroken by Four Decades in Solitary Confinement. My Story of Transformation and Hope* (New York: Grove Press, 2019), 301.

19

A CULTURE OF ABUSE IN OUR NATION'S PRISONS AND JAILS

Kathy Foer-Morse

"FALSE COMPLAINTS Next Challenge for N.J. Prison Trying to Change Culture of Abuse."[1] When I read the article in a New Jersey newspaper, I had a sickening feeling in the pit of my stomach. It's stories like these that add to the skepticism in the community regarding sexual abuse or assault in jails and prisons across the country. It discredits the stories of victims who report on the abuse. If all the complaints had in fact been false, the need to establish the Prison Rape Elimination Act (PREA) would never have arisen in the first place.[2]

Congress passed PREA in 2003, the first federal law addressing sexual assault in jails and prisons across the country. The law also created the National Prison Rape Elimination Commission, tasking the commission with drafting standards for eliminating prison rape. In 2012, the U.S. Department of Justice published the final PREA standards. PREA aims to "prevent, detect, and respond to sexual abuse" in jails and prisons in the United States.[3] It sets a zero-tolerance policy within correctional facilities, identifies hiring and training requirements, and authorizes the development of standards for responding to reported abuse. Additionally, for the first time, incarcerated people are now required to receive educational materials regarding the dynamics of sexual abuse within the facility.[4] These materials also lay out their constitutional rights if they are a victim of such abuse as well as instruct incarcerated individuals, community members, and staff how to report suspected abuse. Despite this landmark legislation and funding to implement the standards, PREA enforcement has been riddled with implementation challenges.[5]

From November 2005 until October 2006, I was detained pretrial at the Rose M. Singer Center for Women (Rosie's) on Rikers Island in East

Elmhurst, New York, one of the jails operated by the New York City Department of Correction. Rikers is notorious for its brutality, abuse, and violence, which occur almost daily.[6] In fact, the Justice Department currently monitors Rikers because of the inhumane conditions there and the repeated violations of detainees' constitutional rights, specifically the Eighth Amendment, which protects the rights of individuals against cruel and unusual punishment.[7]

My time at Rosie's was fraught with pain (both physically and mentally), a loss of dignity, self-esteem, self-respect, heartbreak, and trauma. I became numb. I had to separate myself from what was going on around me and how illegal and morally wrong it all was, because at the time I could do nothing to stop it. I had to turn off my emotions and any indignation I might have at how not only I was being treated but how others were treated as well. I was threatened, verbally and physically. I was bullied. I was taunted and spit on. I had property stolen from me: multiple Walkmans, spare batteries, commissary items, socks brought in from home, and packaged underwear. I was extorted. I was preyed upon. And yes, I was sexually assaulted (once) and mentally abused on an almost daily basis. Someone told me about four years ago that the only reason I survived Rosie's is that I "was worth more to them alive than dead." He did not mean correctional staff.

I spent my time at Rosie's living in a dormitory type housing unit. There was no privacy; it was all out there in the open to share with sixty-one other women. For someone like myself who is rather modest about their body, it was uncomfortable to get used to. Trying to use the toilet while the person next to you wants to have a conversation as if you were sitting next to each other on the subway is a bit uncomfortable. Taking a shower with six other women—strangers—in an open room is overwhelming.

I was raped at Rosie's in the shower. When I moved from reception after clearing my tuberculosis test, I asked an officer where I was going and he replied, "Don't worry, you are going to the 'Hilton' of housing units, the girls there will take good care of you." At the time I wondered what he meant by this comment and why he was looking out for me. Why me? Who was I but a white middle-aged mother from New Jersey who stole money from her employer? What was it about me that made him want to send me to the Hilton of housing units? I walked into the unit and was greeted by a variety of facial expressions, none of which I found to be overly friendly. It was downright frightening, overwhelming, and yes, intimidating as hell, from the correctional officers to the women who were housed there. I was petrified.

I was placed in minimum custody and housed in one of the dorms, similar to a gymnasium with row after row of metal cots. The officers worked in the front of the room in an area known as the bubble. It was a long, narrow room with plexiglass windows on four sides. One exception to their visibility of the dorms was the bathrooms, as frosted glass partially covered the window to that area. The day after I arrived on that unit, I heard muffled conversations referring to me as "Martha, Martha Stewart." Why? Because I was white? Because I was a middle-aged woman? I kept quiet and to myself. I only got up to use the bathroom and telephone. I could not eat. Anything I tried to eat came right out of me. The name *Martha* continued to be mentioned when someone passed me. I tried to strategically plan a good time to shower, when there would be the least traffic in the bathroom during the available shower time hours, when I could shower alone. I sat on my bed and tried to figure it out, to see if there were popular and quiet times. There had to be a block of ten minutes when I could take a shower alone. I thought I had it figured out. It was a weeknight when a popular television show was on. The bathroom was deserted, and I made my move to take a shower.

I went into the bathroom when it appeared the coast was clear. Others were either in the dayroom yelling at the television, talking on the telephone, laying on their beds, or playing cards with others. I got undressed, turned on the water, felt the warm water hit my face and run down the front of my body when I was grabbed from behind. One person got my face and neck while another person pulled my arms behind my back and someone else grabbed my ankles. Someone else pushed me in the back of my knees causing me to fall. I tried to struggle out of their hold to break my fall, but it was not possible. They were pulling my hair and jerking back my head whispering in my ear to be quiet, to not struggle or yell out. They kept saying, "Martha, Martha, we are going to teach you a lesson; this is what we do to snitches."

At this point they had me down on all fours. One person was grabbing at my breasts while another tried to shove the handle of the mop into my anus. I was struggling, trying to yell out in pain, but couldn't speak. I had lost my voice and could only feel the searing pain in my backside. I could feel it being shoved in there, and they switched to the handle of the toilet plunger and shoved it in as well. At this point, I was seeing stars, and the pain was unbearable. I smelled blood. I could feel its stickiness on my kneecaps. It felt like it went on for hours: the in and out of the wooden poles, the yanking of my hair, the grimy hand over my mouth, and the yanking of my breasts. Their last words to me were, "Have you had enough, Martha?" and then they let me go and walked away. I lay there on the wet tile floor like a torn apart rag doll, bleeding from my mouth and my backside. I pulled myself together, and I washed away the blood and feces. It was then that I glanced at the floor and saw the mop and plunger they had used to assault me. They both had my blood and body fluids on them. I simply did not care as I stumbled out of the shower, grabbed some sanitary pads to soak up my blood, and crawled into my cot. I lay there too afraid to move. The pain was unbearable as was the bleeding and stickiness between my thighs. I was numb, cold, shivering, and could not get warm.

I lay awake that night and many thereafter afraid to sleep, afraid that they would come get me for round two. I heard their voices mocking me, calling me Martha. The next few days were a blur. I got out of bed to change the sanitary pads. I drank as much water as I could, and I returned to bed. It simply hurt too much to move, to walk, to even go to the bathroom. I was afraid that I was going to die. I laid in my bed at night, in pain, bleeding, and had conversations with my father who had died fifteen years earlier. I asked him to protect me. I had children at home who needed me. I needed to stay alive, but at the same time I wanted the pain to go away and did not want this to happen to me again. I was losing weight and did not care. I was afraid to shower and did not care. I would soap up a washcloth and use that. I knew who did this to me, but my will to live outweighed my right to report them. It simply was not worth it.

I made the decision that I would tell no one. My attackers would walk past me and taunt me. I had to ignore them. I no longer cared. I figured they had already violated me. What more could they possibly do to me? Gradually the bleeding stopped, the bruises faded, but the ache in my chest remained. It would not go away. I had almost weekly visits with my husband and twenty-two-month-old daughter, and I never told him.

When I saw my lawyer in court, I pleaded with him to get me out, and at every court appearance the judge would deny our request for release or bail. I wondered if I told the judge in open court what happened to me, whether it would change the decision. I sincerely doubted it. Each court appearance became worse. I started having panic attacks and hyperventilated on several occasions, yet no one asked what was wrong. They simply assumed it was because I did not want to be in jail, at Rosie's.

I kept this story to myself for years. I always felt shame, and that no one would believe me. This was why when I read the headline in June of 2022, I felt that I had made the right choice to not report it when I was at Rikers.

Who would believe me? I knew that PREA would not protect me, just like it has failed to protect so many other people in jails and prisons across the country.

I now know that the officer who promised me that I was going to the Hilton of housing units had set me up. I know now that those women who attacked me thinking I was a snitch were wrong. Do I forgive them? Yes. I am at that point where I need to forgive and move on, to heal, and I am okay with that. It has been eight years since my release, and I am no longer numb. I am gradually thawing.

I firmly believe that the trauma of my incarceration is still with me and will be for the remainder of my life. What this experience has helped me do is to bring my story and that of so many other currently and formerly incarcerated women to the community. I can now educate them on what it really is like to be incarcerated in America. I can shed light on the horrors and the trauma. It is also important to me to tell my story as a testament to the brutality, abuse, and violence that is our carceral system. Asia Johnson, who was incarcerated in a women's prison in Michigan, wrote in her essay (see chapter 20), "Every incarcerated individual, no matter their gender identity, is surviving a daily storm. So, I ask the question, when will the rain cease?"

My story illustrates the punitive excess of America's criminal justice system. Where is the justice in my suffering a horrible sexual assault because of a sentence ordered by a judge? How does this embody the rule of law? How have we failed so spectacularly to ensure the dignity and humanity of those sentenced to incarceration in America?

Most people are under the impression that prisons and jails are rehabilitative places where programming and therapy are prevalent. The exact opposite is true. The environment encourages survival of the fittest. Corrections officers sometimes encourage those housed behind bars to fight. I was treated with total disregard for any sense of humanity or dignity.

The things I experienced, witnessed, and heard in jail can never be taught in a classroom or read in a textbook. It can't be fully understood by those who are charged with investigating it and those investigating reports under PREA. It certainly can never be understood based on the numbers reported annually by the Department of Justice.

On an almost daily basis I realize that I was not the only woman incarcerated in this country to experience such abuse and witness such violence and brutality. When I read or hear accounts of incarcerated women who have been abused, I know it is never, ever consensual.

Some think I am blunt. I take that as a compliment. Abuse, brutality, and violence happen in jails and prisons. Stories need to be told honestly. Most important, when someone says they were assaulted, abused, or the victim of violence in jail or prison, please give them the benefit of the doubt.

NOTES

1. Joe Atmonavage, "False Complaints Next Challenge for N.J. Prison Trying to Change Culture of Abuse," *NJ Advance Media for NJ.com*, June 2022, https://www.nj.com/news/2022/06/false-complaints-next-challenge-for-nj-prison-trying-to-change-culture-of-abuse.html.
2. Prison Rape Elimination Act of 2003, 42 U.S.C. § 15601 (2003); National PREA Resource Center, "Prison Rape Elimination Act," accessed December 16, 2022, https://www.prearesourcecenter.org/about/prison-rape-elimination-act.
3. 34 U.S.C. Ch. 303: "Prison Rape Elimination," citing Memorandum of President of the United States, May 17, 2012, 77 F.R. 30873, https://uscode.house.gov/view.xhtml?path=/prelim@title34/subtitle3/chapter303&edition=prelim.
4. National PREA Resource Center, "PREA Standards," § 115.33 Inmate, detainee, and resident education, accessed December 16, 2022, https://www.prearesourcecenter.org/standard/115-33.
5. Colette Marcellin and Evelyn F. McCoy, "Preventing and Addressing Sexual Violence in Correctional Facilities: Research on the Prison Rape Elimination Act" (Washington, DC: Urban Institute, 2021), https://www.urban.org/sites/default/files/publication/104230/preventing-and-addressing-sexual-violence-in-correctional-facilities.pdf.
6. Jan Ransom and Bianca Pallaro, "Behind the Violence at Rikers, Decades of Mismanagement and Dysfunction," *New York Times*, December 31, 2021, https://www.nytimes.com/2021/12/31/nyregion/rikers-island-correction-officers.html.
7. Matt Katz, "NYC Taxpayers Have Paid a Federal Monitor $18 Million to Help Fix Rikers. What Went Wrong?," *Gothamist*, November 17, 2012, https://gothamist.com/news/nyc-taxpayers-have-paid-a-federal-monitor-18-million-to-help-fix-rikers-what-went-wrong; Jonah E. Bromwich and Jan Ransom, "Rikers Still 'Unstable and Unsafe' Under New Jails Chief, Watchdog Says," *New York Times*, March 16, 2022, https://www.nytimes.com/2022/03/16/nyregion/rikers-jail-violence-report.html.

20

SURVIVING A DAILY STORM

Asia Johnson

MOTHERS, DAUGHTERS, SISTERS, WIVES: more than two thousand women holding these titles resided with me at Michigan's only prison for women: the Women's Huron Valley Correctional Facility. The prison is located in the city of Ypsilanti, eight miles southeast of Ann Arbor, and has a population of a little more than twenty thousand people.[1] In this prison, we were packed into cells—some holding as many as sixteen women at a time.

In the Midwest, severe storms are a regular occurrence. Has a storm ever caused you to experience a Wi-Fi interruption or cell service outage? Do you remember how frustrating it was not being able to connect to the outside world? Could you imagine if your only source of information, even under the best of circumstances, was cable news? That's the difficult situation that I and so many others experienced in prison. Prison is like a town that has been hit by a massive storm, only the damage is permanent.

Unlike in the "real world" where it costs nothing to send an email, JPay charges both incarcerated people and those on the outside to send emails. Five dollars gets an incarcerated person just twenty electronic stamps in Michigan prisons.[2] And calling your loved ones? It used to cost $3 for a fifteen-minute phone call.[3] The financial burden of being an incarcerated person for both the individual and their family is overwhelming. As Alexes Harris points out in her essay (see chapter 29), these criminal justice departments disproportionately burden and harm women, especially Black women. This is so even when Black women are not the ones themselves behind bars or criminally convicted; often they are supporting family members who are struggling to pay off these fees and fines.

The extent of the harm of the criminal justice system causes women doesn't stop there. The place I lived in for nine years, the place that some women were sentenced to die in, was not designed with our gender in mind. Necessities, such as some feminine hygiene products, had to be purchased. Mothers visiting with their children sometimes had to endure the termination of their bonding time because the visiting room was overcrowded. Expecting mothers had to walk to the chow hall in rain, sleet, snow, or hellish heat along with the rest of us. Prenatal care is inadequate in many jails and prisons in this country. A recent study about health-care practices for pregnant women in nineteen state prisons found that living conditions, health care, and counseling practices failed to meet their basic needs.[4] Although progress is slowly being made across the United States, shackling pregnant women is still legal across much of the nation: as of April 2022, more than twelve states did not have laws prohibiting the shackling of pregnant women who are incarcerated.[5] This is despite the fact that the practice contravenes the United Nations convention against torture.[6] Imprisoned men do not have to endure our female misery.

One morning, while chatting with a dear friend who was incarcerated on a murder charge in the death of her abusive husband, the subject of sentencing disparities between men and women came up. My friend said, "If I had been a man who'd killed his wife, I'd have an out date." (An out date is essentially the day you can leave prison.) My friend is serving life without parole. Others joined our conversation, and, before I knew it, we all had concluded that women are sentenced more harshly than men.

Now, I recognize that as true as it may have felt to us, data does not support my friend's assertion. An often-cited study from the National Coalition Against Domestic Violence showed that whereas the average prison sentence is two to six years for men who killed their female partners, women who killed their partners, on average, are sentenced to fifteen years.[7] That study was published more than thirty years ago, however, and more recent studies have not replicated these results. After the implementation of the U.S. Sentencing Commission's standardized guidelines in 1992, sentencing disparities between men and women seemingly began to erode.[8]

I went back to my cell to dwell on our morning talk. I had stayed mostly mum during our earlier conversation. I didn't feel like I had been harshly sentenced. I knew that with my violent crime I could have—and some would argue, should have—been sentenced to die in prison. In the midst of a mental health crisis, I had turned violent and taken the life of a loved one. As a result, I was sentenced to nine to thirty years of incarceration. The question I asked myself was, "Had I been treated more harshly than a man would have been in similar circumstances?"

But was that really a material question? While in prison, I spent countless hours listening to the stories of women who had killed, stolen, struggled with addiction, and suffered from mental health issues. They all—we all—had been thrown away. We were all losing time we'd never get back. The men, we thought, got to do their short time and get back to life as they knew it. Now I see that this was not the case: we were all suffering equally under the same excessive system of punishment.

We've been conditioned to think that because harm occurs, we need to throw someone in a cage or in a prison, and then the harm has been healed. That is not the case. Healing cannot happen in a jail cell or in a prison cell, in a six by eight foot space. Every day, I felt as if I was growing closer and closer to complete invisibility. The days are spent in these dark areas, these dark rooms where you're forced to think about your humanity. But as you're thinking about it, you know that you don't have it anymore because you are being treated terribly by the people who are supposed to be helping you heal. And you start to internalize this treatment; you start to think, "Wow, I belong here."

Those people who made mistakes will come home. They're going to be our neighbors. They're going to be the people in the grocery store, shopping alongside us. They're going to be working alongside us.

I was released from prison on October 9, 2018. Because I had tried to do everything right—to become a model prisoner and to do a great deal of self-work—I was able to walk out of prison exactly nine years after I went in. I was stronger, healthier, and ready for the world. However, my personal growth was not the result of the institution but of the time I spent in therapy and self-reflecting. I joined peer groups, formed friendships that became a support system for me, and read every self-help book I could find. I wish I could say that I came out of prison as an expert on incarceration, rehabilitation, and remediation, but that knowledge didn't come until later. When I was released, I was still grappling with the experience and the issues that had affected me so deeply. One issue in particular nagged at me: there are women who did not commit a crime nearly as violent as mine who are serving more time than I did. I still struggle with this survivor's guilt. Why and how did I get so lucky? How did I escape spending the rest of my life locked away in a cage alongside the two thousand other women in the United States who are currently serving life-without-parole sentences, meaning that they are likely to die in prison?[9]

More than 150,000 women are in jail and prison in the United States.[10] That number skyrockets if you include the women under the control of the criminal legal system via probation and parole. In fact, more than one million women are on probation or parole—and those on probation represent "three out of four women under any sort of correctional supervision."[11] According to The Sentencing Project, from 1980 to 2020, "the number of incarcerated women increased by more than 475 percent."[12] In state prisons, women's incarceration rates have been increasing at twice the rate of men's.[13] Racial disparities are stark: Black women and Latinas are 1.7 and 1.3 times more likely, respectively, to end up in prison than white women.[14]

After I was released, I faced significant barriers and collateral consequences that made it difficult to rejoin my community. How was I going to rent an apartment if I didn't have a job? How was I going to rent an apartment if they don't rent to people with a felony conviction? How was I going to get a job if they don't hire people with criminal records?

Shortly after my return home, I began working for The Bail Project, a nonprofit organization whose mission to end cash bail is succinctly captured by its motto: "Freedom should be free."[15] I also spent time working closely with the Detroit Justice Center, learning about how to create the world I wanted to live in—one that is more just and equitable and where freedom can truly be attained by everyone. I realized that the question of who has it worse in prison—men or women—has been beside the point all along. What is more important is the sad truth that too many are more willing to build prisons than to dismantle the conditions which fill them. This is evidenced by the sheer number of sites of incarceration in the United States; as of March 2022, there were "1,566 state prisons, 102 federal prisons, 2,850 local jails, 1,510 juvenile correctional facilities, 186 immigration detention facilities, and 82 Indian country jails, as well as . . . military prisons, civil commitment centers, state psychiatric hospitals, and prisons in the U.S. territories."[16]

Angela Davis wrote, "Homelessness, unemployment, drug addiction, mental illness, and illiteracy are only a few of the problems that disappear from public view when the human beings contending with them are relegated to cages. . . . Prisons do not disappear social problems, they disappear human beings."[17] As one of those people who was relegated to a cage, I know firsthand that prisons do not work. America has a tragic obsession with vengeance and punishment. This infatuation continues to ruin the lives of men and women all over the country. Shouldn't prisons attempt to restore people to their wholeness and not break them apart and make them feel like they're nothing? Everyone is capable of redemption and growth and change.

Every incarcerated individual, no matter their gender identity, is surviving a daily storm. So I ask the question: when will the rain cease?

NOTES

1. U.S. Census Bureau, "Quick Facts: Ypsilanti City, Michigan," Population estimates, July 1, 2021, https://www.census.gov/quickfacts/fact/table/ypsilanticity michigan/AGE295221.
2. Michigan Department of Corrections, "Available JPay Services," accessed December 14, 2022, https://www.jpay.com/Agency-Details/Michigan-Department-of-Corrections.aspx.
3. Michigan Department of Corrections, "Michigan Department of Corrections Lowers Prisoner Phone Rates by Nearly 40%," press release, September 29, 2022, https://www.michigan.gov/corrections/press-releases/2022/09/29/michigan-department-of-corrections-lowers-prisoner-phone-rates-by-nearly-40-percent.
4. Ginette G. Ferszt and Jennifer G. Clarke, "Health Care of Pregnant Women in U.S. State Prisons," *Journal of Health Care for the Poor and Underserved* 23, no. 2 (May 2012): 557–69, https://muse.jhu.edu/article/474039.
5. Joe Hernandez, "More States Are Restricting the Shackling of Pregnant Inmates, but It Still Occurs," NPR, April 22, 2022, https://www.npr.org/2022/04/22/1093836514/shackle-pregnant-inmates-tennessee.
6. As Rule 47 makes explicit, "The use of chains, irons or other instruments of restraint which are inherently degrading or painful shall be prohibited." UN Office on Drugs and Crime, *The United Nations Standard Minimum Rules for the Treatment of Prisoners*, adopted December 17, 2015, 15, https://www.unodc.org/documents/justice-and-prison-reform/Nelson_Mandela_Rules-E-ebook.pdf.
7. American Civil Liberties Union, "Words from Prison—Did You Know . . .?," June 12, 2006, https://www.aclu.org/other/words-prison-did-you-know.
8. Myrna S. Raeder, "Gender and Sentencing: Single Moms, Battered Women, and Other Sex-Based Anomalies in the Gender-Free World of the Federal Sentencing Guidelines," *Pepperdine Law Review* 20, no. 3 (1993): 905–90, http://digitalcommons.pepperdine.edu/plr/vol20/iss3/1.
9. Ashley Nellis, "In the Extreme: Women Serving Life Without Parole and Death Sentences in the United States" (Washington, DC: The Sentencing Project, 2022), 5, https://www.sentencingproject.org/app/uploads/2022/08/In-the-Extreme-Women-Serving-Life-without-Parole-and-Death-Sentences-in-the-United-States.pdf.

10. The Sentencing Project, "Incarcerated Women and Girls," updated May 2022, https://www.sentencingproject.org/app/uploads/2022/11/Incarcerated-Women-and-Girls.pdf.
11. Aleks Kajstura, "Women's Mass Incarceration: The Whole Pie 2019" (Northampton, MA: Prison Policy Initiative, October 29, 2019), https://www.prisonpolicy.org/reports/pie2019women.html.
12. The Sentencing Project, "Incarcerated Women and Girls."
13. Nazish Dholakia, "Women's Incarceration Rates Are Skyrocketing. These Advocates Are Trying to Change That" (New York: Vera Institute of Justice, May 17, 2021), https://www.vera.org/news/womens-voices/womens-incarceration-rates-are-skyrocketing.
14. The Sentencing Project, "Incarcerated Women and Girls."
15. The Bail Project, accessed December 14, 2022, https://bailproject.org.
16. Wendy Sawyer and Peter Wagner, "Mass Incarceration: The Whole Pie 2022" (Northampton, MA: Prison Policy Initiative, March 14, 2022), https://www.prisonpolicy.org/reports/pie2022.html.
17. Angela Davis, "Masked Racism: Reflections on the Prison Industrial Complex," *Colorlines*, September 10, 1998, https://web.archive.org/web/20150321103120/http://colorlines.com/archives/1998/09/masked_racism_reflections_on_the_prison_industrial_complex.html.

21

COVID-19 AND THE STRUGGLE FOR HEALTH BEHIND BARS

Homer Venters

IN THE FIRST WEEKS of the COVID-19 pandemic, I left my job as president of a nonprofit so that I could respond full time to the spread of the virus in jails, prisons, and immigration detention centers. Since then, I've conducted about fifty inspections of facilities to assess their COVID-19 responses and provide recommendations, including things that could be done inside the facilities and how to protect high-risk people via release and other approaches. This work has also evolved into providing recommendations about other potential outbreaks, from influenza to monkeypox, and addressing some alarming developments behind bars relating to health impacts of short staffing and violence.

How do things look from this perspective? Regarding COVID-19, almost every system made some effort to implement Centers for Disease Control and Prevention (CDC) guidelines, with varied impact, but almost none took steps to address the existing barriers to health care that made COVID-19 much more deadly. With only a few exceptions, the reliance on isolation and punitive responses to new COVID-19 outbreaks was common throughout the pandemic. Most facilities worked to transfer people with known or suspected COVID-19 into a separate space for medical isolation, consistent with CDC recommendations. But almost all the housing areas people were transferred into were punitive and isolating, and people were often put into the actual solitary confinement units, with loss of their property, family contact and social support, laundry, and shower access. One person I interviewed in medical isolation said that experience was worse than the many times he had been put in solitary by security staff. Only a handful of the inspections I conducted revealed a genuine effort to make medical isolation nonpunitive. In one facility, they made the simple but important decision to keep the doors to medical isolation cells unlocked so that people known to have COVID-19 were not in twenty-four-hour cell isolation. Another facility let people bring their property into medical isolation and made sure people had phone access. Often, these efforts came far too late, when people had learned that reporting symptoms of COVID-19 meant punishment response. I inspected one facility during the initial Omicron wave where hundreds of people in a small area, some of whom became very ill, didn't report their COVID-19 symptoms because of the fear of punishing response.

In terms of vaccinations, most of the facilities I inspected were able to secure adequate doses of COVID-19 vaccine for detained people, often because supply intended for correctional officers went unused. In some institutions, though, the way vaccines are offered—usually to large groups of individuals, such as everyone in a housing area or dining hall—is itself a problem. This approach often leaves little room for people with questions about vaccine safety or complex medical problems to ask their own questions about vaccination. As a result, some of the people who need the vaccine the most, such as those with multiple serious health problems and those taking numerous medications, end up not being vaccinated simply because they are denied the opportunity to learn what they wish to know. It didn't take long for vaccination rates among detained people to exceed those of correctional staff, itself a serious problem, but these rates often obscured that facilities didn't track or prioritize vaccination for the people most likely to die from COVID-19.

These vaccination challenges, as well as the tendency to rely on solitary confinement for medical isolation, can be addressed with engagement. An engagement approach, which entails eliciting the individual's input and participation in his or her health care, is standard for community health clinics, hospitals, and other health organizations. But in jails, prisons, and immigration detention facilities, the very notion of individualized engagement can be seen as a threat to the paramilitary approach of corrections. In one facility where my role was more ongoing, I promoted one-on-one encounters between high-risk patients and health staff regarding vaccine hesitance, and health staff made significant progress in protecting this group of people. This very basic element of health assessment and promotion butts up against the natural tendency toward dehumanization that characterizes incarceration. It can be seen in many other aspects of substandard health services beyond COVID-19.

For example, a common response to a patient exhibiting suicidal behavior is to lock them in a cell, naked except for a rough "suicide smock," with the goal of depriving them of ways to harm themselves.[1] This approach not only fails to address the actual mental health crisis but also adds additional humiliation and isolation for a person who desperately needs treatment and engagement. For people entering jails and prisons who need medications for opiate use disorder, this type of locked cell treatment is also common as they are denied evidence-based medications and instead experience untreated withdrawal.[2] In this book (see chapter 11), Morgan Godvin describes her harrowing experience with withdrawal when she was denied medication for her opiate use disorder after entering jail. These common practices drive jail- and prison-attributable death and, for people who survive their incarceration, increase the risk of illness and death after release.

Some penal systems are working to increase COVID-19 vaccine engagement via one-on-one meetings with high-risk patients. These sessions are often added into the existing visits that people with chronic health problems already have in order to target high-risk patients who may have questions about their health problems, medications, and COVID-19 vaccines. Some law enforcement agencies have also conducted surveys of their staff to understand attitudes and reluctance and to provide incentives for vaccination.[3] Most American correctional health services, though, remain under the authority of security forces, which often have little appetite for public health and infection control.

These types of efforts are crucial, not only to respond to outbreaks such as COVID-19, but also for the coming wave of heat-related illness and death that facilities will experience with climate change. At least fourteen states still do not have air conditioning in their prisons, including prisons in the American South, such as a number of facilities in Florida.[4] I was recently in a prison in the northwest where the temperature approached 120°F, an unheard-of situation and one that reminded me that many places we consider moderate are experiencing high heat periods. Whether or not a facility has air conditioning, during high heat periods air conditioners can break down. Knowing the identity of (and protecting) those most likely to die from heat-related illness is a necessary but rarely performed job. This issue also dovetailed recently with supply chain issues due to the pandemic, meaning that repairs of air conditioners that usually occurred in hours or days could take weeks to complete, all the while leaving heat sensitive patients at risk.

Overall, the current state of COVID-19 efforts leaves me concerned that the opportunity we had to address basic failures in carceral health services has passed by. Central to this vanishing opportunity is the tepid involvement of the CDC and state departments of health in protecting and promoting the health of people behind bars. The CDC just updated its COVID-19 recommendations and leaves it to facilities to determine whether the local rates of infection and their own facility factors should lead them to follow a lower level of everyday precautions or maintain an enhanced level.[5] These updated recommendations also call for some sort of monitoring of how many high-risk people are in the facility. Virtually none of the fifty or so facilities I inspected did these two things during the height of COVID-19, and I have no confidence that the CDC or local and state departments of health will ensure they do so now. Also, despite clear evidence of the increased risk of illness and death from COVID-19 behind bars, the CDC has been all but silent on the most effective tool: release. Release of high-risk patients has been essential to protect the most vulnerable people from serious illness and death from COVID-19, and to allowing facility administrators the room to establish medical isolation and quarantine units when the need arises.[6]

This lack of oversight and interest among national and state health bodies has reinforced the horrible reality that harming health is part of the punishment of incarceration. People are routinely incarcerated with and even because of health problems for which they will never receive treatment; instead, they are exposed to new health risks that can cause them to suffer serious illness, long term disability, or death.

I recently told European colleagues working on COVID-19 about two aspects of the U.S. system that shocked them—and should shock all of us into action. The first was that the most recent data on deaths in U.S. jails is half a decade old.[7] Just recall the controversy over how deaths from COVID-19 were reported in New York nursing homes; imagine waiting five years to learn of those deaths. The second shocker: COVID-19 is estimated to have reduced the life expectancy of prisoners in Florida's state system by four years.[8] Both of these facts indict a national public health apparatus that has turned its back on incarcerated people, inevitably widening racial disparities in the process.

We must make an affirmative decision to apply the same lens of health expertise and transparency to carceral settings as we do to other parts of society. Concretely, we can begin to address this failure by setting up an office of detention health in the CDC charged with tracking the health of incarcerated people nationwide and the care provided them. This is in fact one of the many interim recommendations we recently made in the Biden-Harris Health Equity Task Force (which I was a member of): to involve the CDC in tracking health outcomes and promoting health among incarcerated people.[9] One of the strongest areas of recommendation to the president from our group was the need for much more coherent data collection on health risks and outcomes inside congregate settings including homeless shelters, inpatient psychiatric facilities, and carceral facilities. These settings represent many thousands of government, nonprofit, and for-profit facilities and both the oversight and data collection from these publicly funded institutions is extremely poor, especially for outbreaks and infection control, which are not part of the core mission.

With federal support, the same monitoring process could be used in state health departments, and then we could join the effort to measure how incarceration harms health, how carceral settings should provide health care, and how undoing mass incarceration can improve individual, family, and community health. But the danger is real that public health funds will continue to be diverted into law enforcement authority and spaces in a manner that fails to improve health or mass incarceration. The state of Alabama diverted about 20 percent of its COVID-19 relief funds ($400 million) toward building prisons.[10] Excitement is considerable over the potential for Medicaid funds to be used behind bars, especially in county jails for treatment of opiate use disorder, but clarity on how the baseline failures of these health systems will be fixed or even monitored as part of this approach is scant.[11] Without independent structures of transparency and accountability, these efforts may only increase the size and power of carceral institutions.

The CDC has a great deal of work to do in this realm. It could start by looking at the rates of what is called long COVID, determining the efficacy of release and other COVID-19 responses during the pandemic, getting involved in suicide prevention (still the number one cause of death among the incarcerated), and analyzing the health needs and costs of care of the enormous and growing portion of elderly people behind bars.

These minimal interventions are crucial to improving our response to COVID-19, as well as the next pandemic, and to informing the nation of public health problems that arise from mass incarceration. They are also small but necessary steps toward addressing the reality that harming health is not a by-product of incarceration but seemingly one of its objectives.

NOTES

1. Jean Trounstine, "Can't We Do Better on Suicide Prevention in Prison?," *Boston Magazine*, February 1, 2013, https://www.bostonmagazine.com/news/2013/02/01/prison-suicide-safety-smocks.

2. American Civil Liberties Union, *Over-Jailed and Un-Treated: How the Failure to Provide Treatment for Substance Use in Prisons and Jails Fuels the Overdose Epidemic* (New York: ACLU, 2021), 6–11, https://www.aclu.org/sites/default/files/field_document/20210625-mat-prison_1.pdf.
3. Meghan McRoberts, "Survey Shows Most Law Enforcement Officers 'Hesitant' to Get Vaccine," WPTV, January 11, 2021, https://www.wptv.com/coronavirus/survey-shows-most-law-enforcement-officers-hesitant-to-get-vaccine.
4. *The Economist*, "Debate Over Air Conditioning in American Prisons Will Heat Up," March 19, 2022, https://www.economist.com/united-states/2022/03/19/debate-over-air-conditioning-in-american-prisons-will-heat-up.
5. Centers for Disease Control and Prevention, "Guidance on Management of COVID-19 in Homeless Service Sites and in Correctional and Detention Facilities," updated November 29, 2022, https://www.cdc.gov/coronavirus/2019-ncov/community/homeless-correctional-settings.html.
6. Leila Miller, "Court Orders Orange County Sheriff to Cut Jail Population in Half to Prevent Spread of Virus," *Los Angeles Times*, December 12, 2020, https://www.latimes.com/california/story/2020-12-12/court-orders-orange-county-sheriff-to-cut-jail-population-in-half.
7. E. Ann Carson, *Mortality in Local Jails, 2000–2018—Statistical Tables*, NCJ 256002 (Washington, DC: Bureau of Justice Statistics, 2021), https://bjs.ojp.gov/content/pub/pdf/mlj0018st.pdf.
8. Emily Widra, "New Data Gives a Detailed Picture of How COVID-19 Increased Death Rates in Florida Prisons" (Northampton, MA: Prison Policy Initiative, April 27, 2021), https://www.prisonpolicy.org/blog/2021/04/27/florida-prison-mortality.
9. Biden-Harris Health Equity Task Force, *COVID-19 Health Equity Task Force: Discrimination and Xenophobia Subcommittee Interim Recommendations* (Washington, DC: U.S. Department of Health and Human Services, Office of Minority Health, 2021), https://www.minorityhealth.hhs.gov/Assets/PDF/May%20COVID%2019%20HETF%20Subcommittees'%20Recommendations_Discrimination%20and%20Xenophobia_final.pdf.
10. Lauren-Brooke Eisen, "Alabama Using Covid Funds to Build New Prisons" (New York: Brennan Center for Justice, October 13, 2021), https://www.brennancenter.org/our-work/analysis-opinion/alabama-using-covid-funds-build-new-prisons.
11. National Association of Counties, "Reinstate Federal Health Care Benefits for Non-Convicted Justice-Involved Individuals," 2019, https://www.naco.org/resources/naco-nsa-one-pager-reinstate-federal-health-care-benefits-non-convicted-justice-involved.

22

INDEPENDENT OVERSIGHT IS ESSENTIAL FOR A SAFE AND HEALTHY PRISON SYSTEM

Michele Deitch

IN 1991, when the Soviet Union still existed, I was invited to present a paper at a criminal justice conference in Leningrad. By the time of the conference a few months later, the Soviet Union had fallen, our gathering was in newly renamed St. Petersburg, and conference participants experienced an emerging openness about life in Russia. In this rapidly changing environment, I had the opportunity to visit a Russian prison with a British colleague as two of the first outsiders allowed inside to see conditions there. Through a translator, the prison administrator expressed deep embarrassment about the shockingly bad infrastructure—six people in a cell meant for one, the use of buckets for toilets in the cells, the deteriorating walls, the dark interior of the building. The administrator did not try to defend what he was showing us, but rather saw in our faces that the conditions we took in as we walked through the facility were inconsistent with international norms and with respect for human decency. He apologized for the conditions and asked what prisons were like in our home countries. He was shocked by some of the stories we told him about our own systems and stunned by the prevalence of brutality and violence and the routine use of force.

This memory has stayed with me over the years because it seems an apt metaphor for what happens when we pull back the, well, iron curtain of our prisons and allow outsiders to see what is happening inside. An independent set of eyes brings in the values of the outside world and brings those values to bear on the way institutions come to understand themselves and their place in that world. Correctional institutions rarely have occasion to have their norms or culture challenged and to imagine other approaches to serving their mission. But seeing yourself as others see you creates an opening for questioning why things are done a certain way and can light a fire for change.

Some thirty years later, most of the Western world has recognized that the protection of human rights in prisons demands transparency and the routine monitoring of conditions. Almost every country in the European Union, for example, has a government entity designated as a National Preventive Mechanism, responsible for inspecting all places of detention and reporting publicly on conditions. These entities shine a light on correctional institutions and help normalize discussions among policymakers and corrections officials about human rights in prison, and about the protection of the dignity of people who are incarcerated.

Similarly, ninety-one countries—but not the United States—are signatories to the Optional Protocol to the Convention Against Torture and other Cruel, Degrading and Inhuman Treatment or Punishment (OPCAT), which requires ratifying states to establish National Preventive Mechanisms.[1] OPCAT also requires states to allow the United Nations' international treaty body, the Subcommittee on Prevention of Torture and other Cruel, Inhuman or Degrading Treatment or Punishment, to make visits to places of detention and examine the treatment of people held in these facilities.[2]

But the United States is an anomaly on the world stage.[3] Jails and prisons in this country are among the most opaque public institutions in our society. We have erected massive walls and razor wire fences around these buildings, placed them in remote corners of each state, limited public access to these spaces, and restricted information that can reveal what is happening inside the walls. We lack reliable data pertinent to the health, safety, and well-being of people in custody and cannot even assess the relative safety or danger of any particular facility. Information about deaths in custody remains elusive in many states.[4] Even data about the spread and toll of COVID-19 behind bars is spotty and unreliable and virtually nonexistent in local jails.[5] In contrast to our peer nations, most states in this country lack oversight mechanisms that can prevent harm in jails and prisons by allowing independent officials to routinely monitor conditions of confinement.[6]

For decades, we relied on federal courts to provide that oversight. In the 1970s and 1980s, many state prison systems operated under the scrutiny of federal judges who had found conditions in correctional facilities in violation of the Eighth Amendment prohibition against cruel and unusual punishment. Cases in Alabama, Arkansas, New York City, and Texas, among other places, revealed and seared into our collective memories appalling practices such as the use of brutal prisoners as guards to control cellblocks; torture devices that deliver electric shocks to the genitals; "hitching posts" to restrain prisoners in the fields, and rampant violence and overcrowding in dilapidated facilities.[7] Long-term court oversight of the detailed consent decrees in these and other cases ensured the dismantling of those practices, often through regular inspections conducted by court monitors and special masters, and by the ongoing threat of contempt fines for agencies that resisted reform.

But court oversight is not enough to fill the gap and promote transparency, for several reasons. First, court oversight is reactive, occurring only after problems have hit constitutional rock bottom; it does not prevent those problems in the first place. Second, increasingly narrow interpretations of the Eighth Amendment by the Supreme Court, and the restrictions imposed by the Prison Litigation Reform Act (PLRA) passed by Congress in 1996, vastly reduce the likelihood of successful lawsuits (the PLRA also limits the extent of ongoing court oversight following a rare judgment against a prison agency).[8] Third, court oversight is timebound, lasting only as long as it takes to remedy the problem, even though conditions can (and do) easily backslide after the court's supervision ends. Finally, the objective of court oversight is to raise institutional conditions to constitutional minimums, not to help the agency implement best practices, or work toward a more humane culture. The courts continue to be essential as a backstop against the worst punitive excesses, but we fool ourselves if we think they can fundamentally change prison culture and transform jails and prisons into places that respect human dignity. One need only look at the horror that is Rikers Island to realize that even court-sanctioned consent decrees do not necessarily solve deep-seated problems.[9]

What's more, court orders are not equipped to address routine conditions that dehumanize people in custody if those conditions do not rise to the level of constitutional violations. As Ram Subramanian has written in another essay in this volume (see chapter 23), "American prison life is built upon the dehumanizing rituals of induction, initiation, hierarchy, degradation and routine, all designed to assert authority and control over the bodies and lives of incarcerated people. Individuality is stripped away upon prison entry, replaced by an inmate number and a standardized, nondescript uniform." These everyday "pains of imprisonment"—and the resulting assault on the dignity of those who are incarcerated—are not susceptible to reform by the courts, though they demand our attention and concern.[10]

In 2008, the American Bar Association called on every jurisdiction to statutorily establish an independent government body to conduct routine, preventive inspections of jails, prisons, and other detention facilities, and to produce public reports about conditions inside these institutions. The ABA Resolution set forth a checklist of the elements necessary to make such an oversight body effective, including requirements that the entity be independent of the corrections agency, have "golden key access" to every part of the facility, be able to inspect without prior notice, and be able to interview incarcerated people and staff confidentially.[11] Such external monitoring is meant to complement other forms of external oversight, including oversight exercised by the courts, the legislature, and accreditation bodies. It also complements internal accountability measures such as internal affairs investigations, audit processes, and grievance systems designed to meet the needs of agency administrators. The goal of external independent monitoring, unlike these other accountability measures, is to enhance transparency of these closed institutions by shining a light on what happens inside, and in doing so, help the agency improve its treatment of people in custody.

In the last decade or so, momentum supporting the establishment of external correctional oversight bodies that serve a preventive monitoring function, often in conjunction with a role designed to address individual complaints, has been increasing.[12] Since 2010, at least six statewide prison oversight bodies, three statewide jail oversight bodies, and nine local jail oversight bodies have been newly created or significantly strengthened, adding to the relatively short list of those oversight entities of longer standing. Serious advocacy efforts are also underway to establish such bodies in other jurisdictions. I have written elsewhere about the status of correctional oversight in the United States and these recent developments.[13]

The Washington State Office of the Corrections Ombuds, created in 2018, has been a model for many other states, and its work is a testament to the importance of external scrutiny of prisons.[14] Even in its short time in existence, that office has drawn legislative attention to the prison agency's challenges managing COVID-19 risks for incarcerated people, helped the agency reduce its use of emergency restraint chairs, addressed concerns about poor food quality, and highlighted issues faced by women in custody.[15] On the other side of the country, the New Jersey Office of the Corrections Ombudsperson was completely restructured and strengthened in 2019, with a new leader appointed in 2022.[16] Its authorizing statute is one of the strongest in the country, and, notably, the legislation creating the New Jersey oversight office was embedded in a bill called The Dignity Act, which addressed the need to ensure the dignity of women who are incarcerated.[17] That office recently issued a report about excessive heat in prisons that has generated public concern about this issue.[18]

The Federal Bureau of Prisons has been extremely opaque about conditions inside its facilities, but in the wake of recent scandals such as the widespread sexual assault of women in the FCI (Federal Correctional Institution) Dublin prison, the suicide and murder of two high-profile individuals in custody, and the deadly impact of COVID-19 on people incarcerated in federal prisons, calls for independent oversight of the Bureau of Prisons have grown louder.[19] In 2022, a bipartisan bill was filed to create an oversight structure for federal prisons, followed the next day by a Senate Judiciary Committee hearing at which senators elicited support for this proposal from the newly appointed director of the Bureau of Prisons, Colette Peters.[20] Passage of this legislation at the federal level would likely provide even greater impetus to efforts to establish statewide prison oversight structures.

Independent oversight of jails and prisons is by no means a panacea that will ensure the safe and humane treatment of people in custody. Monitoring bodies alone cannot curb the abuses they bring to light; they cannot force the spending of necessary resources to fix problems; and they cannot make correctional administrators dismantle systems of solitary confinement or reduce racial tensions, for example. We should not ask them to be enforcers: the power to address the problems of jails and prisons should remain with correctional leaders, legislators, and governors; the oversight entity should not become a supra-management body ultimately responsible for the cleanup of an agency beyond repair.

What oversight bodies can do, though, is to be our eyes and ears. They can provide a window into these dark places and deny elected officials the option of remaining purposefully ignorant about correctional conditions. Their frequent presence in the jails and prisons can act as a form of informal social control over the actions of staff, helping to restrain staff misconduct. They can break down some imagined barrier between the inside and outside worlds, and question the way things "have always been done." They can identify troubling practices early and bring these concerns to administrators' attention for remediation before the problems turn into scandals, lawsuits, or deaths. They can share best practices and strategies that have worked in other facilities to encourage a culture of improvement. They can draw attention to an unhealthy culture that perpetuates or tolerates abuse or a failure to follow policies, and they can bring outside values to bear on the closed confines of a prison environment. They can assess unmeasurable facets of corrections in a holistic way, such as whether people are being treated with dignity and respect, whether they are being held safely, and whether they are being prepared adequately for release. They can help humanize everyone connected to incarceration, including both people in custody and the staff who supervise them. And they can inform us about what is being done in our names and with our tax dollars.

As legal scholar Michael Mushlin has so eloquently written, Franz Kafka noted this same phenomenon in his story "In the Penal Colony": the simple presence of an outside observer changes what happens inside a prison environment.[21] It also can show us who we really are. Our extraordinarily punitive jails and prisons are this way because we have allowed them to become so; it is time for us to feel shame about that—and to take the urgent and necessary steps to prevent future harm.

NOTES

1. Suzanne Jabbour, "Chairperson of the Subcommittee on Prevention of Torture's Statement to the 77th GA Session," United Nations, 77th Session of the General Assembly, New York, October 14, 2022, https://www.ohchr.org/en/statements/2022/10/chairperson-subcommittee-prevention-tortures-statement-77th-ga-session.
2. United Nations, "Subcommittee on Prevention of Torture," accessed December 16, 2022, https://www.ohchr.org/en/treaty-bodies/spt.
3. Jonathan Simon, "Penal Monitoring in the United States: Lessons from the American Experience and Prospects for Change," *Crime, Law, and Social Change* 70, no. 2 (2018): 161–73, https://link.springer.com/article/10.1007/s10611-017-9724-0.
4. Eyal Press, "A Fight to Expose the Hidden Human Costs of Incarceration," *New Yorker*, August 16, 2021, https://www.newyorker.com/magazine/2021/08/23/a-fight-to-expose-the-hidden-human-costs-of-incarceration.
5. Michele Deitch and William Bucknall, *Hidden Figures: Rating the Covid Data Transparency of Prisons, Jails, and Juvenile Agencies* (Austin: University of Texas Lyndon B. Johnson School of Public Affairs, 2021), 5, https://repositories.lib.utexas.edu/handle/2152/85094.
6. Michele Deitch, "But Who Oversees the Overseers?: The Status of Prison and Jail Oversight in the United States," *American Journal of Criminal Law* 47 (2020): 207–74, https://law.utexas.edu/faculty/publications/2020-but-who-oversees-the-overseers--the-status-of-prison-and-jail-oversight-in-the-united-stat.

7. Bruce Cory, "Texas Prison System Being Challenged in Civil Rights Suit," *Washington Post*, October 9, 1978, https://www.washingtonpost.com/archive/politics/1978/10/09/texas-prison-system-being-challenged-in-civil-rights-suit/bd926f76-443d-441b-9c0f-f565e4aad966; *TIME*, "Prisons: Hell in Arkansas," February 9, 1968, https://content.time.com/time/subscriber/article/0,33009,844402,00.html; Adam Nossiter, "Judge Rules Against Alabama's Prison 'Hitching Posts,'" *New York Times*, January 31, 1997, https://www.nytimes.com/1997/01/31/us/judge-rules-against-alabama-s-prison-hitching-posts.html; Wendell Rawls Jr., "Judges' Authority in Prison Reform Attacked; Courts on Trial Third of Four Articles on Efforts; to Restrain the Federal Judiciary," *New York Times*, May 18, 1982, https://www.nytimes.com/1982/05/18/us/judges-authority-prison-reform-attacked-courts-trial-third-four-articles-efforts.html.
8. Andrea Fenster and Margo Schlanger, *Slamming the Courthouse Door: 25 Years of Evidence for Repealing the Prison Litigation Reform Act* (Northampton, MA: Prison Policy Initiative, 2021), https://www.prisonpolicy.org/reports/PLRA_25.html.
9. Beth Schwartzapfel, "Dispatch From Deadly Rikers Island: 'It Looks Like a Slave Ship in There'" (Washington, DC: The Marshall Project, October 5, 2021), https://www.themarshallproject.org/2021/10/05/dispatch-from-deadly-rikers-island-it-looks-like-a-slave-ship-in-there.
10. Gresham Sykes, *The Society of Captives: A Study of a Maximum-Security Prison* (Princeton, NJ: Princeton University Press, 1958).
11. Stpehn J. Salzburg, Chair, Criminal Justice Section, "Report to the House of Delegates" (Chicago: American Bar Association, 2008), 6–10, http://www.ongov.net/jcoc/documents/ABAResolutionandOversight104b.Final.2008.pdf.
12. Deitch, "But Who Oversees the Overseers?"
13. Deitch, "But Who Oversees the Overseers?"
14. Washington State Office of the Corrections Ombuds (Washington Correction Ombuds), accessed December 16, 2022, https://oco.wa.gov.
15. For more, see Washington Corrections Ombuds, "Reports & Publications," accessed December 16, 2022, https://oco.wa.gov/reports-publications/publications/ocos-input-doc-policies.
16. State of New Jersey, "Governor Murphy Names Terry Schuster to Lead the Office of the Corrections Ombudsperson," news release, May 5, 2022, https://www.nj.gov/governor/news/news/562022/20220505a.shtml.
17. Dignity for Incarcerated Primary Caretaker Parents Act, S. 2540, NJ S. Res., 2018) https://pub.njleg.gov/bills/2018/PL19/288_.htm; State of New Jersey, "Governor Murphy Signs Dignity for Incarcerated Primary Caretaker Parents Act," January 9, 2020, https://nj.gov/governor/news/news/562020/approved/20200109b.shtml.

18. Terry Schuster and Kristin King, "Special Report: Summer Heat in New Jersey Prisons" (Trenton: New Jersey Office of the Corrections Ombudsperson, September 6, 2022), https://www.nj.gov/correctionsombudsperson/documents/Jail%20Inspection%20Reports/DOC%20Ombudsperson%20Special%20Report-%20Heat.pdf.
19. Lisa Fernandez, "Dozens of Women Detail Rape and Retaliation at Dublin Prison, Real Reform Is Questioned," KTVU FOX 2, updated September 25, 2022, https://www.ktvu.com/news/dozens-of-women-detail-rape-and-retaliation-at-dublin-prison-real-reform-is-questioned; Luke Barr, "Jeffrey Epstein's Suicide Still Looms Over the Federal Bureau of Prisons 1 Year Later," ABC News, August 11, 2020, https://abcnews.go.com/Politics/jeffrey-epsteins-suicide-looms-federal-bureau-prisons-year/story?id=72289201; Editorial Board, "Whitey Bulger's Death Was Not Justice. It Was a Betrayal of Justice," *Washington Post*, November 2, 2018, https://www.washingtonpost.com/opinions/whitey-bulgers-death-was-not-justice-it-was-a-betrayal-of-justice/2018/11/02/136e149e-dd3b-11e8-b3f0-62607289efee_story.html; Meg Anderson and Huo Jingnan, "As COVID Spread in Federal Prisons, Many At-Risk Inmates Tried and Failed to Get Out," NPR WNYC, March 7, 2022, https://www.npr.org/2022/03/07/1083983516/as-covid-spread-in-federal-prisons-many-at-risk-inmates-tried-and-failed-to-get-.
20. Michael R. Sisak and Michael Balsamo, "New Federal Prisons Chief Vows to Fix Troubles, Regain Trust," Associated Press, September 29, 2022, https://apnews.com/article/health-crime-prisons-covid-judiciary-233404fbc44b5c39b658c2b86a1958f5.
21. Michael B. Mushlin, "'I Am Opposed to This Procedure': How Kafka's *In the Penal Colony* Illuminates the Current Debate About Solitary Confinement and Oversight of American Prisons," *Oregon Law Review* 93 (2015): 571–630, https://digitalcommons.pace.edu/lawfaculty/989.

PART SIX

PRISON REFORM IN THE UNITED STATES

23

HOW SOME EUROPEAN PRISONS ARE BASED ON DIGNITY RATHER THAN DEHUMANIZATION

Ram Subramanian

ON A COLD MORNING IN FEBRUARY 2013, I led a group of American policymakers and criminal justice practitioners—judges, public defenders, legislators, corrections officials, law professors—on a visit to a juvenile prison in eastern Germany.[1] We met with a group of young men, largely between the ages of eighteen and twenty-one, who were serving between two and five years at the facility; most had been convicted of a violent offense.

Although these young men certainly looked like teenagers or very young adults—wearing jeans, cargo pants, colorful T-shirts, sweatshirts, and baseball caps—they would not have been considered juveniles in the American system of punishment, where at the time many states capped the upper age of juvenile status at seventeen, and where children as young as twelve and thirteen can be tried in the adult system for some crimes.[2] Nor would they have been allowed to dress as they did—in their own clothes, or to walk as freely as they did around the facility. A striking aspect of German law extends the ambit of juvenile justice—centered on minimum intervention and diversion—to young adults up to age twenty-one. Nearly two-thirds of young Germans in this age group who are involved in the justice system typically benefit from this ambit.[3] Prison sentences are the exception rather than the rule; even if young people are placed in custody, as these young men were, education and vocational training are central to their lives behind bars.[4]

The young men were brimming with excitement. They were eager to show the visitors where they worked and studied, how they decorated their rooms, and where they cooked their meals. They even introduced us to some of the animals they attentively looked after. They also had a million questions for our group, but one stood out: they wanted to know what sentence they would have received had they been convicted in the United States. It was a stark and confronting question.

One judge seemed almost unnerved by her response as she told a young man serving a four-year sentence that he likely would have received forty-three years for grievously assaulting a fellow young person and causing brain injury. By contrast, the median time served on a life sentence in Germany fluctuates between seventeen and nineteen years—but, as the group learned, such long sentences are exceedingly rare.[5] Nearly two-thirds (66 percent) of people sentenced to a term in custody are given prison sentences of two years or less; nearly 90 percent receive sentences of five years or less.[6] When pressed why she would have doled out such a long sentence, the judge tried to summon an answer, but hesitated, casting around for assistance from her fellow Americans. She could only say what sentence was both mandated by the law and typical of sentencing practices in her state. But she didn't know why. The conspicuous disparity in the scale of punishment revealed how absurdly punitive criminal sentences are in the United States as a matter of choice and shattered some of the Americans' assumptions of what constitutes proportional punishment.

Between 2013 and 2019, I organized four such study trips to introduce American criminal justice officials to several northern European corrections systems. One of the most striking encounters was a November 2018 visit to the neat and well-appointed living and working quarters of Halden Prison in southern Norway, a maximum-security facility that has received much international attention for being the "most humane prison in the world."[7]

Our delegation was surprised not only by the physical aspects of the place—open, well-lit, and bright, with lots of green spaces—but also the high degree to which the conditions of confinement were organized around the normalization principle, which recognizes the inherent harms of incarceration and requires that life in prison approximate the positive aspects of life in the community.[8] Under this principle, punishment is restricted to the separation from society mandated by the custodial sentence itself. Conditions of confinement should themselves be neither punitive nor onerous. Instead, the aim of the incarceration experience is to enable smooth reintegration of people upon release and to model a life of social responsibility.

Consequently, life at Halden is organized around the promotion of safety, well-being, and personal development, orchestrated to mimic life on the outside. Incarcerated individuals live in private rooms with doors and private bathrooms. Small groups share communal living spaces that include fully equipped kitchens. A well-outfitted music studio, dubbed Criminal Records, is even available for recording albums or producing a radio show.[9]

They are also encouraged to maintain a healthy measure of autonomy and personal agency in organizing their daily lives—they cook their own meals and are provided with an array of vocational training and educational programs, as well as various treatment options. They are given ample opportunities to maintain contact with family and friends, and they can all earn the award of brief periods of temporary leave from prison.

Meanwhile, wardens—many of them trained lawyers, social workers, and mental health professionals—and corrections officers are encouraged to develop strong social relationships with the people they supervise, which helps create a respectful, supportive, communicative, and caring environment.[10] Almost half of the approximately 290 prison staff are women.[11]

Discipline is very finely graded and disciplinary measures are closely tied to violations. Least restrictive sanctions are preferred, such as reprimands, brief restrictions on money, property, movement or leisure activities, or delays in scheduled home leave. Punitive solitary confinement is almost never used and is tightly restricted to a maximum of three days.[12] Unsurprisingly, violence is rare.

Contrast this with the U.S. corrections system, where penal life and settings are ordered around the paramount goals of "custody and order." American prison life is built on the dehumanizing rituals of induction, initiation, hierarchy, degradation and routine, all designed to assert authority and control over the bodies and lives of incarcerated people.[13] Individuality is stripped away upon prison entry, replaced by an inmate number and a standardized, nondescript uniform.

Life in a U.S. prison is filled with an endless parade of security measures (caging, handcuffing, shackling, strip and cell searches, and lock-downs) punctuating a daily routine marked by enforced idleness, the ever-present risk of violence, often adversarial relationships with prison staff, and only sporadic opportunities for constructive activities offering rehabilitation, education, or treatment.[14] Solitary confinement is often used as punishment for minor violations of prison rules, such as talking back, being out of place, or failure to obey an order.[15] Incarcerated individuals in America live in a harsh, dystopian social world of values and rules, designed to control, isolate, disempower, and erode a person's sense of autonomous self.[16]

At different points in U.S. history, the community's collective eyes have been opened to this stark but hidden world of what it's like in America's prisons. In 1967, President Johnson's Commission on Law Enforcement and Administration of Justice described life in America's prison as "at best barren and futile, at worst unspeakably brutal and degrading," providing the "poorest possible preparation for . . . successful reentry into society."[17] Later, in 2004, the American Bar Association Justice Kennedy Commission concluded that "correctional systems too often fail to do any correcting," instead "warehous[ing] inmates" while "increase[ing] the chances that prisoners, once released, will be neither equipped nor inclined to conform their conduct to the law."[18] In 2006, the Commission on Safety and Abuse in America's Prisons, an inquiry led by the Vera Institute of Justice, detailed the punishing and often inhumane conditions of confinement in U.S. prisons, shining a spotlight on the pervasive violence, significant overcrowding, poor health care, and regular use of long-term segregated housing and isolation.[19]

Changing this reality has been too slow, and very challenging. What's more, given the location of most of America's more than 1,600 prisons in areas far from large cities, it has been too easy for policymakers and communities to keep prisons—and the people inside them—out of sight and out of mind.[20] Can northern Europe's "human dignity" approach to corrections guide America down a pathway to help undo the degrading, disempowering, alienating, and brutalizing nature of confinement?[21] Experiments across the country at the prison unit level—in Connecticut, North Dakota, Oregon, Pennsylvania, and elsewhere—are trying to implement this human dignity ethos, despite critiques of too many differences—in politics and law, penal philosophy and punishment culture, in crime types or rates, in system scale and correctional resources, and even culturally with a diverse population.[22]

Many of those who have sought to translate lessons to American prisons, however, recognize that many of these differences obscure some important similarities, both current and historical. Many European systems, even those currently held up as models, once had much higher incarceration and recidivism rates than they do today.[23] They also continue to face challenges similar to those in the United States, including overcrowding, overrepresentation of people with mental illness, and a growing and increasingly diverse population of foreign-born individuals.[24] Participants on visits also witnessed these aspects.

In all my European trips with fellow criminal justice scholars and practitioners, two questions were always on the lips of every member of the American delegations: "Does human dignity work?" and "How much does it cost?" Reform-minded correctional practitioners and policymakers often require political cover, usually in the form of evidence-based practices or cost-effective solutions, to justify proposed changes.

How, though, do you study the goal of human dignity? Can you isolate the appropriate variables to truly measure cause and effect? If studies came back that showed that new practices focused on human dignity made little change, or if methods were found to cost too much, would one stop treating people humanely? Although European corrections officials are also interested in "what works," German and Norwegian officials specifically explained that they simply cannot and would not do some things to another person on principle, such as punishing people by keeping them in solitary confinement (twenty-three hours a day in a cramped cell smaller than the size of a standard parking space) indefinitely.[25]

Instead, they point to other evidence. Aggression and physical violence—between incarcerated people or against staff—are rare. Recidivism is lower than in many other countries.[26] Prisons are in large part calm, quiet, even strangely congenial places with high degrees of trust between staff and the incarcerated population. Perhaps illustrative of this was the one word the delegation visiting Halden kept on hearing, from corrections officers and prisoners alike: "hopeful." One young man was "hopeful" he would be "better" and make his family "proud." He was "hopeful" that he would be forgiven by the person he hurt. He was also "hopeful" that one day he could forgive himself. Prison staff, too, expressed hope—hope that their efforts would help the people they supervised and, on a larger level, hope that they were making a meaningful contribution to the overall safety of the community.

When confronted with what they saw in various facilities, most of the American visitors eventually came around, despite their initial skepticism. The spectrum of what was possible had widened. To treat people humanely and with respect and dignity, they needn't wait to build a facility like Halden, nor wait for a legislature to thickly weave a human dignity approach into the skein of their penal laws. Although it may require an adjustment in training, treating people on a person-to-person basis with respect and dignity is essentially free. This is the attitude adopted by the corrections agency and research in Pennsylvania, as detailed in the essay in this volume highlighting the Little Scandinavia approach (see chapter 24). With the assistance of Amend, a nonprofit that brings international public health practices to change the culture in U.S. prisons, North Dakota has applied the normalization principle to an entire facility, transforming conditions of confinement in the Missouri River Correctional Center to more directly approximate or relate to outside life.[27] It also revamped correctional training to focus on dynamic security, a philosophy based on the idea that allowing people to make choices and giving them the opportunity to do better will lead to a safer prison because a person who is treated humanely is less likely to be violent.[28] Amend also played a key role in culture change in Oregon. Since 2019, the Oregon Department of Corrections has applied a new philosophical approach to corrections inspired by Norway that centers on the belief that humanizing and normalizing the prison environment is beneficial for employees and the people who are incarcerated in prisons. Oregon has begun to implement some practical applications to one unit at Snake River Correctional Institution and is in the beginning stages of doing so at Oregon State Penitentiary.[29]

The simple fact is that Finland, Germany, the Netherlands, and Norway have all made a deliberate choice to do things differently. To be sure, Germany's turn toward a human dignity approach was largely directed and deeply informed by the postwar political arrangements and human rights consensus that emerged after World War II. Norway and Finland, on the other hand, demonstrate that a country need not suffer cataclysmic events—genocide, military defeat, foreign occupation—to induce fundamental change.[30] Proactively inducing this transformation is the goal of many of the homegrown initiatives seeking to adapt aspects of northern Europe's humanistic prison model to some prison units in America.

Although putting the brakes on American punitive excess can and should be accomplished by centering human dignity as a foundational, organizing principle of the nation's corrections system, the tentative steps that have been taken across the country will not likely stop the dominant punishment culture that helped give rise to mass incarceration.

Challenges abound in bringing this model to scale. To develop, sustain, and support all the services in a prison like Halden—systemwide, rather than limited to one or two units, or just one facility—would require significant state resources. Budget cuts or the withdrawal of agency or political support would likely endanger the life of current pilot programs and prevent more widespread uptake. Additionally, such projects require a huge paradigm shift in the culture of corrections that would require the participation of a much wider segment of operational staff. This goal is difficult both to implement and measure without wider political or legal reforms. For example, only a select few countries, such as Germany, commit to human dignity in a manner that affirmatively shapes their prison policies and practices.[31]

Failing to center human dignity as a new positive legal standard of treatment for people behind bars risks perpetuating the status quo of security and control prevailing too easily over concerns about dignity or fairness in our prisons. The force of that power is too strong. Fundamental changes to the "soul-chilling inhumanity" of America's prisons, as one judge has described it, will certainly require much more.[32]

NOTES

1. Ram Subramanian and Alison Shames, *Sentencing and Prison Practices in Germany and the Netherlands: Implications for the United States* (New York: Vera Institute of Justice, 2013), 4–5, https://www.vera.org/downloads/publications/european-american-prison-report-v3.pdf.
2. "Raising the Age of Juvenile Court Jurisdiction," *NCSL LegisBrief* 23, no. 39 (2015), https://www.ncsl.org/research/civil-and-criminal-justice/raising-the-age-of-juvenile-court-jurisdiction.aspx; Jeree Thomas, Jasmine Aswad, Katie Rankin, and Hannah Roberts, "Raising the Floor: Increasing The Minimum Age of Prosecution as an Adult" (Campaign for Youth Justice, 2019), 1–2, http://www.campaignforyouthjustice.org/images/Raising_the_Floor__Final.pdf. As of 2021, only three states—Georgia, Texas, and Wisconsin—had failed to pass Raise the Age legislation increasing the jurisdiction of the juvenile court system past the age of seventeen. Chuck Carroll, "Raise the Age: Where Legislation Stands in The Final Three States," *The Imprint*, February 24, 2021, https://imprintnews.org/justice/raise-age-where-legislation-stands-final-three-states/52186.
3. Jörg-Martin Jehle, *Criminal Justice in Germany* (Berlin: Federal Ministry of Justice and Consumer Protection, 2019), 41–43, http://dx.doi.org/10.15496/publikation-9832.
4. Frieder Dünkel, "Germany," in *Juvenile Justice Systems in Europe: Current Situation and Reform Developments*, vol. 2, ed. Frieder Dünkel, Joanna Grzywa, Philip Horsfeld, and Ineke Pruin (Mönchengladbach: Forum Verlag Godesberg, 2011), 562–63.
5. Axel Dessecker, "Dangerousness, Long Prison Terms, and Preventive Measures in Germany," *Champ Pénal* 6 (2009): 27, https://journals.openedition.org/champpenal/7508.
6. Jehle, *Criminal Justice in Germany*, 58–59.
7. Stephen A. Carter, "Welcome to Halden Prison" (paper presented to the Department of Corrections and Rehabilitation Review Committee, Bismarck, North Dakota, October 22, 2019), 21–23, https://www.ndlegis.gov/files/committees/66

-2019/21_5063_03000appendixb.pdf; Amelia Gentleman, "Inside Halden, the Most Humane Prison in the World," *The Guardian*, May 18, 2012, https://www.theguardian.com/society/2012/may/18/halden-most-humane-prison-in-world.

8. Narianne Vollan, "Full Rights Citizens: The Principle of Normality in Norwegian Prisons," interview, *Justice Trends*, July 24, 2018, https://justice-trends.press/full-rights-citizens-the-principle-of-normality-in-norwegian-prisons.
9. Steve Urquhart, "Criminal Records," Listentosteve, February 26, 2014, https://listentosteve.wordpress.com/2014/02/26/criminal-records. See also Steve Urquhart, "Reducing Offending: Listening to Europe, Broadcasting to the UK," Winston Churchill Memorial Trust, 2014, https://media.churchillfellowship.org/documents/Urquhart_S_Report_2013_Final.pdf.
10. Deborah Berlioz, "We Are More Like Social Workers Than Guards," *HesaMag* 19 (2019): 24–25, https://www.etui.org/sites/default/files/Hesamag_19_EN-23-26.pdf.
11. Emma Jane Kirby, "How Norway Turns Criminals into Good Neighbours," BBC, July 7, 2019, https://www.bbc.com/news/stories-48885846.
12. Are Høidal, "Prisoners' Association as an Alternative to Solitary Confinement—Lessons Learned from a Norwegian High-Security Prison," in *Solitary Confinement: Effects, Practices, and Pathways Toward Reform*, ed. Jules Lobel and Peter Scharff Smith (New York: Oxford University Press, 2019), 309, https://academic.oup.com/book/35060/chapter/298996748.
13. Ruth Delaney, Ram Subramanian, Alison Shames, and Nicholas Turner, *Reimagining Prison* (New York: Vera Institute of Justice, 2018), 19–20, https://www.vera.org/downloads/publications/Reimagining-Prison_FINAL3_digital.pdf.
14. John J. Gibbons and Nicholas deB. Katzenbach, *Confronting Confinement* (New York: The Commission on Safety and Abuse in America's Prisons, 2006), 11–12, https://www.vera.org/downloads/publications/Confronting_Confinement.pdf; Leah Wang, "The State Prison Experience: Too Much Drudgery, Not Enough Opportunity" (Northampton, MA: Prison Policy Initiative, September 2, 2022), https://www.prisonpolicy.org/blog/2022/09/02/prison_opportunities.
15. Alison Shames, Jessa Wilcox, and Ram Subramanian, *Solitary Confinement: Common Misconceptions and Emerging Safe Alternatives* (New York: Vera Institute of Justice, 2015), 14, https://www.vera.org/downloads/publications/solitary-confinement-misconceptions-safe-alternatives-report_1.pdf.
16. Delaney et al., *Reimagining Prison*, 19.
17. Nicholas deB. Katzenbach et al., *The Challenge of Crime in a Free Society* (Washington, DC: The President's Commission on Law Enforcement and Administration of Justice, 1967), 159, https://s3.documentcloud.org/documents/3932081/Crimecommishreport.pdf.
18. Justice Kennedy Commission, *Reports with Recommendations to the ABA House of Delegates* (Chicago: American Bar Association, 2004), 79, https://www

.americanbar.org/content/dam/aba/publications/criminaljustice/justice-kennedy-commission-reports.pdf.

19. Gibbons and Katzenbach, *Confronting Confinement*, 11–14.
20. Wendy Sawyer and Peter Wagner, *Mass Incarceration: The Whole Pie 2022* (Northampton, MA: Prison Policy Initiative, March 14, 2022), https://www.prisonpolicy.org/reports/pie2022.html. For prison siting, see John M. Eason, *Big House on the Prairie: Rise of the Rural Ghetto and Prison Proliferation* (Chicago: University of Chicago Press, 2017).
21. Shon Hopwood, "How Atrocious Prisons Conditions Make Us All Less Safe" (New York: Brennan Center for Justice, August 9, 2021), https://www.brennancenter.org/our-work/analysis-opinion/how-atrocious-prisons-conditions-make-us-all-less-safe.
22. Maurice Chammah, "The Connecticut Experiment" (Washington, DC: The Marshall Project, May 8, 2018), https://www.themarshallproject.org/2018/05/08/the-connecticut-experiment; Cinnamon Janzer, "North Dakota Reforms its Prisons, Norwegian Style," *U.S. News & World Report*, February 22, 2019, https://www.usnews.com/news/best-states/articles/2019-02-22/inspired-by-norways-approach-north-dakota-reforms-its-prisons; Oregon Department of Corrections, "The Oregon Way," accessed November 30, 2022, https://www.oregon.gov/doc/about/Pages/oregon-way.aspx; DOC Staff, "Little Scandinavia Opens at Chester," Pennsylvania Department of Corrections, May 31, 2022, https://www.cor.pa.gov/CorrectionalNewsfront/Pages/Article.aspx?post=1820.
23. Marc Mauer, "Incarceration Rates in an International Perspective" (Washington, DC: The Sentencing Project, June 28, 2017), https://www.sentencingproject.org/policy-brief/incarceration-rates-in-an-international-perspective.
24. Jan R. Strømnes, "Nordic Correctional Policies, Values, Methods, and Practice: What Are They—and Can and Should They Be Transferred to the US?" (presentation at the American Correctional Association Winter Conference, New Orleans, LA, January 11–15, 2019), 3, https://waynenorthey.com/wp-content/uploads/2019/02/Halden-prison-ACA-Winter-Conference-New-Orleans-januar-2019-pdf-version.pdf; Jehle, *Criminal Justice in Germany*, 13–14, 56–57.
25. Alison Shames, Jessa Wilcox, and Ram Subramanian, *Solitary Confinement: Common Misconceptions and Emerging Safe Alternatives* (New York: Vera Institute of Justice, 2015), 8, https://www.vera.org/downloads/publications/solitary-confinement-misconceptions-safe-alternatives-report_1.pdf.
26. Meagan Denny, "Norway's Prison System: Investigating Recidivism and Reintegration," *Bridges: A Journal of Student Research* 10, no. 10 (2016): 22–37, 23, https://digitalcommons.coastal.edu/cgi/viewcontent.cgi?article=1032&context=bridges.
27. Delaney et al., *Reimagining Prison*, 77–92.
28. Janzer, "North Dakota Reforms Prisons."

29. Oregon Department of Corrections, "The Oregon Way"; Ariel Bleicher, "Norway's Humane Approach to Prisons Can Work Here Too," *UCSF Magazine*, Summer 2021, https://magazine.ucsf.edu/norways-humane-approach-prisons-can-work-here-too.
30. Strømnes, "Nordic Correctional Policies," 3; Tapio Lappi-Seppälä, "Imprisonment and Penal Policy in Finland," *Scandinavian Studies in Law* 54 (2009): 334–79, http://www.antoniocasella.eu/nume/Lappi-Seppala_2012.pdf.
31. Grundgesetz für die Bundesrepublik Deutschland (Basic Law), Article 1 (1949), https://www.gesetze-im-internet.de/englisch_gg/index.html#gl_p0014. See also Strafvollzugsgesetz (German Prison Act) of 1976, §§ 2–4. The German Prison Act sets the standards by which not only detention facilities must operate but also prison managers and staff must behave.
32. Inmates of Suffolk County Jail v. Eisenstadt, 360 F. Supp. 676, 684 (D. Mass. 1973), https://law.justia.com/cases/federal/district-courts/FSupp/360/676/1887570.

24

EMBRACING DIGNITY

Pennsylvania's Experiment with Scandinavian Correctional Principles

Steven L. Chanenson, Jordan M. Hyatt, and Synøve N. Andersen

AS WE WALKED PAST THE MUSTARD YELLOW WALLS of Anstalten Kumla, the largest prison in Sweden, the surroundings were simultaneously familiar and foreign to us, a group of correctional officers and leaders from Pennsylvania. As a maximum-security facility, Kumla prison houses people convicted of some of the most serious offenses in all of Sweden, and its physical security measures—including a panopticon-like maximum-security wing—seemed more like an American prison than the bucolic correctional campuses, such as Norway's Halden Fengsel, where they had previously spent time.[1]

Although the observable contrasts were stark, the culture and operations of Kumla, like all the Scandinavian institutions they visited, emphasized human dignity for incarcerated people and officers alike. Thus it reflected a sharp break from their experiences working in a correctional institution in the United States. That, however, was about to change.

We are part of the Scandinavian Prison Project (SPP) research team. Our goal is to integrate research and policy by exploring whether Scandinavian correctional principles and practices can work effectively in Pennsylvania.[2] To make this change happen, staff at the Pennsylvania Department of Corrections visited multiple Scandinavian prisons and, for several weeks, worked alongside officers in Norwegian institutions.[3] On returning to the United States, correctional officers and leaders worked together and identified discrete policies and practices to borrow from Scandinavia and adapt to their context. With support from a range of academic, correctional, and subject-matter experts, they took these "legal transplants" and implemented them in one housing unit, now known as Little Scandinavia, at the State

Correctional Institution at Chester (SCI Chester), a medium-security prison just outside Philadelphia.[4]

Little Scandinavia is home to dozens of people whose incarcerated experience differs significantly from their peers who live in other parts of SCI Chester and facilities across the state. The SPP "aims to be both a window and a mirror. It provides a window into what is possible for a correctional facility—one inspired by a different culture but adapted to thrive in Pennsylvania. It also provides a mirror. What will we discover about corrections in the Keystone State and America more broadly?"[5]

The Scandinavian approach to corrections emphasizes human dignity over punitiveness. The logo of the Swedish Prison and Probation Service (Kriminalvården) speaks volumes about the correctional culture it strives to establish. Two keys dominate the image. The top one is golden and faces upward, signifying letting people out when they have served their sentence and the goal of reintegration; the bottom one is silver and faces downward, signifying locking people in and Kriminalvården's obligation to protect public safety. As one of our Swedish hosts told us, this is consistent with one of their prevailing slogans, *bättre ut* (better out).

Fundamental to the Scandinavian model of corrections is the principle of normality, which the Norwegian Correctional Service (Kriminalomsorgen) defines this way:[6] "The punishment is the restriction of liberty; no other rights have been removed by the sentencing court. Therefore, the sentenced offender has all the same rights as all other[s] who live in Norway. No-one shall serve their sentence under stricter circumstances than necessary for the security in the community. Therefore . . . life inside will resemble life outside as much as possible."[7]

The physical, programmatic, and cultural aspects to the goals of the normality principle take different forms in the various Scandinavian systems. It is, under even the best of circumstances, just an approximation of a true noncustodial experience. With this in mind, a Pennsylvania correctional leader remarked after visiting a Danish prison, "one of the things that obviously [matters] in this correctional system, the belief system, is that the more normal [your experience is inside], the better you're going to be as a human being [back home]."[8]

On the physical side, some Scandinavian prisons resemble college campuses; others look like medieval fortresses, boarding schools, or American-style prisons.[9] Regardless of the shape of the walls or the layout of the facility, however, common elements support the development of a distinctive carceral environment. For example, incarcerated people are typically provided with their own cell, sometimes with a private toilet and shower. In certain facilities, people in custody are allowed to wear civilian clothing and prepare their own meals with a full array of kitchen tools, including tethered knives.

On the cultural front, "strengthening the normality principle means organizing a daily routine in prison that as far as possible reflects the society outside the walls."[10] That routine includes regular participation in work and school within the facility, often away from the housing area. In another reflection of noncustodial life, many staff members knock before opening cell doors, except in emergencies, and seek to establish living, cooking, and recreation norms that both prepare people for life outside prison and facilitate typical human interaction between staff and incarcerated people.

Respectful interaction between staff and incarcerated people is arguably central to the success of the Scandinavian approach to corrections.[11] This is fundamental for both the security of their institutions and the cultures within them. For example, some staff at Kumla seek to foster an environment of human dignity by commonly referring to incarcerated people as *clients* as opposed to *inmates*. Officials highlighted that *client* can be seen as a more neutral, as opposed to a demeaning, term.

All of this is consistent with a dynamic security approach, which relies on a positive relationship between officers and incarcerated people to promote safety and rehabilitation.[12] Thus Scandinavian staff seek to know and support the relatively small number of incarcerated people for whom they are directly responsible, which can produce a calm and relatively low-stress environment for everyone. To meet their goals, Scandinavian correctional authorities provide their staff with multiple years of extensive academic and practical training, though the length and nature of the curricula vary by jurisdiction.

After determining which legal transplants from Scandinavia might succeed in Pennsylvania, the SCI Chester team pursued a form of the normality principle. The physical environment that would become the Little Scandinavia housing unit received a significant makeover. Two-person cells were retrofitted for single occupancy and furnished with a mini refridgerator, small TV, and a standard movable desk chair. The common area was transformed with better lighting, sound-dampening tiles, soft Nordic-inspired seating, plants, and an aquarium. After the installation of a full commercial kitchen, SCI Chester partnered with a local grocery store so the residents can purchase fresh food of their choosing and then cook it.

Among the many changes implemented in the Little Scandinavia unit, the most vital are those that might escape the untrained eye. The significance of a new approach to officer-resident interactions can hardly be overstated. During their time in Scandinavia, the Pennsylvanians recognized that they can interact with the people in their charge more respectfully and effectively. In fact, after sharing a meal for the first time with an incarcerated person while working in a Norwegian prison, one officer reflected, "At that moment, I didn't feel like I'm superior to you or I'm in a position of authority over you. We were all just eating a meal. And it was really nice. We don't ever have moments like that [in traditional American corrections]." That was not possible in the Pennsylvania prison system because such interactions would have been prohibited as inappropriate fraternization.[13]

That fraternization policy is broad.[14] One Little Scandinavia officer commented that under Pennsylvania regulations, "We can't talk to [incarcerated people] for more than a five-minute span at any given time or it'll be considered fraternization."[15] Another officer asserted that the fraternization policy needed to be changed "because there's no way that our staff can engage and socialize and really get to know someone on that level that's expected under dynamic security in the current system."[16]

The Little Scandinavia team pursued two tracks. Working with the leadership at the facility and state level, the officers suggested a new framework for these encounters, one that would allow for more communication but remains within the regulation parameters. The resulting redefinition in Little Scandinavia of what constitutes fraternization, though perhaps falling short of what they saw during their trips abroad, provided the officers the opportunity to develop new rapports and patterns of communication. In support of these objectives, the Little Scandinavia officers received a range of training not typically available, including sessions on conflict resolution, Yield Theory, and suicide prevention. They were also afforded the time necessary to put those skills to use through heightened staffing levels.

The day-to-day life of Little Scandinavia's residents and staff differs from a stereotypical American prison. In addition to cooking many of their own meals, people living in Little Scandinavia are each expected to go to work, treatment, or school, just like many in the community. Consistent with Kriminalvården's example and the parameters of dynamic security, officers refer to incarcerated people as residents. In contrast to some Scandinavian facilities, however, street clothes are not permitted in Little Scandinavia. At the same time, everyone working and living in Little Scandinavia has access to distinctive attire in the form of different-colored polo shirts (each with the logo of the unit), pants, and jackets. Although a seemingly small change, they have been a welcomed addition to the unit.

Elsewhere in this volume (see chapter 23), Ram Subramanian asks a crucial question. How can efforts at respecting human dignity in prison be studied and evaluated? As part of the SPP, we are deploying mixed methods to assess Little Scandinavia from a variety of perspectives. When the correctional officials were in Scandinavia, we collected various data, including surveys, semi-structured interviews, and audio diaries from the participants.[17] Now that Little Scandinavia houses a group of residents selected from the general population, in addition to six individuals serving life sentences who act as trained peer mentors, we are monitoring official data as well as conducting regular interviews and administering an externally validated survey developed to measure prison climate in a consistent and replicable way.[18]

Recidivism, of course, is a policy-relevant outcome. Nevertheless, we do not view it as the animating goal or infallible touchstone for either the efforts at SCI Chester or prison reform in general. First, recidivism in the community is a complex process, especially when the prison environment, where programming is delivered, is isolated from the community and its distinct challenges. Little Scandinavia reflects a black box package of reforms, some mundane and some extraordinary, and many confounding factors are involved in teasing out which elements matter the most for reducing crime in the community. Furthermore, recidivism measures neither human dignity nor officer-resident wellness.

Developing an understanding of prison climate, both in Little Scandinavia and within other Pennsylvania prisons, tracks the experience of those who live in prison across several key areas: "relationships in prison, safety and order, contact with the outside world, facilities, meaningful activities, and autonomy."[19] Additionally, we are conducting regular interviews to understand more fully the impact of living in Little Scandinavia. These data provide important insights into how prisons function in varying ways—and can highlight opportunities for short- and long-term reforms.

We are intentionally including correctional staff in our research. Often overlooked in correctional reform efforts, officers suffer alarming levels of stress, mental health challenges, substance abuse, domestic violence, and a reduced life expectancy, including due to suicide.[20] Based on data collected while the correctional officials were in Scandinavia, there is reason to believe that adapting a Norwegian-style approach could reduce stress and improve wellness.[21]

The Little Scandinavia housing unit opened to its first cohort of residents in May 2022 and was fully populated in November 2022, so much remains to be learned about how experiencing heightened dignity in prison can change the trajectory of people's lives. Yet preliminary findings from the SPP are encouraging. They make us optimistic about one potential future for elements of American corrections. We can envision a time when all jails and prisons embrace the normality principle and prize human dignity for everyone.

Some of the changes in Little Scandinavia cost money; some do not. However, these Scandinavian legal transplants require formal institutional support to take root and flourish. Little Scandinavia enjoyed that commitment and leadership at every level of the Pennsylvania government.[22] Unfortunately, incarcerated people and even the staff responsible for their safety are not consistently viewed as political priorities in the United States. Not only must the correctional culture pivot toward dignity, but society at large must as well.[23] As former Justice Anthony Kennedy said, "[Prisons are] the concern and responsibility . . . of every citizen. This is your justice system; these are your prisons."[24]

Under the right conditions, American prisons—our prisons—can in fact move toward a system that prioritizes human dignity. Armed with that knowledge, we have an obligation to move these efforts to the forefront of correctional conversations, policies, and actions.

NOTES

1. Jordan M. Hyatt, Synøve N. Andersen, Steven L. Chanenson, Veronica Horowitz, and Christopher Uggen, "'We Can Actually Do This:' Adapting Scandinavian Correctional Culture in Pennsylvania," *American Criminal Law Review* 58, no. 4 (2021): 1743, https://www.law.georgetown.edu/american-criminal-law-review/wp-content/uploads/sites/15/2021/07/58-4_Hyatt-et-al-We-Can-Actually-Do-This.pdf.
2. Hyatt et al., "We Can Actually Do This."
3. Jordan M. Hyatt and Synøve Nygaard Andersen, "A Pennsylvania Prison Gets a Scandinavian-Style Makeover—and Shows How the US Penal System Could Become More Humane," The Conversation, October 7, 2022, http://theconversation.com/a-pennsylvania-prison-gets-a-scandinavian-style

-makeover-and-shows-how-the-us-penal-system-could-become-more-humane -187834.

4. Jonathan M. Miller, "A Typology of Legal Transplants: Using Sociology, Legal History and Argentine Examples to Explain the Transplant Process," *American Journal of Comparative Law* 51, no. 4 (2003): 839–85, https://doi.org/10.2307/3649131.
5. Hyatt et al., "We Can Actually Do This," 1728–29.
6. Are Høidal, "Normality Behind the Walls: Examples from Halden Prison," *Federal Sentencing Reporter* 31, no. 1 (2018): 61, https://doi.org/10.1525/fsr.2018.31.1.58.
7. Kriminalomsorgen, "About the Norwegian Correctional Service," Kriminalomsorgen.no, accessed January 24, 2023, https://www.kriminalomsorgen.no/index.php?%20cat=265199.
8. Hyatt et al., "We Can Actually Do This," 1743.
9. Jessica Benko, "The Radical Humaneness of Norway's Halden Prison," *New York Times*, March 26, 2015, https://www.nytimes.com/2015/03/29/magazine/the-radical-humaneness-of-norways-halden-prison.html.
10. Norwegian Ministry of Justice and the Police, "Punishment That Works—Less Crime—A Safe Society," *Federal Sentencing Reporter* 31, no. 1 (2018): 54, https://doi.org/10.1525/fsr.2018.31.1.52.
11. Høidal, "Normality Behind the Walls," 63, 65; Kenneth Gustafsson, "The Role of the Prison Officer in Different Epochs," in *Getting Here: An Anthology on the Swedish Approach to Offenders*, ed. Gustav Tallving (Stockholm: Kriminalvården Förleg, 2018), 6–22.
12. Veronica L. Horowitz, Emily R. Greberman, Patrick E. Nolan, Jordan M. Hyatt, Chris Uggen, Synøve N. Andersen, and Steven L. Chanenson, "A Comparative Perspective on Officer Wellness: American Reflections from Norwegian Prisons," *Criminal Justice Studies* 34, no. 4 (2021): 477–97, https://doi.org/10.1080/1478601X.2021.2001231; UN Office on Drugs and Crime, *Handbook on Dynamic Security and Prison Intelligence*, 2015, https://www.unodc.org/documents/justice-and-prison-reform/UNODC_Handbook_on_Dynamic_Security_and_Prison_Intelligence.pdf.
13. Horowitz et al., "A Comparative Perspective."
14. Pennsylvania Department of Corrections, "Offender Contact and Relationship Reporting Requirements," Section 1—Responsibilities and Training, February 7, 2014, 1–1, 1–2. https://www.cor.pa.gov/About%20Us/Documents/DOC%20Policies/01.01.14%20Offender%20Contact%20and%20Relationship%20Reporting%20Requirements.pdf.
15. Horowitz et al., "A Comparative Perspective," 488.
16. Horowitz et al., "A Comparative Perspective," 488.
17. Hyatt et al., "We Can Actually Do This," 1739.

18. Anouk Q. Bosma, Esther Van Ginneken, Hanneke Palmen, Amanda J. Pasma, Karin A. Beijersbergen, and Paul Nieuwbeerta, "A New Instrument to Measure Prison Climate: The Psychometric Quality of the Prison Climate Questionnaire," *The Prison Journal* 100, no. 3 (June 2020): 355–80, https://doi.org/10.1177/0032885520916819.
19. Bosma et al., "A New Instrument," 357.
20. Horowitz et al., "A Comparative Perspective," 480–81.
21. Horowitz et al., "A Comparative Perspective," 486, 490.
22. See, for example, Dave Ross, "This Secretary of Corrections Takes His Job Quite Literally," MyNorthwest, December 28, 2015, https://mynorthwest.com/152920/this-secretary-of-corrections-takes-his-job-quite-literally.
23. Ruth Delaney, Ram Subramanian, Alison Shames, and Nicholas Turner, "Human Dignity as the Guiding Principle," (New York: Vera Institute of Justice, September 2018), https://www.vera.org/reimagining-prison-web-report/human-dignity-as-the-guiding-principle.
24. Anthony M. Kennedy, "Speech Delivered by Justice Anthony M. Kennedy at the American Bar Association Annual Meeting: August 9, 2003," *Federal Sentencing Reporter* 16, no. 2 (December 2003): 126, https //doi.org/10.1525/fsr.2003.16.2.126

PART SEVEN

PUNISHMENT OF YOUNG PEOPLE

25

TREATING ALL KIDS AS KIDS

Kim Taylor-Thompson

AMERICA'S MISTREATMENT OF BLACK CHILDREN is chronic and casual. Sadly, it is an American phenomenon—a handed-down thing—deeply rooted in American soil and in the American psyche. Virtually every system that touches Black children in this country—public schools, foster care, immigration—treats them more harshly than white children. Arguably, though, the most acute harm occurs in the criminal justice system, where we routinely exercise the power to designate and derail.

On a daily basis, the system prematurely labels Black children as adults, ignoring the child in the offender. It carelessly discards young Black offenders in a structure never designed for children. There, these young people lose much more than their freedom. They lose the opportunity to develop in a healthier environment. They can expect lifelong challenges associated with less education, increased mental health problems, higher rates of suicide, and greater financial instability. To interrupt this persistent pattern of mistreatment, we need to adopt a bright line rule prohibiting the prosecution of anyone under twenty-one in the adult criminal justice system.

Children have the right to be children. The U.S. criminal justice system, though, routinely ignores that reality when applied to Black children. Both brain science and common sense confirm that an adolescent's brain differs significantly from that of a mature adult. Adolescents are works in progress who exhibit signature traits. They are impulsive, they have greater difficulty recognizing and regulating emotional responses, and they fail to appreciate fully the risks of their behavior, favoring short-term rewards over potential costs. Adolescents succumb more readily to negative external influences such as the behavior of peers—even their very presence, in fact—and the influence of unstable environments.

But neuroscience tells us that the regions of the adolescent brain governing impulse control and risk avoidance have not yet fully formed. The good news is that these traits are not fixed; volatility and impetuosity are transitory. As young people mature into their mid-twenties, they are better able to resist emotional impulses and regulate their behavior thanks to the development of brain structures and systems involved in executive function and impulse control.[1] By the time young people reach their mid-twenties, most will stop engaging in criminal conduct.[2]

In recent years, this evidence has begun to persuade a growing number of courts and policymakers to question the national reflex to designate younger and younger people as adults in the criminal justice system. But the dark underbelly of that hopeful story is that not all children enjoy the benefits of that new approach. Even as we see a reduction in the youth justice population, racial disparities persist.[3] The prism of race distorts our perception of the Black youthful offender and misshapes the Black child's experience of justice. Three intersecting phenomena are at play: stereotypical assumptions, dehumanization, and "adultification."

The "Black person as criminal" stereotype, which equates dangerousness with skin color, has demonstrated remarkable resilience over time. It persists even in light of conflicting data. Indeed, the narrative is so pervasive and culturally ingrained in America that we implicitly make the connection even when we explicitly reject the view. We see young Black boys and girls as animals or savages who engage in "wilding" behavior. The process of dehumanization turns Black children into undifferentiated objects. It deprives them of their individual features, those qualities that make them valuable and unique. Instead, we brand them as nameless predators.

When we add adultification to the mix, the justice experience for Black children warps even further. Research reveals that we see Black boys and girls as older than their actual chronological age. Participants in a series of comprehensive studies misperceived thirteen-year-old Black boys as seventeen-year-olds.[4] Just as important, the older the participants considered the child, the more culpable the child seemed. In a separate set of studies of Black girls, respondents considered Black girls more adult than white girls at almost all stages of development.[5]That adultification led respondents to conclude that Black girls needed less nurturing and protection than their white peers. The bottom line is simple: together, these phenomena prematurely strip Black children of the privilege and protections of childhood, provoking dangerous ramifications for them in the justice context.

We can trace an indelible through-line from this country's racist origins to today's racialized mistreatment of young people in the justice system. During slavery, white slavers separated Black children from their mothers because a child could garner a greater profit. This was not just profiteering; it was an explicit insistence that Black children were chattel, not human. During Jim Crow, white mobs lynched Black children if they dared cross a racial boundary that white society invented and ruthlessly enforced. Again, the declaration: Black children were not like other children. They needed to "know their place" in the racial caste or risk the ultimate sanction. Our history primed this nation to expect and accept the disparate treatment of Black children as somehow appropriate or deserved.

The twentieth-century justice system delivered on that expectation. Politicians, academics, and the media created and spread a superpredator mythology forecasting a tidal wave of violence by a new breed of offenders. This mythology contended that Black children were more predatory, more dangerous, more adult-like than white children. Although juvenile crime rates actually dropped in this period, the threat stoked fear that white America was in danger. That mischaracterization allowed Americans to withstand any tug of moral constraint in the rush to charge Black children as adults in the criminal justice system—children as young as eight.[6] Politicians pushed "adult time for adult crime" legislation and then filled U.S. prisons with young Black kids.[7]

Even as recently as the summer of 2020, we continue to trip over reminders of this racialized treatment. When a white seventeen-year-old, Kyle Rittenhouse, opened fire on protesters in Kenosha, Wisconsin, killing two protesters, conservative pundits and political operatives were quick to describe him as a "little boy out there trying to protect his community."[8] Even when he walked past police toting a semi-automatic rifle, they did not stop or question him; almost certainly, an armed Black seventeen-year-old would not have lived to tell the story. Rittenhouse, though, was not perceived as dangerous. He was seen as a child. Contrast that with twelve-year-old Tamir Rice, a child playing with a toy gun in his neighborhood park.[9] A Cleveland police officer sized up Tamir in an instant and considered him dangerous, shooting and killing him within two seconds of getting out of his patrol car—evidence, once again, of the pernicious power of racialized perceptions in our discretionary calls.

Retaining the discretion to charge a young person accused of a crime in adult court leads to an untenable form of racial exceptionalism: an adolescent's signature traits will be treated as "mitigating qualities" unless the accused is Black. Adolescent characteristics skew differently when we add race to the mix. Impulsivity morphs into dangerous unpredictability. Misbehavior in the company of peers becomes "gang activity." The inability to appreciate long-term risks devolves into intrinsic irresponsibility. As long as we allow the discretionary call to charge some children accused of crime in the adult system, we will continue to see prosecutors in juvenile court weaponizing adult prosecution as a way to coerce a more severe outcome in juvenile court. We will continue to see Black kids shouldered out of rehabilitative care even when they engage in the exact same behavior as white children. We will continue to see prosecutors misperceiving Black children's wrongful conduct as willful rather than the product of immaturity. Breaking this racism habit requires us to prohibit the prosecution of anyone under twenty-one in the adult criminal system.

NOTES

1. Coalition for Juvenile Justice, "What Are the Implications of Adolescent Brain Development for Juvenile Justice?," 2006, 3, http://www.juvjustice.org/sites/default/files/resource-files/resource_134.pdf.
2. Jeffery T. Ulmer and Darrell Steffensmeier, "The Age and Crime Relationship," in *The Nurture Versus Biosocial Debate in Criminology: On the Origins of Criminal Behavior and Criminality*, ed. Kevin M. Beaver, J. C. Barnes, and Brian B. Boutwell (Thousand Oaks, CA: Sage, 2014), 377, https://www.sagepub.com/sites/default/files/upm-binaries/60294_Chapter_23.pdf.
3. Eli Hager, "Racial Inequality in US Youth Detention Wider Than Ever, Experts Say," *The Guardian*, March 8, 2021, https://www.theguardian.com/us-news/2021/mar/08/us-juvenile-detention-race-marshall-project.
4. Phillip Atiba Goff, Matthew Christian Jackson, Brooke Allison Lewis Di Leone, Carmen Marie Culotta, and Natalie Ann DiTomasso, "The Essence of Innocence: Consequences of Dehumanizing Black Children," *Journal of Personality and Social Psychology* 106, no. 4 (2014): 526–45, https://bma.issuelab.org/resources/21336/21336.pdf.
5. Rebecca Epstein, Jamilia J. Blake, and Thalia González, *Girlhood Interrupted: The Erasure of Black Girls' Childhood* (Washington, DC: Georgetown Law Center on Poverty and Inequality, 2017), 1, https://genderjusticeandopportunity.georgetown.edu/wp-content/uploads/2020/06/girlhood-interrupted.pdf; Center on Gender Justice and Opportunity, "Adultification Bias," Georgetown Law,

accessed November 11, 2022, https://genderjusticeandopportunity.georgetown.edu/adultification-bias.

6. Equal Justice Initiative, *All Children Are Children: Challenging Abusive Punishment of Juveniles* (Montgomery, AL: Equal Justice Initiative, 2017), 5, https://eji.org/wp-content/uploads/2019/10/AllChildrenAreChildren-2017-sm2.pdf.
7. Office of Juvenile Justice and Delinquency Prevention, "Arrests of Youth Declined Through 2020," U.S. Department of Justice, 2022, https://www.ojjdp.gov/ojstatbb/snapshots/DataSnapshot_UCR2020.pdf.
8. Aris Folley, "Former Florida Attorney General Calls Kyle Rittenhouse 'A Little Boy Out There Trying to Protect His Community,'" *The Hill*, September 24, 2020, https://thehill.com/blogs/blog-briefing-room/news/518006-former-florida-attorney-general-defends-kyle-rittenhouse-a.
9. Shaila Dewan and Richard A. Oppel Jr., "In Tamir Rice Case, Many Errors by Cleveland Police, Then a Fatal One," *New York Times*, January 22, 2015, https://www.nytimes.com/2015/01/23/us/in-tamir-rice-shooting-in-cleveland-many-errors-by-police-then-a-fatal-one.html.

26

TREAT KIDS LIKE KIDS

The United States Is One of the Only Countries That Gives Life Sentences to Juveniles

Michael Mendoza

IN THE LATE 1980S, the United States had an opportunity to prevent countless children from receiving life sentences as adults by joining more than a hundred other countries in the ratification of the Convention of the Rights of the Child.[1] The United Nations General Assembly, the largest governing body in the world, reaffirmed then a young person "by reason of his physical and mental immaturity, needs special safeguards and care, including appropriate legal protection, before as well as after birth."[2] To this day, the United States is one of the only countries in the world that has yet to ratify a treaty that would implement special safeguards across the globe that protect children, who are our hope for the future.[3] Since then, countless children have been separated from their families, transferred from juvenile court, and convicted in adult court as "inmates" of their state adult correctional departments. The United States remains in violation of international human rights standards, found within the Convention of the Rights of the Child, by still sentencing children to life sentences, even life without the possibility of parole.

I should know because I was one of those children.

In 1996, a month after my fifteenth birthday, I made the worst decision of my life and participated in a crime that resulted in someone's losing their life. I was immediately arrested and held accountable—as I should have been. However, I found myself standing before a judge and was tried as an adult. The judge sentenced me to spend the rest of my life in prison. The thought of possibly dying in prison didn't quite register through my young mind at the time. Instead, I felt as if the whole world had given up on me and thrown me away without hope.

I'll never forget the night of my arrest. After being ordered out of the car, with my hands in the air, I could feel the cold steel of a million gun barrels aimed at the back of my head. The arresting officer awkwardly yanked my left arm into an unfamiliar position and pushed my face onto the back of the car's trunk. Then everything else became a blur as I was thrown into the back of a police car.

At the time, we were labeled superpredators, unworthy of second chances.[4] We were kids who were supposedly "godless, fatherless, heartless monsters" born in moral poverty.[5] This dehumanizing language against children resulted in creating fear in many communities, further justifying a need to separate children from their families by placing them in adult prison in lieu of holding them accountable in age-appropriate settings that provide trauma-informed care and family services.

On my seventeenth birthday, almost a week after a judge sentenced me to life in prison, I was transferred from the county jail where I had been detained for twenty-three months to California's Wasco State Prison reception center, designed to house 2,984 adults and still overcrowded to this day.[6] I was asleep in the juvenile "tank" section of the adult county jail when the sheriffs barged in and woke up all the kids that were being transferred that night. We were immediately shoved into the hallway and told to strip naked, squat, cough, and jump into a paper-thin jumpsuit. I'll never forget how cold, dark, and afraid I was being wrapped in chains and thrown onto a bus with the rest of society's outcasts—rejected and expelled.

Back then, California wasn't separating kids from adults in state prisons. My first cellmate was old enough to be my grandfather and would mostly try to school me in preparation for "life" in prison. I quickly realized that I had to worry more about my own safety than rehabilitation. At seventeen years of age, I had to begin serving my sentence in a level IV maximum security adult state prison. These prisons were designed to house people who committed serious and violent crimes. Most of the people there were serving lengthy sentences or life without the possibility of parole. Tension was constant on the yard between prison gangs, and survival meant always being fully aware of your surroundings.

According to Article 37 of the UN Convention on the Rights of the Child, "Every child deprived of liberty shall be treated with humanity and respect for the inherent dignity of the human person, and in a manner which considers the needs of persons of his or her age. In particular, every child deprived of liberty shall be separated from adults unless it is considered in the child's best interest not to do so and shall have the right to maintain contact with his or her family through correspondence and visits, save in exceptional circumstances."[7]

During the time I was in prison, which was from 1998 to 2014, the adult prison population in California skyrocketed and prisons became grossly overcrowded. In 2011, the U.S. Supreme Court ruled in *Brown v. Plata* that conditions in California's overcrowded prisons violated the Eighth Amendment's ban on cruel and unusual punishment.[8] At that point in time, California's prison system held approximately 156,000 people; it was designed to hold about eighty-five thousand.[9] I soon found out for myself how badly overcrowded and violent prisons were at the time—especially for people incarcerated as children.

When I was in prison, long lines and waiting lists—often six months to a year—to get into rehabilitation programs, educational classes, and jobs were the rule. The jobs paid about $10 a month after a 55 percent deduction toward restitution. Lock-downs meant no visits, no phone calls, no access to the canteen store, and not even shower heads. People in prison are usually denied showers for days, which is why we would use our sinks in the cell and take a "bird bath." Visiting rooms would be packed with long lines of people waiting to get in for their turn to see their loved ones. Gymnasiums were filled with rows of double bunks, and other buildings were fashioned with triple-racked bunks to provide more capacity to house people. I spent most of my time early on during my incarceration on lock-down due to violence in the yard or security concerns. It was difficult to participate in meaningful programs in prison even when the yard was peaceful because it would never last long enough before someone was stabbed or a riot ensued.

The consensus among incarcerated people serving a life sentence was that participating in rehabilitation programs didn't really matter because the California Board of Parole Hearings (Board) had a conservative reputation that rarely found people to "no longer pose a risk to society" and be suitable for parole no matter how stellar one's behavior in prison. Even more appalling was how frequently a governor would reject the Board findings and deny people parole whom the Board had found suitable to reenter society.[10] There was no hope of finding mercy, redemption, or freedom, only further dehumanization and punishment.

In 2012, the Supreme Court ruled in *Miller v. Alabama* that it is unconstitutional to have a statutory sentencing scheme that requires a judge to sentence a child under the age of eighteen to incarceration for life without parole.[11] Instead, sentencing laws must permit judges to consider the unique status of children and their potential for change as mitigating factors when sentencing them. During the same year, California enacted S.B. 9, authored by then State Senator Leland Yee, which ended the practice of sentencing children to life without the possibility of parole in California.[12] The bill was spurred on by a Human Rights Watch report, *When I Die . . . They'll Send Me Home,* which drew on six years of research finding that children in California sentenced to life without parole were disproportionately of color, had not been previously arrested, and were usually accompanied by an adult during the commission of the crime.[13]

More recently, the Supreme Court ruled in *Montgomery v. Louisiana* that *Miller* applies retroactively to thousands of people who are currently incarcerated serving a life without parole sentence for a crime committed when they were under the age of eighteen.[14] The petitioner, Henry Montgomery, had just been released after serving fifty-seven years in the Louisiana State Penitentiary, often called Angola or The Farm, after the plantation it succeeded, for a crime committed when he was seventeen. He was initially sentenced to the death penalty before being resentenced to life without parole until the Board of Pardons and Committee on Parole voted unanimously for his release in 2022 at the age of seventy-five.[15]

I grew up in San Juan Capistrano, in California. It was an immigrant community mostly of people from Mexico. Most of the kids I grew up with attended the same high school as I did; most of our parents worked several jobs to make a living and provide housing. By the tenth grade, I had experienced sexual, physical, and gang-related abuse while being groomed by adults to join a gang. The sexual and physical abuse left me feeling ashamed and worthless. It was much easier to hang around with other kids who felt just as broken and angry at the world. Most of us had no access to family counselors, therapists, or adults who could help unravel the negative impact of this abuse. Instead, the streets passed on generational trauma and provided drugs, alcohol, and other ways to learn to cope with our emotional pain.

A 2020 report by the Center for American Progress found that "exposure to adversity can have a lasting, lifelong impact on children's physical, emotional, and social well-being."[16] The report emphasizes that exposure to four or more adverse childhood experiences (ACEs) before reaching the age of eighteen "is considered clinically significant."[17] The Centers for Disease Control and Prevention defines ACEs as "potentially traumatic events" such as violence, abuse, or neglect, "that occur in childhood (0–17 years)."[18] When

I found myself standing before a judge being convicted as an adult during the mid-1990s, I had no clue what ACEs were or that I desperately needed help addressing childhood trauma. I was never treated for the trauma I suffered as a young person, nor while growing up in nine adult prisons for nearly two decades. I had to worry more about my safety rather than rehabilitation. Despite receiving a GED, self-help certificates, and staying out of trouble, in 2010, the Board denied my release back into society without taking my age, maturity, and growth into consideration. I would have stayed in prison for the rest of my days if a policy change hadn't transformed my life.

In partnership with Human Rights Watch, in 2013, the Anti-Recidivism Coalition, which is a nonprofit organization working to end mass incarceration in California, worked with then California Senator Loni Hancock to advocate for the passage of S.B. 260.[19] The law passed the California legislature and implemented Youth Offender Parole, which directed the Board of Parole Hearings to give great weight to the hallmark features of young people during a parole suitability hearing for those who committed their crime before reaching age eighteen. This significant change in the law gave hope to thousands of people in California—people like me—by providing an opportunity to prove they were no longer the same kids who they were when they first entered prison. The spirit of the law emphasizes an important message that legal experts and scholars across the globe agree on and what Mr. Montgomery, myself, and so many others have proven, that "children who commit even heinous crimes are capable of change."[20]

In 2014, I earned my release under S.B. 260. The Board considered my age at the time of the crime, along with my growth and maturity while in prison. They deemed that I was no longer a danger to public safety. They found me suitable to reenter society with lifetime supervised parole. On June 11, 2014, I was released from California's Men's Colony, the state prison near San Luis Obispo. I came home to a changed world from the one I had left on October 6, 1996. Technology was far advanced, and people communicated and socialized very differently and at a much faster pace. Since then, I have earned my bachelor's degree in political science at San Francisco State University and have helped pass more than thirty pieces of legislation in California and across the country.

Since California passed its law in 2013, twenty-four other states and the District of Columbia have legislatively ended the practice of sentencing children under eighteen to life without the possibility of parole.[21] These efforts have been empowered by communities directly affected by mass incarceration and emboldened by formerly incarcerated people who have been given an opportunity through legislative changes to be released, reunited with their families, and civically engaged in our democracy. This movement is also filled with passionate attorneys, family members, survivors, and even law enforcement urging America onto a path of redemption and hope for a safer future.

Despite these victories, it is still critical for the United States to ratify General Assembly Resolution 44/25 of the UN Convention on the Rights of the Child. This universal declaration would provide the crucial guidance our states need to provide age-appropriate services to children across the country. It would provide recognition that "childhood is entitled to special care and assistance."[22]

NOTES

1. UN General Assembly Resolution [UNGA Res.] 44/25, Convention of the Rights of the Child (September 2, 1990), https://www.ohchr.org/en/instruments-mechanisms/instruments/convention-rights-child.
2. UNGA Res. 1386 (XIV), Declaration of the Rights of the Child (November 20, 1959), https://www.refworld.org/docid/3ae6b38e3.html.
3. UN Human Rights Office of the High Commissioner, "Status of Ratification Interactive Dashboard," accessed October 30, 2022, https://indicators.ohchr.org.
4. Carroll Bogert and Lynnell Hancock, "Superpredator: The Media Myth That Demonized a Generation of Black Youth" (Washington, DC: The Marshall Project, November 20, 2020), https://www.themarshallproject.org/2020/11/20/superpredator-the-media-myth-that-demonized-a-generation-of-black-youth.
5. Robert Mackey and Zaid Jilani, "Hillary Clinton Still Haunted by Discredited Rhetoric on 'Superpredators,'" *The Intercept*, February 25, 2016, https://theintercept.com/2016/02/25/activists-want-hillary-clinton-apologize-hyping-myth-superpredators-1996.
6. California Department of Corrections and Rehabilitation, "Monthly Report of Population as of Midnight October 31, 2022," 2, https://www.cdcr.ca.gov/research/wp-content/uploads/sites/174/2022/11/Tpop1d2210.pdf.
7. UNGA Res. 44/25, Article 37.
8. Brown, et al. v. Plata, et al., 563 U.S. 493 (2011).
9. Pendarvis Harshaw, "Facing Life: The Project Showing the Cracks in California's Incarceration System," *The Guardian*, May 20, 2022, https://www.theguardian.com/us-news/2022/may/20/facing-life-california-incarceration-system-project.

10. Matt Levin, "Behind California's Dramatic Increase in Lifers Freed from Prisons," KQED, May 15, 2014, https://www.kqed.org/news/135494/behind-californias-dramatic-increase-in-murderers-freed-from-prisons.
11. Miller v. Alabama, 567 U.S. 460 (2012), https://tile.loc.gov/storage-services/service/ll/usrep/usrep567/usrep567460/usrep567460.pdf.
12. California S.B. 9, 2011–12 Leg., Reg. Sess. (Cal. 2012).
13. Christine Back and Elizabeth Calvin, *When I Die . . . They'll Send Me Home* (New York: Human Rights Watch, 2008), 3–5, https://www.hrw.org/reports/2008/us0108/us0108web.pdf.
14. Montgomery v. Louisiana, 577 U.S. ___ (2016).
15. Elyse Carmosino, "Convicted of Murder at 17, His Case Changed Juvenile Sentences. Louisiana Freed Him at Age 75." *The Advocate*, November 17, 2021, https://www.theadvocate.com/baton_rouge/news/article_8b7188a8-47b5-11ec-ac41-6befdfb0d59c.html.
16. Colin Seeberger, "Release: More Than 1 in 4 American Children Experience Adversity, Driven Most by Economic Hardship," Press release (Washington, DC: Center for American Progress, August 27, 2020), https://www.americanprogress.org/press/release-1-4-american-children-experience-adversity-driven-economic-hardship.
17. Cristina Novoa and Taryn Morrissey, *Adversity in Early Childhood: The Role of Policy in Creating and Addressing Adverse Childhood Experiences* (Washington, DC: Center for American Progress, 2020), 6, https://www.americanprogress.org/wp-content/uploads/2020/08/EarlyChildhoodAdversity-report.pdf.
18. Centers for Disease Control and Prevention, "Fast Facts: Preventing Adverse Childhood Experiences," last reviewed April 6, 2022, https://www.cdc.gov/violenceprevention/aces/fastfact.html.
19. California S.B. 260, 2013–14 Leg. Reg. Session (Cal. 2013), https://leginfo.legislature.ca.gov/faces/billNavClient.xhtml?bill_id=201320140SB260.
20. Montgomery v. Louisiana, 577 U.S. ___, slip op. at 21 (2016), https://supreme.justia.com/cases/federal/us/577/14-280/case.pdf.
21. Campaign for the Fair Sentencing of Youth, "States that Ban Life Without Parole for Children," accessed December 4, 2022, https://cfsy.org/media-resources/states-that-ban-juvenile-life-without-parole.
22. UNGA Res. 44/25, Preamble.

PART EIGHT

ECONOMIC INJUSTICE AND COLLATERAL CONSEQUENCES

27

MONETARY SANCTIONS AS A POUND OF FLESH

Alexes Harris

IN THEIR CONCLUSION TO THIS BOOK, Jeremy Travis and Bruce Western ask readers to question the purpose of punishment.

"Punishment," they write, "not only describes what criminal justice institutions do, but also signifies a relationship between the state and its citizens."[1]

Few aspects of the U.S. criminal legal system illustrate that as vividly as the system of monetary sanctions, which requires financial payments from most people who interact with the system. These punishments range from traffic citations to fees associated with juvenile cases and serious felony convictions. In addition to fines associated with specific offenses, people are charged for their court processing, for DNA testing, for required postsentencing rehabilitative programs (such as drug and alcohol assessment and treatment), and, even in some instances, for the costs of defense, prosecution, and incarceration itself.[2] To use Travis and Western's measure, the relationship between the state and citizen in the United States, particularly when the citizen is poor or negatively racialized, is one of control, marginalization, and perpetual punishment.

In most states, all monetary sanctions must be paid in full before a person is released from court supervision. The individual must remain in constant communication with court officials about their living and financial arrangements. Monetary sanctions are not only frequently appended to jail or prison time, but also associated with probation and other court mandated requirements, such as electronic home monitoring.

In many states, this means that people are unable to vote until all costs are paid. For example, in 2018, Florida citizens voted to allow people the right to vote once they have served their sentences.[3] However, within a year of citizens voicing their support of felony voter reenfranchisement, the state legislature moved to define this policy revision as including full payment of all court debt related to a felony conviction.[4] Researchers have estimated that approximately 1.1 million people are not able to vote given the mandate that people must pay before they can exercise their right to vote.[5] Worse, in Florida, those with fines and fees often can't even figure out what they owe, given that Florida does not have a centralized database where those with criminal records can look up their debts.[6]

Since the 1980s, paralleling the massive growth in convictions and incarceration, state and local jurisdictions expanded the types of fees and fines demanded of people convicted of traffic violations, juvenile offenses, misdemeanors, and felonies. At the same time, the cost to local jurisdictions of the expanding conviction and incarceration rate accelerated as well. As a result, policymakers turned to the very people convicted to pay for the costs of their own processing and punishments. For example, Washington State has a mandatory victim penalty assessment that must be charged for each misdemeanor ($250) and felony ($500) conviction, even if there is no direct victim of the crime in question.[7]

In some states, judges even have discretion to assess criminal defendants for the cost of a public defender—in other words, an individual who cannot afford to pay a lawyer is expected to pay for the lawyer that the state is constitutionally required to provide.[8] Furthermore, many jurisdictions charge per night of jail or prison.[9] For those too poor to pay, interest, per payment fees, and nonpayment penalties become penal debt that hangs like a cloud over their families' lives. In addition are the warrants regularly issued for those who are not paying, which set people up for negative police interactions.

Many states also allow cities and counties to engage in contracts with private collection companies, and when debt is transferred to these agencies, additional collection fees are assessed—as much as 50 percent of the principal owed.[10] These public-private debt collection arrangements affect individuals' credit scores, limit their employment opportunities, and inhibit their abilities to access housing, education, and transportation. The price of services such as telephone calls, electronic communication, video visitation, and health care include kickbacks from the private companies to local jurisdictions—the price the collection agencies pay to win exclusive contracts.[11] This private profiteering from public punishment and individual suffering is a common dimension to states' use of monetary sanctions.

The system of monetary sanctions reinforces our two-tiered system of justice: one for people with financial means and one for those without.[12]

Within a society riven by so much inequality, as the United States is, a system of punishment based on economic resources can never be fair or just. This "coerced financialization" perfectly and purposefully places the freedom of poor and racially marginalized people on a perpetual layaway plan.[13] It's a system so fully embedded in our criminal legal system that the American Rescue Plan Act, passed by Congress in March 2021 to alleviate the financial pains of the COVID-19 pandemic, allowed private collectors and courts to seize the $1,400 stimulus grants from people burdened with unpaid penal debt, either public or private.[14]

PAINFUL CONSEQUENCES

When they are unable to pay penal debt, people entangled with the criminal legal system—already stressed by daily financial choices they must make regarding food, health, and childcare—incur additional legal consequences. In many states, they lose their right to drive; then, if apprehended while driving with a suspended license (even to the job that might enable them to pay their debt), they face renewed incarceration and further financial sanctions.

Consequences accelerate, tethering people to the criminal legal system: not only are people who are behind in their payments sent regular court summonses, but in some instances even those making their monthly payments must also regularly report to the court about their employment and living arrangements. This requires many to miss work and to find childcare and transportation (particularly if their driver's licenses are suspended) just to attend court hearings. When people have been summoned to court but failed to receive notice or chose not to attend out of fear of incarceration, bench warrants are issued for their arrest.[15]

An additional legal consequence related to monetary sanctions is the overpolicing that plagues so many communities of color.[16] Because local governments have come to rely so heavily on revenue generated from fines and fees, traffic citations have become a tool for profit-making. This "pocketbook policing" encourages police to use their authority and discretion to make "pretextual" traffic stops—judgment calls that often involve such things as a faulty taillight, expired license tabs, or even an air freshener suspended from the rearview mirror.[17] And when police use their discretion to decide whom they are going to pull over, they pull over Black drivers disproportionately more often than white drivers. Black drivers are consequently searched one and a half to two times more often than white drivers.[18] Costly citations for fines and fees fall most heavily on those least able to pay them. These fines and fees lead to perpetual state surveillance, wealth extraction, and the social control of people who are poor and racially marginalized.

Recent research suggests that not only are individuals harmed by the practice of monetary sanctions, but communities are significantly affected as well.[19] A 2021 study found that in communities where residents were sentenced to large amounts of fines and fees, the poverty rate overall in those communities increased over time.[20] The researchers found a relationship between fines and fees and community poverty rates. Moreover, this relationship was strongest in nonwhite communities. Nationally, the picture is clear: fines and fees are sentences that affect individuals, their families, and their broader communities. They all experience this intense form of punishment.

From an intersectionality lens, it is also important to note the extra burden and harms borne by women, particularly Black women, via the punishment of fines and fees. Black women have a 1.7 times higher incarceration rate than white women, and thus carry a disproportionate burden of fines and fees.[21] However, even when Black women are not themselves convicted or incarcerated, evidence suggests that they are the ones helping support family members who are.[22]

In sum, understanding who is most harmed by monetary sanction policies and in what ways, from convicted people and their loss of fundamental civil rights such as driving and voting, to their children and communities, to Black women more specifically, helps us better understand this purposeful policy decision for what it is—an excessively punitive system of marginalization, control, and wealth extraction. However, we can also see clear pathways for needed and realistic reforms.

NEEDED POLICY REFORM

Set within the context of the criminal legal system, this system of punishment is nuanced but not complicated. Policy implications are clear. In fact, recognizing this system as a purposeful mechanism designed by both policy and statute allows us to clearly see that it can be dismantled. This set of guiding principles and practices should be established by state and local policymakers and court leadership.

First, statutes need to be revised to discontinue monetary sanctions associated with felony convictions. There is no reason that someone sentenced to incarceration should also receive financial penalties, much less be charged daily room and board fees. Fines and fees charged to people who are sentenced to live behind bars, without access to employment and a living wage, are prima facie excessive.

Second, monetary sanctions are also excessive when imposed on children, the unemployed, the unhoused, or those with mental health or chemical addiction disorders. Burdening people who are unable—and who may never be able—to pay fiscal debts is a cruel punishment.

Third, fiscal penalties attached to lower-level offenses that do not call for incarceration, such as traffic violations or misdemeanors, should be calibrated to individuals' abilities to pay the total sum within, say, two years. Countries around the world rely on day fine systems that calculate a score based on both the severity of the offense and the daily wage of the convicted individual.[23]

Fourth, state and local jurisdictions need to discontinue the practice of suspending driver's licenses related to nonpayment of any court fine and fee and cease issuing warrants related to nonpayment. In the last five years, twenty-two states and the District of Columbia have passed reforms to reduce debt-based driving restrictions.[24] In 2020, several states passed driver's license suspension reforms, which included discontinuation of suspending licenses for unpaid traffic violations or for nonpayment of court fines and fees.[25]

Fifth, state and local jurisdictions, along with law enforcement agencies, need to review and revise practices related to pretextual traffic stops. Less than a month after the police killing of Daunte Wright in Brooklyn Center, Minnesota, the mayor and city council enacted an ordinance to create a new Department of Community Safety and Violence Prevention.[26] Among other things, this restructuring of police duties transferred the responsibility of traffic enforcement to an unarmed civilian unit. Further, several prosecutors across the United States have indicated that they will not prosecute people based on evidence collected in pretextual stops.[27]

Finally, states need to require all jurisdictions to report (without names attached, to protect individual privacy) all monetary sentences and fees, regularly and systematically, to a state-monitored database. Such data should include amounts collected, amounts waived, means of levy (fine, fee, surcharge, restitution, and so on), and any additional charges imposed related to nonpayment, such as late fees, interest, and collection fees. Without transparency of this process and who is sentenced to what, we cannot have system accountability.

The evidence is clear. The American system of monetary sanctions is a purposeful punishment aimed at extracting wealth from individuals, their families, and communities—a pound of flesh that many just do not have left to give.[28] It is a system that valorizes those "deserving" of redemption (people with financial means) and stigmatizes those deemed not deserving of redemption (people living in poverty).

Impoverished citizens who are sentenced to monetary sanctions clearly understand their relationship to the state—they are forever indebted, forever subjected to court and police surveillance, control, and punishment. We have alternative punishment and rehabilitative options; we just need the will to make these changes.○

NOTES

1. Jeremy Travis and Bruce Western, "The Era of Punitive Excess" (New York: Brennan Center for Justice, April 13, 2021), https://www.brennancenter.org/our-work/analysis-opinion/era-punitive-excess.
2. See, for example, Chris Mai and Maria Rafael, "The High Price of Using Justice Fines and Fees to Fund Government in New York" (New York: Vera Institute of Justice, 2020), https://www.vera.org/downloads/publications/the-high-price-of-using-justice-fines-and-fees-new-york.pdf.
3. Florida Amendment 4, Voting Rights Restoration for Felons Initiative (2018).
4. Florida S.B. 7066 (Fla. 2019); Gabriella Sanchez, "In Florida, the Right to Vote Can Cost You" (New York: Brennan Center for Justice, September 7, 2022), https://www.brennancenter.org/our-work/analysis-opinion/florida-right-vote-can-cost-you.
5. Christopher Uggen, Ryan Larson, Sarah Shannon, and Robert Stewart, *Locked Out 2022: Estimates of People Denied Voting Rights* (Washington, DC: The Sentencing Project, 2022), 2, 16, https://www.sentencingproject.org/app/uploads/2022/10/Locked-Out-2022-Estimates-of-People-Denied-Voting.pdf.
6. Bianca Fortis, "A Government Official Helped Them Register. Now They've Been Charged With Voter Fraud," ProPublica, July 21, 2022, https://www.propublica.org/article/florida-felonies-voter-fraud.
7. Rev. Code Washington § 9.94A.760.
8. Devon Porter, "Paying for Justice: The Human Cost of Public Defender Fees" (Los Angeles: American Civil Liberties Union of Southern California, 2017),

1–2, https://law.yale.edu/sites/default/files/area/center/liman/document/pdfees-report.pdf.

9. Brennan Center for Justice, "Is Charging Inmates to Stay in Prison Smart Policy?" September 9, 2019, https://www.brennancenter.org/our-work/research-reports/charging-inmates-stay-prison-smart-policy.

10. Alexes Harris, Tyler Smith, and Emmi Obara, "Justice 'Cost Points:' Examination of Privatization Within Public Systems of Justice," *Criminology & Public Policy* 18, no. 2 (2019): 343–59, https://finesandfeesjusticecenter.org/articles/justice-cost-points-examination-of-privatization-within-public-systems-of-justice. For an example of these fees see Rev. Code Washington § 19.16.500.

11. Robert N. Weiner, Leigh Ann Buchanan, Kevin J. Curtain, Marcella A. Holland, Charles A. Weiss, Adrienne Nelson, Lisa Foster, and Adam Abelson, *Privatization of Services in the Criminal Justice System* (Washington, DC: American Bar Association Working Group on Building Public Trust in the American Justice System, 2020), 16, https://www.americanbar.org/content/dam/aba/administrative/legal_aid_indigent_defendants/ls-sclaid-def-aba-privatizaton-report-final-june-2020.pdf.

12. Alexes Harris, *A Pound of Flesh* (New York: Russell Sage Foundation, 2016), https://www.russellsage.org/publications/pound-flesh.

13. Mary Pattillo and Gabriela Kirk, "Layaway Freedom: Coercive Financialization in the Criminal Legal System," *American Journal of Sociology* 126, no. 4 (2021): 889–930, https://www.journals.uchicago.edu/doi/10.1086/712871.

14. Shahar Ziv, "$1,400 Stimulus Checks Could Be Seized By Debt Collectors," *Forbes*, March 15, 2021, https://www.forbes.com/sites/shaharziv/2021/03/15/beware-1400-stimulus-checks-could-be-taken-from-you/?sh=57939ed7155e; Naomi Jagoda, "Treasury: States Can Seize Stimulus Payments to Provide Criminal Restitution," *The Hill*, May 3, 2021, https://thehill.com/policy/finance/551578-treasury-states-can-seize-stimulus-payments-to-provide-criminal-restitution.

15. Karima Modjadidi, Brandon L. Garrett, and William Crozier, "Undeliverable: Suspended Driver's Licenses and the Problem of Notice," *UCLA Criminal Justice Law Review* 80 (2019): 1–18, https://papers.ssrn.com/sol3/papers.cfm?abstract_id=3489255.

16. Magnus Lofstrom, Joseph Hayes, Brandon Martin, and Deepak Premkumar, *Racial Disparities in Law Enforcement Stops* (San Francisco: Public Policy Institute of California, 2021), 1, https://www.ppic.org/publication/racial-disparities-in-law-enforcement-stops.

17. Josh Pacewicz and John N. Robinson, "Pocketbook Policing: How Race Shapes Municipal Reliance on Punitive Fines and Fees in the Chicago Suburbs," *Socio-Economic Review* 19, no. 3 (2021): 975–1003, https://watson.brown.edu/stoneinequality/files/stone/imce/resources/bibliography/Pacewicz_and_Robinson_article_pocketbook_policing_2021.pdf. See also Stephen Rushin and Griffin Edwards, "An Empirical Assessment of Pretextual Stops and Racial

Profiling," *Stanford Law Review* 73 (2021): 637–726, https://lawecommons.luc.edu/cgi/viewcontent.cgi?article=1686&context=facpubs.

18. Emma Pierson, Camelia Simoiu, Jan Overgoor, Sam Corbett-Davies, Daniel Jenson, Amy Shoemaker, Vignesh Ramachandran, Phoebe Barghouty, Cheryl Phillips, Ravi Shroff, and Sharad Goel, "A Large-Scale Analysis of Racial Disparities in Police Stops Across the United States," *Nature Human Behaviour* 4 (2020): 736–45, https://www.nature.com/articles/s41562-020-0858-1.
19. Kate K. O'Neill, Alexes Harris, and Ian Kennedy, "Lift the Burden of Legal Fines and Fees," *Seattle Times*, February 18, 2022, https://www.seattletimes.com/opinion/lift-the-burden-of-legal-fines-and-fees.
20. Kate K. O'Neill, Ian Kennedy, and Alexes Harris, "Debtors' Blocks: How Monetary Sanctions Make Between-Neighborhood Racial and Economic Inequalities Worse," *Sociology of Race and Ethnicity* 8, no. 1 (2021): 43–61, https://journals.sagepub.com/doi/10.1177/23326492211057817.
21. The Sentencing Project, "Fact Sheet: Incarcerated Women and Girls," 2022, 2, https://www.sentencingproject.org/app/uploads/2022/11/Incarcerated-Women-and-Girls.pdf.
22. Saneta deVuono-Powell, Chris Schweidler, Alicia Walters, and Azadeh Zohrabi, *Who Pays? The True Cost of Incarceration on Families* (Oakland, CA: Ella Baker Center, 2015), 9, https://forwardtogether.org/tools/who-pays.
23. Beth A. Colgan, "Graduating Economic Sanctions According to Ability to Pay," *Iowa Law Review* 103 (2017): 53–112, https://ilr.law.uiowa.edu/assets/Uploads/ILR-103-1-Colgan.pdf.
24. Fines and Fees Justice Center, "Free to Drive: National Campaign to End Debt-Based License Restrictions," accessed November 1, 2022, https://finesandfeesjusticecenter.org/campaigns/national-drivers-license-suspension-campaign-free-to-drive.
25. Free to Drive, "2020 Victories: Six States Pass Driver's License Suspension Reforms," 2020, 1, https://freetodrive.org/wp-content/uploads/2020/11/Free-to-Drive-2020-DLS-Reforms-Final2.pdf.
26. Olafimihan Oshin, "Brooklyn Center approves police reform package after shooting of Daunte Wright," *The Hill*, May 16, 2021, https://thehill.com/homenews/state-watch/553791-brooklyn-center-approves-police-reform-package-after-shooting-of-daunte.
27. Nicholas MacDonald, "As Part of Vera Institute Initiative, Progressive County Attorney Will Stop Prosecuting Non-Public Safety Traffic Stops to Address Systemic Bias, Honoring Philando Castile and Others," Press release, Vera Institute of Justice, accessed November 1, 2022, https://www.vera.org/newsroom/as-part-of-vera-institute-initiative-progressive-county-attorney-will-stop-prosecuting-non-public-safety-traffic-stops-to-address-systemic-bias-honoring-philando-castile-and-others.
28. Harris, *A Pound of Flesh*.

28

COLLATERAL CONSEQUENCES AND THE ENDURING NATURE OF PUNISHMENT

Cameron Kimble and Ames Grawert

A DECADE AGO, a Virginia man served about a year in jail for distributing marijuana. After release, he found that his conviction record made securing affordable housing virtually impossible. He could not chaperone his son's school field trip. More recently, a limousine service denied him employment despite his five years of professional driving experience and eight years of freedom. He now pays $575 for a room that has a leak over his bed.[1]

Unfortunately, this tragic story is all too common, representative of a forbidding edifice of thousands of state and local rules, laws, and regulations that blocks people from opportunities of all types based on a criminal record.[2] These collateral consequences of mass incarceration create a form of social exclusion that traps people in poverty and makes reentry after incarceration that much more difficult. Indeed, more than half a million people leave prisons every year hoping that their punishment has ended, only to face barriers to jobs, housing, and fundamental participation in political, economic, and cultural life.[3]

Collateral consequences powerfully illustrate the excessively retributive nature of American criminal justice. From the inability to acquire a driver's license (and thus to drive to work legally) to limits on access to college or even military service, these repercussions remind people with criminal records of their permanent status as Other.[4] Peggy McGarry draws out this argument in her essay on the punitive turn of probation and parole (see chapter 29.) Monetary sanctions such as fines and fees are another common collateral consequence, as further explored by Alexes Harris in chapter 27. These financial obligations trap people in cycles of poverty, years of court process, and sometimes even reincarceration, "tethering people to the criminal legal system" long after their release from prison.[5]

Truly ending mass incarceration will require eliminating these consequences and ensuring that we welcome people with a criminal record back into society. Ultimately, it will mean shifting our criminal justice paradigm away from retribution and toward restoration.[6] As Jeremy Travis notes, in the modern, developed, welfare state of the twentieth century, the collateral consequences faced by formerly imprisoned Americans amount to a variant of the anachronistic tradition of "civil death," in which returning citizens are "defined as unworthy of the benefits of society, and [are] excluded from the social compact."[7] It is time to move past this archaic and cruel system.

LIMITS ON EMPLOYMENT OPPORTUNITIES

In a 2018 survey, 86 percent of human resources professionals reported that their company conducted background screening on all full-time employees.[8] Despite a compelling rationale for these checks in some cases, in others they screen people out of the workforce unnecessarily, turning a conviction record into a scarlet letter. In her seminal work, *The Mark of a Criminal Record*, the late Devah Pager found that a criminal conviction reduced the likelihood of a job applicant receiving a callback interview by 50 percent for white applicants and by nearly 65 percent for Black applicants.[9]

Government also works to limit opportunities for those with a criminal record. Starting in the mid-1980s, state legislatures accelerated the number and breadth of occupational restrictions for people with convictions. In the 1970s, roughly 1,950 discrete laws limited job opportunities for people with a criminal record.[10] Today, more than twenty-seven thousand rules bar formerly justice-involved people from holding professional licenses.[11] This includes a California law that forbids people who put their lives on the line to fight wildfires while incarcerated from becoming licensed emergency responders after release—subject to only limited exceptions.[12]

These limitations and the corresponding lack of job opportunities can trap people in poverty for decades after incarceration. As of 2019, nearly one-fourth of those serving time in prisons were between age twenty and twenty-nine.[13] Most of them will be released at some point—many will enter the job market, and some will find success. But even then, they are likely to begin their working lives earning roughly $7,100 less per year than those of similar socioeconomic status without a criminal record and end them trailing these peers by more than $20,000 a year.[14] As recent Brennan Center research suggests, a criminal conviction is devastating to an individual's earning prospects; a prison record all but ensures a lifetime straddling the poverty threshold.[15]

Even when work is secured after a stint in prison, "it is often temporary, part-time, and low paying," thus lacking in prospects for upward mobility.[16] Those who find decent jobs may still face limits on career progression given that people with a record may be less likely to be considered for the promotions, raises, and credentials that drive wage growth. Indeed, licensing restrictions and criminal background inquiries make people who have spent time in prison unlikely to see the same return on investment from professional training or credentialing as their peers.[17]

THE TATTERED SOCIAL SAFETY NET

English sociologist T. H. Marshall observed in 1950 that as Western societies evolved, so had the notion of citizenship. Whereas citizenship in the eighteenth and nineteenth centuries was defined by civil and political rights, he concluded that the idea of citizenship in an advanced twentieth-century society also entailed social rights. That extension brought with it "a general reduction of risk and insecurity, an equalization between the more and less fortunate at all levels," such as "between the healthy and the sick, the employed and the unemployed."[18] Yet more than seventy years later, many American states continue to exclude people with criminal convictions from the social tools, such as welfare benefits, that make this part of citizenship real. The result is material deprivation that compounds social isolation.[19]

Job and housing insecurity make it more likely that someone with a criminal record might need to rely temporarily on government programs designed to provide relief from poverty. But since 1996, people convicted of certain drug crimes have been ineligible for government assistance through the Temporary Assistance for Needy Families program and Supplemental Nutrition Assistance Program.[20] Congress permitted states to opt out of this framework partially or wholly and, thankfully, many states have done so.[21] In nearly half the states, however, modified bans continue to compound disadvantage and set up a self-perpetuating cycle of poverty and recidivism.[22] Given how many people involved with the justice system also stand on the edge of poverty—in one study, more than half of formerly imprisoned people surveyed report annual earnings less than $500 just before their incarceration—these restrictions are especially damaging.[23]

Moreover, formerly incarcerated people face a significantly elevated risk of homelessness, in part because another critical part of the social safety net, public housing, is often unavailable to them.[24] Beginning in the 1980s, Congress passed and public housing authorities implemented one-strike-and-you're-out rules providing for the eviction of people who became involved in criminal activity. Those policies have slowly been tempered, but they still permanently exclude people convicted of certain crimes.[25] Homelessness and housing insecurity make it that much harder for people to stay connected to family, maintain employment, and enjoy the basic necessities of life—the very definition of social exclusion.

Things are beginning to change.[26] After completing a pilot program launched in 2013, the New York City Housing Authority began liberalizing its rules for allowing people with criminal records back into public housing, helping reunite families in the process.[27] Further reforms were announced in 2020, and others are being contemplated.[28] Additionally, a few years ago, the public housing authority in New Orleans eliminated its blanket ban on housing assistance for people with a criminal record.[29] In many states, however, the exclusions remain in place. In another sign of progress, states across the country, from Pennsylvania to Utah, have adopted what are called clean slate laws that would automatically remove criminal records after several years have passed—helping ease many collateral consequences at a stroke.[30] Similar proposals have been introduced and found broad support in New York State and at the federal level. Business leaders such as JPMorgan Chase and Verizon have even helped make the employer's case for these laws.[31]

VOTING RIGHTS

The practice of felony disenfranchisement traces its roots back to ancient times but found new life in the Jim Crow era.[32] After enslaved Black people were freed, states quickly implemented so-called Black Codes, which legalized the baseless arrest and conviction of Black citizens. Building on this structure, many states adopted laws to strip voting rights from people with a criminal record. Some states, like Virginia, expanded laws to encompass offenses such as petty theft because white politicians believed many Black people could be easily convicted of such crimes.[33]

Unfortunately, this racist legacy endures. Currently, thirty states disenfranchise at least some people based on convictions.[34] The work to change these laws has proceeded in fits and starts, though with increased momentum in recent years, as the governors of Iowa and Kentucky, among others, issued executive orders restoring voting rights to people with convictions. In 2018, a supermajority of Floridians voted to restore voting rights to as many as 1.4 million people with felony convictions.[35] Shortly after the referendum, though, Florida legislators passed a law that made voting rights restoration contingent on people's paying all fees, fines, and restitution owed due to their conviction, which the overwhelming majority of Floridians with convictions cannot afford to pay.[36] Many do not even know what they owe, or whether they owe anything at all, because the state has no centralized database for tracking court debt.[37] The threat of prosecution looms over those who take a risk at the ballot box. Several Floridians have been arrested for allegedly registering or voting while ineligible—some of whom believed they were eligible and say they were even told so by state officials.[38]

Collateral consequences of criminal conviction or incarceration are not unique to the United States. But as with America's overly punitive approach to crime and punishment, they are unique here for their depth, severity, and pervasiveness. British citizens, for example, are deemed ineligible for welfare benefits only if convicted of a welfare fraud offense.[39] Their ineligibility is also temporary, just four weeks. In 2002, Canada's Supreme Court found "Denial of the right to vote on the basis of attributed moral unworthiness" incompatible with Canadian democratic values.[40] In Germany, too, though loss of voting rights may be ordered by a court, it is temporary, rare, and in any event not automatic.[41] Even the American norm of public, permanent criminal records is exceptional. Unlimited access to criminal records is unheard of in Germany outside government institutions, and records are automatically expunged after enough time has passed.[42] In Spain, "criminal records are considered personal information and treated confidentially," their disclosure limited by rights to privacy and honor.[43]

In the United States, however, after finishing a prison sentence, citizens face continued de facto punishment given that their criminal record increases the likelihood that they suffer homelessness, restricts their access to the social safety net, and strips them of their right to vote, further damaging their sense of civic inclusion. This fixation on continued punishment is not inevitable: it is a policy choice, and it is one that can be changed.

NOTES

1. Rob Poggenklass, "A Criminal Record Is Its Own Sentence: The Case for Automatic Expungement in Virginia," Legal Aid Justice Center, January 2021, accessed November 21, 2022, https://www.justice4all.org/wp-content/uploads/2021/01/A-Criminal-Record-is-its-Own-Criminal-Sentence.pdf.
2. National Inventory of Collateral Consequences of Conviction, "Collateral Consequences Inventory," accessed November 21, 2022, https://niccc.nationalreentryresourcecenter.org/consequences.
3. E. Ann Carson, "Prisoners in 2020—Statistical Tables," NCJ 302776 (Washington, DC: U.S. Department of Justice, Bureau of Justice Statistics, 2021), 19, https://bjs.ojp.gov/content/pub/pdf/p20st.pdf.
4. U.S. Commission on Civil Rights, *Collateral Consequences: The Crossroads of Punishment, Redemption, and the Effects on Communities*, briefing report (Washington, DC: Government Printing Office, 2019), 1–2, https://www.usccr.gov/files/pubs/2019/06-13-Collateral-Consequences.pdf.
5. Alexes Harris, "Monetary Sanctions as a Pound of Flesh" (New York: Brennan Center for Justice, July 26, 2021), https://www.brennancenter.org/our-work/analysis-opinion/monetary-sanctions-pound-flesh.
6. For an introduction to these concepts, see Donald H. J. Hermann, "Restorative Justice and Retributive Justice: An Opportunity for Cooperation or an Occasion for Conflict in the Search for Justice," *Seattle Journal for Social Justice* 16, no. 1 (2017): 71–103, https://digitalcommons.law.seattleu.edu/sjsj/vol16/iss1/11.
7. Jeremy Travis, *Invisible Punishment: The Collateral Consequences of Mass Imprisonment* (New York: The New Press, 2002), 25.
8. HR.com, "How Human Resource Professionals View the Use and Effectiveness of Background Screening Methods," 2018, 4, https://pubs.thepbsa.org/pub.cfm?id=9E5ED85F-C257-C289-9E8E-A7C7A8C58D00.
9. Devah Pager, "The Mark of a Criminal Record," *American Journal of Sociology* 108, no. 5 (2003): 937–75, https://scholar.harvard.edu/files/pager/files/pager_ajs.pdf.
10. Jonathan Haggerty, "How Occupational Licensing Laws Harm Public Safety and the Formerly Incarcerated," Policy Study no. 143 (Washington, DC: R Street Institute, 2018), 2, https://www.rstreet.org/wp-content/uploads/2018/05/Final-No.-143-for-posting.pdf.
11. Haggerty, "Occupational Licensing Laws," 2.
12. See Jaime Lowe, "What Does California Owe Its Incarcerated Firefighters?," *The Atlantic*, July 27, 2021, https://www.theatlantic.com/politics/archive/2021/07/california-inmate-firefighters/619567; see also Gurrola v. Duncan, 519 F. Supp. 3d 732, 735–37 (E.D. Calif. 2021), https://www.ca9.uscourts.gov/cases-of-interest

/gurrola-v.duncan (reviewing the legal background behind these rules), aff'd 2022 WL 2072729 (9th Cir. June 9, 2022) (affirming grant of motion to dismiss complaint related to these exclusions; Ruth Sangree, "Prison Inmates Fighting California's Wildfires Can't Do It Once They're Released" (New York: Brennan Center for Justice, August 17, 2018), https://www.brennancenter.org/our-work/analysis-opinion/prison-inmates-fighting-californias-wildfires-cant-do-it-once-theyre.

13. E. Ann Carson, "Prisoners in 2019" (Washington, DC: U.S. Department of Justice, Bureau of Justice Statistics, 2020), 15, table 9, https://bjs.ojp.gov/content/pub/pdf/p19.pdf.
14. Terry-Ann Craigie, Ames Grawert, and Cameron Kimble, *Conviction, Imprisonment, and Lost Earnings: How Involvement with the Criminal Justice System Deepens Inequality* (New York: Brennan Center for Justice, 2020), 18, https://www.brennancenter.org/sites/default/files/2020-09/EconomicImpactReport_pdf.pdf.
15. Craigie, Grawert, and Kimble, *Conviction, Imprisonment*, 17–19.
16. Craigie, Grawert, and Kimble, *Conviction, Imprisonment*, 18.
17. Craigie, Grawert, and Kimble, *Conviction, Imprisonment*, 18.
18. T. H. Marshall, *Citizenship and Social Class* (Cambridge: Cambridge University Press 1950), 10–14, 46–48, 56.
19. For a short discussion of this policy issue and sources for further reading, see Craigie, Grawert, and Kimble, *Conviction, Imprisonment*, 22, nn. 126–28.
20. Marc Mauer and Virginia McCalmont, "A Lifetime of Punishment: The Impact of the Felony Drug Ban on Welfare Benefits" (Washington, DC: The Sentencing Project, November 2013, updated September 2015), 1–2, https://www.sentencingproject.org/app/uploads/2022/08/A-Lifetime-of-Punishment.pdf.
21. Chesterfield Polkey, "Most States Have Ended SNAP Ban for Convicted Drug Felons," National Conference of State Legislatures, *NCSL Blog*, July 30, 2019, https://www.ncsl.org/blog/2019/07/30/most-states-have-ended-snap-ban-for-convicted-drug-felons.aspx.
22. Molly Born, "In Some States, Drug Felons Still Face Lifetime Ban on SNAP Benefits," National Public Radio, June 20, 2018, https://www.npr.org/sections/thesalt/2018/06/20/621391895/in-some-states-drug-felons-still-face-lifetime-ban-on-snap-benefits; Cody Tuttle, "*Snapping Back: Food Stamp Bans and Criminal Recidivism*" (working paper, University of Maryland, 2018), 6, http://dx.doi.org/10.2139/ssrn.2845435.
23. Adam Looney and Nicholas Turner, *Work and Opportunity Before and After Incarceration* (Washington, DC: Brookings Institution, 2018), 8, https://www.brookings.edu/wp-content/uploads/2018/03/es_20180314_looneyincarceration_final.pdf.

24. Lucius Couloute, "Nowhere to Go: Homelessness Among Formerly Incarcerated People" (Northampton, MA: Prison Policy Initiative, 2018), https://www.prisonpolicy.org/reports/housing.html; Craigie, Grawert, and Kimble, *Conviction, Imprisonment*, 8, 22.
25. Rebecca J. Walter, Jill Viglione, and Marie Skubak Tillyer, "One Strike to Second Chances: Using Criminal Backgrounds in Admission Decisions for Assisted Housing," *Housing Policy Debate* 27 (2017): 4–6.
26. Sarah Gonzalez, "New York Eases Rules for Formerly Incarcerated to Visit Public Housing," WNYC, April 21, 2017, https://www.wnyc.org/story/new-york-city-felonies-visit-family-public-housing.
27. John Bae, Margaret diZerega, Jacob Kang-Brown, Ryan Shanahan, and Ram Subramanian, *Coming Home: An Evaluation of the New York City Housing Authority's Family Reentry Pilot Program* (New York: Vera Institute of Justice, 2016), 10, https://www.vera.org/downloads/publications/NYCHA_report-032917.pdf; Gonzalez, "New York Eases Rules."
28. Chelsia Rose Marcius, "NYCHA Seeks to Ease Rules Barring People with Criminal Records from Living in Public Housing," *New York Daily News*, September 16, 2020, https://www.nydailynews.com/new-york/ny-nycha-to-ease-some-restrictions-for-applicants-criminal-records-20200916-bg6ej52wofdwvfdy4p4udua6te-story.html.
29. Richard A. Webster, "HANO Approves New Criminal Background Check Policy," *Times-Picayune/New Orleans Advocate*, updated July 19, 2021, https://www.nola.com/news/politics/article_eb9dc4f4-9e6c-54d2-97c9-f70df68cda14.html.
30. Ames Grawert, "Parole Reform and 'Clean Slate' in New York" (New York: Brennan Center for Justice, April 21, 2021), https://www.brennancenter.org/our-work/research-reports/parole-reform-and-clean-slate-new-york.
31. Stephanie Wylie and Ames Grawert, "Why New York's Clean Slate Act Is Essential for Economic Justice" (New York: Brennan Center for Justice, September 16, 2022), https://www.brennancenter.org/our-work/analysis-opinion/why-new-yorks-clean-slate-act-essential-economic-justice. As this book went to press, the New York State legislature had passed its own clean slate law. Luis Ferré-Sadurní and Grace Ashford, "N.Y. Lawmakers Pass Clean Slate Act as Session Fizzles to an End," *New York Times*, June 9, 2023, https://www.nytimes.com/2023/06/09/nyregion/ny-legislature-2023-session.html.
32. Sarah C. Grady, "Civil Death is Different: An Examination of Post-Graham Challenge to Felon Disenfranchisement Under the Eighth Amendment," *Journal of Criminal Law and Criminology* 102, no. 2 (2012): 443–51.
33. Erin Kelley, "Racism and Felony Disenfranchisement: An Intertwined History" (New York: Brennan Center for Justice, 2017), 2, https://www.brennancenter.org/sites/default/files/2019-08/Report_Disenfranchisement_History.pdf.

34. Brennan Center for Justice, "Can People Convicted of a Felony Vote? Felony Voting Laws by State," updated September 26, 2022, https://www.brennancenter.org/our-work/research-reports/can-people-convicted-felony-vote-felony-voting-laws-state; Eliza Sweren-Becker, "One State Still Permanently Bars Everyone with Convictions from Voting. That's About to End" (New York: Brennan Center for Justice, June 18, 2020), https://www.brennancenter.org/our-work/analysis-opinion/one-state-still-permanently-bars-everyone-convictions-voting-thats-about; Brennan Center for Justice, "Kentucky Governor Andy Beshear Signs Executive Order Restoring Voting Rights to More than 100,000 People with Past Convictions," Press release, December 12, 2019, https://www.brennancenter.org/our-work/analysis-opinion/kentucky-governor-andy-beshear-signs-executive-order-restoring-voting.
35. Tim Mak, "Over 1 Million Florida Felons Win Right to Vote with Amendment 4," NPR, November 7, 2018, https://www.npr.org/2018/11/07/665031366/over-a-million-florida-ex-felons-win-right-to-vote-with-amendment-4.
36. Lawrence Mower, "Being Poor Shouldn't Stop Florida Felons from Voting, Judge Rules in Amendment 4 case," *Tampa Bay Times*, October 18, 2019, https://www.tampabay.com/florida-politics/buzz/2019/10/19/being-poor-shouldnt-stop-florida-felons-from-voting-judge-rules-in-amendment-4-case; Jones v. DeSantis, 462 F.Supp.3d 119, 1219 (N.D. Fla. 2020), rev'd in part sub nom Jones v. Governor of Florida, 975 F.3d 1016 (11th Cir. 2020) (as to holding that restrictions on voting violated the Equal Protection Clause and 24th Amendment), aff'd in part sub nom Jones v. Governor of Florida, 15 F.4th 1062 (11th Cir. 2021) (as to denial of gender discrimination claims).
37. Gabriella Sanchez, "In Florida, the Right to Vote Can Cost You" (New York: Brennan Center for Justice, September 7, 2022), https://www.brennancenter.org/our-work/analysis-opinion/florida-right-vote-can-cost-you.
38. Sanchez, "In Florida, the Right to Vote."
39. Michael Pinard, "Collateral Consequences of Criminal Convictions: Confronting Issues of Race and Dignity," *New York University Law Review* 85, no. 2 (2010): 496, https://digitalcommons.law.umaryland.edu/cgi/viewcontent.cgi?article=1820&context=fac_pubs.
40. Sauvé v. Canada (Chief Electoral Officer) [2002] 3 S.C.R. 519, 2002 SCC 68, https://scc-csc.lexum.com/scc-csc/scc-csc/en/item/2010/index.do.
41. Nora V. Demleitner, "Continuing Payment on One's Debt to Society: The German Model of Felon Disenfranchisement as an Alternative," *Minnesota Law Review* 84 (2000): 760–62.
42. Alessandro Corda and Johannes Kaspar, "Collateral Consequences of Criminal Conviction in the United States and Germany," in *Core Concepts in Criminal Law and Criminal Justice*, vol. 2, ed. Kai Ambos, Antony Duff, Alexander

Heinze, Julian Roberts, and Thomas Weigend (Cambridge: Cambridge University Press, 2022), 410–411.

43. James B. Jacobs, "American Criminal Record Exceptionalism (I): A Spanish Comparison," Collateral Consequences Resource Center, December 30, 2014, https://ccresourcecenter.org/2014/12/30/american-criminal-record-exceptionalism-spanish-comparison.

29

PROBATION AND PAROLE AS PUNISHMENT

Peggy McGarry

COMMUNITY SUPERVISION—generally speaking, our systems of probation and parole—began in the nineteenth century as a peer-to-peer system of support. Community members came forward to assure the court or prison that they could help those convicted of crime to live lawfully outside jail or prison.

In 1841, for example, John Augustus, a Boston shoemaker, persuaded the court to release a man to his care, convinced he could cure the man of his drunkenness. When he was successful, the Boston courts began using community care to suspend criminal sentences. In 1859, Massachusetts passed the first bill enacting probation. The law was largely credited to his decades-long effort to improve outcomes and reduce incarceration.[1] In 1876, Zebulon Brockway, the warden of the prison in Elmira, New York, prevailed on the authorities to release to community care men whom he believed were "rehabilitated."[2] It was not until the early twentieth century that counties and states established formalized systems of support and surveillance as the population of towns and cities grew.[3]

Despite the transition to government agencies with professional staff and budgets, the fundamentally supportive nature of those systems remained in place well into the twentieth century. For people released from jail or prison, staff were available to "reintegrate" them, to help them with the problems that might have led to their crimes in the first place, and to help ensure that they succeeded. Today, however, many of those agencies are more primed to find and punish failure than to promote success. The length of supervision and the nature of the conditions have grown more onerous and punitive, and the consequences of failure more severe.

So, we ask, what happened?

CIVIL RIGHTS, VOTING RIGHTS, AND THE NIXON ADMINISTRATION

A focus on crime and "urban unrest"—code for fear of people of color—grew in the aftermath of the upheavals of the 1960s and the passage of the Civil Rights Act and the Voting Rights Act. Faced with the potential for people of color having power, the policies and rhetoric of the Nixon administration, particularly its Southern strategy and war on drugs effort, were aimed at making sure that they didn't. As the Republican candidate for the presidency in 1968, Richard Nixon and his team realized the potential of turning southern, traditionally Democratic voters against the party by calling attention to the role that the Democratic president, Lyndon Johnson, and party members in Congress had played in advancing the Civil Rights and Voting Rights Acts. Calling attention to crime, especially urban crime, built on the anger many white voters felt after civil rights disturbances in many northern cities. This fear of "Black crime" was taken up by the media and by policymakers of both political parties at the state and federal levels.[4] It led to the passage of harsher sentencing laws, including the recategorization of offenses to make them incarceration-eligible, criminalization of more kinds of behaviors, and longer terms of incarceration.[5]

Jail and prison populations increased, and local and state budgets were hit hard. The era's political rhetoric about race and crime made it much easier to consider those caught up in the system as Other rather than as members of the same community. Instead of an opportunity to restore lives, release on probation or parole became a privilege that could be taken away. Any violation, no matter how trivial, could be seen as an affront to the generosity and forbearance of the court or paroling authority.

The budget hits from the growth in incarceration and the building of more jails and prisons, with the assistance of nearly state and federal funding for construction but not operations, meant fewer dollars for community supervision; from 1990 to 2005, the number of state and federal jails and prisons increased by 43 percent.[6] In practical terms, this means fewer staff, larger caseloads, less money for services, housing assistance, and items such as special clothing (such as work boots), protective equipment (such as helmets and gloves) or other sorts of tools people may need for jobs, such as hammers and specialized screwdrivers, all of which help those released remain stable in the community. In 1976, 1,461,459 people were on probation and parole.[7] By the beginning of 2020, an estimated 4,167,100 adults were on probation or parole.[8] Born of budget cuts, probation and parole agencies saw big increases in caseloads: from forty-five supervisees per officer in the 1970s for parole to seventy in 2003, when probation officers averaged 130.[9] Agencies once structured to provide assistance were reduced to offering surveillance and enforcement.

The trend to punish harshly did not end with sentencing.[10] Laws passed at the state and federal levels closed off many public benefits once been offered to people who were newly released, such as public housing, public assistance, and Pell Grants, making a successful term of supervision difficult to achieve. During the Reagan administration, those benefits were cut for everyone, reducing access even further for those with criminal records.

THE CHANGING NATURE OF SUPERVISION

As "tough on crime" became the rallying cry in many political campaigns, and as state and federal legislatures and agencies made changes to laws and policies, the resulting climate affected the actions and decisions of both judges and parole boards. Worried about their elections and appointments, judges looked to longer terms and more rigid standard conditions of supervision as insurance. Although in recent years this has begun to change, governors often filled parole board positions with political allies who had little education or experience in criminal justice. They often make headlines for their release decisions, but parole boards also determine the conditions of supervision and the responses to any violations of them.

Long lists of conditions—the rules for living while on probation or parole—have become the structure of supervision: surveil for adherence, punish for violation. Standard conditions do not address the specific needs of each person but impose the same rules of conduct on everyone. Although some are sensible, most are controls on noncriminal behavior. "Do not associate with felons"—though the individual's only place to live might be a family home or shelter also occupied by people with felony convictions. "Do not move your place of residence without permission from your parole officer"—though in the crowded housing of poor communities, frequent moves are more common than in society at large. "Do not consume alcohol"—though alcohol use may have been in no way connected to the individual's crime. "Do not leave the county without prior approval," curfews, frequent reporting, and random drug testing—even if the original crime had nothing to do with drugs. These are but a few of the common conditions that can interfere with a person's ability to keep a job or fulfill family obligations such as childcare.[11]

Apart from standard conditions of release, the judge or parole board usually imposes additional requirements, such as treatment, classes, electronic monitoring, and more. In most places, the person on supervision is expected to cover the costs of such programs and even the cost of the supervision itself.[12] As Professor Alexes Harris notes in her essay (see chapter 27), in most states, all monetary sanctions must be completely paid off before someone is released from court supervision, extending their probation or parole. To someone struggling to find housing and employment, to keep a job or initiate family reunification, these obligations and fees can guarantee failure and reincarceration.

This is the result of the budget reductions for staff and services that arose from tough-on-crime rhetoric. Politicians denounced services to those on supervision that "regular" people could not get, simultaneously pushing for a "mess up and you're back" approach. With larger caseloads and fewer resources, officers had significant motivation to yank a "difficult" case—a person struggling to comply with conditions—and recommend revocation and a return to jail or prison. For a judge or parole board, that recommendation was easy to approve because it was politically safer than continuing a difficult case—even if the "difficult" circumstance was a noncriminal violation of conditions.

THE TRANSITION TO LAW ENFORCEMENT

As the duties of probation and parole officers became more about surveillance and enforcement of conditions rather than the original concept of community care and reintegration, the recruitment and training of new officers changed as well. They were no longer hired for their helping skills or orientation. In many places, new officers were trained alongside institutional corrections officers and law enforcement personnel. The focus of such training is on finding and responding to crime: surveillance techniques, use of force, use of firearms, and how to subdue the Other. Beginning in the mid-1980s, their unions and associations successfully lobbied for arming supervision officers.[13] Although these officers certainly do encounter dangerous situations at times, their desire to be armed was driven mostly by the difference in the pay and benefits available to those in public safety. The subsequent arming of probation and parole officers completed the transition of those agencies from a service orientation to identification as law enforcement.

Without time and resources, with scant encouragement from their agencies, officers have had little reason to work patiently with those under their supervision to help them stabilize and successfully reintegrate into their communities. Officers are not given raises or promotions based on the successes achieved by people on their caseloads, and the decision to revoke someone back to jail or prison at the first sign of trouble is affirmed by how often their revocation recommendations are approved. The reasoning is circular: the judge, parole board member, or regional supervisor assumes that the officers in the field know best how to respond to violations; the officers assume their responses and recommendations are correct because the judge or parole board member approves them.

These problems have been exacerbated in recent years by the moves in states alarmed by soaring corrections budgets to reduce prison spending by making more people eligible for probation and parole supervision. In many cases, however, this new eligibility comes with longer terms of supervision. The original sentence may still need to be met in its entirety, and judges, with cases they may have previously sentenced to incarceration, are ordering longer terms. The greater numbers, especially on probation, reflect not only fewer people sent to prison but also more people with minor offenses receiving sentences to supervisory probation with reporting requirements, exposing even more people to revocation to incarceration. Despite the original premise of returning the savings to community services, the resources and the inclination for effective and humane supervision have not reappeared. According to the Pew Trust's Public Safety Performance Project, from 2000 to 2018, twenty-eight states increased the length of their probation sentences.[14] As of 2019, nearly 25 percent of prison admissions nationwide were due to technical violations of conditions of supervision.[15]

The same political and fiscal pressures that have changed community supervision transformed prisons as well—leaving those released on parole in no better, and in most cases worse, condition than before. Without supportive services and providing access to basic needs like employment, housing, and health care, the argument for long periods of supervision—whether probation or parole—is strictly one of control. For example, New York City instituted "kiosk reporting" to reduce the obligation of low-level probationers to come to the office and disrupt their lives further. This benefits people who don't have to miss work or who can continue with childcare obligations but does not provide supportive services to the person checking in. Day reporting centers, once viewed as models of one-stop destinations to meet with supervision staff, receive information and referrals, and participate in programming have today become places to sign in and take a drug test.

CONCLUSION

A different approach to community care is critical if we are to make it a useful tool for preventing future crime and enhancing both family and community well-being. Efforts have been made in recent decades to limit supervision terms, change how paroling authorities make decisions, how supervision is conducted, and how revocations are handled. We know how to use officer time effectively to engage with the people on their caseloads, how to assess who needs more time and who can be left alone, how to intervene in ways that are helpful rather than punitive, and how to encourage stability and success.[16] We also know how to work with communities, religious organizations, and health care and social service agencies to improve lives, rather than to destroy them.

That change, though, isn't happening in enough places. We will continue to see these trends until we intentionally recruit officers who are more interested in prevention than enforcement, until we invest in officer training that focuses on how to help those on supervision to succeed, until we change our reward structure to incentivize those whose clients succeed, and until we stop ordering long terms of supervision and onerous conditions.

We have not done these things primarily because we seem to be content to waste the lives of those who have broken the law. The damage we continue to do is of little concern to us. They are considered Other. To some, their lives don't really matter.

NOTES

1. County of San Mateo, California, "The History of Probation," accessed December 10, 2022, https://www.smcgov.org/probation/history-probation.
2. Connecticut Humanities, "Zebulon Brockway: A Controversial Figure in Prison Reform," January 2, 2014, https://connecticuthistory.org/zebulon-brockway-a-controversial-figure-in-prison-reform.

3. County of San Mateo, "History of Probation."
4. Ruth Delaney, Ram Subramanian, Alison Shames, and Nicholas Turner, *Reimagining Prison* (New York: Vera Institute of Justice, 2018), 44–45, https://www.vera.org/downloads/publications/Reimagining-Prison_FINAL3_digital.pdf.
5. Elizabeth Hinton and DeAnza Cook, "The Mass Criminalization of Black Americans: A Historical Overview," *Annual Review of Criminology* 4, no. 1 (2021): 261–86, https://www.annualreviews.org/doi/10.1146/annurev-criminol-060520-033306; Mark J. Perry, "The Shocking Story Behind Richard Nixon's 'War on Drugs' That Targeted Blacks and Anti-War Activists," American Enterprise Institute Ideas, June 14, 2018, https://www.aei.org/carpe-diem/the-shocking-and-sickening-story-behind-nixons-war-on-drugs-that-targeted-blacks-and-anti-war-activists.
6. Suzanne M. Kirchhoff, *Economic Impacts of Prison Growth*, CRS Report no. R41177 (Washington, DC: Congressional Research Service, 2010), 15, https://sgp.fas.org/crs/misc/R41177.pdf.
7. Margaret Werner Cahalan with Lee Anne Parsons, *Historical Corrections Statistics in the United States, 1850–1984*, NCJ 102529 (Washington, DC: U.S. Department of Justice, Bureau of Justice Statistics, 1986), 180, https://bjs.ojp.gov/content/pub/pdf/hcsus5084.pdf.
8. Danielle Kaeble, *Probation and Parole in the United States, 2020*, NCJ 303102 (Washington, DC: U.S Department of Justice, Bureau of Justice Statistics, 2021), 1, https://bjs.ojp.gov/library/publications/probation-and-parole-united-states-2020.
9. Center on Sentencing and Corrections, *The Potential of Community Corrections to Improve Safety and Reduce Incarceration* (New York: Vera Institute of Justice, 2013), 11, https://www.prisonpolicy.org/scans/vera/potential-of-community-corrections.pdf.
10. Cecelia Klingele, "Rethinking the Use of Community Supervision," *Journal of Criminal Law and Criminology* 103, no. 4 (2013): 1015–70, https://scholarlycommons.law.northwestern.edu/cgi/viewcontent.cgi?article=7463&context=jclc.
11. Abd'Allah Lateef, "Parole Is Better Than Prison. But That Doesn't Mean I'm Free" (Washington, DC: The Marshall Project, May 13, 2021), https://www.themarshallproject.org/2021/05/13/parole-is-better-than-prison-but-that-doesn-t-mean-i-m-free.
12. Mack Finkel, "New Data: Low Incomes—But High Fees—for People on Probation" (Northampton, MA: Prison Policy Initiative, April 9, 2019), https://www.prisonpolicy.org/blog/2019/04/09/probation_income.
13. Shawn E. Small and Sam Torres, "Arming Probation Officers: Enhancing Public Confidence and Officer Safety," *Federal Probation* 65, no. 3 (2001): 25, https://www.uscourts.gov/sites/default/files/65_3_4_0.pdf.

14. Monica Fuhrmann et al., *States Can Shorten Probation and Protect Public Safety* (Washington, DC: The Pew Charitable Trusts, 2020), 1, https://www.pewtrusts.org/-/media/assets/2020/12/shorten_probation_and_public_safety_report.pdf.
15. Council of State Governments Justice Center, "Confined and Costly: How Supervision Violations Are Filling Prisons and Burdening Budgets," June 2019, https://csgjusticecenter.org/publications/confined-costly.
16. The Pew Charitable Trusts, "Comprehensive Polices Can Improve Probation and Parole," Fact sheet, April 2020, https://www.pewtrusts.org/en/research-and-analysis/fact-sheets/2020/04/comprehensive-policies-can-improve-probation-and-parole.

30

A HOLISTIC APPROACH TO LEGAL ADVOCACY

Blake Strode

ON A SPRING AFTERNOON IN 2014, a husband and wife left a local community center in St. Louis County, Missouri, to return home to their seven children. Within seconds, they were stopped by a police squad car. When officers approached the vehicle, they went to the passenger's side and asked the husband for his name, citing a recent report about someone who matched his description. Despite his assurances that he was not the man in question, the husband was asked to step out of the car and was placed under arrest moments later. (He was, indeed, never charged with any of the wrongdoing that formed the pretext for the stop.) When his wife stepped out of the car in protest, she, too, was placed under arrest.

The couple was taken to a local jail, placed in filthy, overcrowded cells, and given bonds of $2,000 each. Recent research indicates that 56 percent of Americans do not have the savings to pay an unexpected $1,000 bill.[1] They would both remain in jail for a month, unable to post bail and not once appearing before a judge. While they were incarcerated, their children were uprooted from their home and taken into the care of multiple relatives. Eventually, exhausted and desperate, they both agreed to plead guilty to a series of municipal charges in exchange for their release. They would still be responsible, they were told, for paying nearly $2,000 each, this time as fines and fees for their supposed offenses.

I met this husband and wife more than a year later, in my very first month as a Skadden Fellow and staff attorney with ArchCity Defenders, a legal advocacy organization in St. Louis. When I met them, their memories from that harrowing month were still fresh. They had lost a full month of earnings for their household, placing them and their entire family under even more dire financial strain than they already had to bear as a large family with inconsistent sources of income. They were struggling to pay rent and utilities, care for their children, and find more stable employment.

Despite all of that, though, their reason for coming to us was that they were still paying hundreds of dollars per month to the local municipal court that had overseen their jailing. The so-called pay docket was approaching. At these monthly dockets, they were expected to make payments of $100 each on their debts, and they could not keep up.

Several elements of this story are particularly egregious, but the basic dynamics—people who are living perilously on the margins being targeted and exploited by the criminal legal system—are in fact not unusual. Susan Butler Plum, the founding director of the Skadden Fellowship Foundation, which places new lawyers in public interest positions across the country, has often underscored the significance of antipoverty legal work by positing, "My definition of poverty is that each thing compounds the next thing."

This definition has returned to my mind many times during my work at ArchCity Defenders. Traffic tickets, court debts, criminal charges, jail, bail, eviction, child support, custody, consumer abuse, homelessness: our clients do not experience these traumatic challenges one at a time—they experience many, all at once or in rapid succession.

We in the legal profession know this, and yet we structure our institutions and interventions as if we do not. The expensive and highly profitable firms that dominate the field of legal practice and the legal institutions they shape are designed not for those who are surviving and overcoming poverty and systemic racism daily, but rather for the wealthy and privileged who largely consider legal action a way of resolving conflict or securing wealth. Legal support can be among the most effective antipoverty interventions; instead, legal institutions are far too often the cause of harm and suffering.[2]

When we know that our field is characterized by systematic underfunding of indigent defense, when 90 percent or more of tenants faced with eviction proceedings must defend themselves without counsel, and when there's a complete dearth of free (or even affordable) legal services for a range of needs, from family law to consumer protection to public benefits claims—when we know all this, how can we possibly justify a system in which the overwhelming majority of people subjected to archaic legal processes are left to navigate those processes with no support whatsoever?[3] How can we stomach a system that does little more than further traumatize, destabilize, and extract from the very people who already have the least? And what can we do differently in the face of entrenched support for the status quo and resistance to structural change?

At ArchCity Defenders, we describe ourselves as a holistic legal advocacy organization.[4] We are an independent, nonprofit civil rights and legal aid organization with a staff of thirty people—about half attorneys and the other half a mix of social workers, paralegals, communications professionals, fundraisers, operations specialists, and organizers. ArchCity Defenders was founded to fill a gap in legal services in the St. Louis region, and even with the significant growth of our team over the past twelve years, that gap continues to exceed by far the scale of services that we can provide. In part for this reason, the word *holistic* is central to who we are, how we understand the world and the system in which we are embedded, and why we believe that traditional legal practice has only deepened some of the most fundamental injustices in this country.

For us, this word also takes on a dual meaning in our daily practice. On one level, we provide holistic defense and legal representation in our work with individual clients. This type of holistic defense is based on the model developed and popularized by the Bronx Defenders.[5] Instead of individual services defined by discrete areas of legal practice, our holistic direct services consist of criminal or municipal defense; civil legal representation for evictions, social security or disability and similar public benefits claims, child support, custody, and other family law matters; and wraparound social support in the form of rehousing services and case management, emergency rental and utility assistance, and supportive referrals to a vast network of social service and treatment providers.

Understanding that the challenges facing our clients are complex and intersecting, our goal is to support people in ways that reflect the reality of their lives. Sometimes, this is as simple as listening to clients and believing what they say about the most pressing issues they are facing, instead of substituting our judgment for theirs. We can only be effective in our work if we develop trusting relationships with our clients, and that requires that we respect them as the experts on their own lives.

The other element of our holistic advocacy is an emphasis on engaging at the systems level as well as the individual level. Over time, we have developed four pillars in our model: holistic direct services (just described), civil rights litigation impact, media and policy advocacy, and community collaboration. If our holistic direct services focus on providing a range of support to clients as they navigate oppressive systems, the other pillars focus on exposing, combating, and dismantling those very systems. In the face of such pervasive injustice, an effective defense is critical but a strategic offense is essential.

Our individual client representation forms the foundation of the fights that we undertake through affirmative civil rights litigation. These cases, often but not always class actions, challenge abusive policing, debtors' prisons, cash bail, unfair housing practices, and a range of practices that criminalize poverty and homelessness.[6] Through litigation, we seek not only policy transformation, but also monetary compensation for our clients and others similarly harmed. Again, we know from our clients that this is a priority.

Our media and policy advocacy with and on behalf of our clients extends far beyond the courts. Having our clients and their families tell their stories fully and honestly is the most powerful mechanism for raising awareness and sparking action, both by policymakers and everyday people. Whether through traditional media, social media, or other creative storytelling means, our aim is to replace the many dehumanizing tropes about our clients with nuanced representations that honor the truth of their experiences. We also seek opportunities to connect these experiences to policy in the form of reports, white papers, open letters, and accessible, illustrated know-your-rights guides.[7]

Last, the efforts aimed at the most lasting and long-term change are those taken in collaboration with partners, clients, and other community members to transform our systems and reimagine what is possible. Ultimately, organized community is the only sustainable way of achieving the change we seek. Eradicating poverty and defeating white supremacy are political projects. They will not be won in the courts. Thus, if we are committed to faithfully serving our clients and pursuing our mission, we need to shed the tired fallacies of neutrality and objectivity and be fully in the fight for our collective liberation. That means supporting the work of organizing campaigns, building coalitions, and shifting power to those we serve.[8]

For people like the couple I described at the beginning of this essay, fairytale endings are rare. Even after resolving the immediate legal issue and successfully fighting back against the city—receiving significant monetary damages for the harm they suffered and securing policy changes preventing the use of secured cash bail to hold anyone in jail on municipal charges—they have continued to face challenges with housing, employment, policing, and even school access for their children during periods of housing instability.

I will never forget one afternoon when I picked this couple up from their home in Black, low-income North St. Louis City to prepare for a court appearance. As we rode down a main thoroughfare lined with closed, boarded-up businesses and check-cashing shops, the husband remarked, almost to no one, "When they start the concentration camps, they're coming here first."

His wife, sitting behind him, narrowed her eyes and looked at him. "What are you talking about?" she asked incredulously. "They've already got concentration camps. We're living in concentration camps."

I share this not for shock value or as political commentary. Whether or not you believe the metaphor to be apt is irrelevant. The point is that poor, Black and Brown, hypercriminalized, and underserved communities across the country understand the immensity of the challenges stacked against them. The only way for us to be of any use as lawyers and advocates is to understand the same and to marshal every tool at our disposal at every turn. Those we serve deserve nothing less.

NOTES

1. Carmen Reinicke, "56% of Americans Can't Cover a $1,000 Emergency Expense with Savings," CNBC, January 19, 2022, https://www.cnbc.com/2022/01/19/56percent-of-americans-cant-cover-a-1000-emergency-expense-with-savings.html.
2. Open Door Legal, *The Anti-Poverty Effect of Legal Aid: A Report*, 2018, 5, https://opendoorlegal.org/wp-content/uploads/delightful-downloads/2018/08/SROI-Report-v1.2.pdf.
3. Bryan Furst, *A Fair Fight: Achieving Indigent Defense Resource Parity* (New York: Brennan Center for Justice, 2019), 1–2, https://www.brennancenter.org/sites/default/files/2019-09/Report_A%20Fair%20Fight.pdf; Heidi Schultheis and Caitlin Rooney, *A Right to Counsel Is a Right to a Fighting Chance* (Washington, DC: Center for American Progress, 2019, 1, https://www.americanprogress.org/article/right-counsel-right-fighting-chance.
4. ArchCity Defenders, "Mission, Vision, Values," accessed November 23, 2022, https://www.archcitydefenders.org/about-us/mission-vision-values.
5. The Bronx Defenders, "About Us: Mission and Story," accessed November 23, 2022, https://www.bronxdefenders.org/who-we-are/.
6. ArchCity Defenders, "What We Do—ArchCity Defenders," accessed November 30, 2022, https://www.archcitydefenders.org/our-impact.
7. Pro Se STL, "Know Your Rights Guides by ArchCity Defenders," accessed November 23, 2022, https://www.prosestl.org.
8. Close the Workhouse, "The Campaign to Close The Workhouse," accessed November 23, 2022, https://www.closetheworkhouse.org; The People's Plan St. Louis, "Home," accessed November 23, 2022, https://www.peoplesplanstl.org.

31

THE DEHUMANIZING WORK OF IMMIGRATION LAW

Jennifer M. Chacón

FOR THE PAST TEN YEARS, I have worked as part of a team of researchers studying the effects of U.S. immigration laws on immigrant families and communities in Southern California. In our book, *Legal Phantoms: Executive Action and the Haunting Failures of Immigration Law,* we explore how people experience the effects of immigration law in their everyday lives and explain how legal service providers and immigrant justice organizations work to navigate and shape immigration policies at the local, state, and national level.[1] We have seen how individuals' encounters with the U.S. immigration and criminal legal systems are affected by factors such as race and gender, and how their immigration and criminal histories in turn shape how they experience changes in immigration enforcement policies.

Many of the immigrants we spoke with had experienced the sundering of their family ties. We heard about parents who were deported. We learned about people unable to visit dying parents, missing weddings and funerals, and going for decades without seeing siblings, all because they did not think they would be allowed to reenter the United States if they visited their home countries. People told us about how long periods of cross-border separation from their children irrevocably strained the bonds between them. Even those immigrants who had not experienced separation firsthand lived in fear of the possibility that they would in the future. Their stories reminded us that most immigration enforcement actions are either breaking families apart or frustrating their reunification. The media and the general public focused on the immediate physical seizure of children from their parents by the Border Patrol during the Donald Trump administration, but family separation is actually an integral part of immigration enforcement in the United States, and ongoing strategy used by U.S. Immigration and Customs Enforcement (ICE) and Border Patrol today.[2]

Public officials regardless of party have justified their participation in our immigration system's daily severing of family ties by invoking the rule of law. A stock talking point of the Republican Party for the past decade is that "we are a nation of immigrants, but we are also a nation of laws."[3] The phrase actually may have originated with President Bill Clinton, a Democrat, who used nearly identical wording in his State of the Union addresses in 1995 and 1996.[4] People who want to be here, we are repeatedly told, need to do it "the right way." Those who violate our laws will face consequences. The comfortable invocation of these bromides in the face of so much human suffering requires the assumption that the law provides sensible avenues for deserving people, particularly those with strong family ties to the United States, to enter or remain legally. The reality, however, is much different. In fact, U.S. immigration laws are exceptionally harsh and often fail entirely to take the needs of people and families into account. The law provides almost no avenues for long-time residents to regularize their immigration status; the U.S. government often ignores the limited protections that immigration laws do provide to noncitizens; and immigration law treats individuals with criminal convictions, even very minor ones, with extreme severity.

NO WAY TO "DO THINGS THE RIGHT WAY"

First, the notion that there is a "right way" to immigrate is simply not true for many people. Most long-term, undocumented residents, for example, do not fit the law's rigid categories for lawful immigration, even though they are long-standing members of our communities and do some of the nation's most essential work. The annals of U.S. immigration history are filled with the stories of men like Oscar Martinez, an undocumented resident in the United States for twenty-five years with a loving family and community, who have nevertheless been deported because they could not navigate a legal path to citizenship.[5] Martinez was an active union member, with significant ties to his family and community, including attending parent-teacher association meetings and involvement in his church.[6]

Even when long-term residents have found a way to regularize their status—such as when marriage to a citizen opens up the possibility of a spousal visa—U.S. laws continue to make it almost impossible to do things "the right way." A noncitizen who marries a citizen generally becomes eligible for a visa sponsored by their citizen spouse. But the law requires anyone who has been in the country for more than a year without authorization to leave the country to process their visa. Once the noncitizen leaves the country, they face a ten-year bar before reentering on that family-sponsored visa.[7] The bar routinely operates as a legal form of family separation in cases where individuals otherwise meet the requirements for family-based immigration status.

Troublingly, although President Joe Biden ran on a platform opposing President Trump's family separation policies in immigration, families continue to be separated physically from their children at the southern border, though in much smaller numbers.[8] More subtly, the Biden administration has embraced legal arguments that facilitate family separation.

For example, under Biden, the Department of Justice effectively argued in favor of family separation before the Supreme Court in April 2021.[9] The legal question concerned the status of noncitizens with Temporary Protected Status (TPS), and in particular, whether they, too, would need to leave the country and face the ten-year bar when applying for family-based lawful permanent residence. The Department of Homeland Security has the power to grant TPS to people in the United States upon a formal finding of a condition in their country of origin that temporarily prevents nationals of that country from returning safely.[10] Because conditions in many of these countries are volatile, some TPS designations have been extended for periods that add up to decades, but no automatic path to more permanent status exists for TPS holders. Still, life happens, and some TPS holders become eligible for family-based or employment-based visas during their time in the United States. Some of these individuals had successfully argued to several federal appeals courts that their admission to the TPS program was a legal admission that allows them to bypass the need to leave the country and face the ten-year reentry bar when processing their family-based visas.

The administration urged that the better reading of an ambiguous statute was to treat TPS holders as if they have not been "admitted" when they seek to adjust their status based on an available visa. The Supreme Court unanimously agreed.[11] This sounds like a banal and technical argument, but the effect is to require TPS holders, many of whom have now lived in the United States for two decades, to leave the country and contend with the ten-year reentry bar when they otherwise qualify for a visa granting lawful permanent resident status. The full weight of the U.S. government was thus brought to bear in favor of a legal position that will require more needless family separations.

THE GOVERNMENT FAILS TO FOLLOW THE LAWS IT CREATES

Second, the United States has not always honored its own legal processes when immigrants are doing things "the right way." For example, U.S. treaty obligations prohibit the government from penalizing asylum seekers who arrive at the border without documents. But under Trump, when Central American asylum seekers presented themselves to U.S. Border Patrol agents at the southern border in 2018 and 2019, as permitted by law, many were criminally prosecuted and thousands of parents were separated from their children.[12] By July 2019, ICE held about fifty thousand people in custodial detention on any given day.[13]

Even though that family separation policy generated a national outcry and drew criticism from the government itself, little public attention was paid to the tens of thousands of others who were turned back and told to remain in Mexico under the so-called Migrant Protection Protocols (MPP).[14] Under MPP, individuals who arrived at the southern border of the United States without entry documents—including those who expressed their desire to claim asylum under existing law—were returned to Mexico pending the adjudication of their claims.[15] Human rights organizations documented the fact that many individuals subjected to MPP faced violence, exploitation, and other perils while awaiting their hearings.[16] The situation went from bad to worse when the U.S. government shut down asylum processing completely, claiming that doing so was necessary as a public health measure to stop the spread of COVID-19.[17] The lack of public health evidence justifying the border shutdown proved no obstacle to the Trump administration's invocation of public health laws to frustrate the efforts of many individuals to do things "the right way" by seeking asylum at the border.[18] Indeed, their efforts to lawfully request asylum at the southern border turned increasingly deadly for them as conditions deteriorated in migrant camps.[19]

Notwithstanding the Biden administration's promise to reverse harsh Trump-era policies, it took the administration until June 1—more than four months—to formally terminate MPP, prolonging the misery of asylum seekers who, by the end of the Trump administration, had already languished in Mexico for as long as two years. Litigation by Republican governors drew the revocation process out even longer.[20] Furthermore, even after President Biden publicly proclaimed the end of the COVID-19 pandemic, a federal court required the administration to keep in place the public health order that, as of late 2022, continued to bar asylum access for many people arriving at the southern border.[21] Those individuals who were exempt from the bar, or who arrived before it, face an overburdened system where they sometimes have to wait years to have their claims adjudicated and where five-year-old children have had to appear without counsel in proceedings.[22] A federal district court recognized the illegalities of the Title 42 program, and struck it down, on November 15, 2022.[23]

IMMIGRATION LAW AMPLIFIES THE EXCESSES OF THE CRIMINAL LEGAL SYSTEM

Third, long-time lawful permanent residents who have contact with the criminal legal system are often denied any chance to do things "the right way." Criminal records, no matter how old or how minor—for instance, for marijuana-related convictions involving conduct that is no longer even criminal in some jurisdictions—are often a barrier to regularizing an immigrant's status and allowing them to remain in the United States. The law also allows for the deportation of long-time residents, including lawful permanent residents, for offenses that were not deportable offenses at the time of their commission. In describing the harsh effects of these immigration laws, Nancy Morawetz, professor of clinical law at the New York University School of Law, discussed a deportation case the government was pursuing in 2000 on the basis of a conviction for possession of a small quantity of drugs in 1978, three years after the immigrant entered the country as a lawful permanent resident.[24] U.S. law requires deportation for a long list of relatively minor offenses regardless of a person's family ties, length in the country, or service in the U.S. military.[25]

Some citizens rejoiced when—in the fall of 2022—President Biden pardoned federal convictions for simple marijuana possession and urged state governors to do the same.[26] But Biden's order expressly excluded both noncitizens who were not lawfully present at the time of their conviction and those who are not now lawful permanent residents or citizens.[27] Thus, even as some states license marijuana dispensaries, noncitizens remain vulnerable to lifelong banishment if they ever incurred convictions for selling marijuana in those same states. Such convictions are considered aggravated felonies, which trigger mandatory detention during removal proceedings, mandatory removal, and a lifetime bar from returning to the United States.[28]

Our national severity toward those charged with crimes reverberates far beyond the criminal legal system, weighing down those who have already served sentences for crimes. The pattern of overpolicing that plagues Black and Latino communities ensures that immigrants from these racial groups are overrepresented among those deported on criminal grounds or barred by criminal convictions from obtaining lawful status and naturalizing.

In 2014, at the same time that President Obama and other members of his administration were critiquing the racial inequities of the criminal legal system, it was dismaying to hear them doubling down on their reliance on a noncitizen's contacts with the criminal legal system as the basis upon which to prioritize them for removal.[29] We were told that the administration would deport "felons, not families. . . . [c]riminals, not children" even though it was clear that families would be separated by the removal of those labeled "felons," and that the felony label itself emerges out of a criminal legal system that is both overly punitive and racially discriminatory.[30]

President Trump's successful 2016 presidential campaign leaned into this framework of good and bad immigrants, dwelling on the bad. He promoted the idea that many immigrants were dangerous, warning that Mexican immigrants were rapists and brought drugs and crime to the country, though some, he "assume[d], are good people."[31] He used this caricatured notion of "criminal aliens" as the basis for his most popular campaign slogan—the call to build a wall on the U.S. southern border. Though his administration never built a physical wall, policies like MPP and the Title 42 order achieved comparable results, and continue to have harsh effects well into the presidency of Joe Biden.

COURTS PLAY A RULE IN DEHUMANIZING IMMIGRANTS

Again and again, notions of the rule of law are invoked to justify the sundering of families and communities that would, in other circumstances, seem unthinkable. Courts have played an essential role in shoring up the dehumanizing narratives that enable our nation's harsh enforcement practices. In fact, U.S. Supreme Court decisions from the 1980s helped lay the groundwork for today's exceptionally severe immigration laws, treating undocumented workers coming to fill jobs in the United States as a grave threat to public safety and security.

In upholding the constitutionality of interior immigration checkpoint stops in the 1976 case of *U.S. v. Martinez-Fuerte*, Justice Lewis Powell justified these stops—including those made on the basis of race—as necessary to address the "formidable law enforcement problems" posed by the "flow" of a population that he describes at the outset of the opinion as "illegal Mexican aliens."[32] In Justice Sandra Day O'Connor's 1984 decision in *INS v. Lopez-Mendoza*, she concludes that illegally obtained evidence can be used against immigrants in their deportation proceedings, analogizing the ongoing presence of an unauthorized immigrant worker to "a leaking hazardous waste dump."[33]

Notably, both of these decisions were handed down before the enactment of the Immigration Reform and Control Act of 1986.[34] At the time, no law prohibited employers from hiring these immigrant workers; indeed, employers were actively recruiting the very immigrant workers whose flow was treated by the Supreme Court as such a toxic menace. Employers hired workers with impunity, yet governmental officials were given license to violate these workers' Fourth Amendment protections when enforcing the immigration laws. Immigrant workers paid a price for perceived lawlessness; those whose recruitment efforts brought them to the United States did not. The price increased when legal changes in the 1980s and 1990s attached expansive penalties to new crimes of migration, made it more difficult for immigrants to regularize their status, and vastly increased the range of criminal violations that would bar immigrants from coming to or remaining in the United States.

Today, people routinely use the term *illegal* not to refer to the law enforcement practices such as the Migrant Protection Policy that openly violate U.S. treaty obligations, nor to the hiring practices of many of the nation's employers, but to describe immigrants as outside the law, always threatening to it. For people thus dehumanized, no legal consequences seem too severe; for them, the law is a threatening sword, not a protective shield.

American economic policies, climate policies, and foreign policy choices play a significant role in shaping the forces that drive people in neighboring countries from their homes. Yet when those displaced persons—many with family and other affective ties to the United States—arrive at our borders, we use law as a cudgel against them and deploy legal language to mask our inhumanity.

NOTES

1. Jennifer M. Chacón, Susan Bibler Coutin, and Stephen Lee, *Legal Phantoms: Executive Action and the Haunting Failures of Immigration Law* (Redwood City, CA: Stanford University Press, 2023).

2. Southern Poverty Law Center, "Family Separation—A Timeline," March 23, 2022, https://www.splcenter.org/news/2022/03/23/family-separation-timeline; Jordyn Rozensky, "The Biden Administration Routinely Separates Immigrant Families," National Immigrant Justice Center, January 19, 2022, https://immigrantjustice.org/staff/blog/biden-administration-routinely-separates-immigrant-families.
3. See James R. Carroll, "Barr: Obama Immigration Move 'Profoundly Disappointing,'" *Courier Journal*, November 20, 2014, https://www.courier-journal.com/story/politics-blog/2014/11/20/kentucky-rep-andy-barr-obama-immigration-move-is-profoundly-disappointing/19326789 (Representative Andy Barr [R-KY] making this statement to register his disapproval of a proposed 2014 plan by the Obama administration to shield parents of U.S. citizens and lawful permanent residents from deportation). See also Deb Fischer, "Anarchy at the Southern Border," United States Senator Deb Fischer Weekly Column, February 22, 2022, https://www.fischer.senate.gov/public/index.cfm/weekly-column?ID=C633AF3D-FA51-4BC1-AF00-6BECA45F213B (Senator Deb Fischer [R-NE] using this statement as part of her critique of the Biden administration's immigration policies).
4. Allison Ehrlich, "State of the Union: Here's What U.S. Presidents Said About Immigration in Their Own Words," *Caller Times*, February 4, 2019, https://www.caller.com/story/news/2019/02/04/their-own-words-presidents-talk-immigration-state-union/2681159002.
5. Bill Ong Hing, "The Failure of Prosecutorial Discretion and the Deportation of Oscar Martinez," *The Scholar: St. Mary's Law Review on Race and Social Justice* 15 (2013), https://papers.ssrn.com/sol3/papers.cfm?abstract_id=2215989.
6. Hing, "Failure of Prosecutorial Discretion," 11.
7. 8 U.S.C. § 1182(a)(9)(B)(II).
8. John Washington and Anna-Catherine Brigida, "Biden Is Still Separating Immigrant Kids from their Families," *Texas Observer*, November 21, 2022, https://www.texasobserver.org/the-biden-administration-is-still-separating-kids-from-their-families.
9. Maryellen Fullerton, "Skepticism and the Shadow of *Chevron* in *Sanchez v. Mayorkas* Argument," *SCOTUSblog*, April 22, 2021, https://www.scotusblog.com/2021/04/skepticism-and-the-shadow-of-chevron-in-sanchez-v-mayorkas-argument.
10. 8 U.S.C. § 1254(a). See also U.S. Citizenship and Immigration Services, "Temporary Protected Status," last updated November 14, 2022, https://www.uscis.gov/humanitarian/temporary-protected-status.
11. Sanchez et ux. v. Mayorkas, Secretary of Homeland Security, et al., 593 U.S. ___ (2021), https://www.supremecourt.gov/opinions/20pdf/20-315_q713.pdf.
12. Human Rights First, "The Rise in Criminal Prosecutions of Asylum Seekers," 2022, https://humanrightsfirst.org/wp-content/uploads/2022/10/hrf-criminal-prosecution-of-asylum-seekers.pdf.

13. U.S. Immigration and Customs Enforcement, *U.S. Immigration and Customs Enforcement Fiscal Year 2019 Enforcement and Removal Operations Report* (Washington, DC: U.S. Department of Homeland Security, 2020), 5, 7, https://www.ice.gov/sites/default/files/documents/Document/2019/eroReportFY2019.pdf.
14. Evaluation and Inspections Division, *Review of the Department of Justice's Planning and Implementation of Its Zero Tolerance Policy and Its Coordination with the Departments of Homeland Security and Health and Human Services*, Report No. 21-028 (Washington, DC: U.S. Department of Justice Office of the Inspector General, 2021), i, https://oig.justice.gov/sites/default/files/reports/21-028_0.pdf; American Immigration Council, "The 'Migrant Protection Protocols,' " 2022, 2, https://www.americanimmigrationcouncil.org/research/migrant-protection-protocols.
15. Kirstjen M. Nielsen, "Policy Guidance for Implementation of the Migrant Protection Protocols," Memorandum (Washington, DC: U.S. Department of Homeland Security, January 25, 2019), https://www.dhs.gov/sites/default/files/publications/19_0129_OPA_migrant-protection-protocols-policy-guidance.pdf.
16. The Biden administration embraced these findings. See Alejandro N. Mayorkas, "Termination of the Migrant Protection Protocols Program," Memorandum (Washington, DC: U.S. Department of Homeland Security, June 1, 2021), 4, https://www.dhs.gov/sites/default/files/publications/21_0601_termination_of_mpp_program.pdf (citing "the lack of stable access to housing, income, and safety" of some MPP enrollees as justification for ending the program).
17. See Notice of Order Under Sections 362 and 365 of the Public Health Service Act Suspending Introduction of Certain Persons From Countries Where a Communicable Disease Exists, 85 Fed. Reg. 17060-02, 17061 (March 26, 2020). See also Michael D. Shear and Zolan Kanno-Youngs, "Trump Administration Plans to Extend Virus Border Restrictions Indefinitely," *New York Times*, May 13, 2020, https://www.nytimes.com/2020/05/13/us/politics/trump-coronavirus-border-restrictions.html.
18. The administration's authority purportedly stemmed from 42 U.S.C. § 265. See Camilo Montoya-Galvez, "What Is Title 42, the COVID Border Policy Used to Expel Migrants?," CBS News, August 16, 2022, https://www.cbsnews.com/news/title-42-immigration-border-biden-COVID-19-cdc (noting the officials' objection to the policy as a public health measure).
19. Megan Diamond, Luke Testa, Carissa Novak, Kathryn Kempton-Amaral, Thalia Porteny, and Alejandro Olayo-Méndez, "A Population in Peril: A Health Crisis Among Asylum Seekers on the Northern Border of Mexico" (Cambridge, MA: Harvard Global Health Institute, 2020), accessed November 30, 2022, https://globalhealth.harvard.edu/wp-content/uploads/2020/07/A_Population_in_Peril.pdf.

20. After the announced revocation of MPP, Republican governors sued to keep it in place. Ultimately, they were unsuccessful, though the effect was to stall the full revocation of the program for another year. Biden v. Texas, 579 U.S. ___ (2022). See also Elizabeth Carlson, Luis Guerra, and Tania Guerrero, "Supreme Court Holds that Biden Administration's Termination of the Migrant Protection Protocols Did Not Violate the Immigration and Nationality Act Authors," Clinic Legal, last updated August 24, 2022, https://cliniclegal.org/resources/litigation/supreme-court-holds-biden-administrations-termination-migrant-protection; American Immigration Council, "Migrant Protection Protocols," 7.
21. Dan Diamond, "Biden's Claim That 'Pandemic Is Over' Complicates Efforts to Secure Funding," *Washington Post*, September 19, 2022 https://www.washingtonpost.com/health/2022/09/18/biden-covid-pandemic-over; U.S. Department of Homeland Security, "DHS Statement on District Court Ruling on Title 42," May 20, 2022, https://sv.usembassy.gov/dhs-statement-on-district-court-ruling-on-title-42.
22. Jerry Markon, "Can a 3-Year Old Represent Herself in Immigration Court? This Judge Thinks So," *Washington Post*, March 5, 2016, https://www.washingtonpost.com/world/national-security/can-a-3-year-old-represent-herself-in-immigration-court-this-judge-thinks-so/2016/03/03/5be59a32-db25-11e5-925f-1d10062cc82d_story.html; Sarah Burr, "Why Are Children Representing Themselves in Immigration Court?," *The Hill*, October 24, 2021, https://thehill.com/opinion/judiciary/578076-why-are-children-representing-themselves-in-immigration-court. For immigration court wait times see TRAC Immigration, "Average Time Pending Cases Have Been Waiting in Immigration Courts as of Oct 2023 [sic]," accessed November 30, 2022, https://trac.syr.edu/phptools/immigration/court_backlog/apprep_backlog_avgdays.php.
23. Huisha-Huisha et al. v. Mayorkas, CV: 21-100 (D.D.C., 2022), https://ecf.dcd.uscourts.gov/cgi-bin/show_public_doc?2021cv0100-165.
24. American Immigration Council, "The Ones They Leave Behind: Deportation of Lawful Permanent Residents Harms U.S. Citizen Children," Fact sheet, April 26, 2010, https://www.americanimmigrationcouncil.org/sites/default/files/research/Childs_Best_Interest_Fact_Sheet_042610.pdf; Nancy Morawetz, "Understanding the Impact of the 1996 Deportation Laws and the Limited Scope of Proposed Reforms," *Harvard Law Review* 113 (2000): 1936–62, https://www.jstor.org/stable/1342314?seq=1.
25. Maria Ines Zamudio, "Deported U.S. Veterans Feel Abandoned by the Country They Defended," NPR, June 21, 2019, https://www.npr.org/local/309/2019/06/21/733371297/deported-u-s-veterans-feel-abandoned-by-the-country-they-defended.
26. Proclamation 10467, Granting Pardon for the Offense of Simple Possession of Marijuana, 87 Fed. Reg. 61441, October 6, 2022, https://www.federalregister.gov

/documents/2022/10/12/2022-22262/granting-pardon-for-the-offense-of-simple-possession-of-marijuana.

27. Proclamation 10467, Granting Pardon for the Offense of Simple Possession of Marijuana, 87 Fed. Reg. 61441, October 6, 2022.
28. American Immigration Council, "Aggravated Felonies: An Overview," Fact sheet, March 2021, https://www.americanimmigrationcouncil.org/sites/default/files/research/aggravated_felonies_an_overview_0.pdf.
29. Eric Holder, "Remarks at the 2014 National Action Network Convention" (speech, New York City, April 9, 2014), https://www.justice.gov/opa/speech/attorney-general-eric-holder-delivers-remarksat-2014-national-action-network-convention.
30. Barack Obama, "Remarks by the President in Address to the Nation on Immigration" (speech, Washington, DC, November 20, 2014), https://obamawhitehouse.archives.gov/the-press-office/2014/11/20/remarks-President-address-nation-immigration.
31. Washington Post Staff, "Full Text: Donald Trump Announces a Presidential Bid," *Washington Post*, June 16, 2015, https://www.washingtonpost.com/news/post-politics/wp/2015/06/16/full-text-donald-trump-announces-a-presidential-bid.
32. United States v. Martinez-Fuerte, 428 U.S. 543, 552, 556, 572 (1976).
33. INS v. Lopez-Mendoza, 468 U.S. 1032, 1046 (1984).
34. Pub. L. 99–603, 100 Stat. 3445 (1986).

32

EXPLORING IMMIGRATION COLLATERAL CONSEQUENCES RELATED TO A CRIMINAL CONVICTION

Khalil Cumberbatch

DURING THE 2016 PRESIDENTIAL CAMPAIGN, the long-term impact of the Violent Crime Control and Law Enforcement Act of 1994 (Crime Bill) received a lot of media attention.[1] This two-decade-old piece of federal legislation has rightfully received considerable criticism. Prior to its passage, incarceration rates in the United States were 360 per hundred thousand people; ten years after, the number was approximately 487 per hundred thousand.[2] During a 2016 Democratic debate in Brooklyn, when Hillary Clinton was on the presidential campaign trail, she was questioned regarding the role she played as first lady in helping advocate for the bill's passage.[3] At the debate, she even apologized for her role in advocating for it, saying, "'I'm sorry for the consequences that were unintended' and that have had a detrimental impact on people's lives."[4]

As Lauren-Brooke Eisen points out in her essay in this book (see chapter 5) on the history of punitive funding to increase enforcement and incarceration, the Crime Bill added financial incentives to expand law enforcement, build prisons, and extend punishments for crimes. Its impact is still felt to this day by communities across the country. In the same vein, the impacts of another piece of federal legislation, passed and signed by the same Democratic leadership, continue to devastate countless individuals, families, and communities. That bill was the Illegal Immigration Reform and Immigrant Responsibility Act of 1996 (IIRAIRA).[5]

IIRAIRA created the immigration enforcement apparatus that exists today, almost thirty years later. Under this law, essentially any immigrant, whether documented or not, who violates U.S. law—in some cases low-level criminal offenses—became eligible for detention and deportation. The law also made it more difficult for those fleeing persecution to apply for asylum and required the government to hold more undocumented people in detention before deporting them. This created an additional barrier for immigrants to obtain counsel.

Prior to its passage, approximately seventy thousand individuals were deported from the United States annually. At the end of President Barak Obama's first term, that number exploded to more than four hundred thousand annually.[6] In 2014, I almost became one of those individuals.

When I was twenty years old, a few weeks before my twenty-first birthday, I committed a robbery in Manhattan, New York. It was an act that would dramatically define my life experiences for the duration of my young adulthood. I would end up serving almost six and half years in prison for the crime. When I was released in 2010, I began my career in advocacy and service delivery to and on behalf of people who had criminal justice involvement. By May 2014, a little over four years after I left prison, I had successfully completed community supervision, become a father, gotten married, completed a bachelor's degree, and was one week from completing a master's degree. Despite these accomplishments, I was still targeted for detention and deportation.

On May 8, 2014, officials from Immigration and Customs Enforcement (ICE) came to my home to detain me. In our living room, where my wife and I sat on the couch, the agents told me they were there to arrest me. The reason was my criminal conviction—that was more than a decade old at that time—coupled with the fact that I was a legal permanent resident. I am from Guyana originally but have lived in Queens, New York, with my family since I was a toddler. This made me eligible for deportation proceedings. You could not imagine the terror and fear I felt in that moment. It was overwhelming. My heart stopped. I was unable to comprehend what they were saying. I could only see their mouths moving. I remember being placed in handcuffs, taken outside my home in front of my family and neighbors and brought to a processing center. By nightfall, I was in a jail cell in New Jersey, miles away from my family.

Many people don't know that ICE leases detention beds from local jails across the country to house detained immigrants.[7] For someone like me, who has served a sentence, I felt as if I were being dragged back into the criminal justice system after I had worked so hard to change who I was and move far away from a life of crime. When I first arrived in the jail, after a painstakingly slow process period, I was brought to an intake housing unit called "the freezer." You take a guess why. It was May, but people were wearing long johns and were covered in blankets because the air conditioning was purposefully kept at chilling temperatures. The reason given for this frigid temperature ranged from "hygiene" to "the air unit is broken."

The food was horrible. There is not a jail or prison in the country where it's good, but the first meal I had there after being out for four years was absolutely disgusting. If you've ever had bad, remicrowaved oatmeal, multiply that experience by one thousand, and you still probably can't fully appreciate how gross this was. Getting quickly adjusted to the jail schedule was another task. Breakfast was served at 5:30 a.m., lunch at 11:30 a.m., and dinner at 4 p.m. That doesn't include the three mandatory counts that took place throughout the day where all movement in the entire facility would stop. All I kept thinking was, yesterday at this time I was in my own home, with my family, enjoying them.

Readjusting to the social culture of jail was also a task I had to remaster. I'm naturally drawn to people. I want to learn about them, about their history, their culture, their stories, their struggles. But in jail you can't allow yourself to be open. At first, I was standoffish because I didn't know how long I was going to be there. I didn't want to answer questions from people who were in the same situation as I was. I also knew I couldn't trust anyone because people were desperate in detention, and my experience taught me that desperation can cause people to act dangerously. Bottom line: it was hard for me to accept that I was reincarcerated.

The hardest part was being away from my family. I couldn't stop thinking of my daughters. They had never been separated from me, and I couldn't imagine what they were going through. My wife, also. She woke up that day in a two-parent household but had gone to sleep as the single caretaker of two little girls. I had promised never to leave my wife and my daughters, and here I was, breaking that vow because of a bad decision I had made as a very different person, at a very different time in my life. That first night was the beginning of a five-month odyssey through the immigration detention system.

Immediately after I was taken away from our home, my wife had to compose herself and start making phone calls. She started with family, then friends, then my coworkers, and classmates, making her way through a long list. What she found was a tremendous amount of support. People started calling other people, sending emails, and even posting on social media. The more people learned I had been taken by ICE, the more they became upset and wanted to help. They weren't just upset because of me, they were upset because of what my situation represented. This is the focal question: how much punishment is enough? My predicament illustrated that the punitiveness of the criminal justice system doesn't end after you serve a sentence. It exists in perpetuity.

In the first few days I was detained, I hoped that I would be released at my next court date. I had to believe that. I couldn't wrap my head around the fact that I was being held after being home for over four years for a conviction that was more than a decade old. I also wanted to get back to my family as soon as possible. However, at that next court date, the judge delivered a devastating blow. He had no discretion to release me from detention, he said. IIRAIRA required that I be mandatorily held and deported. We were all devastated. By this time, we had been able to acquire a lawyer to represent me, which wasn't easy. Many lawyers we spoke to said there wasn't anything they could do, and my outcome would be deportation. Our supporters, though, refused to believe that. After every setback, there was more optimism. They used that optimism to ensure I had adequate representation.

Then, one day, with little explanation, I was released. I remember being awakened early in the morning and told simply to pack up all my stuff. The officer didn't know where I was going. It was 3:30 a.m. By 6 a.m., after a long bus ride, I was in a courthouse. By 11 a.m., I was released into the custody of my family.

However, most people and families don't have the ending we did. For example, during the 2020 fiscal year, 156,158 people were deported, approximately 11,629 of them because of a prior criminal conviction.[8] Under the Obama administration, more than 2.5 million people were deported, more than under all previous administrations combined.[9] Bolstered by decades of tough-on-crime rhetoric and most recently by the war on terror, the deportation apparatus exploded. The IIRAIRA in 1996 had vastly expanded the criminal offenses, otherwise referred to as aggravated felonies, that made a person deportable. It also severely restricted the ability of a judge to waive a person's potential deportation. Between the creation of the Department of Homeland Security (DHS), which houses ICE and Customs and Border Patrol (CBP), in 2003 and 2021, the federal government has spent around $333 billion on these agencies.[10] Between 2003 and 2019, the number of CBP agents doubled and ICE tripled its number of enforcers.

Almost two million people populate America's jails and prisons, but the statistics don't often include the thousands of people locked behind bars in immigration detention.[11] Under former President Donald Trump, more than fifty thousand people were held in custody on any given day.[12] Just as America has taken a punitive turn with its overreliance on jails and prisons, it has as well with undocumented individuals.

The Biden administration's deportation rates have dropped significantly but don't mean that families aren't being affected by these deportation policies.[13]

The consequences of deportation can be devastating. Unfortunately, little research focuses on the long-term impacts of deportation to the families and communities left behind. Even the detention of a family member for short periods can cause disruptions to a family's life that may prove irreversible.

Additionally, the psychological impacts can last much longer. For me, I can still remember the calls with my daughters when I was detained. My youngest was no more than three years old, and every time she would get on the phone with me, she'd ask, "Daddy, when are you coming home?" My wife had done the most humane thing she believed she could do, which was to tell them that I'd gone on a business trip. In a child's mind, when you choose to leave home, you can also choose to return. So my youngest daughter wanted to know when I was going to choose to return to them. I didn't know what the outcome was going to be; all I knew was that the likelihood that I wouldn't be coming home to her was high and that what she was suffering through was going to last her entire life. To this day, almost ten years later, that daughter, now the second oldest of four children, still gets anxious and nervous when I travel for work. And it's not just her—so do my wife and I.

Of course, the legal ramifications are also significant. IIRAIRA made it almost impossible for documented and undocumented immigrants with criminal convictions to achieve citizenship. Some argue an immigrant who commits a crime shouldn't be allowed to become a legal U.S. citizen. It's critical, though, to consider the impact of decades of punitive enforcement policies and overpolicing of Black and Latino people, particularly in communities where both documented and undocumented immigrants reside. Given this backdrop to policing strategies in America, it's not surprising that so many immigrants get swept into a policing apparatus whose net is very wide.

NOTES

1. Violent Crime Control and Law Enforcement Act of 1994, Pub. L. 103-322, 103rd Congress (1994), https://www.congress.gov/bill/103rd-congress/house-bill/3355/text.
2. E. Ann Carson and Joseph Mulako-Wangota, "Corrections Statistical Analysis Tool (CSAT)—Prisoners," Bureau of Justice Statistics, November 22, 2022, https://csat.bjs.ojp.gov/quick-tables.
3. CNN, "Hillary Clinton Apologizes for Husband's Crime Bill," April 15, 2016, https://www.cnn.com/videos/politics/2016/04/14/brooklyn-democratic-debate-hillary-clinton-sorry-1994-crime-bill-6.cnn.

4. Eileen Rivers, "Clinton Apology for Support of Crime Bill Enough?" *USA Today*, December 15, 2016, https://www.usatoday.com/story/opinion/policing/community-calls/2016/04/15/clinton-apology-support-crime-bill-enough/83064232.
5. Illegal Immigration Reform and Immigrant Responsibility Act, Pub. L. 104-208, Div. C, 110 Stat. 3009-546 (1996).
6. Dara Lind, "The Disastrous, Forgotten 1996 Law That Created Today's Immigration Problem," Vox, April 28, 2016, https://www.vox.com/2016/4/28/11515132/iirira-clinton-immigration.
7. Ellyn Jameson, "ICE Detention Through U.S. Marshals Agreements," *Georgetown Immigration Law Journal* 35, no. 1 (2019): 280–315, https://www.law.georgetown.edu/immigration-law-journal/wp-content/uploads/sites/19/2021/04/07-ICE-Detention-Through-U.S.-Marshals-Agreements.pdf.
8. Transactional Records Access Clearinghouse, "Latest Data: Immigration and Customs Enforcement Removals," accessed November 21, 2022, https://trac.syr.edu/phptools/immigration/remove; "Criminal Grounds for Deportation," accessed November 21, 2022, https://trac.syr.edu/immigration/reports/685.
9. Serena Marshall, "Obama Has Deported More People Than Any Other President," ABC News, August 9, 2016, https://abcnews.go.com/Politics/obamas-deportation-policy-numbers/story?id=41715661; U.S. Department of Homeland Security, "Yearbook of Immigration Statistics," accessed December 8, 2022, https://www.dhs.gov/immigration-statistics/yearbook.
10. American Immigration Council, "The Cost of Immigration Enforcement and Border Security," Fact sheet, 2021, 1, https://www.americanimmigrationcouncil.org/sites/default/files/research/the_cost_of_immigration_enforcement_and_border_security.pdf.
11. Wendy Sawyer and Peter Wagner, "The Whole Pie 2022" (Northampton, MA: Prison Policy Initiative, March 14, 2022), https://www.prisonpolicy.org/reports/pie2022.html.
12. Tara Watson, "Immigrant Deportations During the Trump Administration," Econofact, March 25, 2021, https://econofact.org/immigrant-deportations-during-the-trump-administration.
13. Stef W. Kight, "ICE Arrests and Deportations Fall Under Biden," *Axios*, March 11, 2022, https://www.axios.com/2022/03/11/ice-arrest-deportation-number-biden-immigration.

PART NINE

BEYOND BARS
ANOTHER WORLD IS POSSIBLE

33

PROVIDING HOPE AND FREEDOM TO OVERPUNISHED PEOPLE

Where Both Seem Impossible to Achieve

David Singleton

MANY OF THE ESSAYS in this volume focus on America's status as a world outlier given the sheer volume of people locked away in the country's thousands of jails and prisons. Although many people believe mass incarceration largely stems from imprisoning those who commit low-level, nonviolent crimes, recent research indicates that the problem results primarily from the overpunishment of people who have committed violent crimes.[1] Indeed, more than half of people in state prisons are there for physically harming someone. At least two hundred thousand are serving life sentences for serious crimes such as murder.[2]

So what's wrong with locking up people who have committed violent crimes, particularly ones that result in loss of life? I don't quarrel with the notion that some period of punishment, including prison time, is appropriate for the most serious crimes such as murder. But how long should we punish? Should we continue to incarcerate a person who has served a decade or more in prison for a homicide or other violent offense if that individual is no longer a danger to the community? What if twenty years into a life sentence the prosecutor no longer believes incarceration is necessary? What if the victim (or victim's family in a homicide case) supports the incarcerated person's release? If one of prison's primary goals is to rehabilitate, shouldn't we release people if that objective has been met?

Ordinarily, judges lose the power to change a sentence after imposing it, unless the conviction is vacated on appeal or through postconviction proceedings, or a statute specifically vests the court with jurisdiction to reconsider the sentence. Five states—California, Illinois, Louisiana, Oregon, and Washington—and the District of Columbia have enacted statutes that revest the court with jurisdiction to reconsider a life sentence under certain circumstances.[3] These statutes, colloquially known as second look provisions, provide hope to people serving life sentences with no other realistic route to freedom.[4]

But is there hope for a person who lives in one of the states without a second look law and who has exhausted all available appeals and postconviction remedies? Can lawyers and judges in these jurisdictions develop creative ways to grant relief to overpunished people who deserve freedom?

On a winter evening in 1997, twenty-one-year-old Robert Jones and several of his associates were dealing cocaine from an apartment located in an Ohio city.[5] Robert's role that particular night was guarding the drugs, which were stashed in the apartment's back bedroom. From behind the closed bedroom door, Robert suddenly heard a commotion near the apartment's front entrance. He heard shouts, followed by gunshots and screams. Although Robert could not see what was happening near the apartment's front door, he believed that a rival group had come to rob them. He was right.

Robert then heard a noise outside the bedroom and reached for his gun. He feared for his life. Guided by his self-preservation instinct, he fired three shots through the door. Then silence. When Robert emerged from the bedroom, he saw a body lying nearby—the corpse of his friend Barbara, whom he had mistaken for one of the robbers.

The state charged Robert with murder and drug trafficking. In view of the circumstances of the shooting, however, the state offered him a plea to the lesser offense of manslaughter with a proposed fourteen-year sentence. Fourteen years seemed like a lifetime to him, though, so he rejected the plea offer and went to trial, where he sought to argue that his intent to defend himself against the intruders justified his accidental shooting of Barbara. To Robert's disappointment, the trial judge refused to instruct the jury on Robert's defense and the jury convicted him on the murder and drug trafficking counts. The court then sentenced Robert to twenty-nine years to life, meaning that Robert would have to serve nearly three decades in prison before becoming parole eligible. Martin Sabelli's essay (see chapter 8) highlights the real consequences of the "trial penalty," which Robert experienced when he was given a more punitive sentence than he would have through a plea deal.[6]

People who enter the Ohio prison system to serve a life sentence have little hope of early release. Nationwide most convictions are affirmed on appeal.[7] Although statistics on Ohio criminal conviction reversal rates are not readily available, my work in the state's criminal legal system for the past twenty years leads me to believe that Ohio is no different. Although a handful of governors across the country have revitalized clemency as an option for release, Ohio governors, based on my experience, have rarely granted clemency for people convicted of violent felonies.[8] Ohio's parole system, like others across the nation, is broken and in need of reform. Again, based on my experience, the Ohio Parole Board rarely releases people at their first hearing; the board frequently denies people parole multiple times before finally granting their release.

In Robert's case, the court of appeals affirmed his conviction, holding that the trial court was correct to refuse his request for a transferred intent self-defense instruction because he brought the situation on himself by dealing drugs.[9] Even though Robert eventually sought postconviction and habeas relief, his various appeals fell on deaf ears in the courts.[10]

When he entered prison, Robert had almost no hope that the parole board would release him at his initial hearing twenty-nine years later; he faced the very real prospect of serving forty years or more. His conduct reflected his hopelessness. He spent eight of his first fourteen years in prison at a maximum-security facility reserved for the so-called worst of the worst.

In year fifteen, though, something changed in Robert. After completing his GED, he became hungrier for more education and read voraciously. He earned a forklift license, learned welding, and completed training in upholstery and bindery. In his free time, he taught himself to play the guitar. In 2012, he began working his way down from maximum-security to minimum-security status two years later. His status never went back up after 2014.

In 2019, the Ohio Justice & Policy Center, the organization I lead, founded a new project called Beyond Guilt.[11] Beyond Guilt works to free overpunished people who have served a significant portion of their sentence, admit (or do not contest) guilt, and who can demonstrate rehabilitation and fitness to return to the community. As we thought of our first clients to represent, Robert's name immediately came to mind. We had represented him some years earlier in a civil rights case challenging the prison system's denial of medical care he needed. I had stayed in touch with Robert through the years and admired his growth and maturity. Every time I would visit him in prison, he would ask me to send him a self-help book so that he could continue to improve as a human being. We decided that Robert would be among the first Beyond Guilt clients we would serve.

We pored through Robert's transcripts and obtained his institutional records, which confirmed what I believed to be true: Robert was a changed man. We even sat down with Barbara's family to see if we could win their support for Robert's release. At first her family resisted. "Why should we help Robert?," one of Barbara's sisters asked. But after learning about his accomplishments, Barbara's immediate family, including both of her sisters, supported Robert's release.

The problem, though, was glaring: Robert had no discernible release mechanism. He had exhausted his appeals and all possible postconviction claims. We never considered clemency seriously, for we were certain it would be denied—even with support from Barbara's family. It appeared that Robert would have to wait for his first parole hearing, which was still seven years away.

Then we had a creative idea. Ohio has a civil procedure rule, Rule 60(B)(5), that allows a court to set aside a judgment in the interest of justice.[12] The state also has a criminal procedure rule, Rule 57(B), that permits the civil procedure rules to apply in criminal cases when the criminal rules do not "specifically prescribe" a procedure.[13] Although no incarcerated person, to our knowledge, had ever used 60(B)(5) to set aside a conviction, we hoped we could persuade the prosecutor to support interests of justice relief for Robert. It was definitely worth a try.

The prosecutor's office in Robert's case is in no danger of being labeled progressive. To the contrary, the elected head of that office seems straight from a central casting call for a tough on crime prosecutor. Surprisingly, though, his office had signaled a willingness to work with us on Beyond Guilt cases, so I met with a top assistant in that office, whom I call Michael, and made my pitch.[14]

Michael was impressed with Robert's growth since his first decade in prison. Michael also found Barbara's family support compelling. Something struck the prosecutor as unfair, though: that at that point Robert had served eight years longer than he would have done had he pled guilty to manslaughter. I proposed that if we could find a way to undo Robert's murder conviction, he would plead guilty to manslaughter and receive time served.

Ultimately, after obtaining his office's approval to support Robert's release, Michael told me to file the 60(B)(5) to get the case before the court as soon as possible. After I filed the motion, however, he informed me that his office, after thinking about it more, would not support 60(B)(5) relief, fearing that it would set a dangerous precedent resulting in a flood of similar motions from other incarcerated people.

The problem, I explained to Michael, was that Robert did not meet the standard for a new trial motion, which required newly discovered evidence of either actual innocence or a violation of either the federal or state constitutions, such as the discovery of exculpatory information suppressed by the state in violation of *Brady v. Maryland*.[15] "Don't worry," Michael told me. "Just file a bare-bones motion asking for a new trial, and we will meet with the judge in chambers and tell him he should grant it."

That's what we did. I filed Robert's new trial motion and set a meeting with the judge. Michael came with me to the meeting and urged the judge to grant the motion because it was "the right thing to do" to achieve justice in Robert's case. Further, although probably unnecessary, Michael added that his office would not appeal the judge's ruling if he granted relief. The judge agreed to grant the motion.

One week later, I stood next to Robert in court. He pled guilty to involuntary manslaughter and drug possession and received time served. He became a free man after serving twenty-two years of his twenty-nine-to-life sentence.

Beyond Guilt has developed a niche skill of devising creative ways to free people from an unforgiving legal system that overpunishes. Robert is not the only person who has benefited from our creativity. Of the forty people Beyond Guilt has freed during its first three years, four—including Robert—walked out of prison early from life sentences, several years before they were eligible for parole. In these cases, prosecutors and judges worked with us to engineer release paths where none existed through traditional legal avenues. Whether you call our efforts creative or subversive, I don't care. We joined forces to do what we thought necessary to achieve justice in a handful of cases.

Some might say that our work has made no progress in meaningfully reducing mass incarceration in Ohio. Strictly based on the numbers, I'm constrained to agree.

A human being, though, is more than a number. Each one is a living, breathing person with hopes and dreams and family and friends who love and adore them. Each is full of possibility and promise. Each has the potential to have an impact on the community in a positive way. Each has a story to tell.

One of the ways we have deepened the impact of our work is through storytelling. With our clients' permission and in full partnership with them, we have lifted up their stories of postprison life following a lengthy time of incarceration. Through video, photography, and written words, we share their successes in obtaining employment and housing, but we also don't hide their struggles. All people experience setbacks during their life journeys—that's what makes us human. In August 2022, we exhibited six of these stories at the National Underground Railroad Freedom Center. The exhibit, aptly named *Beyond Guilt*, will travel throughout the state as we lay the foundation needed to convince the public, and ultimately legislators, that Ohio should enact second look legislation. We must replace the dominant punishment narrative—that people who commit violent crimes should be locked away forever—with stories showing that people who commit such offenses are capable of redemption and real change.

With support we provided, Robert found a well-paying job soon after his release, one that sent him to college, where he earned straight As. He saved his money and bought a small brick house. He was finally free and living his version of the American dream.

The last time I spoke with Robert, approximately three years after his release, he told me that he was going to make me proud. I told him, "You already have. But don't worry about pleasing me. Just live your life." Within the month, Robert died suddenly. Those of us who got to know him are still reeling.

Robert left behind family and friends who loved him, including me and my colleagues. He also has left something else important: a story of hope, redemption, and transformation. Hopefully we will continue to free more people like Robert, people who are overpunished and deserve to be free.

NOTES

1. John F. Pfaff, *Locked In: The True Causes of Mass Incarceration and How to Achieve Real Reform* (New York: Hachette Book Group, 2017), 185–89; see also, discussing Pfaff's book, Bill Keller and Eli Hager, "Everything You Think You Know About Mass Incarceration Is Wrong" (Washington, DC: The Marshall Project, February 9, 2017), https://www.themarshallproject.org/2017/02/09/everything-you-think-you-know-about-mass-incarceration-is-wrong.
2. Ashley Nellis, "No End in Sight: America's Enduring Reliance on Life Sentences" (Washington, DC: The Sentencing Project, February 17, 2021), https://www.sentencingproject.org/reports/no-end-in-sight-americas-enduring-reliance-on-life-sentences.
3. California Penal Code § 1170(d), 1170.03 (2018; 725 Illinois Compiled Statutes 5/123 (2021); Louisiana Revised Statutes § 15:574.4 (2021); Oregon Revised Statutes 137.218 (2021); Revised Code of Washington, 9.94A.730 (2014) and 36.27 (2020); and District of Columbia, § 24-403.03.

4. See, for example, FAMM, "Second Look Sentencing," accessed December 29, 2022, https://famm.org/secondlook.
5. Robert Jones is a pseudonym. Although the person identified here as Robert Jones gave the author permission to use his real name, the author has chosen to use a fictitious name to protect the identities of the other people mentioned here. Thus, all the names of the parties discussed here are pseudonyms. The author has maintained the relevant file materials and has shared them with the editors of this book.
6. The National Association of Criminal Defense Lawyers defines the trial penalty as "the substantial difference between the sentence offered in a plea offer prior to trial versus the sentence a defendant receives after trial." "The Trial Penalty: The Sixth Amendment Right to Trial on the Verge of Extinction and How to Save It" (Washington, DC: NACDL, July 10, 2018), https://www.nacdl.org/Document/TrialPenaltySixthAmendmentRighttoTrialNearExtinct.
7. Nicole L. Waters, Anne Gallegos, James Green, and Martha Rozsi, "Criminal Appeals in State Courts," NCJ 248874 (Washington, DC: U.S. Department of Justice, Bureau of Justice Statistics, 2015), 1, https://bjs.ojp.gov/content/pub/pdf/casc.pdf.
8. Jorie K. Johnson, "Review of Governor Pritzker's Clemency Grants from 1/1/21 through 6/14/22," *Illinois Expungement Lawyer Blog*, June 22, 2023, https://www.illinoisexpungementlawyerblog.com/?refPageViewId=7804e22b762a2012; Restoration Rights Project, "50-State Comparison: Pardon Policy & Practice," updated October 2022, https://ccresourcecenter.org/state-restoration-profiles/50-state-comparisoncharacteristics-of-pardon-authorities-2. For context, see Amanda Waldroupe, "The Story of One US Governor's Historic Use of Clemency: 'We Are a Nation of Second Chances,'" *The Guardian*, September 28, 2022, https://www.theguardian.com/us-news/2022/sep/28/oregon-governor-kate-brown-clemency.
9. This concept allows for the transfer of the defendant's intent from the intended focus of the force to the eventual victim.
10. As described by Cornell University's Legal Information Institute, "A writ of habeas corpus is used to bring a prisoner or other detainee . . . before the court to determine if the person's imprisonment or detention is lawful. . . . Although the Constitution does not specifically create the right to habeas corpus relief, federal statutes provide federal courts with the authority to grant habeas relief to state prisoners" ("Habeas Corpus," updated March 2022, https://www.law.cornell.edu/wex/habeas_corpus).
11. Ohio Justice & Policy Center, "OJPC," accessed December 27, 2022, http://www.ohiojpc.org; "Beyond Guilt," accessed December 27, 2022, https://ohiojpc.org/our-work/beyond-guilt.
12. Supreme Court of Ohio, "Ohio Rules of Civil Procedure: Rule 60, Relief from Judgment or Order," accessed December 27, 2022, https://www.supremecourt.ohio.gov/docs/LegalResources/Rules/civil/CivilProcedure.pdf.

13. Supreme Court of Ohio, "Ohio Rules of Criminal Procedure: Rule 57, Rule of Court, Procedure Not Otherwise Specified," accessed December 27, 2022, https://www.supremecourt.ohio.gov/docs/LegalResources/Rules/criminal/CriminalProcedure.pdf.
14. Michael is a pseudonym. As discussed in note 5, this essay uses fictitious names to protect the identities of the people mentioned. The author has maintained the relevant file materials and has shared them with the editors of this book.
15. 373 U.S. 83 (1963), https://supreme.justia.com/cases/federal/us/373/83.

34

COUNTERING EXCESSIVE PUNISHMENT WITH CHANCES FOR REDEMPTION

Carlton Miller

"CARLTON, I NEED TO TELL YOU SOMETHING." No eight-year-old son wants to hear these words from his mother, her face marred with distress, her voice trembling. Sitting on the side of her bed anticipating what she was soon to disclose, I looked in her eyes and held my breath.

She said, "Kendrick is not coming home for a while." In disbelief and bewilderment, I replied, "What do you mean? What happened? How long is 'a while?' " The tears she attempted to hold back burst into a river of emotions.

Later that evening, I saw my eldest brother's face plastered across the local evening news. I do not remember the news anchor's words, but I will never forget seeing Kendrick handcuffed and escorted from a building into the back of a police car. I felt like the floor beneath me had opened and swallowed me, sinking me deeper into a pit of shame, helplessness, and frustration. What lay ahead was unfathomable.

My brother's absence would have devastating emotional, financial, and health impacts on my family. It was this pain that led me to encounter America's peculiar taste for punishment, which plagues 113 million adults who have or have had a loved one in jail or prison.[1] In this pain, I found my purpose and dedicated my life to becoming an attorney and champion for criminal justice reforms not only in my home state of Louisiana, but also across the country.

Considering the quantifiable and qualitative generational impact of excessive punishment on families and communities around the country, this issue is more than a criminal justice issue: it is a human rights issue. We are in a crisis—a crisis that has defined the trajectory of my life.

Kendrick's excessive sentence was a direct result of unspeakable policies, beginning with one enacted in the intense wave of racism that engulfed the southern states in the wake of Reconstruction. He was effectively consigned to life in prison even though the jury in his trial did not come to a unanimous verdict. Among the "Black codes" and convict-leasing laws of the Jim Crow era that enabled a white society to imprison Black people virtually on a whim—for offenses such as loitering, breaking curfew, and failing to carry proof of employment—Louisiana waived the requirement for a unanimous jury in all but capital cases.[2] It was an especially effective way for Black people to be convicted and consigned to an equivalent of slavery, the state leasing them to plantations, coal mines, and railroad companies.[3]

This scheme was embedded in the law not merely by legislative act, but also by its insertion into the state constitution. The right to a jury trial may be a fundamental guarantee of the Sixth Amendment of the U.S. Constitution, but Louisiana's constitutional convention of 1898 came up with its own view of how a jury might operate. Article 116 had a clear origin: according to one committee chairman, the 1898 constitution was specifically designed "to establish the supremacy of the white race."[4] Non-unanimous jury verdicts, which allowed punishment based on a 10–2 jury vote, would deny thousands of Black Louisianans their right to a unanimous jury, increase Louisiana's convict leasing labor force, and intensify the disenfranchisement of Black citizens.

In the spring of 1999, just over a hundred years after Article 116 was adopted, a nonunanimous jury convicted my brother of armed robbery and two counts of attempted murder. Two jurors voted to acquit because they had reasonable doubts about his culpability due to inconsistent statements by the survivors and testimony about the accused's identity. This was during the heart of the tough on crime era, when federal and state policymakers engaged in an unprecedented expansion of prisons and prison populations. Mandatory minimums, sentencing enhancements, and restrictive parole release policies were the order of the day.[5]

Consequently, because of his prior convictions, Kendrick's sentence was enhanced to sixty-four years and eleven months, and an administrative determination made him ineligible for parole. My brother wrestled with untreated addictions and repeated interactions with the justice system as a young man, but he was still a young man, just twenty-eight years old. No one had been killed in the crime for which he was sentenced. No unanimous jury had ever determined that he was in fact guilty. Yet he was given a de facto life sentence with little hope of ever coming home. In short, he was convicted and sentenced to die in prison—and my family had to serve this time with him.

Kendrick was consigned to a prison system that is notoriously violent, lacks independent oversight, and undermines the health and well-being of those housed and staffed in them. Much of my brother's incarceration was spent at Louisiana State Penitentiary, a former slave plantation better known as Angola, the largest maximum-security prison in the nation.[6] It is considered one of America's most violent and abusive prisons. During my brother's incarceration, I learned of the harsh realities of prison labor.[7]

Present-day prison labor practices are directly tied to the history of chattel slavery and convict leasing. The Thirteenth Amendment of the U.S. Constitution expressly permits unpaid and forced labor as "a punishment for crime."[8] Even more, federal statutes governing minimum wage, overtime pay, and workplace safety exclude protections for incarcerated workers. Consequently, incarcerated workers are provided meager wages ranging from two cents to a dollar an hour while producing an estimated $2 billion a year in goods and commodities and more than $9 billion a year in services for the maintenance of the prisons where they are warehoused.[9] If an incarcerated worker refuses to work, they are subjected to additional punishment, such as solitary confinement and loss of family visitation, or denied opportunities for other programming to reduce their sentence. Because incarcerated workers earn little wages for their work, they are inhibited from affording necessities for survival such as clothing, food, and toiletries and must either rely on their families to bear the costs or resort to an underground prison economy.[10]

The current system of prison wages not only fails to make prisons safer but also nearly ensures indigence after release and strains family connection, despite income and family connection being important indicators of successful reentry and public safety. Louisiana's prisons, like many others in the United States, rely on incarcerated people's labor for farming and food service, laundry, janitorial duties, prison maintenance, and other tasks to offset operational expenditures. Kendrick was subjected to working in its fields and paid pennies an hour, supervised by shotgun-toting correctional officers riding on horseback. He was one of many who would rather risk solitary confinement than work in those torturous fields.

Finally, in 2021, after he had served nearly twenty-four years, life came full circle for Kendrick and for our family. Building on the historic Louisiana justice reforms of 2017 that I was fortunate to play a role in shaping, justice advocates secured the enactment of Act 122, a landmark elder parole law that retroactively provided a pathway home for an estimated three thousand incarcerated people who were sentenced to prison for more than thirty years.[11]

In particular, incarcerated individuals who had served at least twenty years and reached the age of forty-five were immediately eligible to apply for parole. On December 14, 2021, thanks to the efforts of organizations like the Louisiana Parole Project, Voices of the Experience, and First72+, I had the pleasure of supporting my brother at his parole hearing. A unanimous decision granted him his release. Two days later, Kendrick walked out of the prison walls and whispered words that shook my core: "Thanks for not forgetting me, little brother!"

In 2018, Louisiana voters overwhelmingly chose to eliminate Article 116 from the state constitution. In 2020, the U.S. Supreme Court in *Ramos v. Louisiana* declared such convictions unconstitutional but left it to Louisiana and Oregon (the only other state allowing non-unanimous jury convictions) whether people currently incarcerated were allowed new trials.[12] In October 2022, the Louisiana Supreme Court refused to apply the *Ramos* decision retroactively, leaving the fate of 1,500 people currently incarcerated because of a non-unanimous jury conviction to the state legislature. Today, the Promise of Justice Initiative, a New Orleans-based legal services and advocacy nonprofit, continues to advocate for a retroactive legal remedy to undo those serving time for non-unanimous jury convictions.

Previous essays in this series highlight the many ways America's excessive reliance on punishment has harmed families and communities and weakened our democracy. In my case, over the past two decades, my brother's incarceration has taught me some essential lessons.

Chief among them is that if we are going to end the incarceration crisis, we need to see that people are redeemable and can be restored because, as Bryan Stevenson says, "each of us is more than the worst mistake we have made." According to Rahsaan Thomas's and Asia Johnson's essays in this series (see chapters 13 and 20), dehumanizing people begins with the language we use to describe people. History is replete with accounts where human atrocities began with dehumanizing language. If we use harmful language that describes people as "less than" or "subhuman," acts that rob people of their dignity may soon follow. Consequently, if we believe that incarcerated people are redeemable, we must interrogate and abandon dehumanizing labels such as *felon*, *criminal*, *inmate*, or *offender*, because they work on a broad misconception that all of those incarcerated for violence are dangerous and irredeemable and fail to account for the fact that so many of the incarcerated have been victims or witnesses of repeated violence in their communities and suffer from untreated trauma.

I witnessed my brother traverse this valley of despair with a resolute hope despite the fact he was ineligible for early release, even though in his years in prison he worked earnestly, earned occupational licenses, and mentored other incarcerated people. His character gained him the respect of the wardens, staff, and others housed in prison. Yet his past excluded him from earning good time credits that could reduce his sentence. But he never gave up hope, and redemption finally arrived.

By centering on redemption and restoration, we can counter excessive punishment through policies that promote racial justice and create release opportunities for those serving long prison sentences for violent offenses. Research by the Urban Institute in 2017 found that one in five people in prison for at least ten years is a Black man incarcerated before age twenty-five.[13] In addition to highlighting the racial disparities in extreme sentencing, this finding also reinforces the harm caused when we "lock people up and throw away the key."

Correctional leaders and parole authorities play an important, often opaque role in American prison policy and have an immense degree of discretion over prison releases. In thirty-four states, these policymakers have legal authority over the ultimate duration of most prison sentences.[14] Any prison reform efforts to reduce the prison population needs to focus a significant degree on prison-release discretion through retroactive and prospective policies that remove parole eligibility exceptions, expand elder parole and compassionate release, allow for second look resentencing, and increase earned and good time credits.

In recent years, we have seen legislators in twenty-five states introduce bills that allow incarcerated people an opportunity to have their sentences reduced or to be considered for early release either through the courts or parole boards.[15] Second look laws have gained traction and are a mechanism to address excessively long sentences head on through the courts. Second look laws provide incarcerated people an opportunity to petition their sentencing judge to have their sentence reduced after serving a certain amount of time in prison, which the Model Penal Code recommends is at least fifteen years. California's 2018 second look law allows prosecutors to initiate resentencing to undo excessively long prison sentences.[16] Most recently, the District of Columbia's local Council unanimously voted to overhaul its criminal laws, including expanding second look for those incarcerated who were twenty-five or older at the time of the crime and have served a minimum of twenty years in prison.[17] DC's historical expansion builds on their 2016 and 2020 laws that expanded the possibility of a reduced sentence for people who were under eighteen years of age to twenty-five years of age, becoming a model for other jurisdictions. Similar to second look, elder parole laws—which are based on research that older people are less likely to pose a public safety risk—provide an opportunity for release to incarcerated individuals after they served a certain period of time in prison and reached a minimum age. Legislative victories in Louisiana and Mississippi can help boost momentum in New York and inform efforts in other parts of the United States that seek to advance elder parole laws.[18] These "levers of change" will reduce the amount of time people spend in prison.[19] In my brother's case, such a law brought him an immediate pathway home.

At the heart of our collective effort to change America's reliance on punitive excess is the acknowledgment of people's humanity, the belief that people can be redeemed and restored. This acknowledgment underpins our shared movement to reconceive what investments in people, not punishment, can do. These bedrock values are the foundation of the constitutional guarantees of equal protection, liberty, and due process. They can serve as a lighthouse beam cutting through the blinding fog of excessive punishment and guiding us over the troubling waters of a fear that seek to divide us. If we can keep our eyes on this light, it can navigate us to the shores of a stronger democracy that is inclusive and equitable and promotes healthy families and communities.

NOTES

1. Brian Elderbroom, Laura Bennett, Shanna Gong, Felicity Rose, and Zoë Towns, *Every Second: The Impact of Incarceration on America's Families* (FWD.us, 2018), 10, https://everysecond.fwd.us/downloads/everysecond.fwd.us.pdf.
2. Angela Allen-Bell, "How the Narrative About Louisiana's Non-Unanimous Criminal Jury System Became a Person of Interest in the Case Against Justice in the Deep South," *Mercer Law Review* 67, no. 3 (2016): 588, https://digitalcommons.law.mercer.edu/cgi/viewcontent.cgi?article=2387&context=jour_mlr.

3. Ruth Delaney, Ram Subramanian, Alison Shames, and Nicholas Turner, *Reimagining Prison* (New York: Vera Institute of Justice), 2018, 37–40, https://www.vera.org/downloads/publications/Reimagining-Prison_FINAL3_digital.pdf.
4. Allen-Bell, "How the Narrative," 596.
5. Arit John, "A Timeline of the Rise and Fall of 'Tough on Crime' Drug Sentencing," *The Atlantic*, April 22, 2014, https://www.theatlantic.com/politics/archive/2014/04/a-timeline-of-the-rise-and-fall-of-tough-on-crime-drug-sentencing/360983.
6. Clyde Tucker, "Louisiana State Prison, Angola (1880–)," Blackpast, June 17, 2021, https://www.blackpast.org/african-american-history/institutions-african-american-history/louisiana-state-prison-angola-1880.
7. Leah Wang, "The State Prison Experience: Too Much Drudgery, Not Enough Opportunity" (Northampton, MA: Prison Policy Initiative, September 2, 2022), https://www.prisonpolicy.org/blog/2022/09/02/prison_opportunities.
8. U.S. Const. amend. XIII.
9. Jennifer Turner et al., *Captive Labor: Exploitation of Incarcerated Workers* (Chicago: ACLU and the University of Chicago Global Human Rights Clinic, 2022), 37, https://www.aclu.org/report/captive-labor-exploitation-incarcerated-workers.
10. Casey Quinlan, "Costs of Incarceration Rise as Inflation Squeezes Inmates, Families," *Oregon Capital Chronicle*, October 17, 2022, https://oregoncapitalchronicle.com/2022/10/17/costs-of-incarceration-rise-as-inflation-squeezes-inmates-families.
11. H.B. 145, 2021 Reg. Sess. (La. 2021), enrolled as Act No. 122, https://www.legis.la.gov/legis/ViewDocument.aspx?d=1234498.
12. Ramos v. Louisiana, 590 U.S. ___ (2020), https://www.supremecourt.gov/opinions/19pdf/18-5924_n6io.pdf.
13. Leigh Courtney, Sarah Eppler-Epstein, Elizabeth Pelletier, Ryan King, and Serena Lei, "A Matter of Time: The Causes and Consequences of Rising Time Served in America's Prisons" (Washington, DC: Urban Institute, 2017), 2, https://apps.urban.org/features/long-prison-terms/a_matter_of_time.pdf.
14. Edward E. Rhine, Kelly Lyn Mitchell, and Kevin R. Reitz, *Levers of Change in Parole Release and Revocation* (Minneapolis: University of Minnesota Robina Institute of Criminal Law and Criminal Justice, 2019), 7–8, https://robinainstitute.umn.edu/sites/robinainstitute.umn.edu/files/2022-02/parole_landscape_report.pdf.
15. Nazgol Ghandnoosh, *A Second Look at Injustice* (Washington, DC: The Sentencing Project, 2021), 4, 6, https://www.sentencingproject.org/reports/a-second-look-at-injustice.
16. A.B. 2942 (Cal. 2018).

17. D.C. Law 23-274. Omnibus Public Safety and Justice Amendment Act of 2020 (D.C. 2000).
18. Alesha Judkins, "As We Celebrate Parole Reform in Mississippi, We Must Continue Our Fight for Freedom," FWD.us, June 2, 2021, https://www.fwd.us/news/mississippi-end-of-session-2021.
19. Rhine, Mitchell, and Reitz, *Levers of Change*, 7–8.

35

EDUCATING FOR JUSTICE IN THE ERA OF MASS INCARCERATION

Karol Mason and Erica Bond

AS WE WERE FINALIZING THIS ESSAY, five Memphis police officers were charged with murder for the beating death of Tyre Nichols, a twenty-four-year-old Black man, whom friends and family also described as the father of a four-year-old son, a FedEx employee, a photographer, and a skateboarder. Elected officials and the news media around the country spent days preparing the public for the release of video evidence of the pain and suffering police officers inflicted on Nichols before he died of his injuries three days later. Many people, particularly in Black and Brown communities, braced for the trauma of witnessing yet another Black man brutalized by police. Local authorities moved relatively swiftly to release information and prosecute the officers responsible for Nichols's death. However, any modicum of justice delivered through the criminal legal process cannot restore Nichols's life and is inevitably overshadowed by the harms our systems of policing and justice continue to perpetuate in communities around the country.

Tyre Nichols's death, and the persistence of racial, ethnic, and gender-based inequities in traditional, government public safety strategies, raise the question as to what role a college, originally founded to educate a new generation of enlightened police officers, can play in ushering in a new era of mass decarceration that makes us all truly safe?[1] We know that the complex political, economic, and racial dynamics that have resulted in—what many other contributors in this series have pointed out—almost two million people incarcerated in local, state, and federal facilities; our rates of incarceration in the United States surpass the rest of the world.[2] However, we also know that our country's current emphasis on police and punishment as the primary response to violence and crime is not working. We must change our playbook in fundamental ways. As a school of criminal justice, we are committed to collaborating with our students, academics, advocates, practitioners, and elected officials to imagine a different way forward.

In 2020, in the wake of the police murders of George Floyd, Breonna Taylor, Ahmad Taylor, and too many others, John Jay College in partnership with the National Organization of Black Law Enforcement Executives, brought diverse voices together from across disciplines and communities to focus on what we should be doing to create safer communities. Agreement was widespread that we needed to continue to improve policing through better hiring, training, and oversight. However, an important consensus also emerged that we need to fundamentally rethink "the future of public safety" by investing heavily in the health and well-being of those communities most affected by violence, too many of which are communities of color; ensuring government is partnering with and empowering community members to devise and lead responses to violence and crime; and minimizing the role of the criminal justice system in addressing many issues for which the system does not offer a solution and can actually undermine public safety by destabilizing people and communities.[3]

At John Jay College, we have long been evolving to meet the need for the kinds of transformational approaches to public safety highlighted in our "Future of Public Safety Report"—approaches that center communities in the quest for safety and justice.[4] Founded nearly sixty years ago as a police college, we now educate the future leaders for justice, safety, and peace, including those who become police or corrections officers as well as people who work in other government agencies, nonprofits, and research organizations. Today, John Jay College students, faculty, and research centers work on all aspects of public safety, offering coursework and majors in policing as just one element of a much broader institutional commitment to educating for justice.

To prepare John Jay College students for leadership roles across a variety of fields, we work to educate them on the historical, political, racial, and economic conditions that shape safety in communities across the country (many of which are covered in detail in other sections of this book). Many John Jay College graduates continue to serve their communities by choosing careers in law enforcement, but a growing number select other fields of employment that are also key to reducing mass incarceration. John Jay College graduates who take on roles as counselors, violence interrupters, and caseworkers help support the expansion of alternative responses to arrests, prosecution, and enforcement.[5] These new approaches are essential to reducing the number of people unnecessarily incarcerated in the United States, including young people and people with behavioral health and substance misuse issues.

Regardless of what students go on to do—whether they wear a uniform, take elected office, or work directly with people affected by the criminal justice system to advocate for reforms—our goal is to ensure that they appreciate a few fundamental facts about public safety. Safe communities are not characterized by the overwhelming presence of police; they exist when peoples' basic needs for housing, health care, education, and employment are met. Further, safe communities require that government institutions, including the police, are responsive and accountable to the neighborhoods they serve. Law enforcement must be prepared to shift and share power with those they serve. This means listening to and taking direction from the public on how they operate in the community.[6]

By educating students, including future law enforcement leaders, on the principles, research, theory, and practices that support safe communities, we empower them to break the cycles of violence and racism that have driven and perpetuate mass incarceration across the United States. This is why John Jay College seeks to expose students to research and programming on everything from community-based violence programs designed to reduce violence among young people, to crime prevention through environmental design (such as, through blight removal) to reentry programs that enable people returning from prison to obtain a college education.[7]

For students who go into law enforcement careers, we seek to prepare them to address the well-documented, negative impacts of mass incarceration on communities of color. From the officers to chiefs, these future leaders need to see themselves not just as guardians of the communities they serve but also as agents of change. They need to be committed to facing the racism embedded in policing's origin story and addressing long-standing community mistrust due to police abuses and racial inequities in enforcement.[8] Because we are a diverse institution, with a student population that is majority Black and Latinx (and almost half are the first in their families to go to college), many of our students are already aware of these dynamics and have chosen law enforcement careers specifically to serve as agents for change within policing and public safety.

At John Jay College, we have been adapting our curriculum to support future law enforcement leaders in developing the knowledge and cultural competency to work with diverse communities. For example, John Jay's students who opt for the law and police science major (the one many students who ultimately enter law enforcement professions choose) are now required to take courses in Africana and Latin American and Latinx studies. In our conversations with our more recent alumni in law enforcement, they spoke about how the updated curriculum helped prepare them to appreciate and respect the cultural differences in the communities they serve. They said that this understanding changed the dynamics of how they approached situations they encountered, and made them better and more effective in their jobs. These students expressed their appreciation for an education that prepared them to work with the community to address community needs so that an arrest is the last option, not the first and only option—a crucial mental shift that all officers need to adopt if we are to unwind mass incarceration. Some police departments have started to do similar work by providing opportunities for officers to learn about the history of race in the United States and its influence on policing through educational trips to civil rights museums in the South.[9] Future generations of law enforcement leaders must expand on this work, including by providing officers with an understanding of how issues of race drive community mistrust at the local level as well as how officers' positive interactions with the community can help in rebuilding trust.[10]

For those students who choose to serve their communities in law enforcement roles, John Jay College encourages them to see themselves as partners with their community. Our hope is that, with a greater understanding of how mass incarceration and police abuse has undermined trust and safety in communities of color, these future leaders can address the ways in which the culture and operations of police departments may permit, and even encourage the kind of conduct that in recent years has resulted in the unjustified deaths of Tyre Nichols, Eric Garner, Michael Brown, Laquan McDonald, Philando Castile, Walter Scott, Freddie Gray, and Tamir Rice, among others. The next generation of law enforcement leaders must be prepared to work proactively and urgently to ensure that the mothers of these men, like Amadou Diallo's mother, are not left questioning why so little has changed twenty years from now.[11]

We also encourage future generations of law enforcement to continue to diversify their ranks with the understanding that it only mitigates some of the harm associated with policing in communities of color. Nonetheless, some evidence indicates that diversifying police forces can benefit communities long accustomed to being policed by people not from their community. It has the potential to improve relationships with communities of color and reduce disparities in enforcement that are essential to mass decarceration. In fact, some research indicates that police officers of color can play an important role in reducing enforcement and police violence. In one Chicago study, Black and Hispanic officers made far fewer stops and arrests and use less force than white officers, especially against Black civilians, when facing otherwise similar circumstances.[12]

Of course, we are mindful of the fact that, even as police departments have diversified across the country, deaths caused by police have remained stubbornly high. In 2022, after years of reforms aimed at reducing police violence, the police still killed 1,192 people.[13] Further, all five of the officers charged with Tyre Nichols death were Black—a powerful reminder that simply changing the demographics of police officers will not automatically result in better outcomes.

Ultimately, and most important, the future generation of law enforcement leaders need to understand that addressing the legacy of mass incarceration requires that we go beyond reforming policing practices and operations. We must ensure that people in our most vulnerable communities—those most affected by crime, violence, and incarceration—have the necessary resources to build strong communities and are empowered to dictate the way they are policed. Our goal should be to ensure that every community has the vibrant schools, housing, jobs, health care, and clean, green spaces that are hallmarks of safety. Every law enforcement interaction with a community member should be approached as an opportunity to shrink the imprint of the carceral state and figure out how to prevent future violence and crime—whether by cleaning up abandoned lots that allow crime and fear to flourish, providing treatment to a person in mental health crisis, or offering young people the necessary employment, education, or therapy to avoid violence.[14] Just as we have invested heavily in the instruments of mass incarceration (prisons, police, courts), we must now invest equally, and equitably, in communities. We must enable community members to organize resources in ways that respond to their public safety needs and desires. Before he died, Tyre Nichols said, "I am just trying to get home." We must transform our approach to public safety and policing so that everybody lives in a community where they can get home safely.

NOTES

1. Charles R. Epp, Steven Maynard-Moody, and Donald Haider-Markel, "Beyond Profiling: The Institutional Sources of Racial Disparities in Policing," *Public Administration Review* 77 (2016): 168–78, https://onlinelibrary.wiley.com/doi/abs/10.1111/puar.12702; Magnus Loftstrom, Joseph Hayes, Brandon Martin, and

Deepak Premkumar, "Racial Disparities in Law Enforcement Stops" (San Francisco: Public Policy Institute of California, 2021), 3–29, https://www.ppic.org/publication/racial-disparities-in-law-enforcement-stops; Lara Vomfell and Neil Stewart, "Officer Bias, Over-Patrolling and Ethnic Disparities in Stop and Search," *Nature Human Behaviour* 5 (2021): 566–75, https://www.nature.com/articles/s41562-020-01029-w; Andrea J. Ritchie and Delores Jones-Brown, "Policing Race, Gender, and Sex: A Review of Law Enforcement Policies," *Women & Criminal Justice* 27, no. 1 (2017): 21–50, https://www.tandfonline.com/doi/full/10.1080/08974454.2016.1259599.

2. Wendy Sawyer and Peter Wagner, "Mass Incarceration: The Whole Pie 2022" (Northampton, MA: Prison Policy Initiative, March 14, 2022), https://www.prisonpolicy.org/reports/pie2022.html.
3. Desmond Ang, "The Effects of Police Violence on Inner-City Students," *Quarterly Journal of Economics* 136, no. 1 (2021): 115–68, https://scholar.harvard.edu/ang/publications/effects-police-violence-inner-city-students; Desmond Ang, "Wider Effects of Police Killings in Minority Neighborhoods," Econofact, June 24, 2020, https://econofact.org/wider-effects-of-police-killings-in-minority-neighborhoods; Aaron Stagoff-Belfort, Daniel Bodah, and Daniela Gilbert, *The Social Costs of Policing* (New York: Vera Institute of Justice, 2022), https://www.vera.org/publications/the-social-costs-of-policing.
4. John Jay College of Criminal Justice, "Future of Public Safety," July 20, 2021, https://www.jjay.cuny.edu/future-public-safety.
5. Akhi Johnson, Mustafa Ali-Smith, and Sam McCann, "Diversion Programs Are a Smart, Sustainable Investment in Public Safety" (New York: Vera Institute of Justice, April 28, 2022), https://www.vera.org/news/diversion-programs-are-a-smart-sustainable-investment-in-public-safety.
6. Maria Ponomarenko and Barry Friedman, "Democratic Accountability and Policing," in *Reforming Criminal Justice*, vol. 2, *Policing*, ed. Erik Luna, 5–25 (Phoenix, AZ: Academy for Justice, 2017), https://law.asu.edu/sites/default/files/pdf/academy_for_justice/1_Reforming-Criminal-Justice_Vol_2_Democratic-Accountability-and-Policing.pdf.
7. Jeffrey A. Butts, Caterina Gouvis Roman, Lindsay Bostwick, and Jeremy R. Porter, "Cure Violence: A Public Health Model to Reduce Gun Violence," *Annual Review of Public Health* 36, no. 1 (2015): 39–53, https://www.annualreviews.org/doi/abs/10.1146/annurev-publhealth-031914-122509; Jeffrey A. Butts et al., *Reducing Violence Without Police: A Review of Research Evidence* (New York: John Jay College Research and Evaluation Center, 2020), 3–25, https://johnjayrec.nyc/wp-content/uploads/2020/11/AV20201109_rev.pdf; Vernisa M. Donaldson and Christopher Viera, *College After Prison: A Review of the Literature on Barriers and Supports to Postsecondary Education for Formerly Incarcerated College Students* (New York: City University of New York,

2021), https://justiceandopportunity.org/wp-content/uploads/2021/10/College-After-Prison-Whitepaper.pdf.

8. Sue Rahr and Stephen K. Rice, "From Warriors to Guardians: Recommitting American Police Culture to Democratic Ideals" (Washington, DC: National Institute of Justice, April 2015), https://www.ojp.gov/pdffiles1/nij/248654.pdf; Olivia B. Waxman, "How the U.S. Got Its Police Force," *Time*, May 18, 2017, https://time.com/4779112/police-history-origins; Jonathan Daniel Wells, *The Kidnapping Club: Wall Street, Slavery, and Resistance on the Eve of the Civil War* (New York: Bold Type Books, 2020); Gary Potter, "The History of Policing in the United States, Part 1," EKU Online, accessed February 1, 2023, https://ekuonline.eku.edu/blog/police-studies/the-history-of-policing-in-the-united-states-part-1; Kala Bhattar, "The History of Policing in the US and Its Impact on Americans Today," *UAB Institute for Human Rights Blog*, December 8, 2021, https://sites.uab.edu/humanrights/2021/12/08/the-history-of-policing-in-the-us-and-its-impact-on-americans-today; Terrence M. Cunningham, "How Police and Communities Can Move Forward Together." *American Bar Association Human Rights Magazine* 46, no. 1 (2021), https://www.americanbar.org/groups/crsj/publications/human_rights_magazine_home/civil-rights-reimagining-policing/how-police-and-communities-can-move-forward-together; Katie Nodjimbadem, "The Long, Painful History of Police Brutality in the U.S.," *Smithsonian Magazine*, July 27 2017, https://www.smithsonianmag.com/smithsonian-institution/long-painful-history-police-brutality-in-the-us-180964098; Jocelyn Fontaine, David Leitson, Jesse Jannetta, and Ellen Paddock, "Mistrust and Ambivalence between Residents and the Police" (Washington, DC: Urban Institute Justice Policy Center, 2017), 1–16, https://www.urban.org/sites/default/files/publication/92316/2017.07.31_legitimacy_brief_finalized_2.pdf.

9. San Francisco Police Department, *Departmental Racial Equity Progress Report: Annual Report for 2021*, 2022, 18–21, https://www.sanfranciscopolice.org/sites/default/files/2022-05/SFPDREAP20220505.pdf; Byron Brown, "Police learn better skills on Civil Rights Museum tour," WJTV, November 11, 2022, https://www.wjtv.com/news/crime-crisis-focused-on-solutions/police-learn-better-skills-on-civil-rights-museum-tour.

10. Ben Bradford, "Policing and Social Identity: Procedural Justice, Inclusion and Cooperation Between Police and Public. Policing and Society," *An International Journal of Research and Policy* 24, no. 1 (2014): 22–43, https://www.tandfonline.com/doi/abs/10.1080/10439463.2012.724068; Daniela Gilbert, Stewart Wakeling, Vaughn Crandall, and Julia Reynolds, "Procedural Justice and Police Legitimacy: Using Training as a Foundation for Strengthening Community-Police Relationships" (Oakland: California Partnership for Safe Communities, 2015), 1–3, https://post.ca.gov/procedural-justice-and-police-legitimacy-resources.

11. Ese Olumhense, "20 Years After the NYPD Killing of Amadou Diallo, His Mom Asks: What's Changed?" *The City*, February 1, 2019, https://www.thecity.nyc/justice/2019/2/1/21211182/20-years-after-the-nypd-killing-of-amadou-diallo-his-mom-asks-what-s-changed.
12. Bocar A. Ba, Dean Knox, Jonathan Mummolo, and Roman Rivera, "The Role of Officer Race and Gender in Police-Civilian Interactions in Chicago," *Science* 371, no. 6530 (2021): 696–702, https://www.science.org/doi/abs/10.1126/science.abd8694.
13. Samuel Sinyangwe, "Mapping Police Violence," Mapping Police Violence, updated January 26, 2023, https://mappingpoliceviolence.us.
14. Charles C. Branas, Michelle C. Kondo, Sean M. Murphy, Eugenia C. South, Daniel Polsky, and John M. MacDonald, "Urban Blight Remediation as a Cost-Beneficial Solution to Firearm Violence," *American Journal of Public Health* 106, no. 12 (2016): 2158–64, https://ajph.aphapublications.org/doi/full/10.2105/AJPH.2016.303434; Ashley Abramson, "Building Mental Health into Emergency Responses," *Monitor on Psychology* 52, no. 5 (July 1, 2021), https://www.apa.org/monitor/2021/07/emergency-responses; AmeriCorps, *Preventing Youth Violence: An Evaluation of Youth Guidance's* Becoming A Man *Program* (Chicago: University of Chicago Crime Lab, 2018), 1–3, https://americorps.gov/sites/default/files/evidenceexchange/BAM_SIF_Final_Report_Revision_20181005_508_1.pdf; Farhana Hossain and Kyla Wasserman, "Using Cognitive Behavioral Therapy to Address Trauma and Reduce Violence Among Baltimore's Young Men: A Profile of Roca Baltimore" (Baltimore, MD: MDRC, 2021), 1–6, https://www.mdrc.org/sites/default/files/ROCA_Baltimore_FINAL.pdf.

36

REDEEMING PUNISHMENT IN AMERICA

Heather Rice-Minus

ROUGHLY ONE-THIRD OF AMERICANS report reading the Bible weekly, a rate nearly the same as in 1993.[1] Almost eighty million—or one in four—adults in the United States remain "practicing Christians," a term the Barna Group uses to describe those who "identify as Christian, agree strongly that faith is very important in their lives, and have attended church within the past month."[2] This sets America apart as "a statistical outlier among affluent and educated societies," points out David Kinnaman, the president of Barna.[3] Christians and those drawing from biblical values remain a significant constituency influencing any national debate—one that policymakers cannot afford to ignore.

The organization where I've worked for more than a decade, Prison Fellowship, is uniquely positioned to educate and mobilize Christ followers on matters of criminal justice. We were founded in 1976 by the late Christian author Chuck Colson.[4] A former aide to President Richard Nixon, Colson spent seven months in federal prison for his role in the Watergate scandal.

We have spent nearly five decades supporting those living and working in prison. Drawing from biblical teachings and our organizational experience, I have found that Christians who follow an orthodox interpretation of the Bible do not pursue justice by abandoning law-and-order principles such as punishment in favor of a total focus on grace and mercy. Despite political sound bites to the contrary, the goals of rule of law and redemption are mutually reinforcing instead of mutually exclusive. Followers of Christ hold them in tension as we seek to live out our duty in the public square.

IMAGO DEI AND PROPORTIONALITY

The Christian worldview holds human beings as created in God's image (*imago Dei*) and demands a just, proportional punishment in response to crime.[5] I make this argument from the perspective of the state, which has a role distinct from that of the church or Christians' interpersonal relationships in biblical teaching. Christians are called to "act justly, love mercy, and walk humbly before God."[6] Jesus instructed his followers to "turn the other cheek" in response to those who harm or insult them.[7] However, "the state was instituted by God to restrain sin and promote a just social order."[8] In response to crime, a just government should promote social order while upholding the dignity of the person responsible for crime, those who are victimized, and the affected community. Christians should work to embody all of Christ's teachings in their personal capacity and seek to influence the government toward Christian values while respecting the government's God-given responsibility to preserve the rule of law.

Some secular and utilitarian understandings of human dignity seek to impose criminal penalties solely or primarily to cure and deter crime. For example, Germany and Norway are often touted by the media as having developed more humane justice systems than the United States, as evidenced by their shorter maximum sentences. But both nations use preventive custody, which allows judges to deprive a prisoner of their liberty beyond the maximum sentence until no threat to public safety remains. Correctional leaders in both countries point out that maximum sentences are rarely applied. Still, deprivation of liberty for the perceived prevention of future crime, when disconnected from a just punishment for the actual crime committed, is disconcerting. Imposing compulsory and potentially indefinite rehabilitation raises justice concerns similar to those accompanying long maximum sentences and risks misuse by bad government actors. For those who rely on an orthodox interpretation of the Bible to impart justice values, utilitarian arguments fall short.

This difference in Christian versus utilitarian viewpoints on justice is not a new debate. Christian author C. S. Lewis warned against the seemingly benevolent intentions of British leaders in the 1950s, who were increasingly rejecting a retributive view of punishment in favor of humanitarian theory. He wrote, "Their very kindness stings with intolerable insult. To be 'cured' against one's will and cured of states which we may not regard as disease is to be put on a level with those who have not yet reached the age of reason or those who never will. . . . But to be punished, however severely, because we have deserved it, because we 'ought to have known better,' is to be treated as a human person made in God's image."[9] Punishment ascribes dignity to the person convicted of a crime by recognizing that person's God-given free will.

Whereas proportional punishment is a legitimate, necessary response to crime, excessive penalties undermine a consistent regard for human dignity. Most Americans, including Christians, have lost sight of what constitutes a proportional penalty. We have grown apathetic to double-digit sentences and the collateral impacts incarceration has on families.[10] But we cannot afford to ignore these realities—not when more than seventy million Americans have a criminal record and one in two Americans have a formerly or presently incarcerated family member.[11]

America's collective definition of crime and its appropriate punishment has expanded significantly over the last several decades. A Pew study found that people released from prison in 2009 had served about 36 percent more time than those released in 1990.[12] This increase in time served was fairly consistent regardless of the crime type. Starting in the late 1960s, as crime rates began to rise, leaders vying for political office began to leverage voters' fear of crime.[13] Fear-based political rhetoric and pandering contributed to misguided reforms like longer mandatory sentences, the abolishment of parole, and the infamous three-strikes laws.

Even though fear of crime is a natural human response, Christians are not to be governed by fear, but instead marked by love, godly wisdom, and discernment.[14] We can learn much from leaning into the data.[15] For example, Texas introduced several reforms that helped reduce the state's imprisonment rate by 12.9 percent from 2010 to 2015.[16] Over the same five years, the state realized a 23.3 percent decline in its crime rate.[17] Ultimately, the biblical belief in human dignity requires Christians to be concerned with proportionality in justice. As it turns out, proportionality yields results.

CONCERN FOR THE VULNERABLE

The Bible is bursting with verses urging concern for the poor and vulnerable. For example, Leviticus says, "Do not pervert justice; do not show partiality to the poor or favoritism to the great, but judge your neighbor fairly."[18] Christians are exhorted to "speak up for those who cannot speak for themselves" and "defend the rights of the poor and needy," ensuring that all receive equal treatment under the law.[19] The late Christian pastor and author Tim Keller went as far as to say, "If I don't care about the poor, if my church doesn't care about the poor, that's evil."[20]

This biblical duty is acutely relevant in America, where poverty often frustrates citizens' ability to navigate a complex justice system, resulting in disparate access to bail, quality defense, and other tools of justice. But poverty is not the only force subverting access to justice in this country; justice system data offers many examples of race-based disparities. Black Americans are more frequently subject to traffic stops, searches, and use of force by police. Federal sentencing data tells us that Black men are more likely to receive harsher sentences than similarly situated defendants of other races. These same groups experience outsized rates of victimization. As Christians evaluate the workings of the U.S. justice system, biblical counsel requires special concern for the vulnerable.

This exhortation to care for the poor and marginalized means that Christians should be just as concerned with ensuring that every child in America receives a true first chance to achieve their potential before they ever need a second chance. This includes cultivating the "seedbeds of virtue," including families, churches, neighborhoods, schools, and other sources of moral formation and advocating for fair access to education, economic opportunity, and the social safety net.[21] Prison Fellowship recently launched the First Chance Network, a group of organizations in strategic urban centers committed to uplifting children who have incarcerated parents, nurturing their success through holistic program offerings, and maximizing their real-life outcomes. Additionally, through Prison Fellowship Angel Tree, we mobilize thousands of churches to serve more than 250,000 children with a gift on behalf of their incarcerated parent every Christmas and to meet families' needs throughout the year.

RETRIBUTION AND RESTORATION

Although retribution is an acknowledged biblical principle of justice, Christians should not support punishment merely for punishment's sake. A Christian view of justice also emphasizes redemption, reformation, and restoration. Scripture authorizes proportional penalties—including an eye for an eye—that include retributive impact. Yet throughout scripture, God frequently redeems those guilty of the most offensive acts and uses their lives in significant ways. Despite having murdered an Egyptian, Moses experienced the physical presence of God while leading his people, the Israelites, to the promised land.[22] David, who conspired to murder an innocent man, was known as a man after God's "own heart."[23] In the New Testament, you'll find Zacchaeus, the Bible's poster child for white-collar crime.[24] To the dismay of many of Jesus's followers, Zacchaeus was given the honor of showing Jesus hospitality. If retribution is an aspect of biblical justice, so is restoration.

One way we promote restoration is to ensure that punishment reflects dignity. Because *imago Dei* means that everyone has intrinsic dignity and a God-given purpose, each person in the justice system should experience safe conditions and opportunities to grow into their giftings. Treating people as human beings and infusing opportunities for rehabilitation does not negate a just punishment; it legitimizes and gives it purpose beyond retribution.

The experience of incarceration in America can often feel far from dignified and purposeful. For example, solitary confinement (or "restrictive housing") generally entails confining a person in a cell for twenty-three hours a day and severely limiting their social interaction and physical exertion. Many studies have documented the severe psychological impact this isolation can have, particularly on those with serious mental illness.[25] In some situations included in the studies, the length of restrictive housing exceeded three years. One study found that from 2011 to 2014, forty-two jurisdictions did not limit the duration of solitary confinement.[26] If we expect incarcerated people to return as better neighbors, conditions of confinement must uphold human dignity and promote safety and prosocial values.

That's why Prison Fellowship has intentionally invested our privately raised funds in more than four hundred participants of Warden Exchange.[27] This program convenes corrections professionals to exchange transformative best practices and join a peer network committed to creating safer communities inside and outside prison. Prison Fellowship has also offered the Prison Fellowship Academy program for more than twenty-five years, teaching the biblically based Values of Good Citizenship to thousands of incarcerated participants annually, leading to safer communities.[28] However, we believe recidivism, essentially a failure rate, is not a high enough bar, and that what you measure matters. Our research team is developing new tools, including a Prison Culture Assessment and the Good Citizenship Inventory, to better assess success in prison and out.

Prison Fellowship is a leading national voice shaping the public debate on justice. We mobilize Christians and equip policymakers to advocate for reforms that advance proportional punishment, constructive corrections culture, and second chances. One recent example is our publication "The Road to Redemption."[29] The white paper highlights research showing that in-prison programming contributes to safe prison environments and postrelease success.[30] When structured well, release incentives such as parole, earned time credits, and good time credits encourage program participation.[31] Another example was our prominent role in the restoration of Pell Grants for incarcerated students.[32] We mobilized Christians to meet with lawmakers and advocate for expanding access to Pell Grants for people in prison. Higher education in prison is a proven tool for improving public safety, developing the workforce, and reducing racial disparities in the criminal justice system.[33] These are just two examples from more than four decades of work to prioritize fair punishment, community safety, and rehabilitation.

SECOND CHANCES

Christians value the principle of redemption. Accepting the Gospel message is an acknowledgment of one's sins and need of God's grace. "Therefore, if anyone is in Christ, the new creation has come: The old has gone, the new is here!"[34] In other words, Christians are the people of a second chance. A Christian understanding of second chances does not apply only to one's first transgression. In Matthew 18:21, Peter, a disciple of Jesus, asks, "Lord, how often will my brother sin against me, and I forgive him? As many as seven times?"[35] Jesus says to him, "I do not say to you seven times, but seventy-seven times." Dr. Mark Batterson, pastor of National Community Church in Washington, DC, says, "God has not, cannot, and will not give up on any one of us. It's not in His nature."[36] Illustrating this point in his Second Chance Sunday sermon, he pointed out that Peter would later deny even knowing Jesus three times, but Jesus forgave him three times. He is the God of second, third, and hundredth chances. We are never beyond the need nor the reach of God's grace.

Unfortunately, a criminal record can lock people out of opportunities through barriers that can last years or decades after their punishment is supposedly complete. The collateral consequences of a criminal conviction number nearly forty-four thousand, such as voter disenfranchisement, inability to obtain professional licensing, and lack of access to higher education, not to mention pervasive social stigma.[37] Many of these postrelease restrictions take effect automatically, without consideration of criminal history, time since the offense, or efforts to make amends. As Chuck Colson pointed out in his last op-ed, barriers such as denying voting rights bear no logical purpose except excessive punishment.[38] These restrictions should be eliminated or narrowly tailored to serve public safety.

Laws must change to provide opportunities for second chances, but so must culture. Failure to gain meaningful employment can be a significant predictor of a return to criminal activity, but 90 percent of those who have been incarcerated struggle to find a job in the first year after release.[39] One study found that only 40 percent of employers are willing to hire someone with a criminal record, and white applicants with a criminal record are half as likely to receive a call back from a potential employer; among Black applicants, that rate was even lower.[40] That's why, in 2017, Prison Fellowship established April as Second Chance Month. Since then, two U.S. presidents and more than twenty-five states have made it an official observance, and more than eight hundred organizations, businesses, and churches have joined as Second Chance Month partners.[41] Our efforts to advance second chances aren't limited to April. At Prison Fellowship, we work diligently to limit barriers affecting housing, education, and employment and have contributed to the successful passage of key occupational licensing legislation in Texas and Oklahoma.[42]

Although it is impossible to achieve perfect justice this side of heaven, Christians are called to publicly pursue a vision of justice that restores. We uphold the *imago Dei* by applying proportional punishment to people who commit crimes and infusing opportunities for rehabilitation and second chances into the criminal justice experience. Perhaps the greatest test of this generation of American Christians will be whether we can overcome distraction, ambivalence, and fear—and step into our calling to "remember those in prison."[43] My prayer for fellow followers of Jesus is that we will.

NOTES

1. Barna Group, "Signs of Decline & Hope Among Key Metrics of Faith," March 4, 2020, https://www.barna.com/research/changing-state-of-the-church.
2. Barna Group, "Signs of Decline." The Barna Group describes itself as "a visionary research and resource company located in Ventura, California." See Barna Group, "Who Is Barna?," accessed June 14, 2023, https://www.barna.com/about.

3. Barna Group, "Signs of Decline."
4. Prison Fellowship, "Our Founder Chuck Colson," accessed June 14, 2023, https://www.prisonfellowship.org/about/chuck-colson.
5. Exod. 21:22–25 (New International Version); Lev. 24:17–22 (NIV); Deut. 19:21 (NIV).
6. Mic. 6:8 (NIV).
7. Matt. 5:39 (NIV).
8. Chuck Colson, *God and Government: An Insider's View on the Boundaries Between Faith and Politics* (Grand Rapids, MI: Zondervan, 2010), 101.
9. C. S. Lewis, "The Humanitarian Theory of Punishment," in *God in the Dock: Essays on Theology and Ethics* (Grand Rapids, MI: Eerdmans Publishing, 1972).
10. Prison Fellowship, "Practicing Christians on Policing, Sentencing, and Other Issues," November 2021, https://www.prisonfellowship.org/2021/11/practicing-christians-on-policing-sentencing.
11. National Conference of State Legislatures, *Criminal Records and Reentry Toolkit*, March 31, 2023, https://www.ncsl.org/civil-and-criminal-justice/criminal-records-and-reentry-toolkit; Fwd.us, "Every Second," accessed June 15, 2023, https://everysecond.fwd.us/#chapter1-1.
12. Adam Gelb, Ryan King, and Felicity Rose, *Time Served: The High Cost, Low Return of Longer Prison Terms* (Washington, DC: Pew Center on the States, June 6, 2012), 2, https://www.pewtrusts.org/-/media/legacy/uploadedfiles/wwwpewtrustsorg/reports/sentencing_and_corrections/prisontimeservedpdf.pdf.
13. Arthur L. Rizer, "Can Conservative Criminal Justice Reform Survive a Rise in Crime?," *Annual Review of Criminology* 6, no. 1 (January 2023): 65–83, https://doi.org/10.1146/annurev-criminol-030920-090259.
14. Ps. 23:4 (NIV); Jas. 3:17 (English Standard Version); Rom. 12:2 (ESV).
15. Pew Charitable Trusts, "National Imprisonment and Crime Rates Continue to Fall," Fact sheet, December 29, 2016, http://www.pewtrusts.org/~/media/assets/2017/03/pspp_national_imprisonment_and_crime_rates_fall.pdf.
16. Pew Charitable Trusts, "National Imprisonment," 2.
17. Pew Charitable Trusts, "National Imprisonment," 2.
18. Lev. 19:15 (NIV).
19. Prov. 31:8–9 (NIV).
20. Tim Keller, "What We Owe the Poor," interview by Kristen Scharold, *Christianity Today*, December 6, 2010, https://www.christianitytoday.com/ct/2010/december/10.69.html.
21. Prison Fellowship, "Responding to Crime & Incarceration: A Call to the Church," June 2017, https://www.prisonfellowship.org/wp-content/uploads/2017/08/Justice-Declaration-White-Paper_FINAL.pdf; Mark E. Kann, review of

Seedbeds of Virtue: Sources of Competence, Character, and Citizenship in American Society, by Mary Ann Glendon and David Blankenhorn, *American Political Science Review* 91, no. 2 (June 1997): 434.

22. Exodus (NIV).
23. Acts 13:22 (NIV).
24. Luke 19 (NIV).
25. Stuart Grassian and Nancy Friedman, "Effects of Sensory Deprivation in Psychiatric Seclusion and Solitary Confinement," *International Journal of Law and Psychiatry* 8, no. 1 (1986): 49–65; Craig Haney and Mona Lynch, "Regulating Prisons of the Future: A Psychological Analysis of Supermax and Solitary Confinement," *N.Y.U. Review of Law and Social Change* 23, no. 4 (1997): 477–570, https://socialchangenyu.com/wp-content/uploads/2017/12/Craig-Haney-Mona-Lynch_RLSC_23.4.pdf; Craig Haney, "Mental Health Issues in Long-Term Solitary and "Supermax" Confinement," *Crime & Delinquency* 49, no. 1 (2003): 124–56.
26. Natasha A. Frost and Carlos E. Monteiro, *Restrictive Housing in the U.S.: Issues Challenges and Future Directions*, NCJ 250315 (Washington, DC: National Institute of Justice, 2016), 9, https://www.ojp.gov/pdffiles1/nij/250316.pdf.
27. Prison Fellowship, "What Is the Warden Exchange," accessed June 16, 2023, https://www.prisonfellowship.org/about/warden-exchange/warden-exchange-details.
28. Prison Fellowship, "The Prison Fellowship Academy," accessed June 16, 2023, https://www.prisonfellowship.org/about/academy. Of the programs studied by the Texas Department of Criminal Justice, the Prison Fellowship Academy had the lowest recidivism rate in the entire state. Texas Department of Criminal Justice, "Evaluation of Offenders Released in Fiscal Year 2013 That Completed Rehabilitation Tier Programs," October 2017 (on file with the author).
29. Chelsea Friske, *The Road to Redemption: Incentivizing Rehabilitation Through Parole, Earned Time, and Good Time Credits* (Landsdowne, VA: Prison Fellowship, 2021), https://www.prisonfellowship.org/wp-content/uploads/2021/03/RoadtoRedemptionReport.pdf.
30. Grant Duwe, *The Use and Impact of Correctional Programming for Inmates on Pre- and Post-Release Outcomes* (Washington, DC: National Institute of Justice, June 2017), https://www.ojp.gov/pdffiles1/nij/250476.pdf.
31. Friske, *Road to Redemption*, 9.
32. Prison Fellowship, "Congress Restores Access to Pell Grants for Incarcerated Students Seeking a Second Chance," December 2021, https://www.prisonfellowship.org/2020/12/congress-restores-access-to-pell-grants.
33. Prison Fellowship, "Congress Restores Access."
34. 2 Cor. 5:17 (NIV).
35. Matt. 18:21 (ESV).

36. National Community Church, "People of the Second Chance with Prison Fellowship—Dr. Mark Batterson," YouTube video, 36:45, April 3, 2022, https://www.youtube.com/watch?v=BBZo-PPqB3A.
37. National Inventory of Collateral Consequences of Conviction, "Collateral Consequences Inventory," accessed June 16, 2023, https://niccc.nationalreentryresourcecenter.org/consequences; American Bar Association, *Collateral Consequences of Criminal Convictions Judicial Bench Book* (Chicago: ABA Criminal Justice Section, March 2018), 2, https://www.ojp.gov/pdffiles1/nij/grants/251583.pdf.
38. Charles W. Colson, "Why Punish Ex-Offenders with a Voting Ban?," *Washington Post*, January 19, 2012, https://www.washingtonpost.com/opinions/why-punish-ex-offenders-with-a-voting-ban/2012/01/19/gIQAvjAqBQ_story.html.
39. John M. Nally, Susan Lockwood, Taiping Ho, and Katie Knutson, "Post-Release Recidivism and Employment Among Different Types of Released Offenders: A 5-Year Follow-up Study in the United States," *International Journal of Criminal Justice Sciences* 9, no.1 (June 2014): 16, 23; Le'Ann Duran, Martha Plotkin, Phoebe Potter, and Henry Rosen, *Integrated Reentry and Employment Strategies: Reducing Recidivism and Promoting Job Readiness* (New York: Council of State Governments Justice Center, September 2013), https://csgjusticecenter.org/wp-content/uploads/2020/02/Final.Reentry-and-Employment.pp_.pdf.
40. Harry J. Holzer, "Collateral Costs: The Effects of Incarceration on the Employment and Earnings of Young Workers" *Institute of Labor Economics*, Discussion paper no. 3118 (October 2007): 14, https://docs.iza.org/dp3118.pdf.
41. Prison Fellowship, "Second Chance Month," accessed June 20, 2023, https://www.prisonfellowship.org/about/justice-reform/second-chance-month.
42. Prison Fellowship, "Prison Fellowship Celebrates Texas Occupational Licensing Law Reforms," 2019, https://www.prisonfellowship.org/2019/07/prison-fellowship-celebrates-texas-occupational-licensing-law-reforms; "Criminal Justice Reform Achievements," accessed June 16, 2023, https://www.prisonfellowship.org/2022/12/justice-reform-achievements.
43. Heb. 13:3 (NIV).

37

CRIMINAL JUSTICE HAS BEEN AND MUST REMAIN BIPARTISAN TO SEE SUCCESS

Jason Pye

ALTHOUGH MOST OF THE WHITE HOUSE PRESS CORPS was focused on the impending government shutdown on December 21, 2018, a group of us were gathered and waiting in the West Wing to be ushered into the Oval Office for the signing ceremony for the First Step Act. To say that our group was unique would be an understatement.

If one looked around the room, one would see the full ideological spectrum represented. Progressives such as CNN commentator and former Barack Obama administration official Van Jones and Senator Sheldon Whitehouse (D-RI); conservatives such as Senator Mike Lee (R-UT) and former Virginia Attorney General Ken Cuccinelli; and libertarians such as my then boss Adam Brandon and I were gathered to witness the signing of a landmark piece of legislation that represented a small but still significant rollback of the excesses of the war on drugs.

Also in the room were people who had been affected by the criminal justice system and become advocates for sentencing and prison reform. Among them were Georgetown Law Associate Professor Shon Hopwood, Right on Crime's John Koufos, and the Ladies of Hope Ministries' Topeka Sam. Many of the justice-affected individuals in the room spoke about what the First Step Act meant to them, often with tears were streaming down their faces. Their stories and advocacy were an endless source of inspiration throughout the legislative effort and beyond.

Being in the Oval Office is an incredibly humbling experience. Although the executive branch is only one of the three branches of the federal government—and its importance shouldn't be elevated above the others—the White House represents the last stop for any piece of legislation that becomes law. The reason our ideologically diverse crew was gathered, to witness the signing of the First Step Act, only added to the amazement of the already awesome and humbling moment.

Many of the people in the room represented a constituency of conservatives or progressive activists. However, the most important constituency that day were those serving time in prison. It was Ms. Sam who reminded us that "we have been fighting and we will continue to fight, and this is just a first step."[1]

The First Step Act was the culmination of years of work. This wasn't a piece of legislation that happened overnight; nor was it an easy accomplishment. It's also not the end of the journey to reform our criminal justice system. We have a lot of work left to do at the state and local levels, as well as continued reform efforts in Congress.

Congress is downstream from the states. When I was at FreedomWorks, we called the states "laboratories of policy innovation," a paraphrase of sorts of Justice Louis Brandeis's famous framing of the states serving as "laboratories of democracy" in *New State Ice Co. v. Liebmann*.[2] With the costs of incarceration rising and anticipated prison construction costs adding up, in 2005, Texas started experimenting with criminal justice reforms, including drug courts and programming in prisons designed to reduce recidivism.[3] As of 2019, according to former state Representative Jerry Madden, who chaired the state House Committee on Corrections when Texas began pursuing criminal justice reform, the initiative led to the closure of eight prisons and an 11 percent decline in the prison population.[4]

More than thirty states have enacted at least some steps to reform their criminal justice systems, although some have gone further than others.[5] Georgia, Rhode Island, and Texas were among the pioneers in the effort and showed others that states could cut prison populations, avert some of the significant costs of corrections, reduce sentences for nonviolent offenses, and reinvest savings into more cost-effective alternatives to incarceration while enhancing public safety.

Two decades ago, Congress took some steps to improve the conditions in prisons and reduce recidivism through evidence-based programs in federal, state, and local prisons and jails with the Prison Rape Elimination Act of 2003 and to support state and local efforts to reduce recidivism with the Second Chance Act of 2007 and the Justice Reinvestment Initiative in the Commerce, Justice, Science, and Related Agencies appropriations bill.[6] All of these efforts were bipartisan and noncontroversial.

In 2010, Congress passed the Fair Sentencing Act, which reduced but did not eliminate the sentencing disparity between crack cocaine and powder cocaine. The Fair Sentencing Act was so rooted in common sense that it passed the Senate without opposition.[7] In fact, some conservative legislators did not believe the bill went far enough. Representative Ron Paul (R-TX) called the bill the "Slightly Fairer Sentencing Act" during the debate in the House, although he supported the legislation.[8]

Bipartisan bills were also introduced in Congress that never passed. In 2013, Senators Dick Durbin (D-IL) and Mike Lee (R-UT) introduced the Smarter Sentencing Act.[9] This legislation, which boasted broad bipartisan support, would have reduced mandatory minimum prisons sentences for nonviolent drug offenses. It also proposed to expand the federal safety valve exception from mandatory minimums for individuals with little to no criminal history. Also in 2013, Senators Sheldon Whitehouse (D-RI) and John Cornyn (R-TX) introduced the Recidivism Reduction and Public Safety Act, a prison reform bill modeled after efforts in their home states.[10]

Despite the lack of legislation in 2014, hopes were renewed for action on criminal justice reform legislation in 2015 and 2016. Senator Chuck Grassley (R-IA), who had taken over the gavel of the Senate Judiciary Committee and had resisted sentencing reform efforts like the Smarter Sentencing Act, worked with Senators Durbin and Lee, as well as Cory Booker (D-NJ), Charles Schumer (D-NY), Lindsey Graham (R-SC), and Patrick Leahy (D-VT) to introduce the Sentencing Reform and Corrections Act.[11] Equally important was that Speaker John Boehner (R-OH) and, after Boehner's resignation, Speaker Paul Ryan (R-OH), voiced their support for broader efforts. Ryan in particular was very involved in working to move criminal justice reform bills like the Sentencing Reform Act forward.[12]

Although the judiciary committees in the House and the Senate moved these bills to the forefront, roadblocks got in the way of their passage. In the Senate, Majority Leader Mitch McConnell (R-KY) showed next to no interest in criminal justice reform legislation, particularly when it divided his conference. Annoyingly, House conservatives, even some who supported the efforts, did not want to hand President Obama, who had prioritized criminal justice reform in his second term, a legacy win.[13]

Adding to our problems, by the time House Republican leadership was prepared to dedicate floor time to the package of criminal justice reform bills that included the Sentencing Reform Act and the Corrections and

Recidivism Reduction Act, we were knee deep in the 2016 presidential election. The Republican nominee, Donald Trump, had made law and order a key part of his campaign messaging. House conservatives were concerned about undermining the campaign message.

No one expected Trump to win. I recall representatives from some progressive groups who were involved in the reform effort telling other advocates that we would get a robust criminal justice reform package done when Hillary Clinton got into the White House. That of course did not happen.

Most who worked hard to advance criminal justice reform bills in 2015 and 2016 did not see much of a window under President Trump. Considering the rhetoric used during the campaign, the pessimism was understandable. For example, during his nomination acceptance speech in July 2016, then candidate Trump said, "I have a message for all of you: the crime and violence that today afflicts our nation will soon—and I mean very soon—come to an end. Beginning on January 20th, 2017, safety will be restored."[14] The rhetoric did not reflect reality, but that did not matter.

However, Holly Harris of the Justice Action Network, Representatives Doug Collins (R-GA) and Hakeem Jeffries (D-NY), #cut50 (now part of Dream.org), Pat Nolan of the American Conservative Union Foundation, a handful of others, and I all believed that there was a possibility to move something, even if it was only prison reform, because of President Trump's boastful posture on his ability to make deals. Added to that, President Trump's son-in-law, Jared Kushner, made reform one of his top priorities and had the president's ear.

I was summoned to the Capitol by Doug Collins's chief of staff, Brendan Belair, in early 2017 to discuss ideas for a criminal justice bill. I walked into the meeting with a wide-ranging list of options, but Collins and his team decided to focus on prison reform. Collins partnered with Jeffries on the Prison Reform and Redemption Act.[15]

We all knew the White House was slowly getting on board with the effort, but the first real public sign of support came in the 2018 State of the Union address. President Trump spoke about job growth and investment and subsequently said, "As America regains its strength, this opportunity must be extended to all citizens. That is why this year we will embark on reforming our prisons to help former inmates who have served their time get a second chance."[16]

After some complaints that the Prison Reform and Redemption Act didn't go far enough, Collins and Jeffries introduced a new bill, the Formerly

Incarcerated Reenter Society Transformed Safely Transitioning Every Person Act, or First Step Act.[17] The First Step Act moved through the House Judiciary Committee in early May 2018. The bill cleared the House on May 22 with limited opposition, the vast majority of which came from Democrats who were frustrated that the bill did not go far enough.[18]

Initially, we hit a wall in the Senate, but Senator Grassley's tenacity and commitment to including sentencing reform in the First Step Act was strong. He held out until he got a commitment from President Trump that he would support adding sentencing reform to the legislation.[19] President Trump publicly announced his support at a press conference in the Roosevelt Room of the West Wing in November 2018.[20]

Despite Majority Leader McConnell's unwillingness to move the legislation on his own, President Trump publicly and privately prodded the Republican leader to move the bill through the Senate.[21] Progressive organizations like the Leadership Conference on Civil and Human Rights and the American Civil Liberties Union got on board with the First Step Act after sentencing reform was added to the legislation.[22] A week before Christmas 2018, the Senate passed an updated First Step Act.[23] Passage in the House came next. With little drama, the First Step Act passed the House and went to President Trump's desk.[24]

Since the First Step Act became law, Congress has accomplished little in the criminal justice reform space. In fact, other than the December 2020 Pell Grant restoration, the only federal criminal justice reform legislation that has passed since the First Step Act is the Fair Chance Act, which was included in the National Defense Authorization Act for FY 2020.[25] This bipartisan legislation spearheaded by Senators Booker and Ron Johnson (R-WI) and Representatives Collins and Elijah Cummings (D-MD) allows applicants for federal government and private-sector jobs tied to a federal contract to get to the conditional offer stage of the hiring process before inquiries can be made about criminal history.

Despite something of a drought recently in federal criminal justice reform accomplishments, the good news is that the bipartisan nature of this work has continued. In the past few years, Senators Rob Portman (R-OH), Thom Tillis (R-NC), and nine other Republicans cosponsored legislation, the Eliminating a Quantifiably Unjust Application of the Law (EQUAL) Act, to eliminate the sentencing disparity between crack cocaine and power cocaine.[26]

Although the EQUAL Act did not move in the Senate, the House passed the bill twice in bipartisan fashion, once in September 2021 as a standalone bill and again as part of an amendment package to the National Defense Authorization Act for fiscal year (FY) 2023.[27] Unfortunately, the Senate did not consider the House version of the EQUAL Act, despite having the support of enough Republican senators to move the bill, and the National Defense Authorization Act for FY 2023 that became law did not include the House amendment.[28]

In 2022, the House passed the bipartisan Prohibiting Punishment of Acquitted Conduct Act, which would have eliminated the use of conduct for which an individual was acquitted in sentencing for other charges, with little opposition.[29] Although the SAFE Banking Act is not a criminal justice bill, the legislation, which normalizes the treatment of cannabis- and hemp-related businesses in the financial system, passed the House on a bipartisan basis, with a majority of the House Republican Conference voting for passage.[30]

Other bipartisan criminal justice reform legislation was marked up by the Senate Judiciary Committee or the House Judiciary Committee but did not move to the floor. These bills included an expungement bill named the Kenneth P. Thompson Begin Again Act, an expansion of the sentencing reforms in the First Step Act through the First Step Implementation Act, and an expansion of home confinement and compassionate release programs in the Safer Detention Act. Unfortunately, there were no votes on these bills in the Senate and the House in the 117th Congress. It remains to be seen whether any action will be taken on them in the current Congress.

Many in Congress doubtless believed that the First Step Act was a one and done effort, that criminal justice reform was out of the way, that there was no reason to revisit the topic in the short term. For those of us who worked on these issues, however, the First Step Act was only the beginning. We recognize that much more needs to be done—from record-sealing and expungement opportunities to further sentencing and prison reforms to civil asset forfeiture and policing reform.

Advocates know the policy prescriptions to address the problems in the U.S. criminal justice system, but Democrats and Republicans and people from across the ideological spectrum must come together if goals are to be accomplished. That may mean it takes time or that we do not get everything we want. Making laws is not easy, nor is it supposed to be. We need to be incremental in our approach. This means that we must be willing to work in bipartisan fashion to achieve what is attainable, even if it is not everything we want. Making policy means building consensus and making compromises, and these are arts that too few are willing to learn in today's toxic hyperpartisan political climate.

Bipartisan work is what leaves me feeling good about what I do. Sadly, hyperpartisanship has infected U.S. politics and has metastasized into a larger societal ill that has manifested itself into misguided populism, in a creeping authoritarianism on the fringes of U.S. politics, and in the cultural wars that appeal to the lowest common denominator.

The only way we are going to be successful, even incrementally, is to pursue criminal justice reform policies that we know we need on the foundation of bipartisanship. Otherwise, we are simply messaging for political purposes. That does no good to our movement or the people who have been affected by the criminal justice system. All messaging does is give politicians an excuse to retreat to partisan corners and set our movement back.

NOTES

1. The White House, "Remarks by President Trump at Signing Ceremony for S. 756, the 'First Step Act of 2018' and H.R. 6964, the 'Juvenile Justice Reform Act of 2018,'" December 21, 2018, https://trumpwhitehouse.archives.gov/briefings-statements/remarks-president-trump-signing-ceremony-s-756-first-step-act-2018-h-r-6964-juvenile-justice-reform-act-2018.
2. New State Ice Co. v. Liebmann, 285 U.S. 262 (1932), https://supreme.justia.com/cases/federal/us/285/262. Justice Brandeis wrote in his dissent, "It is one of the happy incidents of the federal system that a single courageous State may, if its citizens choose, serve as a laboratory; and try novel social and economic experiments without risk to the rest of the country."
3. Jerry Madden, "Prison, Probation, and Parole Reforms: The Texas Model," *Trust Magazine*, May 20, 2019, https://www.pewtrusts.org/nb/trust/archive/spring-2019/prison-probation-and-parole-reforms-the-texas-model.
4. Madden, "Prison, Probation."
5. Pew Charitable Trusts, "35 States Reform Criminal Justice Policies Through Justice Reinvestment," Fact sheet, July 2018, https://www.pewtrusts.org/-/media/assets/2018/07/pspp_reform_matrix.pdf.
6. Prison Rape Elimination Act of 2003, Pub. L. 108–79, September 4, 2003, https://www.prearesourcecenter.org/resource/prison-rape-elimination-act-public-law-108-79-sept-4-2003-full-text-law; Second Chance Act of 2007, Pub.

L. 110–199, 122 Stat. 657 (2007), https://www.congress.gov/110/plaws/publ199/PLAW-110publ199.pdf. The Justice Reinvestment Initiative, originally referred to as "criminal justice reform and recidivism reduction," between FY 2010 and FY 2013, is a specific earmark in the Commerce, Justice, Science, and Related Agencies appropriations bill each fiscal year. The Justice Reinvestment Initiative has been funded with bipartisan support since FY 2010. In FY 2023, $35 million was appropriated for the initiative (see P. L. 117–328, Division B, Title II, https://www.congress.gov/bill/117th-congress/house-bill/2617/text).

7. Fair Sentencing Act of 2010, S. 1789, 111th Cong. (2009–2010), August 3, 2010, https://www.congress.gov/bill/111th-congress/senate-bill/1789.
8. 156 Cong. Rec. H6203 (daily ed. July 28, 2010) (statement of Rep. Paul), https://www.congress.gov/congressional-record/volume-156/issue-112/house-section/article/H6196.
9. Smarter Sentencing Act of 2014, S. 1410, 113th Cong. (2013–2014), https://www.congress.gov/bill/113th-congress/senate-bill/1410.
10. Recidivism Reduction and Public Safety Act of 2014, S. 1675, 113th Cong. (2013–2014), https://www.congress.gov/bill/113th-congress/senate-bill/1675.
11. Sentencing Reform and Corrections Act of 2015, S. 2124, 114th Cong. (2015–2016), https://www.congress.gov/bill/114th-congress/senate-bill/2123.
12. Sentencing Reform Act of 2015, H.R. 3713, 114th Cong. (2015–2016), https://www.congress.gov/bill/114th-congress/house-bill/3713.
13. Some may dispute this, but several House conservative members and staff explicitly told me in private conversations that giving President Obama a victory for his legacy was the very reason that they would not support the bills moving to the floor.
14. Philip Bump and Aaron Blake, "Donald Trump's Dark Speech to the Republican National Convention, Annotated," *Washington Post*, July 21, 2016, https://www.washingtonpost.com/news/the-fix/wp/2016/07/21/full-text-donald-trumps-prepared-remarks-accepting-the-republican-nomination.
15. Prison Reform and Redemption Act, H.R. 3356, 115th Cong. (2017–2018), https://www.congress.gov/bill/115th-congress/house-bill/3356.
16. The White House, "President Donald J. Trump's State of the Union Address," January 30, 2018, https://trumpwhitehouse.archives.gov/briefings-statements/president-donald-j-trumps-state-union-address.
17. Formerly Incarcerated Reenter Society Transformed Safely Transitioning Every Person Act, H.R. 5682, 115th Cong. (2017–2018), https://www.congress.gov/bill/115th-congress/house-bill/5682.
18. Clerk of the U.S. House of Representatives, "Roll Call 215, H.R. 5682," 115th Cong. (May 22, 2018), https://clerk.house.gov/Votes/2018215.
19. Nicholas Fandos and Katie Rogers, "Senator Says He Has Trump's Backing for Prison Bill Vote Late This Year," *New York Times*, August 23, 2018, https://www

.nytimes.com/2018/08/23/us/politics/trump-criminal-justice-prison-reform.html.

20. Nicholas Fandos and Maggie Haberman, "Trump Embraces a Path to Revise U.S. Sentencing and Prison Laws," *New York Times*, https://www.nytimes.com/2018/11/14/us/politics/prison-sentencing-trump.html.
21. Ames Grawert and Tim Lau, "How the First Step Act Became Law—and What Happens Next" (New York: Brennan Center for Justice, January 4, 2019), https://www.brennancenter.org/our-work/analysis-opinion/how-first-step-act-became-law-and-what-happens-next.
22. Leadership Conference on Civil and Human Rights, "The ACLU and The Leadership Conference Urge Members of Congress to Support S. 756, the First Step Act," December 19, 2018, https://civilrights.org/resource/the-aclu-and-the-leadership-conference-urge-members-of-congress-to-support-s-756-the-first-step-act.
23. First Step Act of 2018, S. 756, 115th Cong. (2017–2018), https://www.congress.gov/bill/115th-congress/senate-bill/756.
24. John Wagner, "Trump Signs Bipartisan Criminal Justice Bill amid Partisan Rancor over Stopgap Spending Measure," *Washington Post*, December 21, 2018, https://www.washingtonpost.com/politics/trump-to-sign-bipartisan-criminal-justice-bill-amid-partisan-rancor-over-stopgap-spending-measure/2018/12/21/234f9ffc-0510-11e9-b5df-5d3874f1ac36_story.html.
25. Ruth Delaney and Allan Wachendorfer, "Congress Lifted the Pell Grant Ban for Incarcerated People. What Now?," *Higher Education Today* (American Council on Education blog), April 22, 2021, https://www.higheredtoday.org/2021/04/22/congress-lifted-pell-grant-ban-incarcerated-people-now; National Defense Authorization Act for 2020, Pub. L. 116-92, Division A, Title XI, Subtitle B (2020), https://congress.gov/116/plaws/publ92/PLAW-116publ92.pdf.
26. EQUAL Act, S. 79, 117th Cong. (2021–2022), https://www.congress.gov/bill/117th-congress/senate-bill/79.
27. Clerk of the U.S. House of Representatives, "Roll Call 297, H.R. 1693," 117th Cong. (September 28, 2021), https://clerk.house.gov/Votes/2021297. The link to the House Armed Services Committee website that tracked amendments is no longer active. However, the EQUAL Act was included in a package of amendments, H. Amdt. 288, which passed the House by voice vote on July 14, 2022. See National Defense Authorization Act for Fiscal Year 2023, H.R. 7900, Division E, Title LVIII, Sec. 5848, https://www.congress.gov/bill/117th-congress/house-bill/7900.
28. Carrie Johnson, "A Bill That Would Have Impacted Racial Disparity in Cocaine Crimes Died in the Senate," *All Things Considered*, January 10, 2023, https://www.npr.org/2023/01/09/1147909174/a-bill-that-would-have-impacted-racial-disparity-in-cocaine-crimes-died-in-the-s.

29. Clerk of the U.S. House of Representatives, "Roll Call 83, H.R. 1621," 117th Cong. (March 28, 2022), https://clerk.house.gov/Votes/202283.
30. SAFE Banking Act, H.R. 1996, 117th Cong. (2021–2022), https://www.congress.gov/bill/117th-congress/house-bill/1996; Clerk of the U.S. House of Representatives, "Roll Call 120, H.R. 1996," 117th Cong. (April 19, 2021), https://clerk.house.gov/Votes/2021120.

38

NO ONE ANSWER TO OVERPOLICING AND MASS INCARCERATION BUT MANY

Alia Nahra and Hernandez Stroud

THE ESSAYS IN THIS BOOK illustrate a clear fact: America is a carceral society. By the end of 2020, the United States held about 5.5 million people under some form of correctional control.[1] We continue to confine people to prisons and jails plagued with inhumane conditions.[2] We rely on criminal punishment to respond to basic human needs and solve social issues, such as homelessness and drug addiction. We penalize people even after they've completed their sentence by permitting limitations on their civil liberties and saddling them with unbearable debt, two burdens that prevent individuals with criminal records from holding full-fledged membership in our polity. We disproportionately punish our society's most disempowered members, the largest share of whom are descendants of the enslaved.

Obviously a problem so complex, so deeply ingrained in the American experience, has no easy solution. Some jurisdictions, though, have already taken steps toward reimagining and unwinding the legal system's reliance on punitive excess by developing hyperlocal, community-led systems of accountability, public safety, and financial and political empowerment. Of course, these officially recognized programs come in addition to—and are often inspired by—the numerous ad hoc and constituent-led initiatives that are less visible, such as mutual aid groups and informal support networks. Individually, these reforms cannot entirely dismantle the phenomenon of mass incarceration, but some of these innovations provide a blueprint to make meaningful change.

In Shreveport, Louisiana, after twenty-three students were arrested at Southwood High School for fighting, families responded by forming a group called Dads on Duty.[3] The dads take shifts "greeting students in the morning and helping maintain a positive environment for learning." Since the initiative launched in September 2021, the school has reported a dramatic decrease in fighting and gang violence on campus has ceased.[4] This shift embodies a welcome break from how things were before the program started: according to the school's principal, Kim Pendleton, troublesome violence had beset the institution at the start of the academic year.[5]

Removing police contact in schools has the potential to drastically reduce what is often termed the school-to-prison pipeline. This phrase encompasses the school policing practices that create a pipeline through which students are criminalized and forced out of school into the criminal legal system. Typical examples of school policing are the use of law enforcement tools (handcuffs, tasers, and the like) for disciplinary purposes, arrests for disorderly conduct following developmentally typical disruptions that would previously have been handled by school administrators, and disproportionate targeting of Black and Brown students or those with disabilities.[6] In the U.S. public school system, the number of law enforcement officers on campus (generally referred to as school resource officers or SROs) has ballooned in recent decades. Fifty years ago, fewer than 1 percent of schools reported having onsite SROs; by 2018, the figure had reached 58 percent.[7] These officers are more likely to be placed in schools with high concentrations of nonwhite students and their presence is the cause of higher rates of exclusionary discipline and arrest; schools with SROs boast arrest rates roughly three and a half times those of schools without SROs.[8] Even the Congressional Research Service has found no evidence that police presence in schools reduces violence or even school shootings.[9] Of course, the consequences of this unnecessary entanglement with the criminal legal system are consequential for students, making them more likely to "drop out of school, earn less money as adults, and end up in the criminal justice system."[10]

Other cities and states have begun to address the school-to-prison pipeline by reducing or removing police officers from their schools. In East Lansing, Michigan, the public school district decided to stop funding SROs and instead invest in developing the district's restorative justice practices.[11] In Oakland, the school board disbanded the Oakland Unified School District Police Force, redirecting the roughly $2.5 million spent each year toward student support services and restorative justice efforts.[12] For the 2021–22 school year, the city decided to implement a new safety plan that funds social workers and psychologists to respond to students in crisis, rather than police.[13] However, the district also voted to continue employing many of the people who had worked as SROs, retraining them in restorative justice and dispute resolution tactics and instead labeling them school security officers.

Outside schools, jurisdictions are recognizing responsibilities currently delegated to police officers that don't benefit from a law enforcement response. For example, traffic enforcement has long been a source of conflict between police and the public; officers killed roughly six hundred people in traffic stops over the past five years and disproportionately targeted Black residents for fines and fees.[14] Both Philadelphia and Pittsburgh voted in 2021 to ban police from making traffic stops for minor violations such as a broken taillight.[15] In Virginia, the legislature in late 2020 barred police from stopping vehicles for a raft of minor charges such as driving with only one working headlight or brake light. This legislation faced significant pushback from the policing lobby but has, according to Justice Forward Virginia, already begun to narrow racial disparities in traffic stops.[16]

Several cities have redirected funding to address the root causes of crime, including housing and job insecurity. Despite a 2021 ballot initiative passed by voters that effectively criminalizes activities tied to homelessness, such as sitting or lying on public sidewalks, Austin's city council also voted in 2021 to use diverted funds to transform two hotels into permanent supportive housing units for individuals experiencing chronic homelessness. There, residents will have access to case management services that include mental health and substance use counseling, workforce development programs, and job placement services.[17] Salt Lake City's city council voted to construct a small community of sixty fully furnished, cottage-style homes, split into two neighborhoods of thirty homes for the chronically unhoused.[18] The community will provide permanent housing and will have various stores providing employment opportunities to develop financial self-sufficiency.

To redress decades of inequitable resource distribution, both Los Angeles and San Francisco have reinvested police funds in youth programming, workforce training, and housing support for historically underinvested communities.[19]

Other jurisdictions, tapping into the growing skepticism that law enforcement is poorly suited to respond to myriad situations, have begun to alter their emergency response systems to reduce police contact that disproportionately harms nonwhite residents.[20] In Eugene, Oregon, the Crisis Assistance Helping Out on the Streets (CAHOOTS) program has redirected a function previously performed by the police by creating a program that sends two-person teams of crisis workers and medics to respond to 911 and nonemergency calls involving people suffering a mental health crisis.[21] CAHOOTS is so successful that the organization has begun collaborating with numerous other cities—like Indianapolis and Denver—to develop similar nonpolicing models of response.[22]

Some jurisdictions have included law enforcement in reform efforts that have boasted "a proven record of reducing unnecessary arrests and emergency hospitalizations while connecting people to appropriate community-based services and treatment," according to the Brennan Center for Justice.[23] Such programs are also growing in popularity. At least fifteen of the fifty largest police departments between January 2020 and July 2022 rolled out new coresponder teams.[24] These models can also produce dramatic cost savings. In 2019, the CAHOOTS program saved Eugene around $14 million in emergency medical services.[25]

Many reforms have embraced elements of restorative justice, a proven method of tackling culpability that works to avoid a reliance on imprisonment.[26] As a systemic response, restorative justice has been embraced as an evidence-based solution by court systems, hospitals, attorneys, and other stakeholders. But even aside from an empirical analysis of its merits, qualitative evidence demonstrates that restorative justice transforms relationships and communities by offering a different approach to redress the often traumatizing and ineffective criminal legal system.[27] It provides crime victims with the opportunity to engage directly with those who have harmed them while still fostering accountability for those who caused the harm.

Many of the guiding principles of restorative justice can be traced to indigenous practices, such as peacemaking and talking circles used to resolve conflict and injury in Native American and First Nation Canadian cultures.[28] However, the contemporary exercise of restorative justice in criminal legal settings comes from a Canadian experiment that began in 1974 and has provided nearly half a century of knowledge that can be used to refine best practices.[29]

Consider New York City's Common Justice, an organization that focuses on reducing and addressing crime without relying on incarceration.[30] Founded in 2017, the group has developed successful alternative-to-incarceration programs that divert cases into a restorative justice process "designed to recognize the harm done, honor the needs and interests of those harmed, and develop appropriate responses to hold the responsible party accountable." It offers restorative justice to crime survivors as a way to heal, giving them the chance to be heard and to help determine the outcome of what happened to them. According to Common Justice, 90 percent of victims to whom it offered restorative justice opted for restorative justice over the alternative: incarceration for the defendant.[31] Save Our Streets, also in New York, is another example. It sends violence interrupters to respond immediately after shooting incidents to prevent further escalation. And in Detroit, the Detroit Life Is Valuable Everyday intervention program operates as a hospital-based approach, connecting with injured people while they are receiving treatment to provide a range of trauma-informed healing supports, such as integrated mental health therapy, transportation, housing, and employment.[32] These are sometimes provided directly, but also often come from partner organizations that help round out a structural approach to understanding how to prevent further violence. These hospital-based violence interventions have been shown to reduce reinjury, future violence, criminal legal system involvement, and posttraumatic stress symptoms.[33]

All told, a wide body of evidence illustrates the growing number of solutions to the nation's reliance on punitive overenforcement and incarceration. To operate at scale, these practices require both government investment and commitment from the public to supplement existing grassroots networks.

We know that these systemic adjustments, even if jurisdictions everywhere implement them, won't entirely transform U.S. society into one that no longer harms its most marginalized groups. Yet the nation's most radical changes—ending slavery, mandating racial integration of public facilities, rooting out racial voter suppression tactics such as literacy tests and poll taxes—arose from incremental steps toward visionary goals. We must start somewhere. Perhaps the best way to do so is to acknowledge where transformative approaches to reduce the justice system's harms are already under way.

NOTES

1. Rich Kluckow and Zhen Zeng, "Correctional Populations in the United States, 2020—Statistical Tables," NCJ 303184 (Washington, DC: U.S. Department of Justice, Office of Justice Programs, Bureau of Justice Statistics, 2022), 1, https://bjs.ojp.gov/content/pub/pdf/cpus20st.pdf.

2. Jan Ransom, Jonah E. Bromwich and Rebecca Davis O'Brien, "Inside Rikers: Dysfunction, Lawlessness and Detainees in Control," *New York Times*, October 11, 2021, https://www.nytimes.com/2021/10/11/nyregion/rikers-detainees-correction-officers.html.
3. Steve Hartman, "Dads Spend Time in Louisiana High School After 23 Students Were Arrested in String of Violence," CBS News, October 22, 2021, https://www.cbsnews.com/news/dads-louisiana-high-school-student-violence.
4. Caroline Fanning, "These Fathers Formed 'Dads on Duty' to Prevent Violence at a Local High School," *Reader's Digest*, May 13, 2022, https://www.rd.com/list/dads-on-duty.
5. Katie Kindelan, "Dads Form 'Dad's on Duty' Squad to Help Stop Violence at Their Kids' High School," *Good Morning America*, October 27, 2021, https://www.goodmorningamerica.com/family/story/dads-form-dads-duty-squad-stop-violence-kids-80787546.
6. Barbara A. Fedders, "The End of School Policing," *California Law Review* 109 (2021): 1467–69, https://clrorg.wpenginepowered.com/wp-content/uploads/2021/08/4-Fedders-postEIC.pdf.
7. Chelsea Connery, "The Prevalence and the Price of Police in Schools" (Storrs: University of Connecticut, NEAG School of Education, 2020), 1, https://education.uconn.edu/2020/10/27/the-prevalence-and-the-price-of-police-in-schools/#.
8. Amit Whitaker, Sylvia Torres-Guillén, Michelle Morton, Harold Jordan, Stefanie Coyle, Angela Mann, and Wei-Ling Sun, *Cops and No Counselors: How the Lack of School Mental Health Staff Is Harming Students* (Los Angeles: American Civil Liberties Union of Southern California, 2019), 5, https://www.aclu.org/sites/default/files/field_document/030419-acluschooldisciplinereport.pdf.
9. Nathan James and Gail McCallion, *School Resource Officers: Law Enforcement Officers in Schools*, CRS Report no. R43126 (Washington, DC: Congressional Research Service, 2013), 26, https://sgp.fas.org/crs/misc/R43126.pdf.
10. American Civil Liberties Union of Washington, "How Do Police Officers Impact Schools?," August 12, 2019, 2, https://www.aclu-wa.org/docs/how-do-police-impact-schools.
11. Mark Johnson, "East Lansing Schools to Defund Resource Officers, Hire More Black Teachers," *Lansing State Journal*, June 17, 2020, https://www.lansingstatejournal.com/story/news/2020/06/17/east-lansing-public-schools-defund-resource-officers-hire-more-black-teachers/3209267001.
12. George Floyd Resolution to Eliminate the Oakland Schools Police Department, Resolution no. 1920-0260 (2020), https://californiaengage.org/wp-content

/uploads/2021/10/Reference-Oakland-USD-Board-Policy-George-Floyd-Resolution.pdf.

13. Samuel Getachew, "Oakland Eliminated Its School Police Force—So What Happens Now?," KQED, March 11, 2021, https://www.kqed.org/arts/13893831/oakland-eliminated-its-school-police-force-so-what-happens-now.
14. Sam Levin, "US Police Have Killed Nearly 600 People in Traffic Stops Since 2017, data shows," *The Guardian*, April 21, 2022, https://www.theguardian.com/us-news/2022/apr/21/us-police-violence-traffic-stop-data; Josh Pacewicz and John N. Robinson, III, "Pocketbook Policing: How Race Shapes Municipal Reliance on Punitive Fines and Fees in the Chicago Suburbs," *Social-Economic Review* 19, no. 3 (2021): 977, https://academic.oup.com/ser/article-abstract/19/3/975/5917153.
15. John Bacon, "Philadelphia to Become First Major US City to Ban Minor Traffic Stops to Promote Equity, Curb 'Negative Interactions' with Police," *USA Today*, October 31, 2021, https://www.usatoday.com/story/news/nation/2021/10/31/philadelphia-ban-minor-police-traffic-stops/6224286001; Julia Felton, "Pittsburgh Bans Traffic Stops for Minor Violations," *Tribune-Review*, December 28, 2021, https://triblive.com/local/pittsburgh-bans-traffic-stops-for-minor-violations.
16. Peter Dujardin, "Police in Virginia Were Barred in 2020 from Stopping Cars for a Range of Violations. Now Lawmakers Look to Undo Those Changes," *Virginian-Pilot*, February 26, 2022, https://www.pilotonline.com/government/virginia/dp-nw-motorist-legislation-senate-20220226-e6p7eag4xzc07hsvy3f3ymisuu-story.html.
17. Allyson Waller and Sophie Park, "Austin Still Struggling to Find Places for People Experiencing Homelessness as It Begins Enforcing Public Camping Ban," *Texas Tribune*, August 9, 2021, https://www.texastribune.org/2021/08/09/austin-texas-camping-ban; Tori Duff, "Austin City Council Approves Purchase of New Hotel to House People Experiencing Homelessness," *Daily Texan*, February 9, 2021, https://thedailytexan.com/2021/02/09/austin-city-council-approves-purchase-of-new-hotel-to-house-people-experiencing.
18. Halisia Hubbard, "A Village for Salt Lakers Experiencing Homelessness Is Designed for Self-Sufficiency," NPR, November 6, 2022, https://www.npr.org/2022/11/06/1134230388/village-salt-lake-city-chronic-homelessness-housing.
19. Office of the Mayor, "Mayor London Breed Announces Spending Plan for Historic Reinvestment in San Francisco's African-American Community," City and County of San Francisco, February 25, 2021, https://sfmayor.org/article/mayor-london-breed-announces-spending-plan-historic-reinvestment-san-franciscos-african; City News Service, "L.A. Council Approves Spending Millions Diverted from LAPD on Community Reinvestment," KCET, May 25,

2021, https://www.kcet.org/l-a-council-approves-spending-millions-diverted-from-lapd-on-community-reinvestment.

20. Ram Subramanian and Leily Arzy, "Rethinking How Law Enforcement Is Deployed" (New York: Brennan Center for Justice, November 17, 2022), https://www.brennancenter.org/our-work/research-reports/rethinking-how-law-enforcement-deployed.
21. White Bird Clinic, "Cahoots—Crisis Assistance Helping Out on the Streets," accessed November 22, 2022, https://whitebirdclinic.org/cahoots.
22. Sigal Samuel, "Calling the Cops on Someone with Mental Illness Can Go Terribly Wrong. Here's a Better Idea," Vox, June 15, 2020, https://www.vox.com/future-perfect/2019/7/1/20677523/mental-health-police-cahoots-oregon-oakland-sweden.
23. Subramanian and Arzy, "Rethinking Law Enforcement."
24. Subramanian and Arzy, "Rethinking Law Enforcement."
25. White Bird Clinic, "Crisis Assistance Helping Out on the Streets: Media Guide 2020," Eugene, Oregon, 2020, 2, https://whitebirdclinic.org/wp-content/uploads/2020/07/CAHOOTS-Media.pdf.
26. International Institute for Restorative Practices, "Community Health & Restorative Practices," accessed November 22, 2022, https://www.iirp.edu/community-health/reports-recommendations.
27. Leila Miller, "He Befriended His Brother's Murderer. In Each Other, They Found Healing," *Los Angeles Times*, October 11, 2021, https://www.latimes.com/california/story/2021-10-11/la-me-col1-victim-offender-dialogue.
28. Henry Gass, "Native Justice: How Tribal Values Shape Judge Abby's Court," *Christian Science Monitor*, March 27, 2019, https://www.csmonitor.com/USA/Justice/2019/0327/Native-justice-How-tribal-values-shape-Judge-Abby-s-court.
29. Restorative Justice Exchange, "What Is Restorative Justice?," accessed November 22, 2022, https://restorativejustice.org/what-is-restorative-justice/#sthash.PV3rk5cu.dpbs.
30. Common Justice, "The Common Justice Model," accessed November 22, 2022, https://www.commonjustice.org/the_common_justice_model.
31. Common Justice, "The Only Way to Tackle Mass Incarceration Is to Address the Issues of Those Convicted of Violent Offenses," accessed December 12, 2022, https://www.commonjustice.org/the_only_way_to_tackle_mass_incarceration_is_to_address_the_issue_of_those_convicted_of_violent_offenses; Danielle Sered, *Accounting for Violence: How to Increase Safety and Break Our Failed Reliance on Mass Incarceration* (New York: Vera Institute of Justice, 2017), 16, https://www.vera.org/downloads/publications/accounting-for-violence.pdf.
32. Amanda Alexander and Danielle Sered, *What Makes a City Safe: Viable Community Safety Strategies That Do Not Rely On Police or Prisons* (New York: The Square One Project, 2021), 18, https://squareonejustice.org/wp

-content/uploads/2021/12/CJLJ9283-What-Makes-a-City-Safe-report-211215-WEB-1.pdf.

33. National Network of Hospital-Based Violence Intervention Programs, "Hospital-Based Violence Intervention: Practices and Policies to End the Cycle of Violence" (Boston: Health Alliance for Violence Intervention, 2019), 2, https://static1.squarespace.com/static/5d6f61730a2b610001135b79/t/5d83c0d9056f4d4cbdb9acd9/1568915699707/NNHVIP+White+Paper.pdf.

CONCLUSION

The Era of Punitive Excess

Jeremy Travis and Bruce Western

DESPITE A DECLINE IN INCARCERATION RATES over the last decade, American criminal justice policy remains historically punitive. The extent of correctional supervision—including community supervision on probation and parole as well as institutional confinement in prison and jails—expanded steadily beginning in the early 1970s for three decades. Today, the total correctional population numbers almost six million adults, including almost two million incarcerated and another four million on probation or parole.[1]

The forty-year growth in imprisonment rates since the early 1970s has been linked to changes in sentencing policy, particularly the widespread adoption of mandatory minimum sentences, often for drug offenses, and then through the enactment of very long sentences, particularly for those convicted of violence and with long criminal histories.[2]

A full accounting of the harsh realities of the modern system of criminal justice in America extends beyond the vast reach of correctional supervision. Today's landscape of punishment also includes the extensive criminalization of social problems such as homelessness and mental illness, intrusive policing policies such as stop and frisk, the imposition of fines and fees that exacerbate poverty, the legislatively defined collateral sanctions that close off opportunities to millions with criminal records, and the new technologies that place the entire public under a form of state surveillance.

As the essays in this volume artfully illustrate, this new reality is what we call the era of punitive excess. In its multiple manifestations, damaging impact, political durability, and unbridled reach into all aspects of American life, the modern expression of society's need to marginalize the poor and people of color through criminalization and punishment has become a stubborn social fact.

The essays in this series mark another step in an overdue reckoning with this history. The era of punitive excess documented in this volume represents the latest chapter in a long history of white supremacy and economic injustice and constitutes a multicount indictment against the system of criminal laws created in its wake. Because the criminal justice system that has emerged over the past half century is so deeply intertwined with the legacy of white supremacy in America, this reckoning necessarily underscores the urgency of recognizing, and repairing, the damage borne by communities of color and marginalized populations. At the most fundamental level, we must ask unsettling questions about the impulse to criminalize and punish, especially as this impulse has been applied selectively throughout American history.

Punishment not only describes what criminal justice institutions do, but also signifies a relationship between the state and its citizens. We define criminal punishment as the infliction of human suffering under the color of law. Criminal punishment describes a coercive relationship between an authority and those subject to its jurisdiction. The unequal distribution of criminal justice supervision across the population is an essential fact about the punishment relationship.

The nature of the punitive relationship lies as much in the qualitative character of who is incarcerated or under justice supervision as in the quantitative extent of the affected population. The punished are often poor, yes, but they are also vulnerable in a variety of other ways that, in the absence of other social supports, exposes them to contact with police, the courts, and prisons. This is punishment as social policy—a way of responding to the range of social problems (including crime) associated with America's particularly severe variety of poverty. The burdens of punitive policy have fallen particularly heavily on low-income communities, especially low-income Black communities. Neighborhood segregation by race and class concentrates a wide variety of social problems—poverty, unemployment, public disinvestment, unaffordable housing, untreated health problems—that contribute to crime and attract the attention of authorities.

The great injustice of the punitive posture of contemporary criminal justice was to attribute a superabundance of moral agency to those who, by virtue of economic, demographic, and social disadvantage, often had the fewest choices to make. In this social world, shot through with racism, severe poverty, and their accompanying constraints on action, the moral agency that punishment regulates is distributed unevenly across the population and is in shortest supply among the most disadvantaged. But harsh punishment was at best indifferent to racism and poverty. In this world of punitive excess, poverty, trauma, and ill health were seen as bad choices by bad people who were then punished by the police, courts, and prisons.

If punishment is not justice in such a world of great socioeconomic inequality, then what is? Here, the answer lies in balancing the jurisprudence of individual culpability with the promotion of human capabilities. If the problems of crime, disorderly behavior, and idleness are characteristic of the social conditions of poverty, then justice is found in abating those social conditions rather than punishing those who live with them.

This suggests a fundamental change in the work of those who are publicly charged with responding to violence and other crimes. First, they would guard against the harms they may inflict on the most disadvantaged. The possibility of undue punishment and the necessity of safeguards are pressing because crime and disorder are more prevalent in poor communities, because of not the moral deficiencies of community residents but instead the social conditions of severe poverty. Second, and more ambitious, the agents of the response to harm might work actively for promoting opportunity, citizenship, and community involvement at the deepest margins of society while recognizing the importance of individual accountability.

The essays in this volume do more than simply document the unprecedented reach and devastating consequences of unbridled punishment in modern America. They also pose a challenge to our collective imagination. As we come to terms with these troubling realities, we must also ask, how does the era of punitive excess come to an end?

On one level, an all-out mobilization is required to roll back the harmful effects of a justice system that causes so much injustice. We applaud the efforts of those who tackle these challenges. Yet a clear-eyed realization of how far the country has strayed from the path of true justice requires more than system reform. The long history of punitive excess with its damaging effects on poor people and in Black and Brown communities is itself the product of a grave democracy deficit. The laws that have brought about the era of punitive excess were all passed by our elected representatives. The prosecutors who enforced these laws and sought long prison terms were all elected, as were many of the sheriffs and judges. Police chiefs were appointed by mayors responsive to the public will. The build-up of police and prison budgets, the starving of public defenders, the continuing atrophy of community supports—all were the product of democratic processes. We necessarily arrive at this disturbing conclusion: we live in an era of punitive excess because the American people, through our democratically elected representatives, have chosen it.

But if our democracy brought us to this point, can we count on our democracy to also provide the means of fundamental change? If the past half century demonstrated the electoral effectiveness of tough-on-crime rhetoric, then reversing the trends we have observed will require a new public discourse about how best to respond to harm. That is a tall order. The status quo has proven impressively durable and resistant to the most modest reforms. Powerful financial incentives sustain the bureaucracy of law enforcement, prisons, and courts, and fuel the economies dependent on massive government spending on criminal justice activities. The legacy of white supremacy that links criminality to skin color allows politicians, overtly and covertly, to respond to public fear by embracing racist policies.

Most challenging of all, those who suffer the deepest effects of punitive excess have been marginalized from political power. Yet in recent years we have seen hopeful signs pointing toward a different future. Prosecutors are being elected on platforms promising deep reform. Their electoral success had depended on strong support from communities adversely affected by crime and the overreach of the system. The historic uprising following the murder of George Floyd tapped into outrage about police brutality, particularly against unarmed Black men, and demonstrated widespread support for fundamental police reform. The Black Lives Matter movement has articulated an agenda that would reverse the punitive policies of the past. Unlike any of its predecessors, the generation now coming into voting age has placed justice reform on its list of urgent demands, along with climate change and gun safety. The reform movement has been strengthened by the emergence of several robust national and local organizations led by formerly incarcerated individuals who have demanded a seat at the policy table. More and more states are adopting legislation that restores the vote to those with criminal convictions. Advocates for voting rights have in turn mobilized the justice-affected community and their allies to embrace a wider justice reform agenda. Even though the spike in violence during the pandemic provided fuel for political resistance to justice reforms, it also ironically created a platform for political support for a new suite of community-led programs designed to reduce violence. A growing segment of the movement is calling for abolition of police and prisons, challenging the fundamental role of the state in providing for safety and responding to crime by use of state power.

The emergence of these new voices, all external to the traditional justice framework, provide hope that the democracy deficit that allowed punitive policies to the national imagination and political discourse over the past half century may indeed be narrowed in the coming years.

To realize these hopes for the future, we need to wrestle with basic questions that have been forcefully presented by the era of punitive excess: What is the purpose of punishment? How does a democracy guard against the inappropriate exercise of that state power? How can a society respond to harm while minimizing the imposition of punishment? Even more, can our society respond to harm in ways that respect the human dignity of all involved, do not exacerbate conditions of poverty, provide communities with agency over communal life, and promote healing and racial justice? Answering these questions will allow our country to repudiate the punitive project and undertake an authentic search for justice.

In December 2021, the city council of Charlottesville, Virginia, voted unanimously to donate the city's statue of Confederate war leader Robert E. Lee to the Jefferson School African American Heritage Center, which proposed to melt it down and use the bronze to create "a new work of art that will reflect racial justice and inclusion." The center's proposal was called Swords into Plowshares. According to Andrea Douglas, executive director of the center, "We're taking something that was harmful, taking something that was the source of trauma, and transforming it into something that is more respective of the democratic, community space."[3]

If mass incarceration is the bronze statue of punitive excess, it should now be melted down and transformed. What has been traumatic and painful should be replaced with a new vision of justice that promotes community well-being, not oppression, and elevates democracy, not racial domination.

To turn the page on this chapter, we propose an honest reckoning with the harms of punitive excess.

Reckoning requires a commitment to truth-telling, beginning with the tangle of fictions that stand in the way of change: punishment keeps us safe; justice is found in courtrooms; conflicts are best resolved through an adversarial process; harmed parties need retribution; prisons are places for rehabilitation; punishment ends once one leaves prison; the rich and the poor receive equal treatment under the law. Perhaps foremost among the fictions of justice is the notion that monumental racial disparities were necessitated by patterns of crime and demanded by communities of color. A reckoning is needed to set the record straight.

Our idea of a reckoning has three key parts.

First, a reckoning is a historical project. History reveals how institutions charged with the task of safety have operated as instruments of control and isolation. History explains why the demographic contours of mass criminalization and incarceration align so neatly with racial exclusion and extreme poverty. The history teaches that police and courts—held up in theory as objective agents of justice—have instead been complicit in upholding the regime of white supremacy. Slave patrols, convict labor, Black codes, the terrorism of lynching, the violent suppression of Black political power after Reconstruction, infiltration of Black liberation movements—all were perpetuated by agencies of the justice system. Understanding history can help propel the demand for a new vision of justice.

Second, a reckoning also supports a demand for sharing power. An honest reckoning can drive a political dynamic in which community representatives have a more central role. We have already glimpsed the propulsive force of historical reckoning in the work of community movements to close jails, reform bail, forgive court debt, and eliminate stop and frisk policies. Articulating the historic harms of punitive excess will lend urgency to these community demands. The fertile ground of community organizing has the potential to encourage a new generation of community-based leadership, steeled to sustain the movement from vision to reality.

Third, a reckoning must also engage the public officials who have staffed the juggernaut of punitive excess. Truth-telling provides a chance for community members to confront authorities with the harm they've suffered. The myth that safety is rooted in punishment can be powerfully exposed if community members speak to how countless police stops, arrests, and incarcerations have put them at risk. The myth that justice is found in courtrooms can be debunked by crime survivors who struggle with the unaddressed trauma of their victimization. Although engaging public officials will be difficult, an honest truth-telling process that invites their participation will provide opportunities for some officials to become champions for change. In a struggle for transformation, the voice of the convert has unique credibility.

A successful reckoning can help create political space for policies that disrupt the logic of punitive excess. Communities themselves would have a much stronger hand in designing how and for whom safety is achieved. The pursuit of justice would draw on community strengths to advance the goals of healing and forgiveness. The accountability of public officials would reflect a commitment to transparency, power-sharing, and civilian authority. Sanctions for those community members who harm others would show unwavering respect for their value and dignity and be proportionate to the harm they've committed.

Disrupting the logic of punitive excess by reckoning with the legacy of economic injustice and white supremacy is as much a process as it is an outcome. A sustained dialogue that is steeped in history, led by the voice of impacted communities, and confronts officials with the harms they have caused or perpetuated will sometimes be halting and often frustrating. But, we hope, such a process can enable fundamental change by sharing power and broadening the coalition for change. Most fundamentally, a process of reckoning could create a new politics of justice to replace the politics of the era of punitive excess.

We recognize that the road to dismantling systems of injustice is long and that progress is not linear. We also believe that dismantling the sturdy architecture of punitive excess will require more than marginal reforms. The statue needs to be taken from its pedestal, melted down, and recast as something new.

The experience of other times and places teaches us that a reckoning with history happens only rarely, and then often in the context of painful regime change, such as a defeat in war, a political revolution, or accumulated moral outrage. One need only consider the history of the Truth and Reconciliation Commission in post-apartheid South Africa, the establishment of a democratic Germany following the horrors of the Holocaust and the revelations of the Nuremberg trials, or America's brief experiment with racially inclusive democracy during Reconstruction before it was destroyed by a century of resurgent white supremacy. These and other examples of nations coming to terms with their historical injustices underscore the complexity—and necessity—of a process of reckoning as a precondition for a new kind of justice.

A reckoning does not determine precisely how the swords of punitive excess are beaten into the plowshares of community empowerment, but we hope it creates a space for such a political process to begin. This process embodies the values of dignity, democracy, and truth-telling. It actively pursues the promise of a multiracial democracy. These values, when infused into a political dialogue, have the transformative power to eclipse the era of punitive excess.

NOTES

1. Jacob Kang-Brown, Chase Montagnet, and Jasmine Heiss, *People in Jail and Prison in Spring 2021* (New York: Vera Institute of Justice, 2021), 1, https://www.vera.org/publications/people-in-jail-and-prison-in-spring-2021; Danielle Kaeble, *Probation and Parole in the United States, 2020*, NCJ 303102 (Washington, DC: U.S. Department of Justice, Bureau of Justice Statistics, 2021), https://bjs.ojp.gov/content/pub/pdf/ppus20.pdf.
2. Jeremy Travis, Bruce Western, and F. Stevens Redburn, *The Growth of Incarceration in the United States: Exploring Causes and Consequences* (Washington, DC: National Research Council, 2014).
3. Eduardo Medina, "Charlottesville's Statue of Robert E. Lee Will Be Melted Down," *New York Times*, December 7, 2021, https://www.nytimes.com/2021/12/07/us/robert-e-lee-statue-melt-charlottesville.html.

ACKNOWLEDGMENTS

MANY OF THE CONCEPTS AND IDEAS in this book stem from conversations with Jeremy Travis and Bruce Western, who graciously devoted their time to dozens of Zoom conversations discussing the ideas that are explored throughout these pages. Starting in 2020, they both weighed in to suggest potential contributors to the series along with topics that should be covered. This book owes them a huge debt of gratitude.

This project originated as an online essay series published by the Brennan Center. Dan Okrent played a pivotal role in editing essays for the online series, working magic to make arguments crisper and somehow managing to cut extraneous words without losing the meaning of all the essays he edited. His dexterity in wordsmithing is evident in so many of the essays in this book.

We are also grateful to the American Bar Association (ABA) for acknowledging the online essay series with the ABA's 2022 Silver Gavel award for commentary.

Thank you to every contributor who penned an essay for this book. We are grateful for your valuable scholarship, insights, and continued contributions to making the world a better place.

This entire project would not have succeeded without Ava Kaufman and Alia Nahra, who both conducted significant research for essays in this book and added a level of organization to this process that ensured we met deadlines, sent essays out for fact-checking, and didn't drop any balls coordinating with contributors. Ava Kaufman ensured that every essay in this series complied with Columbia University Press formatting, created citations for dozens of essays, and highlighted typos and errors in essays throughout this process. Alia Nahra coauthored an essay, coordinated with contributors, assisted with research to pick authors, and worked closely with Lisa Vosper to produce the Brennan Center online video series. Ava and Alia were truly the backbone of this project.

Special thank you to Maris Mapolski and Jules Verdone, who fact checked the essays in this book, reading every fact, figure, and claim made by each contributor to ensure they were properly cited and accurate. More than one contributor remarked on their detail-oriented and spectacular catches and additions to the essays in this volume.

Thank you to Sabrina Alli, Susan Augenbraun, Josh Bell, Lisa Benenson, Bianca Gomez-Nachand, Matt Harwood, Brian Palmer, Jeanne Park, Alexandra Ringe, Derek Rosenfeld, Lisa Vosper, Alden Wallace, and Pinky Weitzman for their tremendous support and assistance putting this project together.

Jeanine Chirlin and Mellen O'Keefe played an instrumental role highlighting this work in public forums and ensuring these words reached more people. Thank you to Elisa Miller for her assistance and always wise counsel on this project.

Numerous Brennan Center colleagues provided research for these essays. Special thanks to Leily Arzy, Terry-Ann Craigie, Jackie Fielding, Emelia Gold, Maylina Graham, Ames Grawert, Josy Hahn, Jinmook Kang, Sarah Mazzarella, Zoe Merriman, Jamie Muth, Noah Kim, Cameron Kimble, Taylor King, Rosemary Nidiry, Tiffany Sanabia, Brianna Seid, Hernandez Stroud, Ram Subramanian, and Stephanie Wylie for their research support.

Thank you to Nausheen Ansari, Ana Sofia Barrios, Britney Brito, Nell Compton, John Donahue, Paulette Hodge, Jaemin Kim, Allison Kruk, Charles Ombwa, Alan Prieto, Hannah Smolar, Katherine Storch, Laura Strausfeld, Chrissy Teeter, and Adrienne Yee for constantly drawing attention to the importance of this project.

Thank you to Brennan Center colleagues Alesya Acero, Amanda Bart, Alicia Bannon, Alan Beard, Jerrell Braithwaite, Jessica Brenner, Okeisha Brown, Tony Butler, Antonio Dell'Agli, Ivey Dyson, Maya Efrati, Liza Goitein, Allison Hertz, Ted Johnson, Tanvi Krishnamurthy, Jessica Lam, Chisun Lee, Ronn Mathew, Manuel Monge, Larry Norden, Ben Nyblade, Faiza Patel, Megan Penney, Ajay Pothuri, Fabienne Ranjit, Angie Rendon, Dan Weiner, Jen Weiss-Wolf, and Wendy Weiser.

We are also appreciative of the research assistance from Emily Bauwens, Clare Downing, Hayden Henderson, Kyle Alexander Hogan, Michael Jeung, Jaden Lessnick, Julian Melendi, Mikaila Smith, and Katja Stroke-Adolphe.

Without the support of Michael Waldman and John Kowal, this project would not have been possible. Their support and championship of this undertaking paved the way for the book to come to life. The Justice Program at the Brennan Center is grateful for their passionate devotion to the idea of books and their power to educate the broader public in the hopes of impacting public opinion.

At Columbia University Press, my thanks to Christian Winting, H. Glenn Court, Kathryn Jorge, and Peter Barrett. We are also appreciative of the wonderful indexing work done by Lee Gable.

Thank you to Stefanie Lieberman at Janklow & Nesbit Associates for ensuring that this project turned into a book and found a home. Thank you also to Adam Hobbins, Michael Steger, and Molly Steinblatt at Janklow & Nesbit Associates. And, of course, thank you to my editor at Columbia University Press, Stephen Wesley, who believed in this project from the beginning and continues to see how criminal legal scholarship can play a role in making the justice system more fair and more humane.

CONTRIBUTORS

Synøve N. Andersen is a postdoctoral fellow in the Department of Sociology and Human Geography at the University of Oslo. She is also a faculty affiliate at the Department of Criminology and Justice Studies at Drexel University, where she teaches on Norwegian corrections and coteaches an intensive course abroad about Scandinavian criminal justice.

Lenore Anderson is cofounder and president of the Alliance for Safety and Justice and founder of Californians for Safety and Justice. An attorney with extensive experience working to reform criminal justice and public safety systems, she is also the author of *In Their Names: The Untold Story of Victims' Rights, Mass Incarceration, and the Future of Public Safety*.

Monica C. Bell is a professor of law and Counselor to the Dean at Yale Law School and an associate professor of sociology at Yale University. Working at the intersection of law and sociology, Bell uses sociological theory and research to explore legal questions regarding race and class inequality. Her scholarship has appeared in the *American Journal of Sociology*, the *Yale Law Journal*, *Journal of Economic Perspectives*, *NYU Law Review*, *Harvard Civil Rights-Civil Liberties Law Review*, and other journals. Her other writing has been published in a variety of popular outlets such as *Politico Magazine*, the *Los Angeles Review of Books*, *Inquest*, and the *Washington Post*. Prior to joining the faculty, Bell was a Climenko Fellow and lecturer on Law at Harvard Law School and a Liman Fellow at the Legal Aid Society of the District of Columbia.

Christopher Blackwell is a Washington-based award-winning journalist currently incarcerated at the Washington Corrections Center whose work has been featured in news outlets nationwide. He is also cofounder of Look 2 Justice, a grassroots organization that provides support to incarcerated people and their loved ones.

Erica Bond is the vice president of justice initiatives at John Jay College of Criminal Justice. Her work on public safety includes a variety of roles, among them as a special advisor for criminal justice to the first deputy mayor of New York City, as a mayoral appointee to New York City's Civilian Complaint Review Board, and as a policy director at John Jay College's Data Collaborative for Justice.

Paul Butler is the Albert Brick Professor in Law at Georgetown University and an MSNBC legal analyst. A former federal prosecutor, he is the author of *Chokehold: Policing Black Men* and lectures regularly for the American Bar Association and the NAACP, and at colleges, law schools, and community organizations across the United States. An appointee of the District of Columbia City Council, Butler serves on the DC Code Revision Commission.

Jennifer M. Chacón is the Bruce Tyson Mitchell Professor of Law at Stanford Law School. Focusing on the nexus of immigration law, constitutional law, and criminal law and procedure, her writings elucidate how legal frameworks on immigration and law enforcement shape individual and collective understandings of racial and ethnic identity, citizenship, civic engagement, and social belonging. An associate at the New York law firm of Davis Polk and Wardwell after clerking for the Honorable Sidney R. Thomas of the Ninth Circuit (1998–99), Chacón has also held appointments as a professor of law at the University of California, Berkeley, School of Law; the UCLA School of Law; the UC Davis King Hall School of Law; and as a Chancellor's Professor of Law and Senior Associate Dean for Administration at the University of California, Irvine, School of Law.

Steven L. Chanenson is a professor of law at Villanova University's Charles Widger School of Law and a leading scholar in the areas of criminal law and sentencing. He also serves as the director of the Villanova Sentencing Workshop and is the former chair of the Pennsylvania Commission on Sentencing, where he was a member for almost fourteen years, having been appointed by three successive governors of Pennsylvania. Chanenson is currently the secretary of the Pennsylvania Prison Society, the oldest organization in the country dedicated to sensible and humane criminal justice policies.

Ed Chung, vice president of initiatives at the Vera Institute of Justice, has two decades of legal and policymaking experience, including positions in the White House Domestic Policy Council and the U.S. Senate Judiciary Committee. As a senior advisor at the U.S. Department of Justice, Chung worked on some of the Obama administration's signature priorities, such as the My Brother's Keeper initiative, the Task Force on 21st Century Policing, and ending the criminalization of poverty.

Andrew Cohen is a senior editor at the Marshall Project. A former senior legal analyst for CBS News and *60 Minutes*, he has won two Edward R. Murrow Awards and two Silver Gavel Awards from the American Bar Association for his coverage of prisons and the death penalty in America. Cohen served as a fellow at the Brennan Center for Justice for ten years.

Khalil A. Cumberbatch is a nationally recognized formerly incarcerated advocate for criminal justice and deportation policy reform. He currently serves as director of strategic partnerships at the Council on Criminal Justice. Pardoned by New York Governor Andrew Cuomo in 2014, Cumberbatch earned a master's degree in social work from Lehman College, City University of New York.

Michele Deitch is a distinguished senior lecturer at the University of Texas with a joint appointment at the Lyndon B. Johnson School of Public Affairs and the UT School of Law. She is the cofounder and director of the Prison and Jail Innovation Lab at the LBJ School, a policy resource center working to transform the way we treat people in custody and to improve correctional oversight. She specializes in independent oversight of correctional institutions, prison and jail conditions, managing youth in custody, and youth in the adult criminal justice system.

Emile DeWeaver is a community organizer, literary writer, and journalist who cofounded prisonrenaissance.org while serving a prison sentence of sixty-seven years to life. DeWeaver participated in the passage of Senate Bills 260 and 261 as well as Proposition 57, the Public Safety and Rehabilitation Act of 2016. DeWeaver's personal essays and op-eds have been published in multiple news outlets. His sentence was commuted by California Governor Jerry Brown in December 2017 for his community service, his productivity, and his story of transformation. DeWeaver is currently working as a product specialist for Pilot.com and as a guest lecturer and freelance writer.

Lauren-Brooke Eisen is senior director of the Justice Program at the Brennan Center for Justice, where Eisen leads the organization's work to end mass incarceration. While creating policies that ultimately shrink the size and scope of the justice system, the Brennan Center's Justice Program focuses on exposing the profound social and economic hardships that affect those who encounter it. Eisen is a former prosecutor who also worked as a journalist and is the author of *Inside Private Prisons: An American Dilemma in the Age of Mass Incarceration*.

Adam Gelb has been working for a more just and effective criminal justice system over his thirty-six-year career as a journalist, congressional aide, senior state government official, and nonprofit executive. Before launching the Council on Criminal Justice in 2019, he led the Pew Charitable Trusts' criminal justice work, helping thirty-five states adopt sentencing and corrections reforms. Gelb has staffed the U.S. Senate Judiciary Committee, led development of public safety initiatives for governors in Georgia and Maryland, and covered crime as a reporter in Atlanta.

Morgan Godvin is the editor of the American Prison Newspapers collection with JSTOR Daily. She also serves on Oregon's drug decriminalization Measure 110 Oversight and Accountability Council and the Multnomah County Local Public Safety Coordinating Council.

Ames Grawert is senior counsel in the Justice Program at the Brennan Center for Justice, where he leads quantitative and policy research focused on trends in crime and the collateral costs of mass incarceration. Grawert also advocates for criminal justice reform policies at the state and federal level. Before joining the Brennan Center, he served as an assistant district attorney in the Appeals Bureau of the Nassau County District Attorney's Office.

Alexes Harris, Presidential Term Professor and professor of sociology at the University of Washington, is the author of *A Pound of Flesh: Monetary Sanctions as a Punishment for the Poor.* In her research, which focuses on social stratification processes and racial and ethnic disparities, Harris investigates how contact with varying institutions (educational, juvenile and criminal justice, and economic) affects individuals' life chances. Her current work examines the loss of driver's licenses as a result of unpaid fines and fee as well as recent legislative impacts on sentencing decisions and outcomes.

Shon Hopwood, a lawyer and law professor, served more than ten years in federal prison and is the author of *Law Man: Memoir of a Jailhouse Lawyer.* Hopwood's research and teaching interests include criminal law and procedure, civil rights, and the constitutional rights of prisoners.

Jordan M. Hyatt is an associate professor in the Department of Criminology and Justice Studies at Drexel University. His research in corrections and reentry focuses on the evaluation of innovative criminal justice interventions and emphasizes randomized experiments.

Asia Johnson is a storyteller, writer, and filmmaker who has worked with several organizations in the criminal justice reform space, including The Bail Project, cut50, Shakespeare in Prison, Prison Creative Arts Program, Hamtramck Free School, and the Michigan Prison Doula Initiative. She is also a 2019 Right of Return Fellow, 2019 Room Project Fellow, and a 2021 Brennan Center for Justice Fellow.

Theodore R. Johnson is a senior advisor at New America and the author of *When the Stars Begin to Fall: Overcoming Racism and Renewing the Promise of America.* A retired U.S. Navy commander after a two-decade career, he served as a White House Fellow and as a speechwriter to the chairman of the Joint Chiefs of Staff. Before New America, Johnson was a senior fellow and directed the Fellows Program at the Brennan Center for Justice.

Cameron Kimble is a senior analyst at the Benenson Strategy Group (BSG) and a former Henry M. McCracken Fellow at New York University's Graduate School of Arts and Science for research in Africana studies. Prior to joining BSG, he worked in the Justice Program at the Brennan Center for Justice, analyzing the social and economic consequences of poverty, interpersonal violence, and mass incarceration.

Karol V. Mason is the president of John Jay College of Criminal Justice, City University of New York. Previously, she served as the U.S. assistant attorney general and head of the U.S. Department of Justice's Office of Justice

Programs, where she oversaw an annual budget of $4 billion to support an array of state and local criminal justice agencies, juvenile justice programs, and services for crime victims, among a wide range of other efforts related to justice and public safety.

Peggy McGarry is the former director of the Center on Sentencing and Corrections at the Vera Institute of Justice. She also served as the director of criminal justice programs at the JEHT Foundation and currently serves as a consultant to the Center for Effective Public Policy, where she was a principal for twenty-three years.

Michael Mendoza is the director of advocacy at Anti-Recidivism Coalition, where he has been a member since 2014—the year he earned his release from prison after serving close to eighteen years. Mendoza was incarcerated at the age of fifteen and treated as an adult, receiving a fifteen-to-life sentence.

Carlton Miller is a director of criminal justice at Arnold Ventures and a former policy advisor for Louisiana Governor John Bel Edwards. Miller develops and manages investments to reduce prison populations, improve prison culture and conditions, increase transparency, and bolster prospects for successful reentry.

Kathy Morse is an advocate for criminal justice reform. Currently based in New Jersey, she is a legal services coordinator for a New Jersey reentry nonprofit. Morse advocates on issues relating to the detention and incarceration of women in the United States, having spent nearly a year detained on Rikers Island and three years incarcerated in other New York State facilities.

Alia Nahra is a JD/PhD joint degree student, Hamilton Fellow at Columbia Law School, and Paul F. Lazarfeld Fellow in the Sociology Department at Columbia University. Before joining Columbia, she worked in the Justice Program at the Brennan Center for Justice, conducting research and policy advocacy aimed at ending mass incarceration.

Jason Pye, the director of rule of law initiatives for the Due Process Institute, has worked on several pieces of legislation that have become law, including the First Step Act and the Fair Chance Act. Previously, Pye served as the vice president of legislative affairs for FreedomWorks, where he was responsible for lobbying on federal legislation, forming relationships with congressional offices, and keeping tabs on congressional activity.

Heather Rice-Minus is the current executive vice president and incoming president and chief executive officer of Prison Fellowship, the nation's largest Christian nonprofit serving people in prison, returning citizens, and their families. A sought-after public speaker on the intersection of faith, justice, and incarceration, Rice-Minus has been a leading voice in advancing significant justice reform legislation.

Martín Sabelli is a criminal defense attorney who has represented individuals in state and federal courts since 1993, including federal RICO capital cases. After receiving its Champion of Justice Award in 2018, he served as president of the National Association of Criminal Defense Lawyers from 2021 to 2022. Sabelli is also a member of the Board of Regents and faculty member of the National Criminal Defense College and, in 2012, established a criminal defense college for Latin American defenders in Argentina.

Alison Siegler is a clinical professor of law at the University of Chicago Law School and the founding director of the Federal Criminal Justice Clinic, the nation's first legal clinic devoted to representing indigent clients charged with federal felonies, pursuing impact litigation in federal court, and engaging in systemic reform of the federal criminal system. Previously, Siegler was an attorney with the Federal Defender Program in Chicago, a Prettyman Fellow at Georgetown Law Center's Criminal Justice Clinic, and a law clerk for U.S. District Judge Robert W. Gettleman.

Jonathan Simon is the Lance Robbins Professor of Criminal Justice Law at the University of California, Berkeley, where he teaches criminal law, criminal procedure, criminology, legal studies, and the sociology of law. Simon's scholarship concerns the role of crime and criminal justice in governing contemporary societies, risk and the law, and the history of the interdisciplinary study of law. He is the author of *Mass Incarceration on Trial: A Remarkable Court Decision and the Future of Prisons in America*.

David A. Singleton is an associate professor of law at the University of the District of Columbia (UDC) David A. Clarke School of Law, where he teaches criminal procedure and evidence. Before joining UDC in July 2023, Singleton served for twenty-one years as the executive director of the Ohio

Justice & Policy Center, a nonprofit public interest law firm that works to reform Ohio's criminal legal system and provides free legal representation to overpunished people. For most of his time in Ohio, he also taught as a professor of law at NKU Chase College of Law. Singleton is a member of the American Law Institute.

David Alan Sklansky is the Stanley Morrison Professor of Law and a faculty codirector of the Stanford Criminal Justice Center at Stanford Law School. He also serves as faculty codirector of the Stanford Criminal Justice Center, a faculty affiliate of Stanford's Center for Comparative Studies in Race and Ethnicity, and is a member of the American Law Institute. Prior to his work teaching and writing about criminal law, criminal procedure, and evidence, Sklansky practiced labor law in Washington, DC, and served as an assistant United States attorney in Los Angeles. He is the author of *A Pattern of Violence: How the Law Classifies Crimes and What It Means for Justice.*

Blake Strode, executive director of ArchCity Defenders, helped establish the Civil Rights Litigation unit at ArchCity, which has brought challenges to a variety of unlawful and predatory practices including debtors' prisons, police misconduct, and inhumane jail conditions, among others. Strode regularly speaks at conferences and panels throughout the country and has published columns and essays on issues of race, policing, and criminal justice.

Hernandez D. Stroud is a senior counsel in the Justice Program at the Brennan Center for Justice and serves on the faculties of Columbia University and New York University Law. Stroud leads work on prisons and jails, correctional oversight, and constitutional law. His research focuses on the scope of the federal government's power to fashion structural and systemic reforms that prevent and remedy the failure of state and local criminal justice institutions in observing the rights of the incarcerated under the U.S. Constitution.

Ram Subramanian is the managing director of the Justice Program at the Brennan Center for Justice where he manages data-driven reports and analyses that examine the racial and economic disparities in the criminal justice system. For a decade, he worked at the Vera Institute of Justice managing projects related to sentencing laws, community corrections, and prison conditions. Earlier in his career, Subramanian worked as a researcher and human rights advocate in Zimbabwe and South Africa, focusing on issues of democracy, judicial independence, and political violence.

Nkechi Taifa is president of the Taifa Group LLC, a social enterprise firm whose mission is to advance justice. The author of the memoir *Black Power, Black Lawyer: My Audacious Quest for Justice*, she is founder and convener emeritus of the Justice Roundtable, a broad network of advocacy groups advancing progressive justice system reform. She is a senior fellow for the Center for Justice at Columbia University and serves on the governing board of the Corrections Information Council, an independent monitoring body that provides oversight over the conditions of District residents imprisoned throughout the Federal Bureau of Prisons and the DC Department of Corrections. Taifa is also a founding member of the National Coalition of Blacks for Reparations in America and an inaugural commissioner of the National African American Reparations Commission.

Kim Taylor-Thompson is a professor of clinical law emerita at New York University School of Law, where she teaches courses related to criminal law and community and criminal defense. Her teaching and scholarship focus on the impact of race and gender on public policy—particularly criminal and juvenile justice policy—and the need to prepare lawyers to meet the demands of practice in and on behalf of subordinated communities. As a member of the MacArthur Foundation Research Network on Law and Neuroscience, Taylor-Thompson engaged in interdisciplinary research examining the ways that immature brain functioning in adolescents influences judgment and criminal behavior.

Rahsaan "New York" Thomas is the cohost and coproducer of the Pulitzer Prize Finalist–podcast *Ear Hustle*, as well as a contributing writer for the Marshall Project, the *San Quentin News*, and *Current*. Thomas also created the Empowerment Avenue program and is featured in the documentary *26.2 to Life*.

Jeremy Travis is a senior fellow at the Columbia Justice Lab, where he works on the role of values in the future of justice reform and the launch of a major research project on the impact of mass incarceration on New York City neighborhoods. Before joining the Justice Lab, Travis served as executive vice president of criminal justice at Arnold Ventures, one of the nation's largest funders of justice reform. While there, he collaborated with Bruce Western to launch the Square One Project at the Columbia Justice Lab, which aims to reimagine the public policy response to violence under conditions of poverty and racial inequality. Travis also chaired the National Research Council's consensus panel exploring the causes and consequences of high rates of incarceration in the United States.

Homer Venters is a federal monitor of health services in jail and prison settings. He also serves as adjunct faculty at the New York University College of Global Public Health and was formerly a member of the Biden-Harris COVID-19 Health Equity Task Force and chief medical officer of the New York City Correctional Health Services. Venters is the author of *Life and Death in Rikers Island.*

Bruce Western is a professor of sociology at Columbia University and director of the Columbia Justice Lab, where he is also cofounder and principal investigator of the Square One Project. Western studies poverty and socioeconomic inequality with a focus on the U.S. criminal justice system. The cochair of a National Academy of Sciences panel on reducing racial inequality in the U.S. criminal justice system, he is the author of *Homeward: Life in the Year After Prison.*

INDEX

GPSR Authorized Representative: Easy Access System Europe, Mustamäe tee 50, 10621 Tallinn, Estonia, gpsr.requests@easproject.com

www.ingramcontent.com/pod-product-compliance
Lightning Source LLC
Chambersburg PA
CBHW022132020426
42334CB00015B/858

* 9 7 8 0 2 3 1 2 1 2 1 7 5 *